Absence and Presence

Absence and Presence

Spanish Women Poets
of the Twenties and Thirties

Catherine G. Bellver

Lewisburg
Bucknell University Press
London: Associated University Presses

Associated University Presses
440 Forsgate Drive
Cranbury, NJ 08512

Associated University Presses
16 Barter Street
London WC1A 2AH, England

Associated University Presses
P.O. Box 338, Port Credit
Mississauga, Ontario
Canada L5G 4L8

The paper used in this publication meets the requirements
of the American National Standard for Permanence of Paper
for Printed Library Materials Z39.48–1984.

Library of Congress Cataloging-in-Publication Data

Bellver, C. G. (Catherine Gullo)
    Absence and presence : Spanish women poets of the twenties and thirties / Catherine
G. Bellver.
        p. cm.
    Includes bibliographical references and index.
    ISBN 0-8387-5463-5 (alk. paper)
        1. Spanish poetry — Women poets — History and criticism. 2. Spanish poetry —
20th century — History and criticism. I. Title.

PQ6055 .B45 2001
861' .62099287—dc21   00-023736

PRINTED IN THE UNITED STATES OF AMERICA

To my parents

Contents

Acknowledgments

I wish to thank the heirs, publishers, and literary agents of the poets studied in this book. I acknowledge the agency Carmen Balcells for its authorization to cite the poetry of Rosa Chacel and the publishing house Biblioteca Nueva for its prompt reply to my request to quote from Carmen Conde's *Obra poética*. I am indebted to the Ministry of Culture and Sports of the government of the Canary Islands for its clarification of the Spanish laws regarding the reprinting of previously published texts. I am grateful to Josefina de la Torre for her personal note granting me permission to quote her poetry. I also thank the heirs of Ernestina de Champourcin: M. Belén Klecker Michels de Champourcin and Jaime Lamo de Espinosa. My belated thanks to Ernestina de Champourcin for granting me an interview in 1993. I regret she did not live long enough to see this tribute to her poetry. Finally, for the permission to cite the works of Concha Méndez, I would like to express my gratitude not only to Hiperión, but also to the poet's daughter, Paloma Altolaguirre, who has extended her friendship to me over the years. I am grateful to Margo Persin for her advice on publishers. Special thanks to my friends Barbara Agonia, for her expertise in English and comments on my manuscript, and Donald Schmiedel, for his knowledge of Spanish and keen eye for detail.

Absence and Presence

1
Introduction

In the works of Spanish women poets of the twenties and thirties, absence and presence are significant phenomena evident on the level of both reception and text. They are factors that encompass the relationship between the literary creation and its public as well as questions of subjectivity, language, thematics, and voice. Presence and absence might appear to be polar opposites identifiable as existence and nonexistence, but rather than these passive states, they are complex, variable, and interrelated conditions of being. Absence and presence on the level of reception point to the interaction between a literary work and certain extratextual forces and between a writer and her milieu. More than a simple situation of inclusion or exclusion, this dynamic incorporates gradations of participation; and its two antithetical components often mirror one another. Marginalization is a degree removed from absence as well as a mark of limited presence. Exclusion from the canon, while rendering previously published works invisible, does not eradicate them. Physical evidence of their presence earlier in the twentieth century remains buried in out-of-date editions and defunct periodicals and, therefore, is available for bibliographical disinterment. On the level of text, the interplay between absence and presence covers interactions involving words, structures, and signs. Presence, in this sense, is a metaphorical construction. Absence corresponds to the symbolic transformations of personal feelings of loss, unfulfilled desire, and emptiness. In the case of text, human connections take place within the intimate space of the poem in the dialogues between the poetic, fictive persona and her textual interlocutors. When applied to female writing, absence and presence, whether manifested within a text or as the critical response toward it, are contained within the frame of the patriarchal concept of woman as lack, passivity, and absence. Therefore, the study of poetry by women has to have as its implied backdrop the efforts of the poet to escape this confinement through both the publication of her verse and the realities she creates within it.

11

The external story of the poets Concha Méndez, Ernestina de Champourcin, Josefina de la Torre, and Rosa Chacel is a drama in which absence figures prominently. Although they enjoyed a modicum of recognition and positive criticism in their own day, they virtually disappeared from the annals of literature after the Spanish Civil War. In Carmen Conde, the story of absence is different, but her first works have been essentially ignored. Therefore, one of the implicit purposes of this study is to create a posthumous literary presence for the early works of these poets buried in Spain's literary past. Although a great deal has been done by Hispanists to resurrect forgotten women writers, to revise the past, and, as the contemporary Spanish novelist Monserrat Roig puts it, "dive" in literary history as feminist archaeologists,[1] most of the work on Spanish women writers has concentrated on writers of the nineteenth century or the period after 1940 rather than on those of the period between these two time frames. Even with the panoramic studies on Spanish women poets by Janet Pérez and John C. Wilcox, decidedly more attention in the growing corpus of feminist studies on Spanish literature has been paid to narrative than to poetry.[2] Spanish poetry written by women illustrates the lingering need for scholars to reenter the second phase of feminist criticism and to continue to focus part of their efforts on the recovery of forgotten writers.[3] The need for women to define a literature of their own that Elaine Showalter discerned in 1977 still exists in Spanish literature, because the need remains to revisit and redefine female self-awareness, to reclaim those works excluded from the literary canon, and to re-establish historical links, so that the tradition of female authorship can be validated.[4]

A discussion of the reception given to the works of Spanish women poets must include two different time frames and environments: the moment in which new writing trends were emerging coetaneous to their publications, and the later years when the process of selection inherent in canon formation imposed limits on their literary longevity. The discrepancy in the response to women writers within these two time frames reveals a subtle but significant difference in the place in Spanish culture experienced by the women poets who began writing in the twenties and thirties. An era of literary experimentation and of modification, albeit minimal, in the status of women in Spain, the twenties afforded women poets the illusion of integration into the culture scene of the day. Under scrutiny, their cultural presence proves to be peripheral and the response to their work ambivalent at best. Nevertheless, this context of marginalization in which they were nurtured contrasts with the erasure the works of most of them suffered in Francoist Spain. Therefore, while I write about an absence definable as exclusion, the dynamics of the backdrop against which the poets Concha Méndez, Josefina de la Torre, Rosa Chacel, Carmen Conde, and Ernestina de Champourcin began was more complex. The lack of response to their

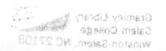

work was often complicated by disparagement or measured tolerance and was only occasionally counteracted by authentic endorsement. In order to understand some of the strategies these poets employed to create a tenuous literary presence for themselves within this atmosphere of mixed reactions to their work, the first chapter of this book is devoted to outlining the problematic context within which they navigated and to documenting their subsequent elimination from the annals of literature.

The absence against which women poets wrote and are now reevaluated is a destructive force that has limited and distorted their poetry, but the other interior, symbolic absence warrants greater attention because of its rich, creative potential. For this reason, after my initial consideration of absence on the level of reception, in the remaining five chapters I turn to the interplays between presence and absence in specific texts by Méndez, de la Torre, Chacel, Conde, and Champourcin. Fundamental to the examination of the poetic works by these poets are two complementary issues: how they create an environment of plasticity, immediacy, and vitality within their verse and how they deal with the psychological and ontological implications of absence, loss, and loneliness. Because the works studied here correspond to the early years in the lives of these women, the temperament of the poetic personae reflects qualities associated with youth: a desire for freedom, exuberance, carefreeness, and the bliss that comes from lack of experience. Consequently, in many cases, the discussion of their poetry is devoid of all evidence of absence or sorrow. Presence, self-assurance, and plenitude prevail. Also because the poets wrote during the era of the vanguardist mode of poetry in Spain, they exploit the visual and sonorous potential of words to generate poems of exceptional pictorial vividness. In accordance with the tendency of the day to elude personal sentiment and embrace instead the image as the primordial ingredient of poetry, they often construct poems as a succession of terse metaphors or as lists of objects and thereby create a strong sense of materiality within the confines of their poetic world. The manner in which they manipulate time to arrest its progression and treat space to produce an impression of proximity enhances the overriding impact of presence in their early poetry. They speak of life, liberty, and desire with youthful verve and confidence. The element of possession—of both the self and the other—implied in the joyful expression of presence connotes autonomy and power, qualities indispensable for self-assertion.

Although the tendency for presence to give way to absence becomes considerably more apparent in their later collections, presence is tempered early in some of these poets by an awareness of absence. The present yields to the past, proximity to distance, and visibility to the invisible. Loss and emptiness annul the sense of fulfillment revealed in the early collections of some, and solitude replaces human connections for others. On the psychological level, the articulation of desire implies need, and the confrontation with the other provokes an awareness of difference and conflict. The intrusion of temporality creates an emotional longing expressed as nostalgia for what has disappeared or was never attained. And finally, a preoccupation with mortality and death can expose the threat of existential nothingness. After 1936, even before the critics would forget them, these poets disappeared into a void of silence: Concha Méndez withdrew into the realm of the private self; Josefina de la Torre abandoned poetry; Rosa Chacel willfully curbed her poetic production; and Ernestina de Champourcin slipped into a sixteen-year hiatus in her publication of poetry. Only Carmen Conde expanded her poetic horizons.

The dynamic interplay of absence and presence within the texts of these women brings to light the difficult struggle of the woman poet to inscribe her own subjectivity, voice, and imprint on her general cultural community. This effort of hers highlights that all-encompassing absence to which all members of her gender have been confined. This type of absence might be called ontological and ideological because it includes both the existential vacuum assigned to women and the patriarchal philosophies responsible for this concept. An inferred confrontation with this long-standing denial of the potential for female presence necessarily underlies any current feminist reading of women writers. For this reason, the theoretical point of departure of this study presupposes a challenge, on the part of the critic as well as the poet, to the institutionalization of woman as absence. Because the very act of poetry writing subverts women's perennial exclusion from creative agency, the discussion of the five poets chosen for this book presumes that, through the establishment of a forceful presence in their work, they unconsciously challenged this pervasive absence. Therefore, the analysis of their five individual poetic personalities and evolutions implicitly uncovers the strategies used by a female poet to become the center of her fictive work and thereby undermine misogynist deprivations.

Western metaphysics, as reflected throughout patriarchal discourse, reserves presence, along with its connotations of autonomy, action, and mastery, for man, while emphatically equating woman with absence and its corollaries of silence, passivity, and nonexistence. As Hélène Cixous has asserted, within the patriarchal binary thought system "either the woman is passive; or she doesn't exist."[5] When women write, they subvert this phallocentricism because they assume the posture of creative subject and, through the written medium, they formulate a female presence that permits them to stand out against a backdrop of broken expectations as well as unprecedented challenges. The writing of poetry by women becomes particularly threatening to established gender differentiations because, as Suzanne Juhasz points out, "woman" and "poet" traditionally denote opposite and contradictory qualities and roles or, as Sandra M. Gilbert and

Susan Gubar explain, the woman poet, even more than the woman novelist, has appeared presumptuous and misguided in that poetry writing suggests the adoption of attitudes long considered inherently masculine, of a posture definable as priestly, aristocratic, aesthetic, assertive, and authoritative.[6]

The female poet cannot yet be subjected to the postmodern decision to declare the author dead, because that, as Nancy K. Miller affirms, forecloses the question of identity for women.[7] The writing female subject cannot be deprived of subjective agency and authoritative canonicity before they are acquired. The authority of the Spanish female poets of the twenties and thirties was never openly realized and their assertion of the self remained tenuous, ambivalent, and compromised. Theirs was an effort to initiate an existence as poets within a social environment that, if not inhospitable, can at best be termed patronizing and within a cultural arena that may be considered tolerant but not particularly supportive. Without a strong sense of their female heritage and only partially attached to the emerging literary circles of their day, these poets struggled through the act of writing for self-identity, literary legitimacy, and creative independence. Therefore, special note will be taken of their attempts not only at self-representation, but also at integration into the prevailing literary trends.

As already stated, writing creates presence. When women write, they are no longer silent, hidden, or immobile; they enter the field of presence traditionally identified as masculine. However, beyond serving as a vehicle of defiance against a system that privileges the masculine, writing provides women a means to create a network of self-generated images and meanings. Instead of the product of male imagination, the "blank page" on which men sketch their myths and fantasies, the woman writer delineates and develops her own pictures of both the self and other.[8] Woman has been the sign of nonexistence, the "you" to which a poem is directed, a second person that is either an object of absence or a fictional representation.[9] But if the speaking voice in poetry by women can be presumed to be female, then woman passes from sign to subject, from represented object to agent of representation. To participate in the stimulating process of self-consciousness and creativity is to grow and gain authority—considered to be incompatible with femininity. Thus female texts, as Ellen G. Friedman has said, look beyond culture, beyond patriarchy, into the unknown, the outlawed.[10] At times, the significance of the poetry of writers like Chacel or Méndez may seem to lie more in the gesture than in the substance of their words. Yet in the embryonic attempts of women to achieve literary recognition, the personal inevitably appears political. In her departure from the male concept of woman, the woman poet subverts gender ideology; her work becomes, in the words of Mary Jacobus, the site of "challenge and otherness."[11]

Poetry, like other acts of communication, performs the three functions that linguists detect: the ideational, the interpersonal, and the textual.[12] It represents a response to a specific time and place; it establishes links among itself, its author, and its readers; and it constructs an interplay of words, structures, and signs. Poets, to be sure, are conditioned by the time and place in which they live. As Toril Moi explains, an author's personal situation and intentions can become "no more than one of many conflicting strands that make up the contradictory construct we call the text." A whole set of different structures (ideological, economic, social, and political) intersect to produce precisely those textual structures.[13] Méndez, de la Torre, Chacel, Conde, and Champourcin are five distinct writers with varying personal circumstances; but as contemporaries, they formed a group of women obliged to confront the same contextual reality. While a glance at their context and biography bestows an historical existence on their works, it must be stressed, at the same time, that for all of its referential potential, for its explicit reflection of reality, literature (and perhaps poetry more than another genre) remains at bottom the symbolic transformation of reality. A vehicle for the configuration of personal visions and the product of collective social realities, poetry is a complex network of symbolic representation. A recognition of poetry's independence from reality and an awareness of the artistry of the writer become particularly important in the case of women poets if their work is to transcend traditional accusations of privacy and banality that have pursued women's poetry. As Alicia Suskin Ostriker has explained, women's poetry has routinely been viewed as busywork, as a private, idle preoccupation to compensate for frustrated love or the lack of fulfillment in motherhood and not as poetry of a "true writer."[14] To consider poetry merely unmediated self-expression not only obscures poetry's real power to create and recreate, to transform and re-form, but it also perpetuates the notion that women fail to distinguish life from art and to subordinate impulse to reflection.

The dual nature of literary discourse as historical product and artistic construct, as referential and symbolic, not only invites an open, flexible reading of their works, it also accounts, in part, for the bifurcation in feminist criticism of recent decades. One approach, often called the Anglo-American position, is linked to social theory and judges texts primarily on their political consciousness and effectiveness. Texts are expected to chronicle the women's personal experience with social oppression. The other approach, usually identified as the French current, is associated with postmodern linguistic and psychoanalytic theories and analyzes texts ahistorically for differences from the male symbolic order. It celebrates the biological features that identify women and recommends that women write about and through their sexual difference. This feminist biocriticism runs the risk of reaffirming the essentialism promulgated by the male theorists engaged in the debate on gender in Spain during the first third of the century, and it tends to reinforce the traditional patriarchal dichotomy between body and intellect, reason and sentiment, that the writers like those studied here diligently tried to subvert. Anglo-American feminism can be equally doctrinaire, because as Moi discerns, underlying it is the assumption that the "good" feminist writers "would present truthful images of strong women with which the reader may identify."[15] This requirement can jeopardize the appreciation of Spanish women poets whose ultra-conservative society did not allow them to fulfill today's expectations of feminist rage nor to display a collective feminist consciousness. Social feminist criticism can lead to the anachronistic censure of what constitutes for it an impoverished vision and thereby perpetuates the exclusion or devaluation of women writers. Since the Spanish women poets of the twenties refused to be confined within the boundaries of traditional feminine literature and they attempted to free themselves, though poetry, from constrictions of various kinds, criticism which requires that they conform to preconceived criteria would form another set of exclusionary conditions depriving them of literary worth.

Nonetheless, references to current feminist theory are decidedly helpful because they alert us to new ways of looking at authors, give useful terminology, and provide a familiar context in which to scrutinize unexplored works. I believe the poets studied here are particularly well served by reading double, as Naomi Schor recommends. By employing a reading that is "a simultaneous assertion and denial of sexual difference," the risks inherent in both are avoided because to read beyond difference runs the risk of reinforcing the canon and its founding sexual hierarchies and exclusions, while to read for difference is to risk relapsing into essentialism and its inevitable consequence of marginalization.[16] Social considerations grant women poets a temporal, albeit marginalized, existence, and an analysis of difference can bestow upon their works a vital distinctiveness; but reading beyond difference permits both. Interpretive adaptability gives their work the greatest visibility and allows for the exposure of variances and evolutions.

***

Having defined the parameters for the concepts of absence and presence as used in this study and identified the theoretical approach best suited to an exploration of the poetry written by Spanish women in the twenties and thirties, I turn to the five specific poets this book treats. Although each will be presented in separate chapters from the perspective dictated by their individual poetic elaborations, together they share certain features that bind them in a group, however loose and undefined it may be. Viewing women as a group has the interpretive advantage of revealing patterns that, as

Showalter has said, would not be perceptible if they are studied only in their relation to male writers,[17] and of giving them a visibility they would not otherwise have. As a group they gain a place on the temporal continuum of changing female consciousness. Concha Méndez, Josefina de la Torre, Rosa Chacel, Carmen Conde, and Ernestina de Champourin were poets who struggled between the two levels of women's self-consciousness some call "feminine" and "female,"[18] never reaching that more recent, feminist stage in the development of poetry by women in which the poet "both validates herself as she is and works toward the revolution, the transformations she desires."[19] They refused to internalize the "feminine" features of passivity, sentimentality, and purity deemed "natural" and beneficial to women, but they were never ready to start any revolution.

Seeing them as a group also relates them to the literary contemporaries of their own time span. These five poets maintained personal and publishing ties with the male writers of their time, but have never been considered members of the Generation of 27. Yet, the caliber of their publishers set them apart from other women poets of their day. They formed varying connections among themselves, but never banded together as a consolidated group intent on advancing the concerns of female poets. The incohesiveness of this group of women poets, the absence of a leader around which to rally, and their lack of responsiveness to historical events prevent the application to them of the German notion of generation as developed in the period by Julius Petersen and discussed in Spain by José Ortega y Gasset and Pedro Salinas. Other factors, however, such as their dates of birth (within a space of a decade from 1898 to 1907); an intellectual formation curbed by marginalization, yet nurtured by male mentors and by a strong desire to read; and a certain amount of personal interrelation create generational-like bonds among them. They adopted aspects of the vanguard language, adapting them to their feminine perspective of life. More importantly, by embracing creativity as an assertive and liberating step toward self-realization, they subverted both the sentimentality of some of their female predecessors and the patriarchal limitations placed on women. They all settled in Madrid; they published in some of the same journals; and they were united by links of friendship. Champourcin and Chacel published in the journal *Héroe*, run by Méndez and her husband; and they attended the couple's wedding, a memorable festival of young intellectuals and bohemians.[20] Chacel wrote a sonnet on Méndez; Champourcin and Méndez saw one another in exile in Mexico; and Champourcin and Conde were friends before the civil war and after the former's return to Spain. In fact, according to Champourcin's account in her *La ardilla y la rosa* [The squirrel and the rose], it was she who accompanied Conde on her first visit to Juan Ramón Jiménez, who had published in *Ley* compositions that later appeared in her book *Brocal* [Well curb]. Afterwards, Conde dedicated to

Champourcin a poem about the visit titled "Guía de la buena amistad" [The guide of good friendship].

To avoid errors of generalization and oversimplification, an examination of female writing, even if historical references are included, must acknowledge the differences and divisions that make their poetry a product of separate individuals. In 1975 Annette Kolodny already warned: "What we have not fully acknowledged is that the variation among individual women may be as great as those between women and men . . . perhaps . . . greater."[21] Therefore it must be stressed that although writing within similar poetic currents and enjoying personal associations among themselves, Concha Méndez, Josefina de la Torre, Rosa Chacel, Carmen Conde, and Ernestina de Champourcin are distinct individuals whose poetry differs in origin and outcome. Méndez, the "free spirit" of the group, celebrates her release from spatial confinement; de la Torre, not coincidentally the singer and actress, will struggle to speak, to break the silence ascribed to her gender, and to find her own voice; Chacel, the intellectual with an interest in philosophy, will forcefully assert her ideas even at the cost of the sustained exercise of poetry writing; Conde, the only female poet of the century to enjoy persistent acclaim, establishes herself early as the speaking and creative subject at the center of her poetic universe; and Champourcin, also a poet of enduring poetic impulse, carves out her own sense of self in the presence of the other, be it human or divine. The contrasting nature of the poetry written by Rosa Chacel and Concha Méndez as well as that of Josefina de la Torre and Ernestina de Champourcin requires that their individual differences prompt differing structures in the chapters devoted to each one.

Méndez articulated a noteworthy voice of freedom and impetuosity during a brief period before the Spanish civil war, earning for herself the passing notice of critics and the bewildered admiration of her male fellow poets. Contradicting perennial stereotypes, the poetry she wrote between 1925 and 1933 escapes confinement, closed spaces, and connectiveness in favor of movement, openness, and autonomy. Unable to sustain her exuberant pose as liberated woman for very long, her carefree poetic persona faded quickly. Multiple lessons in loss and the lack of a kindred literary milieu compelled her to withdraw into the shadowy zones of her inner spiritual world. Only the celebration of motherhood relieves the dark tones of her later poetry. A precocious and admired poet, Josefina de la Torre displays an evolution similar to Méndez's in that an initial phase of vibrant presence slowly unravels as feelings of absence and nostalgia begin to dominate and the tone of her poetic voice grows increasingly somber. The question of silence and voice is central to her poetry. At first, nature and the word provide a timeless refuge from the world, but soon she becomes preoccupied with time, its loss, and finiteness. In contrast to Méndez and de la

Torre, Chacel eschews the disclosure of personal feelings and autobiographical detail and steadfastly denies throughout her long life the existence of
gender difference in any aspect of literature. Yet, an examination of the
collection of sonnets she published in 1936 reveals that she also forged,
through poetry, an image of strength and self-assertion. In her case, technical dexterity and self-censorship prove to be masks for an underlining urge
to exert control on every level of her art. Rather than exposing personal
sentiment in her poetry, she follows the dictates of her intellect and curtails
her poetic development. Champourcin embraces the personal. She asserts
her presence as an emotional being intent on self-fulfillment and plenitude
through an amorous relationship with the other. She textualizes erotic desire at the same time she pursues her ultimate goal of spiritual transcendence. In her later poetry, her desire is directed to the divine other, but
consciousness of the terrestrial coupled with an intense aspiration for eternal union persists in her poetry. Carmen Conde also displays greater depth
and sobriety in the poetry she wrote after the civil war, when a broad gamut
of concerns, both personal and collective, social and existential, floods her
verses. In her pre-civil war works, she portrays the female self as a cosmic
woman delighting in a pantheistic union with nature.

***

Exile, after 1936, cut off Méndez, Chacel, and Champourcin physically
from their homeland, and a shift in their poetic focus guaranteed their separation from mainstream poetry in Spain. In the aftermath of the civil war,
poetry in Spain centered on the effects of that event, on issues of social
justice, and on philosophical themes. However, these women poets turned
to introspection and concerns traditionally associated with women—abandonment in love, motherhood, and religion. Carmen Conde, who wrote,
from within Spain, about human suffering and problems of the national
consciousness, publicly embraced a poetics of difference and espoused the
mother as the universal paradigm for the female poet. Only for these reasons was she able to attract critical recognition in the early years of the
Franco dictatorship. Yet during the twenties and thirties, they all exemplify
the efforts of the female poet to inscribe herself, as woman and artist, within
the masculine cultural arena and to declare, with exuberance, their sense
of energizing self-affirmation. As Conde testifies, "cortando los hilos del
pasado, lejano o inmediato, dos o tres poetas brotamos con la ilusión que
todo lo joven pone en renovar el mundo en que ha nacido" [cutting the
remote or immediate links to the past, two or three of us poets emerged
with the illusion anyone young invests in renewing the world in which he or

she is born].[22] Their tangential contacts with the leading male writers of the times and their assimilation of the vanguardist principles did not secure their access to the canon, just as their divergence did not earn them literary acclaim. Confined to an environment of conflictive ambivalence, they modified or rejected traditional views of women only with restraint and hesitancy. However, within the climate of misogyny, tepid support, or total disregard that surrounded them, their efforts at self-affirmation represent a venture more noteworthy than what a superficial consideration might suggest. For a brief moment of a little more than ten years, they earned a modicum of artistic recognition and they depicted woman as free, active, and powerful. As women and as poets, they converted absence into presence and became creative subjects within their own poetic world.

2

Spanish Women Poets in Context: Navigating Choppy Waters

Literary texts are symbolic creations that textualize reality and formulate their own distinctive visions; they are also historical products that in some way chronicle and reflect the world around them. Literary production, like other human endeavors, is shaped by experiential circumstances, social constructs, and conceptual supports. Because the ideological framework underpinning culture projects the interests of the dominant ruling group of a society, a consideration of context is particularly fruitful for the study of literature by women, for whom the steadfast restriction of patriarchal precepts and practices long limited their participation in literature. An examination of the dynamic between women and their context leads to an understanding of their absence from the canon, of the poetics of women's writing, and of their implicit struggle for textual identity. Also, any reconsideration of the circumstances in which women wrote rescues them from oblivion and restores them to history.

The work of Spanish women poets of the twenties and thirties rests within two time frames: the moment of production of their specific texts and the subsequent period in which the canon is established. Raw data on the exclusion of women poets from anthologies, literary histories, biobibliographic dictionaries, and general studies on poetry document their absence from the canon; but the pressures to exclude women from the public arena of their time constitute a more complex process requiring a consideration of different factors. These include the nature of the social and cultural environment in which they wrote, the extent of their participation in the literary mainstream of their day, and the strategies they used to negotiate their entry into that realm. A review of the context surrounding these poets reveals that their works were hidden from sight by the later established canon, but in their day the presence of their poetry was not totally concealed. The social situation of women in Spain, especially with regard to education, improved noticeably in the first third of the century, but the ideological tenets of both the general public and of most of the country's intellectuals remained adverse to women's poetry. Within a contradictory context of support and rejection, women writers tried valiantly to etch for themselves a small mark on the cultural map of their day.

WOMEN POETS AND THE CANON

The absence of Spanish women poets from the annals of literary history may be their most prominent feature, for as José-Carlos Mainer accurately observes, "brillan por su ausencia" [they are conspicuous by their absence].[1] They are only present as the void their absence implies. The examples of the exclusion or neglect to which they have been subjected are seemingly endless and sometimes startling. In one of the few insightful studies on the work of Ernestina de Champourcin, Andrew P. Debicki bemoans the neglect her work has suffered, duly noting her conspicuous absence from books on the period and perceptively observing that the few critics who have noticed her speak not of her poetry but of her associations with her mentor, Juan Ramón Jiménez, or her husband, the poet Juan José Domenchina.[2] If omission and oversight are the hallmarks of the criticism of the poetry of Ernestina de Champourcin, the work of the other female poets of her generation has encountered similar or sometimes greater disregard. The case of Josefina de la Torre is extreme; she is left out of most histories of literature as well as studies on the poetry of the period.[3] Bibliography on her consists of mere notes and passing references. When she is remembered, it is usually as one of the two women included in Gerardo Diego's 1934 landmark anthology of contemporary poets or perhaps as a founder of a theater group.[4]

Given the revival of interest in the work of Rosa Chacel after her return to Spain in 1974 and her receipt of the Premio Nacional de las Letras in 1987, she fared better in recent decades than the other women writers of the twenties and thirties. She is included in volumes in which the others do not appear and sometimes she receives greater attention.[5] Nevertheless, she has been studied almost exclusively as a novelist and essayist, not as a poet; and before 1970, she was overlooked as much as the others.[6] Concha Méndez is a particularly disturbing case of neglect. Despite the critical commentary elicited by her works when they were published in the twenties and thirties, and her significant role as a publisher during the period, her work has experienced some glaring examples of exclusion. Besides the omissions she shares with the others, she is inexplicably left out of major dictionaries of literature.[7] An effort has been made to publish some of her poetry posthumously, and a flurry of newspaper notices and magazine reviews appeared when her memoirs, written with the aid of her granddaughter, appeared in 1990.[8] Even Josefina de la Torre was resurrected from total obscurity by an anthology published in the Canary Islands, her birthplace.[9] Ernestina de Champourcin also enjoyed a revival of her poetry with the publication of her complete works, prefaced by a fine panoramic study written by José Angel Ascunce.[10]

Other than a few recent editions of their poetry, some isolated studies in journals, and a number of newspaper articles—usually reviews or interviews—the bibliography on the major women poets of the twenties and thirties, until the appearance of the books by Pérez and Wilcox, was limited to entries in literary dictionaries and histories.[11] The publication of bio-bibliographical dictionaries on women writers reflects a conscious attempt to rectify the neglect these writers have suffered,[12] but on the whole, the appearance of Spanish women poets in the volumes that establish the canon has been extremely scant and therefore not particularly informative. Anthologies are telling indicators of the institutionalized canon of Spanish poetry. Much has been made of the symbolic importance of the inclusion of Champourcin and de la Torre in Gerardo Diego's 1934 anthology of the Generation of 27, but this early concession to a female presence in poetry did not guarantee its longevity among the ranks of male canonical poets.[13] This passing acknowledgment soon waned. According to his survey of a hundred anthologies of Spanish and Spanish American poetry published between 1940 and 1980, Howard Mancing found that the only Spanish woman poet of the twentieth century anthologized is Carmen Conde.[14] As with dictionaries, the publication of anthologies devoted exclusively to women opens opportunities for the publication of their verses, although not necessarily for incorporation into the canon.[15]

When not invisible, women poets are isolated from mainstream poetry or in some way diminished. In histories of literature, they are often relegated to names on a list: a concluding list of poets of the Generation of 27, a list of "puristas" [purists], and a list of novelists in the case of Chacel.[16] In one literary manual, Chacel secures a place on three different lists.[17] The most common practice is to marginalize women by confining them to the separate category of feminine poets, not in an attempt to highlight a divergent, alternative literary practice, but as a patronizing gesture of condescension.[18] Sometimes they are dismissed with a cursory allusion;[19] other times the poets are granted a few well-sounding words that do little to promote either an understanding of their art or an interest in their works. For example, in a subsection of "intimate and sentimental" poetry, Guillermo Díaz-Plaja lists fifteen women poets whom he quickly describes with epithets that for the most part reinforce the stereotype of female poetry as sweet, sentimental, and secondary; he uses phrases such as "la elegante delicadeza sentimental," "la gracia ligera," and "la delicada ternura" [elegant sentimental delicacy, light grace, and delicate tenderness].[20] This isolation of women poets from substantive discussions of literature implicitly carries with it a negative assessment of their value as writers.

In addition to being slight, references to these poets can contain inaccuracies that compound the general lack of awareness of their work. For example, Angel Valbuena Prat's assumption that Champourcin's Basque origins influenced her works is repeated by Federico Carlos Sainz de Robles and in the Oxford Companion to Spanish Literature.[21] She was indeed born in Vitoria, in the Basque province of Alava, but only because her parents were vacationing there in the summer of 1905.[22] Criticism that is minimal, misguided, or misleading leaves the work of poets like Champourcin in a vacuum that not only separates them from the canon in which they tried to insert themselves, but also hampers our understanding of the period in which they evolved.

THE DISAPPEARING ACT

Before Spanish women poets virtually disappeared from the canon, they made a modest, peripheral appearance on the cultural stage. Their association in the Generation of 27 was always marginal, but poets like Concha Méndez and Ernestina de Champourcin did enjoy a certain amount of literary attention during the twenties and thirties. Never possessing the commanding presence of the novelist Emilia Pardo Bazán at the end of the last century, or the name earned by the prose writers Carmen de Burgos or Concha Espina in the first decades of this century, they nonetheless published the books they wrote, occasionally appeared in literary journals, and mingled with the major proponents of the new generation. Yet, even though they wrote on some of the same themes and used some of the same poetic techniques as their male counterparts, these women have not been granted membership in the famed Generation of 27.

The reasons for their disappearance are literary, social, and political.[23] Blame for much of the exclusion of these women poets can be placed on the gender bias underlying canon formation and on the prevailing notion of the time that the role of poet was at odds with the literary potential of women. Central also to the marginalization of the female writer in Spain was the ideological and theological aversion to women that institutionalized misogyny on all levels, despite the influence of liberal thought within intellectual circles. The effects of exile on the tenuous links between women and the writers of official culture cannot be underestimated nor can the exclusionary policies of Franco's authoritarian government toward all exiled Spaniards.

The role of exile in the absence of these women from the canon was decisive. At the outset of the Spanish civil war in 1936, the alliances that

Concha Méndez, Ernestina de Champourcin, and Rosa Chacel had forged with vanguard literature broke. The three of them went into exile and their literary production waned or ceased drawing attention.[24] Cut off from their native country and the collective evolution of its poetry, they could only write within the vacuum of personal, inner experience. Economic necessity demanded that Champourcin involve herself in the more practical work of translator. Méndez, for her part, found herself in unreceptive foreign milieus. Speaking of Cuba, she says "aquellos hombres tenían una dosis de machismo muy grande" [those men had a very large dose of machismo]; and as Emma Rodríguez has noted, it was extremely difficult for this woman of nearly fifty to find a niche in the cultural life of Mexico.[25]

Exiled male writers of the Generation of 27 were also withdrawn from national attention, and many of their works were censored or banned, but to a much lesser extent and for less time than in the case of the women.[26] While most men were eventually reintegrated into the literary consciousness, women poets were virtually obliterated. Only Chacel returned to Spain to be honored, rewarded, and appreciated, and then only for her prose. Ernestina de Champourcin returned to live in Spain but remained nearly invisible. Concha Méndez visited Spain after exile, yet left no imprint there. Josefina de la Torre never left Spain, but her voluntary disappearance from poetry erased her name as a poet. The fact that Carmen Conde, who remained in Spain and wrote of motherhood and the suffering caused by the war, gained acceptance would suggest that exile was important in the erasure of the names of the female poets associated with the defeated republic.

Even before 1936, the literary response to the work of women poets was uneven and contradictory. While many respected critics took note of their poetry, their works did not make a strong impact on readers, nor were all responses impartial. The very nature of Modernism has been blamed for this tepid response. Critics have pointed out that the displacement of the Victorian aesthetic that prized sentimentality, conventionality, melodrama, religiosity, and pathos (qualities associated with women's writing) by a new aesthetic of authorial detachment, verbal sophistication, emotional restraint, originality, and complexity jeopardized the appreciation of works by women. Modernism in Spain, as elsewhere, says Bieder, was "a singularly male movement."[27] Before recent feminist observations, in 1931 Rosa Chacel already sensed that a crucial change had taken place in literature at the turn of the century; she wrote that "el arte fue quedando libre de la mujer" [art was slowly left without women]. Eros, she said, was no longer the center of man's life nor the nucleus of what he wrote.[28]

Although a change in aesthetics had occurred, one thing had not changed in Spain—its perennial conservatism. While some of the younger male poets supported the literary efforts of their female contemporaries, many critics displayed unabashed condescension, bias, and sexism in their comments about women writers. Paradoxically some of the critics, writers, and intellectuals with whom these women maintained otherwise cordial professional dealings uttered some of the most negative comments on them.[29] By 1925, it was acceptable for a woman to engage in certain "feminine" occupations, at least until marriage, or to be the helpmate in her husband's profession, after marriage, but creative activity was still off limits. Writing during the period, María del Pilar Oñate perceived the problem clearly: "La capacidad intelectual femenina . . . se acepta en la actualidad con la salvedad de la aptitud de la mujer para el trabajo creador y original propio del genio" [Female intellectual capacity is accepted nowadays except for women's aptitude for original and creative work characteristic of a genius.].[30]

At the time, public declarations of female artistic ineptitude were loud and direct. A particularly reactionary writer, Edmundo González Blanco, asserted that "Cierto, la mujer es un ser esencialmente receptivo, y, por ello, triunfará siempre en la asimilación utilitaria de conocimientos elementales. Pero cuando se trata de facultades creadoras, tiene que contentarse con el segundo rango" [Certainly, woman is an essentially receptive being, and, therefore, will always triumph in the utilitarian assimilation of basic knowledge. But when it is a question of creative faculties, she has to be content with second rank.].[31] Unable to conceive of women as writers, male critics tended to pay tribute to them through praise of the traditional feminine attribute of beauty, but their patronizing winks of approval constituted little more than a subtle, softened version of the overt affirmations of women's lack of intellectual ability. Luis Franco de Espés credited the success of a lecture given by María Teresa León in 1929 at the Círculo de Bellas Artes to her beauty, not her intellect.[32] Melchor Fernández Almagro wrote, "La primera obligación de la mujer es ser guapa. La inteligencia es la gracia que añade, o el suplemento con que se excusa" [A woman's first obligation is to be beautiful. Intelligence is an added grace or a supplement with which she tries to justify herself].[33] Intellectual capacity was considered nothing but an accessory to a feminine essence rooted in beauty. The bias to which women writers were subjected was at times so subtle as to be nearly imperceptible. As a student of art, Rosa Chacel was included in an interview with young writers on architecture, but besides being segregated by gender at the end of the article in a section titled "Damas" [ladies], she was asked different questions, questions referring to domesticity and personal preference, not architectural precepts.[34] Although a period of literary innovation and artistic liberation, 1920 to 1936 was a time of condescension and deceptive acceptance for the woman poet. She had to navigate cautiously the choppy waters of the reactionary social context in which she lived.

If Spanish women poets had to write against prevailing currents before 1936, after that date their names were drowned in a sea of oblivion beyond critical view. No matter how slight the recognition of their work before 1936, a difference nonetheless exists between the tepid reception of their early work and their subsequent exclusion from literary histories and anthologies. Like any history, the literary canon reflects the ideological and cultural perspectives of those responsible for determining its boundaries.[35] Therefore any divergences from patriarchal norms that women writers achieve during their lifetime can be expunged later, once the framers of literary history set literature back on the track of the interests of the cultural and social groups to which they belong. If, as Elaine Showalter has shown, it is common for celebrated women writers to vanish without a trace from the records of posterity, it should not surprise that marginalized poets disappear.[36] For instance, Concha Méndez was relegated to mere administrative assistant in the studies that accompany the 1977 facsimile edition of their journal *Héroe*, despite her work with her husband to launch many of the figures of the new generation through their publishing efforts.[37] Although two reviews of *Presencia a oscuras* [Presence in the dark] were published in the 1950s, Champourcin also did not appear in the literary press of Spain until the seventies, when she returned to Spain toward the end of the Franco regime. Some belated attempts were made to recognize earlier female narrators Rosa Chacel, Mercè Rodoreda, and María Zambrano, but women poets in Spain have been forgotten to a great extent, even by their literary descendents.[38]

The Status of Women in Spain in the Twenties

The understanding of the cultural situation of the female poet in Spain in the 1920s can be enhanced by a brief examination of the status of women as it related to the larger context of their social, economic, and political circumstances. To appreciate its reactions to and difficulties with the dominant male discourse, women's writing needs to be located within the "regime of truths" that Michel Foucault insists each society enforces through its systems of power and employs to predetermine individual responses to one's human environment.[39] Specifically, to gauge the precise effects of gender dynamics on women writers in a given historical moment, as Joan Kelly affirms, certain factors must be considered: women's economic and political roles, their cultural roles and access to education, and the ideology about women displayed and advocated in society.[40]

In the first decades of the twentieth century, Spain continued to be essentially a country of conservative thought wedded to the dogma of the Catholic Church. The leader of the Counter-Reformation, Spain had a long tradition of staunch resistance to the modification of female roles and to women's self-determination. The aspirations of women were set centuries ago by Fray Luis de León's notions of "la perfecta casada" [the perfect wife], who goes to mass early in the morning and then stays at home cooking, tending children, and doing household chores. Moral obligation dictated that abnegation, modesty, and asexuality predispose women to an existence of silent devotion to domesticity and of restricted mental development.

Economically, Spain did not display an open attitude toward women either. José Manuel López Abiada suggests that the differences in social and economic structures of Spain and Anglo-Saxon countries contributed strongly to the delay in a women's rights movement in Spain. Without the industrial and democratic basis of these countries, Spain lacked a well-developed middle class and its characteristic demands for improved labor conditions and educational possibilities.[41] Besides providing domestic labor as servants and housewives, women worked in factories, primarily in textile and tobacco factories, and a substantial percentage worked in the agricultural sector. Men, however, not only restricted the types of jobs women could hold, they also attempted to block their participation in collective action on behalf of the working class. Thus, joining the work force did not alter women's exclusion from avenues to power or improved conditions. Conservative forces, led by the Church, reinforced male bias; and leftist labor movements, while promoting class struggle, disregarded the issue of women's rights.[42]

Nevertheless, the beginning of the twentieth century saw the slow incorporation of middle class women into the work force and a slight expansion in the kinds of occupations to which women were allowed access. According to Rosa Capel, the number of women working in occupations deemed nonthreatening to a woman's femininity (namely teacher, librarian, office worker, sales clerk, and civil servant in the telephone, telegraph, postal, and transportation fields) doubled between 1910 and 1920 and surged again from 1920 to 1930.[43] Work outside the home was acceptable only in the case of absolute economic necessity and as a temporary phase before marriage, yet certain changes in the economic and demographic structure of the country, like a decrease in the marriage rate, forced more women to work outside the home. By 1936, laws on behalf of women had changed their legal status appreciably, but their application was more hypothetical than real; and, as Capel notes, laws were easier to change than attitudes. The Spanish woman continued to live in "un mar de contradicciones entre las ideas que le inclucaron y sus necesidades materiales" [a sea of contradictions between the ideas that were inculcated in her and her material needs].[44]

Education, not civil rights, was the first area of women's lives that moved toward equality in Spain. In the second half of the nineteenth century certain ideological and economic changes supported the growth of education for women. Women began to speak out on their rights to education;[45] the revolutionary movements of socialism, Marxism, and anarchism saw advantages in molding women's minds; and the economic evolution of bourgeois society required more and more women to work and therefore to receive professional training. After 1858, a number of schools for women were founded; middle schools were opened to women; and a general debate on education took place. To counteract the growing tendency to modernize and secularize schooling, the Catholic church enacted a few experiments without truly changing its essential principles.[46] It was, however, a small group of enlightened male intellectuals known as "krausistas" [followers of the philosophy of Krause] who would bring the first concrete changes to education of women in Spain.[47] Even before the creation of their extraordinary school, the Institución Libre de Enseñanza [Free Institute of Learning], in 1876, one of their proponents, Fernando de Castro, began to redesign education for women. In 1869 he organized a series of lectures at the University of Madrid on the education of women, and he created the Escuela de Institutrices [Teachers' College].[48] His most significant contribution was the creation of the Asociación para la Enseñanza de la Mujer [Association for the Instruction of Women], an association that not only reformed general education for young women but also prepared them for a number of "suitable" trades.

The reforms adopted by the "krausista" pedagogues were limited to a small group of upper middle-class children and were not endorsed officially by the government. The illiteracy rate for women in 1900 was still 71%.[49] Secondary education was not encouraged for women and the university was all but inaccessible to them. As María Angeles Durán puts it, the history of women and the university was "an absence of a thousand years."[50] Although the number remained small, the percentage of women attending universities increased more than a thousandfold in Spain between 1900 and 1930.[51] María de Maeztu can be singled out for her dedication to higher education for women. Using American colleges like Smith and Vassar as her model, she fashioned the Residencia de Señoritas [Women's Residence] into a center that served not only as a residence hall for women attending the university or preparing entrance exams, but as a nondegree granting college offering lectures, scholarships, laboratories, field trips, sporting events, and other social and intellectual activities. With close ties to both the Institución Libre de Enseñanza and the Instituto Internacional, the Residencia de Señoritas fostered the development of the total woman—the development of her mental, physical, and moral capacities. In 1920 she also organized university women into a group called Juventud Universitaria Femenina.[52]

Despite the efforts of people like Maeztu, the overall level of education for women remained lamentably low because of rigid restrictions administered in the home. As Pilar Folguera explains, the social class and ideological bent of the family were the determining factors in the kind of education girls received, with those belonging to the middle class more likely than those of the upper classes to further their studies.[53] Within this context, it is not surprising that women writers of the twenties and thirties did not necessarily benefit from a college education. They acquired their knowledge of literature outside the classroom either by reading on their own or through personal contact with writers. Rosa Chacel, for example, for health reasons received her academic schooling at home under the tutelage of her parents. She began attending art school at the age of eight, but her appreciation for the written word came from her home. Ernestina de Champourcin also came from a family environment that nurtured an interest in literature. Proficient in French and English from an early age, she longed to attend college, but refused to succumb to the prevailing custom that women be chaperoned to class. Carmen Conde obtained a teaching degree, but most of her intellectual development was achieved on her own.

The Feminist Debate

The discussion of women's issues sustained in Spain throughout the first third of the century confirms the threat of the growing presence of women in society. Spain, however, never has had a vigorous and organized feminist movement. Nothing resembling the suffragette movement of the United States and England existed in Spain. Except for the writings of Concepción Arenal and some of the articles of Pardo Bazán, little was done to improve the social conditions of women until reformers influenced by "krausismo" began to take concrete steps to develop education for women. Women, themselves, regardless of their class, educational level, or cultural involvement, displayed little consciousness of the unifying problems of their gender.[54] Nevertheless, the growing need of middle class women to earn a living fostered the introduction of pragmatic feminist arguments, and the political advances made by women in other countries inevitably influenced the debate on women's issues in Spain.[55] The ideological dimensions of Spanish feminism were, however, diluted, if not dubious.

The term "feminism" surfaced in Spain in 1899 in a book by Adolfo González Posada.[56] But no movement of any sort can be said to have existed in Spain until 1918, and then only in a very moderate form consisting essentially of proposals to enhance rather than to modify women's traditional roles as wife and mother. The perennial impact of the church, the conservatism of the female elite and the apathy of the general female popu-

lation, the general indifference to women's issues on the part of leftist political parties, and the late arrival of international feminist thought formed
a composite of factors converging to make the Spanish brand of feminism
a timid, mildly reformist, and unsubstantial phenomenon.

Nonetheless, around 1918 certain changes in the conditions of women
and attitudes toward them took place in Spain.[57] An intensification in the
process of urbanization, a series of demographic changes, and the introduction of foreign models of liberation began to release a few Spanish
women from the long-standing physical, social, and intellectual strictures
that would continue to condemn the vast majority to a life consumed in
drudgery or banality.[58] As a result of patterns assimilated from other coun-
ties and in response to a new emphasis on sports, women's mode of dress,
their conduct, and even their bodies changed. Corsets were abandoned,
rudimentary versions of slacks were designed, and short hair became styl-
ish. The aloof, hourglass figure as a paradigm of female beauty gave way to
the "garçonne look," the adolescent boyish image of slender hips, flat chest,
and exposed legs. Women used makeup freely, became physically more active, and appeared more cheerful. During the "roaring twenties," an array
of exciting, new carefree activities—tennis, aviation, dancing, night clubs—
became fashionable among the youth of means. As a woman who swam,
skied, and rode in airplanes, Concha Méndez, among the poets studied
here, is the prototype of this modern woman.

At this time women also mingled more freely with men, not only in sports,
but at the university and in cultural affairs. This new freedom marked the
beginning of what Julián Marías terms "amistad intersexual" [friendship
between the sexes] and the creation of what Luis Aranguren calls the
"revolución de promoción de la mujer y revolución erótica" [revolution to
promote women and sexual revolution].[59] This new, emancipated woman
fascinated some, but was condemned by many as "the modern Eve," an
adulteration of essential feminine identity and national traits, a masculin-
ization of women imposed by fashionable, but immoral, foreign modes of
conduct.[60]

The appearance of the "modern woman" as well as the general feminist
agenda of the early twentieth century elicited a lively debate in the general
press and in intellectual circles of Spain.[61] The nineteenth-century misogynist premises of phrenology, according to which women were structurally
and organically weak, deficient, and limited, still predominated.[62] Many
doctors, essayists, and scholars continued well into the twenties to subscribe
to these pseudoscientific justifications for the deprecation of women
and for their exclusion from all spheres but the domestic one. The an-
tifeminists, however, could not keep from recognizing the importance
of the threat of feminism to the established male hegemony. Edmundo
González Blanco, for instance, called feminism "el principal de todos los

problemas sociales que traen revuelto al mundo" [the foremost among social problems upsetting the world]. He indicts feminists for their selfish destruction of the family and their "absurd" aspiration to equality and individualism.[63]

The preeminent twentieth-century Spanish intellectual José Ortega y Gasset, on a number of occasions, outlined the differences between the sexes that he saw as verifying the superiority of men, and he used his journal, *Revista de Occidente*, to broadcast views on essentialism and to circulate the justification for feminine subordination.[64] In its initial year, 1923, the *Revista de Occidente* published articles by Georg Simmel, who identified the feminine as undifferentiated nature trapped in gender and the masculine as both individualized and universal, the force of action and intellect. In 1929 Ortega included an article by Waldo Frank criticizing feminism in the United States, an essay by Manuel G. Morente outlining the distinction between feminine culture and feminism, and a study by Carl Jung urging the preservation of the separation of the sexes and warning of the harmful consequences of its elimination.

More moderate intellectuals supported the idea, not of equality but of complementarity. A more modern disguise for the perpetuation of the inequality of women, the theory of complementarity delineated essential differences between men and women, primarily on the basis of biology, supposedly without moral judgment as to superiority or inferiority of those traits. Nevertheless, this notion of gender difference essentially maintained the unshakeable belief in gender difference as a means to preserving patriarchal authority. For example, the priest Graciano Martínez declared that he supported equality of women; but, while conceding that women might display their intelligence "discreetly," he chided feminists for not focusing on their natural function and charm, which lay in their distinctive role as mother.[65] The major exponent of complementarity, Gregorio Marañón, argued that psychological and intellectual differences between the sexes, although not confirming the inferiority of women, did nonetheless reinforce the desirability of the sexes expressing their "natural" temperament and attitudes. For him, any deviation from these "norms" signified sexual abnormality.[66] According to Campo Alange, Dr. Marañón's theory of differentiation caused quite a stir, falling "como una bomba en esta sociedad a un tiempo pervertida y timorata" [like a bomb in this society, at one and the same time perverted and prudish].[67]

Although considered highly controversial, a small group of moderate, male intellectuals began earnestly to defend the emancipation of women and to argue that changes in women's social roles need not erase their feminine nature. The term "feminism" itself, however, never gained favor, and no document appeared in Spain that could be considered an authentic feminist manifesto.[68] Furthermore, the few thinkers who supported the expansion of women's rights did not espouse radical change, but adhered to the notion of "complementarity." José Francos Rodríguez, for example, refuted the Spanish truism that "la carrera de la mujer es casarse" [marriage is woman's profession], stressing the need, particularly for middle-class women, to resolve their economic difficulties through work rather than unhappy marriages.[69] He also ardently defended women's right to vote. The most well-known defender of women's rights during the twenties was Gregorio Martínez Sierra. In 1919 he delivered a famous lecture in which he defined feminism as women helping other women in need and as the opportunity for all women to reach their full potential.[70] Martínez Sierra and his fellow progressive writers favored a "feminismo sensato" [sensible feminism], a program of conservative change that improved women's social conditions but neither altered their traditional social roles nor disrupted existing relations between the sexes.

Women were also involved in the feminist debate of the twenties, but they were cast in the role of respondent to the declarations made by men, and their arguments did not carry authoritative weight. María Luisa Navarro de Luzuriaga, for example, confronted Ortega y Gasset in *La Gaceta Literaria* on two occasions. She responded to his remarks on the negative impact of women's "porosidad mental" [mental porosity] on Spanish culture; she contradicted his contention that biology disqualifies women from public affairs and insisted that femininity and feminism are not incompatible.[71] In an essay published in 1931 in *Revista de Occidente*, Rosa Chacel also addressed the theories on the nature of women defended by Ortega. Questioning both Simmel and Jung, she rejected their essentialist differentiation between the sexes. She argued that Eros and Logos cannot be assigned a gender and that these two principles manifest themselves in both males and females. Frank in her appraisal of the theories that disallow feminine intelligence, she ascribed to them "mil temores pueriles sin fundamento lógico alguno" [a thousand puerile fears lacking in any logical basis].[72] Women like Carmen de Burgos, María de Maeztu, María Lejárraga, Carmen Díaz de Mendoza —the Condesa de San Luis—and Margarita Nelken dealt with more concrete issues. While upper-middle-class women like Maeztu strove to improve women's access to education and culture, Nelken and other women of the left were critical of moderate reforms that failed to change social structures and ideologies more radically.

The twenties witnessed a flurry of ventures including books, magazines, events, and organizations that focused on women. In 1920 a noteworthy meeting, sponsored by Acción Social Femenina [feminine social action], took place in Madrid, at which a number of male and female speakers publicly denounced the low cultural and educational levels of women and called for an improvement in both these areas. A variety of women's issues—education, family, hygiene, paid work—were addressed in women's magazines, usually with a conservative, if not religious, slant, but they inevitably created a new awareness of women's social circumstances. Women themselves founded feminist magazines—namely *La Voz de la Mujer*, the foremost among them begun in 1917 by Celsia Regis, and *Mundo Femenino*, a moderate, apolitical publication started by María Espinosa in 1921.[73] Women were writing as journalists in greater numbers, and literature by women was appearing occasionally in prestigious journals.

Around 1920 many different women's organizations were formed. Most Spanish women joined one of the Catholic women's organizations, which under the guise of charity delivered religious indoctrination to poor women on morality and family life. Of the more progressive organizations, the most important was the Asociación Nacional de Mujeres Españolas [National Association of Spanish Women]. Founded in 1918, it promoted equal civil and political rights for women through its magazine *Mundo Femenino* and formed a confederation of five leading women's groups in an attempt to consolidate efforts on a national level.[74] Another very important women's group of the time was the Lyceum Club Femenino, formed in 1926 by María de Maeztu on the model of comparable clubs in England and the United States. A well-educated group of women with professions, writing careers, or close ties to the cultural world, it represented the female cultural elite. Among its members were the poets Concha Méndez and Ernestina de Champourcin, who served as secretary of its literature section. The Lyceum Club was designed as a center to promote the social and cultural concerns of women and as a pleasant place where women could exchange ideas without the interference of men.[75] This group of open-minded female intellectuals and its library collection were condemned as immoral and subversive. The Catholic newspapers printed an attack on the club for its secularism and denounced it as a "verdadera calamidad para el hogar y enemigo natural de la familia, y en primer lugar del marido" [real calamity for the home and the natural enemy of the family, and especially of husbands]. It went as far as to suggest that the moral climate of the city would be improved if these "féminas excéntricas y desequilibradas" [eccentric and unbalanced females] were hospitalized or confined.[76] Between 1926 and 1936 the Club effectively united a variety of ideological perspectives in a collective attempt to advance the feminist movement in Spain. It brought together female writers, professional women, and educated women interested in advancing their intellectual status.[77] However, its efforts were admittedly isolated and limited.

The twenties and thirties, therefore, represent a brief and slightly open window in the history of Spanish conservatism, a gestation period for an embryonic feminism that would be aborted by the totalitarian efforts of the Franco regime. Against the advances made by feminists outside Spain, the development of Spanish feminism pales in comparison. Although displaying a cohesion greater than anything known before, the movement remained limited to a small, privileged minority who failed to convert liberal theory into widespread practice.

WOMEN AND LITERATURE

Of the three public arenas—the work force, politics, and culture—into which Spanish women began to tread, the latter was particularly inhospitable because literature continued to be a forbidden zone for women. Yet women were beginning to figure more prominently in the publishing industry. Not only did urban newspapers begin to devote sections to women's interests, but women were launching their own periodicals.[78] Women were also involved in the publication of mainstream or avant-garde journals: Concha Méndez, with her husband Manuel Altolaguirre, published *Héroe, 1616,* and *El Caballo Verde para la Poesía;* Carmen Conde with her husband Antonio Oliver started a small journal called *Presencia;* and María Teresa León founded the leftist political magazine *Octubre* with Rafael Alberti.

Poetry by women was being published in leading journals of the day. Given the taboo against women writing poetry and the fact that poetry does not lend itself to public notoriety, the minimal appearance of women poets in the literary magazines of the period becomes noteworthy. For example, the magazine *Noreste,* published in Zaragoza, devoted one of its fourteen issues to poetry by women, providing us in this way a list of some of the women poets of the era: Dolores Arana, Carmen Conde, Maruja Falena, Elena Fortún, María Luisa de Buendía, Margarita de Pedroso, Rosario Suárez-Castiello, María Teresa Roca de Togores, and Josefina de la Torre. *La Gaceta Literaria,* the foremost literary magazine of the Generation of 27, published poetry of women on a number of occasions. The issue of 1 April 1927, published poems by Ernestina de Champourcin, Pilar de Valderrama, Claire Gol, and Norah Lange under the title "Mapa de poetisas" [map of poetesses]; later that year in the issue of 15 September, under the heading "Mapa en rosa" [pink map], poems by Concha Méndez, Pilar de Valderrama, and María Luisa Muñoz de Buendía were published; and on 1 March 1928, poems of Fernanda de Castro, Ernestina de Champourcin, and Carmen Conde were included in a section called "Mapa de carmín" [crimson map]. Occasionally their names appeared alone, instead of being grouped with other women poets. Champourcin, for instance, in addition to the examples quoted above, had poems published in issues 47, 70, and 84. Conde appeared in number 37, Méndez in numbers 21 and 53, and de la Torre in number 76. Even Rosa Chacel, who has always been known primarily as a prose writer, had three of her earliest poems included in the 1 February 1928, issue of *La Gaceta Literaria.* Their poetry was published also in other periodicals, including *Alfar, Héroe, España, Manantial, Meseta, El Mono Azul,* and *Verso y Prosa.*

The recognition of their worth as poets would also seem to be confirmed by the occasions on which they were sought to answer published surveys taken of young writers. Champourcin appeared alongside names such as Melchor Fernández Almagro and César M. Arconada in a survey that asked "¿Qué es vanguardia?" [what is avant-garde?], and Méndez's comments were solicited for a survey on the cinema and for a tribute to Armando Palacio Valdés.[79] Again, it may be the paucity of women in the press that makes their limited appearances conspicuous. Such was the case when three female poets—Champourcin, María Teresa Roca de Togores, and Cristina de Arteaga—published books of poetry the same year. Men took notice because they were women, as Champourcin attested many years later in an interview: "Fuimos las tres que publicamos y les sentamos muy mal a los hombres, a los chicos jóvenes les molestaba mucho. No me explico por qué, pero así era" [We were the three who published, and that didn't sit well with the men, the young fellows were quite upset. I don't know why, but that's how it was].[80] What the male reader saw was not the poet but a novelty, if not an anomaly. Women poets were indeed accomplishing surprising things. They were publishing not in marginal magazines intended only for a feminine readership, but in the select journals of Spain's new intelligentsia, such as *La Gaceta Literaria, Revista de Occidente,* and *Héroe.* Of the five poetic portraits he wrote as prefaces to the issues of *Héroe* and later collected in his *Españoles de tres mundos* [Spaniards from three worlds], Juan Ramón Jiménez dedicated two to women—Rosa Chacel and Concha Méndez. Perhaps more important, in his landmark anthology of new poetry of 1934, Gerardo Diego included two women poets—Champourcin and de la Torre. The poetry of these women captured the attention of the leading critics of the day, names like Francisco Ayala, Rafael Cansinos-Assens, Ernesto Giménez Caballero, and Juan Ramón Jiménez.

As gender dynamics began changing in the 1920s, men and women began to work together in shared professional endeavors. For example, Rafael Alberti became Méndez's friend and poetry mentor. She also formed close associations with other male members of her generations—with García Lorca, Luis Buñuel, Luis Cernuda, and of course with her future husband, Manuel Altolaguirre.[81] No anecdote illustrates better the intimate rapport she had with the men of the Generation of 27 than what Carlos Morla Lynch calls her "parto literario." While Méndez was suffering labor pains in her bedroom, her male friends shouted encouragement from the next room.[82] Also during these years the position of wife was becoming recognized publicly as an occupation. The magazine *Estampa,* for example, paid tribute with feature stories to the women who were wives of famous men. So many wives of eminent men belonged to the controversial Lyceum Club

Femenino that it became known as the "club de las maridas" [club of the husbandettes]. A woman could be subsumed under a man's identity, as in the case of María de la O Lejárraga, who was the ghost writer of most if not all of her husband Gregorio Martínez Sierra's plays; but all in all, within the context of the times, it can be said that women were slowly passing from nonentity to shadow, from chattel to helpmate.

Much has been made of the fact that many women writers married men who were also writers. Of the poets, Méndez was married to Manuel Altolaguirre, Champourcin wed Juan José Domenchina, and Conde became the wife of the poet Antonio Oliver. Chacel married a painter, Timoteo Pérez Rubio; and although de la Torre married an actor, it was her novelist brother Claudio who brought her into contact with many of the important writers of the time. Critics John C. Wilcox and Biruté Ciplijauskaité blamed these liaisons for the marginalization of the female poet; and Concha Méndez lamented in her memoirs that she was seen only as a poet's wife, not a poet in her own right.[83] The full impact of their marriages on their marginalization is difficult to judge. Without husbands they might have gained a firmer sense of their identity as individuals, but it is unlikely that they would have been granted canonical status. Unmarried women poets of the twenties did not gain access to the canon either; and Carmen Conde, who was married, became the first woman voted into the Real Academia de la Lengua [Royal Academy of Language]. Being married to fellow writers meant that the women poets' names became forever linked to that of their husbands, but it also provided opportunities for introduction to other writers, publishing opportunities, and professional support.[84]

Women poets were not, to be sure, major actors on the literary stage, but they were visible as minor players in the drama of the evolution of Spanish poetry. They shared with male poets the pages of leading periodicals, some common professional activities, and many different personal relationships. Yet their involvement must be called ancillary and tenuous. Women did not take part in the events that transformed Spain's literature; it was the men who initiated dialogues on the need for new directions in literature, made public gestures on behalf of innovations, and worked together to effect change. The Generation of 27 came about basically as a result of a few activities that bonded together a relatively small group of men: the crucial trip to the Ateneo in Seville, the preparations for the tricentennial celebration of the death of Luis de Góngora, the café conversations with Rafael Cansinos-Assens, and life together at the Residencia de Estudiantes. Men engaged in scandalous iconoclastic attacks on the literary establishment while women remained among the bystanders, as occurred for example on the occasion of Alberti's outrageous lecture before the Lyceum Club Femenino in 1929. Between 1927 and 1935 Josefina de la Torre gave singing recitals at the Residencia de Estudiantes, but did not enjoy the camaraderie that daily contact meant for the male boarders and regulars of this breeding ground for new ideas. By her own admission, Rosa Chacel, despite her cordial relationship with Ortega y Gasset, had very little contact with those who published in his *Revista de Occidente* and did not attend his "tertulias."[85] Concha Méndez opened her home to the writers of her day, but she does not figure in any of the substantive events that set new literary trends.

As a result of their exclusion from the center of literary activity, women poets did not establish a firm footing for themselves in mainstream culture nor did they develop a sense of community with their fellow female writers. Individual poets emerged as isolated exceptions within a male-dominated literary milieu, and the bonds the women did form were kept on the level of personal friendship. Champourcin and Méndez joined the Lyceum Club Femenino in an effort to enrich themselves culturally, but neither they nor other women poets of the period intruded aggressively into the public arena on behalf of women. Within their poetry they inevitably project a female worldview; but they do not directly attack the limitations placed upon them as women. Even though they themselves did not always adhere to the traditional role and language of women, in their works they did not satirize the traditional role of women or vent anger at the masculine society that restricted them. Their subversion of social convention was achieved more by example than by message and more by tentative gesture than by audacious statement. Their male counterparts, as Carmen Bravo-Villasante observes, had no interest in the social problems of women: "están más preocupados en problemas existenciales, en los que el hombre es el protagonista . . . que en introducir en sus textos problemáticas sociales que afectan al otro 50 por 100 de la humanidad, como es la lucha por la obtención del derecho al voto" [they are more concerned with existential problems, in which men are the protagonists . . . than in introducing into their writing the social problems that affect the other 50 percent of humanity, like the struggle for the right to vote].[86] And the female political activists of the period moved in different circles than those of women poets, and, for the most part, strove to assist leftist political parties or workers' movements, not to solidify a feminist advocacy for equality.

The problematic relationship to masculine culture that women poets experienced on the empirical level is reiterated in the ambiguities and contradictions they displayed within their art toward male and female literary traditions. During the period of the Generation of 27, women poets consciously assumed subjectivity in consonance with males. They assimilated generational prosodic structures, particularly the brief, fragmented verse; they incorporated vanguardist images and metaphors, specifically those of an *ultraísta* or surrealist nature; and they adopted prevailing attitudes of emotional restraint, authorial detachment, and assertive optimism. This imitation of male models implies not so much subservience as subversion, because through appropriation of mainstream techniques, the women undermined the shunning of female writing. Their female presence, on the social level, challenges the equation of high poetry with male poets and, on the textual level, manifests itself in the form of protagonists who actively seek physical movement (as in the case of Méndez), who articulate their own expressions of desire (as occurs in Champourcin), who flaunt their technical virtuosity (as Chacel does), who position themselves at the center of the world (as seen in Conde), or who struggle for personal communication (as evidenced in de la Torre). Nonetheless, while many of the elements of their poetry mimed the paradigms established by their male contemporaries, certain images, tonalities, and attitudes would inevitably rise from their female experience.

Their "double-voiced discourse," confirms Elaine Showalter's observation that women inevitably embody both the muted and the dominant discourse; they are "not inside and outside of the male tradition; they are inside two traditions simultaneously."[87] Further evidence of the complexity of the discourse of Spanish women poets of the twenties and thirties is the fact that while they indirectly articulated their feminine difference from within masculine poetic discourse, they overtly turned their backs on their female predecessors in the hope of widening their emotional, intellectual, and physical horizons. They rejected the prevailing image of the female poet as sentimental, sad, and sensitive and embraced instead the seductively liberating masculine modes of the Generation of 27.[88] In an article written during the period, Champourcin criticizes her literary mothers for not knowing freedom and limiting their emotional register exclusively to love in its mournful contours. She appeals for the erasure of "el viejo y desacreditado tópico que nos presta una alma tímida, reconcentrada, temiendo el eco de sus propias vibraciones" [the old and discredited cliché that gives us a timid, withdrawn soul that is afraid of the echoes of its own vibrations]. She believes that the timid, melancholy "poetisa" has been replaced by the lively and cheerful "poeta": "La pantalla se cubre de sol y un tropel de muchachas ágiles, vigorosas, llenan el mundo. Es el triunfo de la juventud. Vence por fin lo sano, lo nuevo" [The screen is bathed in sunlight and a throng of agile, strong women fills the world. It is the triumph of youth. Good health and innovation finally prevail].[89] Their desire for dissociation between the feminine and the poetic is understandable, but it was impossible to eradicate. For instance, when Guillermo de Torre reviewed two of Champourcin's books in 1936, he judged her focus on "el vivir en su dimensión más tangible" [life in its most tangible dimension] to be a weakness confirming Simmel's contentions on women's inability to transcend their personal emotions.[90] And even in an otherwise laudatory review of 1932, Ernesto Salazar y Chapela perceives the poetic and the feminine as fortunately separate tonalities in Champourcin.[91] The refusal of male critics to equate woman and poet explains why poets like Champourcin rejected the mark of gender. Since to profess to write as a female would negate their validity as poets, Champourcin insisted that "La auténtica poesía no prefiere al hombre ni a la mujer. Prefiere, sencillamente al Poeta" [Authentic poetry doesn't prefer either the male or the female. It simply prefers the Poet].[92]

Since the feminine tradition was unpalatable to women poets, the "new" women poets that Champourcin heralded turned for moral support and artistic guidance to their contemporary brethren who championed liberation from the literary past. Following the examples of their male peers, women poets in Spain during the twenties could break away from a limited and limiting feminine past and participate in the vitalizing trends of their own times. The emerging Modernist canon provided them with models of youthful optimism, self-assertion, and various kinds of freedom that contradicted their feminine heritage of melancholy, restraint, and enclosure. Thus masculine modes and mannerisms represent for them an escape from the ghetto of disparaged feminine tradition. Imitation became the entry fee for gaining access into the men's literary "club" of the day and for enjoying a modicum of legitimacy there as professional practitioners.

Although it may be true that long-lasting self-definition is realized by a woman writer only through a connection with the feminine, through a return to her female past or to an exploration of gender difference, for the women poets under consideration this path meant subordination to fixed stereotypes. Just as women in general were discarding constricting feminine clothing, the poets needed to reject the tightness of the narrow range of registers and postures characteristic of poetry by women. Changing the gender of their models did not necessarily secure for them a stable place in the canon, for by using innovation as the sole criterion for the appraisal of texts, critics can effectively exclude female works modeled on male texts just as easily as they reject, on the basis of their difference, those works adhering to patterns of traditional feminine style. Thus the coincidences between the verse of women poets of the Generation of 27 and that of their male counterparts earned them only secondary roles on the literary stage, roles easily overlooked. By walking in the footsteps of their contemporaries, they left the quiet house of sentimentality of their literary mothers and embarked on a brief and, for the most part, forgotten adventure into the poetic waters of freedom, exuberance, and innovation. This excursion into forbidden territory constitutes a valiant expansion of poetic possibilities, in consonance with the emergence of the image of the modern woman in Spain.

* * *

Against the backdrop of the sociocultural reactions to female creativity ranging from institutionalized erasure to ambivalent tolerance that has been
outlined in this chapter, the subsequent analyses of the early texts of Concha Méndez, Josefina de la Torre, Rosa Chacel, Carmen Conde, and
Ernestina de Champourcin gain breadth. We find that despite all their efforts to align themselves with male-defined trends, these poets created a
female presence through some of the images they chose, the poetic personae filing though their verses, and their expressed desire to love, live, and
communicate. Even though some indications of existential absence, insecurity, and loss emerge, self-identity and liberation were the hallmarks of
their early poetry. Even though their stance may not fulfill the more recent
expectations of a feminist consciousness and a denunciation of collective
injustice, their interjection of a female presence into the poetic discourse
of the day defied the widespread negation of the poetic capabilities of
women and challenged the milieu in which they wrote, a milieu on the
whole disinterested in the advancement of women either as citizens or as
artists. These women poets navigated the choppy literary waters in which
they traveled with a mixture of assimilation and self-assertion.[93]

3

Concha Méndez: Plotting the Route from Open Spaces to the Realm of Shadows

The poetry of Concha Méndez incorporates both absence and presence. Absence, in her later works, represents a loss of self and provokes retrospection, but in her first three books the poetic speaker, impelled by an undefined urge to freedom, eagerly dashes toward distant and alluring spaces. The desire for advancement toward a remote, and usually elevated, goal compels the speaker to assert her presence as well as to progress in a linear fashion within concrete landscapes. Her early movement across open spaces subsides as she retreats into the secluded realm of shadows. Throughout Méndez's poetic production, space is a significant feature of her changing view of life and of herself.

The phenomenon of space reveals the conception of status of the self in the world. Traditionally the relationship between women and space has hindered their creative development and their possibilities for self-affirmation. Across cultures and over the centuries, outer, public space has been considered the "natural" male domain, while inner domestic space has been reserved for females with such consistency that "an illusion of inevitability and revealed truth" has been produced.[1] This spatial partition with its inseparable corollary of the opposition between freedom and confinement manifests itself on a variety of levels. On the concrete, physical level of architecture, enclosed spaces have been divided according to functions that reinforce male privilege.[2] On the level of philosophy, Western metaphysics has been dominated by an equivalence between the visible occupation of space or the state of presence on the one hand, and power and masculinity on the other. Presence connotes a potential for visibility, audibility, and mobility—attributes traditionally deemed unnatural and undesirable for women. Within this scheme, woman is absence; she forms the silent, hidden, and compliant object of masculine desire or the mysterious, scorned, and threatening origin of masculine dread. In literature, confinement has a

43

long history as a stereotype for femininity, even in literature by women. Mary Ellman, for example, finds confinement not only a social axiom but a literary constant even in literature by women. Of women narrators, she writes: "Their experience is narrow, their characters never leave 'the bedroom and the salon.'"[3] In Spain, a country entrenched in medieval religious morality and overlaid with an Arabic perspective toward women, the reality of the cloistered woman persists throughout its history and literature. To confirm this persistence, one needs only recall Federico García Lorca's masterful dramatization of the absolute confinement of Spanish women in his 1936 play *La casa de Bernarda Alba* [The house of Bernarda Alba], a stark work in which women are figuratively buried alive behind thick walls that transform the house into a convent, a jail, and a living hell.[4]

Studying the subtext of nineteenth-century women's works, Sandra M. Gilbert and Susan Gubar laid the groundwork for the exploration of women writers' obsession with spatial imagery of enclosure and escape as a dramatization of their own personal discomfort, their sense of powerlessness, and their fear that, as writers, they inhabit incomprehensive places.[5] In the early twentieth century, Anglo-American women writers began to interact with both their matrilineage and their patrilineage in a complicated and arduous process of self-discovery,[6] but Spanish women lag behind their northern counterparts both in social development and literary boldness. Susan Kirkpatrick explains that nineteenth-century Spanish women writers experienced a different kind of conflict. They found themselves constrained by Spanish tradition and by new Romantic models that portrayed women as objects of desire or as symbols of men's fears and aspirations.[7] Examples of nonconformist women increase with time, but the tradition of encloisterment continues in Spanish literature into the post-civil war period.[8] What Carmen Martín Gaite calls the "condición ventanera," the image of woman veiled from the world by window curtains, typifies the Spanish woman and metaphorically represents the Spanish woman writer until the end of the Franco era.[9] Critics have analyzed the efforts of women writers to negotiate and overcome the silence prescribed for their sex and to deconstruct persistent stereotypes, but the emphasis of these explorations has most frequently been on oppression and exclusion, on inner exile, and subversion.[10] Few images of women of exuberant independence and free movement emerge in Spanish literature before the seventies. The portrayal of the physical mobility of women has been generally excluded, restrained, or somehow compromised in works by women as well as those by men. This paucity in Spanish literature of the image of woman moving through open spaces makes the poetry Concha Méndez wrote in the 1920s especially noteworthy.

SETTING THE STAGE FOR POETIC PRESENCE

Images of movement and expansiveness endow Concha Méndez's poetry with a spirit of adventure and freedom that permits joyful self-affirmation. Her depiction of open spaces through the clear delineation of directions establishes a vast field in which to trace movements upward and outward. The poetic speaker asserts herself within these expansive spaces as a discrete, mobile being who travels across them freely and without intimidation. *Inquietudes* [Restlessness] (1926) and *Surtidor* [Fountain] (1928), Méndez's first two collections, set the stage for the independence of this poetic persona by an overwhelming emphasis on outdoor scenes and by creating an environment of physical presence through the accumulation of visual images, the inclusion of human figures in motion, and the development of a poetic style that heightens concreteness.

Concha Méndez disengages the poetic "I" from her landscapes. Only occasionally does nature serve in her earliest poetry as an empathetic backdrop for a human drama or a metaphorical vehicle for emotion; most often nature stands alone without witnesses. An emphasis on the description of external, sensorial reality precludes direct revelation of intimate, personal feelings, avoids subjectivity, and minimizes allusions to temporality while creating a poetic environment of substantiality, detachment, and dispassion. Often no more than a loosely linked series of images, her poems appear to be catalogues of visual impressions or annotations for stage settings. In many of the compositions of *Inquietudes*, the poet crafts pithy lists of visual images that, almost in the manner of haiku poetry, create moods obliquely, through the implications derived from juxtapositions rather than through overt analogies, as her poem called "Toledo" illustrates:

> Calles estrechas.
> Rinconadas.
> Rejas.
>   Faroles encendidos.
> La noche.
> Ya la luz se ha dormido . . .
>   Doblar de campanas.
> Variedad
> de estilos.
>   El Tajo:
> Caprichoso
> recinto.
>   Las rejas misteriosas.
> Siglos.
> Sombrías mariposas.

La vega.
(¡Ni hay lirios
ni rosas!)
                        (*Inquietudes*, 20–21)

[Narrow streets.
Corners.
Window grilles.
    Lit street lamps.
Night.
The light has fallen asleep already . . .
    The ringing of bells.
Variety
of styles.
    The Tagus:
Whimsical
place.
The mysterious window grilles.
Centuries.
Gloomy butterflies.
The meadow.
(There are neither lilies
nor roses!)]

In her preference for syntactical condensation, lexical simplicity, and authorial detachment, Méndez was not only following the model of traditional Spanish poetry, but she was also assimilating the antisentimental posture evinced by her male counterparts. Poets assumed a new authorial detachment that expressed itself in the anonymity of the poetic voice, the erasure of the "I," and the eschewal of sentimentality. The intellectual authority of the day, José Ortega y Gasset, diagnosed this "deshumanizacion del arte" [dehumanization of art] as a victory over the human, and he declared that all great periods of art have avoided having the human as the center of gravity.[11] A distance between poetry and the self fosters the transcendence of the poet as conscious generator and manipulator of the resources of the craft. This detachment and an awareness of the creative potential of a poet become particularly important in the case of women poets, who have perennially been linked to a poetic expression firmly circumscribed by emotions and personal experience. Margaret Homans cautions against the dangers of the demands that poetry by women report on the poet's experience as a woman, ably arguing that all language is inherently fictive and insisting that only through the separation of self and poem can women abandon the disadvantageous position as other.[12]

Spanish critics have been reluctant to recognize Concha Méndez's efforts to break out of gender-bound limits. The poet Jorge Guillén insists on equating what he discerns as femininity in her poetry with sentimentality,[13] and José-Carlos Mainer deems her excursions into the masculine realm of playful vanguard extravagance to be superficial poems "salidos de un bazar de los años veinte" [emerging from a bazaar of the twenties].[14] Few recognize that, in her early works, motivated by a strong but generalized desire for freedom, Méndez evolved a poetic mask of an agile, mobile, and spirited figure who moved quickly across outdoor scenes, particularly the sea and the seashore, with surges of energy, exuberance, and joyous affirmation. The assertiveness of her poetic persona does not turn self-awareness into brash defiance, and the images of advancement and intrusion that surface in her early poetry do not cede to visions of aggression. Hers is a poetry of co-existence more than dominion, of alternations rather than alternatives.

In Méndez's first three collections, there is evidence of darkness among the rays of sunshine that bathe her landscapes, of silence within her animated scenes, and of an occasional expression of nostalgia alongside the strong sense of palpable presence. Similarly, among the shadows that prevail in her later poetry, there is light and some sense of energy. What changes is the emphasis, the origin, and the impact of those shadows; as dark tones increase in prominence, their attachment to personal meaning deepens and their influence on poetic outcome broadens. As Méndez's poetry moves from presence to absence, from delight to despair, and from open spaces to the realm of the shadows, impetuosity and confidence subside and the poetic persona turns her eyes from the future toward the past. At the beginning of her poetic production, however, the poet's affirmative outlook colors even her nocturnal scenes with empowering light and a humanized pulse. Like her sun-drenched daylight scenes, her nocturnal ones are defined by concrete, material substances: darkness is onyx; the sky is punctuated with stars, moonbeams, and airplanes; and night assumes the form of a butterfly, phantom, or a colorfully dressed male figure.

Presence is the known or knowable that exists in a time and space contiguous to the perceiving subject; presence is verifiable, visible, or material. In poetry, the mere accumulation of unadorned substantives and an abundance of objects creates a sense of bulk that lends materiality to the textual environment. Méndez often structures her early poems as brief lists of objects: of plazas, avenues, and trolleys, of a bar on the wharf, pipe smoke, and lanterns. More than developed descriptions, her landscape poems are enumerations of images, as in "Primavera" from *Surtidor:*

Primavera.
Tarde de añil,
inflada de globos
en el parque infantil.
Primavera.
Almendros de nieve.
La brisa de tierra,
¡dejadla que juegue!
Primavera.
Florecer de canciones.
Brote de capullos
en los corazones.
Primavera.
¡Qué loca gira en el balcón
la rehilandera!

(*Surtidor,* 51)

[Spring.
Indigo afternoon,
inflated with balloons
in the children's park.
Spring.
Snowy almond trees.
Land breeze,
let it play!
Spring.
A flowering of songs.
An outbreak of buds
in our hearts.
Spring.
How wildly the pinwheel revolves
on the balcony!]

The absence of conjugated verbs in her early poetry intensifies the impact of the substantives. The compression of time to an eternal present and the use of the imperative form function as a strategy to reinforce presence, for present and presence are interrelated in their affirmation of existence.

The human figures who move across Méndez's landscapes are invariably engaged in physical activity. Skaters, skiers, and dancers emerge in her first three collections and, as the theme of the sea gains prominence, sailors, swimmers, and boatmen also make their appearance. Motifs of movement are accompanied by active verbs connoting bodily propulsion—"deslizar," "saltar," "volar" [to slide, to jump, to fly]. A descriptive style often yields to a

more assertive voice when finite verbs are replaced by imperative forms
that articulate notes of impending urgency. Nature and humans can merge,
but their temporary fusion does not jeopardize the wholeness of either. In
one early poem, the skier carries the sounds and rhythms of the mountains
in her skirt, and in another her lost white scarf returns to the snow, its
rightful element:

> Van los patinadores
> con trajes de colores.
>   Una blanca bufanda
> cayó en el ventisquero.
> Voló como velita
> que empujaran los vientos,
> y allá quedó hecha nieve
> que vuelve a su elemento.
>   Van los patinadores
> con trajes de colores.
>
> (*Inquietudes*, 37)

> [There go the skiers
> dressed in colors.
>   A white scarf
> fell in the snow drift.
> It flew like a little sail
> propelled by the winds,
> and there it stayed turned into snow
> that returns to its element.
>   There go the skiers
> dressed in colors.]

The skiers do not forfeit their essence, for only an article of their clothing
fuses with nature. The repetition of the poem's short second stanza at the
end creates a sense of continued motion that the verb "ir" reinforces and
the colorful outfits enhance. Among the few times that a poetic "I" speaks
in *Inquietudes*, it is as a swimmer who enjoys her freedom and mobility:

> Deslizándome en el agua
> hasta la Isla he venido.
> He vagado entre sus brisas.
> Y por su costa he corrido.
>   Del mar salí llena de algas,
> con el bañador ceñido.
> Y tras de andar por la Isla,
> bajo un árbol he dormido.
>   ¡Qué soledad suntuosa!
> ¡Qué espléndida soledad!

Y que fatigosa vida
la vida de la ciudad!

(*Inquietudes*, 36)

[Slipping into the water
I have come as far as the Island.
I have wandered among its breezes.
And I have run along its coast.
    I came out of the sea full of algae,
with my bathing suit clinging to me.
And after walking around the Island,
I slept under a tree.
    What sumptuous solitude!
What splendid solitude!
And what a tiresome life
the life in the city!]

The poem concludes with the swimmer in joyful rest, but she conceives of herself essentially as moving smoothly through water, an active body headed for a specific place.

    Despite this occasional suggestion of fusion with her environment, the poetic speaker in Méndez's first three collections displays a strong sense of self and a consciousness of her own body, of her physicality, and of her vitality. Her awareness of her body as a solid object capable of forceful movement may stem in part from the poet's own experience as an athlete. Her contemporaries record an image of someone active and dynamic at work as well as at play. In one of his lyrical sketches of his fellow Spaniards, Juan Ramón Jiménez portrays Concha Méndez as "la niña desarrollada que veíamos, adolescente, con malla blanca, equilibrista del alambre en el casino de verano; la que subía con blusa de marinero del aire, prologuista de la aviación, en el trapecio del Montgolfier cabeceante y recortaba su desnudo chiquito blanco negro sobre el poniente rojo . . . la campeona de natación, de jiujitsu, de patín, de jimnasia sueca" [a grown-up child, an adolescent, whom we used to see, with her white tights, tightrope walker at the casino in the summer, the one who used to go up, with her blouse like a sailor of the airways, forerunner of aviation, in the Montgolfier trapezoid with her head tossed and her little white figure outlined darkly against the red sunset . . . the swimming, jujitsu, skiing, Swedish gymnastics champion].[15] She belonged to the Spanish middle class of means who could spend vacations in the winter in the mountains and in the summer at the beach. In her memoirs, Concha Méndez recalls summers in San Sebastian during her youth, usually in the company of Luis Buñuel, going to the car races, the beach, the casino, and concerts.[16] She caused quite a stir in San Sebastian when she swam to a party held on board a boat and once she even tried to jump out of an airplane.[17] As sports ceased being the exclusive domain of the aristocracy, and as sports and other forms of amusement became emblems of writers' rejection of the past, sports came to characterize a large portion of culture. According to Antonio Gallego Morell, during the twenties the sport theme reflected the very spirit of the era—the celebration of youth, the body, and hygiene.[18] The case of Concha Méndez, though not unique, was noteworthy; one writer calls her the "excepcion femenina" [female exception] and another an "anormalidad" [abnormality].[19]

Besides provoking amazement among her contemporaries, Méndez's nonconventional involvement in athletics and other activities unlikely for women understandably transferred to her poetry images commonly associated with men, images such as verticality, advancement, and unrestraint. Much of the carefree exuberance in her poetry must also be credited to the spirit of the age and exaltation of motion, speed, and modern means of communication.[20] Jazz, movies, automobiles, and airplanes represented wondrous inventions that incorporated the originality, openness to the future, and radical change that fascinated the poets of the twenties. Participating in this delight for modern gadgets and forms, Méndez includes poems on cars, planes, and yachts. The energy associated with this new technology goes beyond imagery to include Méndez's choice of poetic techniques and structures. Short lines, the accumulation of disconnected images, and the exchange, superimposition, or combination of the distinctive natures of objects and humans by means of personification, animalization, or dehumanization create a quick pace, a fragmented structure, and a playful disruption of syntactical and conceptual relations. Two short compositions illustrate the timbre of Méndez's earliest poetry, one titled "Lo mismo que una granada" [Like a pomegranate]:

> El corazon se me ha abierto
> lo mismo que una granada.
> Y siento caer su sangre
> —mi sangre—cristalizada . . .
> (Surtidor, 25)

> [My heart has opened up
> like a pomegranate.
> And I feel its blood drip
> —my blood—crystallized . . .

and another titled "La noche" [Night]:

La noche viene llorando.
Si es que perdió el corazón
y no ha podido encontrarlo,
la puedo ofrecer el mío,
que no sé donde dejarlo . . .
(*Surtidor,* 27)

[Night arrives in tears.
If it has lost its heart
and cannot find it,
I can lend it mine,
for I don't know where to leave it . . .]

This poetry provided a medium of expression for Méndez's enthusiasm for physical activity and her urge for youthful rebellion. Poetry written under the spell of the spirit of the early twenties becomes a verbal game without any apparent serious mission and an outburst of joy, marking the triumph of sports and youthfulness that Ortega y Gasset identifies with the "deshumanización del arte." For Francisco Ayala, youthfulness is precisely what characterizes *Surtidor:* "Un espléndido catálogo de valores: vitalidad, fuerza, decisión, entusiasmo. Valores jóvenes en suma" [A splendid catalogue of values: vitality, strength, decisiveness, enthusiasm. Youthful values, in short].[21] For others, the collusion of sports and poetic playfulness made her a modern woman who transferred her free spirit to her poetry: "Esta es una muchacha actual, ceñida y tensa por el deporte y el aire libre. Como sus telas alegres muy exiguas, como sus palabras que tienen aristas de metal y concavidas turbadoras, así son sus poemas [She is a modern girl, tight and taut from sports and fresh air. Her poems are like her scanty, colorful fabrics, like her words with their metallic edges and disturbing cavities].[22] The image of Concha Méndez, the champion swimmer, the international traveler, the bride dressed in green with parsley for a bouquet, "rayaba con el mito" [bordered on the mythical], according to María Dolores Arana.[23] Her personality made more of an impact on her contemporaries than her poetry, but it is in her poetry that she immortalizes the figure of the liberated woman, the new woman freed from bourgeois models of conduct and from literary expectations for female poetry.

THE SEA AS A UTOPIAN PLACE

By means of artistic elaboration, Concha Méndez creates a myth of the sea in her first three collections. The sea begins in her poetry as a utopian space of love and joy and soon becomes, in *Canciones de mar y tierra* [Songs of the sea and the earth], an escape route, an avenue to freedom, adventure, and self-affirmation. The theme of the sea in her early poetry has been discounted as a mere imitative homage to her friend Rafael Alberti.[24] However, important differences between her poetry and his exist and reveal a discernible contrast of training and perspectives. Alberti, on the one hand, absorbed the influence of canonical Spanish poetry—of Gil Vicente, other Spanish poets of the Golden Age, and the whole corpus of "romances"[25]— but Méndez, on the other hand, had to turn for inspiration to an unrecognized, living poet because her access to the literary tradition was restricted by the limits placed on her education. She recounts in her memoirs how her mother beat her when he found out her daughter was auditing a literature class at the university.[26] Only after making personal contact with the poets associated with the Residencia de Estudiantes was Méndez openly exposed to literature. A poem of Méndez's like "Mi barca" [My boat], from *Inquietudes,* displays a resemblance to the themes, rhythms, and motifs of *Marinero en tierra* [Sailor on land] that confirms this contact, but careful scrutiny reveals a contrast between her poetry and Alberti's that must be traced to their gender differences. Although Méndez's poetry may be an echo of Alberti's *Marinero en tierra,* her response constitutes a feminized reply. He dreams of dressing like a sailor, a symbol of masculine energy that passes across the vital life force of the sea; she imagines herself dressed as the moon, a traditional symbol of woman. His poetic voice coincides with that of a land-locked youth who longs to be a mariner and a lover who often laments the distance of his beloved. Her poetic speaker intones a female voice; she is at once the beloved waiting on shore and leaving the port, and she identifies herself with the siren rather than simply invoking her. Beyond these readily identifiable gender differences, there lies a distinction in focus, perspective, and flavor in their works.

The impetus for *Marinero en tierra* was nostalgia for the sea left behind with childhood and recoverable only through memory and dreams. The sea symbolizes a submarine paradise inhabited by a siren more childlike than seductive, a beneficent harbinger of "la nueva vida vegetal recién creada" [the new plant life recently created] and a sober reminder of death by drowning.[27] Throughout his poetic production, the sea was for Alberti his "arsenal," a repository of his happy childhood memories and the nurturing medium of his existence, the maternal womb from which he will forever feel exiled. In sharp contrast to this overriding nostalgic orientation, a sense of presence and realization, especially in Méndez's third collection, *Canciones de mar y tierra,* emerges in her verses. The sea, for Méndez, rises before her as an ideal space close at hand or within reach. The dream of return to Eden is substituted by a dream of Utopia. Alberti's relationship with the sea is one of distance, separation, and distinction. In the poem "El mar. La mar. . . . " [The sea. The sea], for example, he reproaches his father for "disinterring" him from the sea and he varies the gender of "sea" to duplicate his own inner fragmentation. Méndez, however, obliterates the discreteness of the sea by making her poetic protagonist enter into physical contact with it and even merge with its essence. The sea for her becomes an extension of the self and a vehicle of self-realization.

The persistent recurrence of the image of enclosure in female literature makes its counterpart, escape, a relentless dream. As dream space, the sea functions for Méndez somewhat like the "green world" archetype Annis Pratt outlines, a zone where a woman feels "a sense of oneness with the cosmos as well as of a place to one side of civilization." Pratt recalls Simone de Beauvoir's observation that nature represents what woman herself represents for man, herself and her negation, and that when she takes possession of nature, she possesses herself.[28] This is what happens in Méndez's poetry; the sea becomes a site where, by unfolding a dream of love and escape, its young protagonist affirms her strength and achieves a sense of dominion.

Méndez casts the sea into an object of desire while at the same time transforming it into a vast, diffuse incarnation of the love force. As an idealized space, the sea is a magical place where night fishing yields a catch of "estrellas fugaces" [fleeting stars] and "una luna redondita / y quieta en un fanal" (*Inquietudes*, 63) [a little round moon, / motionless inside a bell glass]. The poetic speaker makes clear her desire to be a close partner of the sea; she wants to be a sea gull, a lark, and a mermaid. The English Hispanist Stanley Richardson observed in 1935 the strong sense of desire coupled in Méndez's poetry with an equally strong decisiveness. "Her main verb," he writes, "is 'Quiero'—'I want,' her most general expression 'Más allá'— 'Further, beyond!' But she is not merely crying for the moon; she is preparing to go there in an autogiro."[29] This sense of initiative is evident from the beginning of her production. For example, in one poem, appropriately entitled "Canto de la libertad" [Song of freedom], a series of imperative verbs issues invitations to escape: "¡Vámonos a la mar! / ¡Vámonos en busca / de su soledad!" [Let's go out to sea! / Let's look for its solitude!]; "Marchemos; ¡la mar nos espera!" [Let's go; the sea awaits us!]; and "Huyamos de la gente; / ¡huyamos de la tierra!" [Let's flee from people; / let's flee from the earth!"]. Besides manifesting a desire to enjoy the freedom offered by the sea, the use of the first person imperative underscores a faith in the potential realization of dreams. The implication, through the plural form, of the presence of a companion dismisses any notion of loneliness. The future tense in these poems enhances the air of confidence and potential for fulfillment that runs through them. The sea is both the origin and destination of love. The beloved comes from and goes out to the sea; she is mariner and traveler as well as the beloved left behind.

Alongside Méndez's idealized transformation of the sea, there exists a referentiality that conceptualizes her social context. Méndez uses the visual signs of her quotidian world as raw materials to create poetry. These realistic, contemporary elements are reflected in the specificity of the types of boat she names. She speaks of canoes, a pirogue, a frigate, and a yacht.[30] Her lovers also appear literal and realistic. Amorous encounters take place on board ship and on shore. In one poem for example, a bather and a sailor converse aboard an anchored ship and then quickly display their passion:

> Conversamos
> en la escalinata.
> Mi jadeante cuerpo
> un bañador cubría.
>   El llevaba
> el blanco uniforme
> que llevan
> los guardias marinas.
> . . . .
>   Nuestras manos
> al fin se abrazaron.
> Y los pulsos
> ardientes latían . . .
> (Inquietudes, 15)

>   [We talked
> on the stairway.
> A bathing suit covered
> my panting body.
>   He wore
> the white uniform
> that the navy
> guardsmen wear.
> . . . .
>   Our hands
> finally embraced.
> And our passionate pulses
> beat.]

The poetic speaker declares herself lover of the sea: "Amante, sólo del mar" [lover, only of the sea], she cries in *Surtidor* (46) and later, in *Canciones de mar y tierra,* she declares, "novia del mar me sentía / novia del mar, o su amante" (49) [I felt like the bride of the sea, the bride of the sea, or its lover]. This loving relationship is reenacted through physical contact and spiritual union. The recurrent image in Méndez's first collections of the swimmer slipping through the silent waters of the sea establishes an intimate, tangible connection between her protagonist and the material substance of the sea. The swimmer metaphorically becomes a ship:

> Mis brazos:
> los remos.
> La quilla:
> mi cuerpo.
> Timón:
> mi pensamiento.
>
>   (*Surtidor*, 31)

> [My arms:
> the oars.
> The keel:
> my body.
> Rudder:
> my thoughts.]

Or the swimmer is a moving object traversing a stationary surface:

> Camino claro de luna
> sobre el esmalte del agua.
> Yo he de pasar, nadadora
> —pequeña nave sin ancla—,
> por ese camino claro
> —camino de luz y escarcha—.
> Y he de perderme en las sombras
> bajo el cielo, sobre el agua,
> en una noche de invierno
> —noche fría—
>   con mi alma.
>
>   (*Surtidor*, 41)

> [Clear path of the moon
> on the enamel of the water.
> I have to pass, a swimmer
> —a small ship without an anchor—,
> along that clear path—
> a path of light and frost—.
> And I have to lose myself
> under the sky, over the water,
> on a winter night
> —a cold night—
>   with my soul.]

Physical contact and motion lead to a smooth, momentary loss of self. The willingness on the part of the poetic speaker in Méndez's early poetry to fuse with her surroundings tends to confirm the premise of those feminists who argue that on the level of social interaction, psychological need, and literary elaboration, women favor weak ego-boundaries.[31] Yet in Méndez's case, fusion does not translate into a total loss of self, for her poems evolve from the perspective of an active, mobile body conscious of her own corporal autonomy, a self-awareness reflecting, perhaps, the author's confidence in the water.[32]

The relationship with the sea depicted in her poetry is loving, personal and immediate. A palpable entity rather than an abstract symbol, the sea is not only perceived from shore but experienced with a sense of temporal immediacy and of physical proximity. The poetic protagonist transforms herself from "bañista" [bather] to "marinera" [woman sailor] to imposing "capitana" [female captain]. This female skipper gains self-assurance as she voices increasingly assertive declarations ranging from hopeful intention:

> que me han hecho capitana
> de la marina mercante.
> y he de marchar en un alba
> por los mares adelante.
> (*Canciones de mar y tierra*, 30)

> [for they have made me captain
> of the merchant marine,
> and I will leave some day at dawn
> to go out to sea.]

to enthusiastic self-affirmation:

> Mi vida en el mar. Yo voy
> saltando de puerto a puerto.
> Y en mi aventura yo soy
> como un corazon despierto.
> (*Canciones de mar y tierra*, 75)

> [My life on the sea. I am
> Jumping from port to port.
> And in my adventure I am
> like a spirited heart.]

to unabashed pride:

> Siete puertos he corrido
> de uno y otro continente.
> Siete luces me han nacido
> y brillan bajo mi frente.
>
> (*Canciones de mar y tierra*, 85)

> [I have traveled to seven ports
> from one continent to another.
> Seven lights have sprung from me
> and shine beneath my brow.]

The sea is a known surface joyfully traveled by the poetic speaker and yielding to her desire.

The sea is her life. As Elena Urrutia has observed, "el destino de Concha Méndez consiste en ir viviendo su vida eslabonando puertos, ciudades, países . . . está en tierra pero siempre de cara al mar, al espacio infinito que se abre ante ella y la llama, y la invita a cruzarlo" [Concha Méndez's fate consists of living her life by linking ports, cities, countries . . . she is on land but always facing the sea, the infinite space that opens before her and calls her, and invites her to cross it].[33] The sea constitutes a dream space where special treasures can be found:

> Toma este sueño tan mío
> y cuídalo bien cuidado,
> que en una noche sin noche
> en altamar lo he encontrado."
>
> (*Canciones de mar y tierra*, 86)

> [Take this dream of mine
> and take very good care of it,
> for in a night without night
> I found it on the high seas.]

or stored:

> Una noche que tenía
> un secreto que guardar,
> porque no me lo robasen
> lo tiré al fondo del mar
>
> (*Canciones de mar y tierra*, 146)

> [A night I had
> a secret to keep,
> so that no one would steal it from me
> I threw it to the bottom of the sea]

The sea responds to Méndez's desire for freedom with an alluring voice of invitation. The sea provides the escape route to exciting, distant places, to adventure, and to a liberation from the laws, limits, and restraints of society. More a medium for travel than a final destination, the sea offers unknown expansive horizons that promise to nurture personal growth. In Méndez's first three collections, dynamic motion, self-assertion, and disengagement from sentimentality signal the adoption of a nonconventional female posture of freedom, exuberance, and mobility.

Voyages, Flights, and Other Patterns of Passage

The very titles of Méndez's first two books—*Inquietudes* and *Surtidor*—verify the importance of motion, change, and verticality in her early poetry. *Canciones de mar y tierra* (1930) represents a culmination of this trend and demonstrates the prominence of patterns of flight and forward-directed movements in her early literary production. Carol Christ has identified the path of women writers' spiritual quest with a metaphorical plunge into the experience of nothingness and a subsequent emergence or awakening,[34] but Concha Méndez's poetic persona, in contrast, assumes a stance that could be described as flying high and standing tall. An enthusiasm for the unknown, a preference for images of flight, and a love of the sea are already evident in *Inquietudes* and expand in *Surtidor*. An expression of yearning continues in *Canciones de mar y tierra* with poems expressing a longing to travel to unknown places, to discover the gardens at the bottom of the sea, and to reach distant heights. A number of poems in the collection also textualize voyages in progress and refer to a personal context of real travel.

Unescorted travel by women was at the time discouraged. Despite the existence of some eccentric "lady travelers" of the Victorian age and writers like Isak Dinesen, until recent times few women traveled alone. Concha Méndez is one of those exceptions. The story of her life during the two years prior to the publication of *Canciones* contains many of the ingredients of an adventure novel: a rebellious spirit, an escape from a stifling home environment, arrivals at strange places, a series of odd jobs, and the creation of numerous friendships. Méndez left her family a farewell note and sailed for England in 1928 without money or knowledge of English. Shortly after returning to Spain, she left for the New World, arriving in Buenos Aires on Christmas Eve of 1929, again with no resources but her "gran bagaje de ilusiones" [huge valise of illusions].[35] She traces her desire to travel to the moment she was born: "Yo debí nacer con el alma viajera. . . . A los siete años ya decía que me iría" [I must have been born with a traveler's soul. . . . At seven, I already was saying that I would leave home].[36] The limitations placed on her education and the condescending responses to her youthful appetite for freedom provoked a burning desire to run away from her stifling environment.[37] Angela Ingram maintains that it is not unusual for women already feeling "exiled" at home, excluded by society from their dreams, to exile themselves literally in an attempt to counteract their feelings of exclusion. In this way, "geographical exile is often more a *getting away from* than *going to* a place."[38] Méndez openly acknowledged that travel, and particularly sea travel, meant independence for her: *Canciones de mar y tierra* opens with the lines "Por los mares quiero ir / corriendo entre Sur y Norte, / que quiero vivir, vivir, / sin leyes ni pasaporte" [I want to go via the seas, traveling from north to south, for I want to live, to live, without laws or passports], and after her return from Buenos Aires, she told an interviewer that her experience "fue el despertar a mi realidad: Emancipación. . . . Libertad . . . el mejor de los deportes" [was my awakening to a new reality: Emancipation. Freedom . . . the best of sports].[39]

In *Canciones* the voyage motif is a comprehensive referent comprised of a beginning, middle, and end. The de-emphasis of the final, arrival phase helps heighten the sense of immediacy, movement, and substantiality running through the collection. By highlighting the initiation phase of travel, Méndez creates scenarios for activity and a future-oriented focus. Even if recounted as a completed act, the voyage in *Canciones* represents an excursion forward to the exclusion of any mention of distancing from the past. In "Canal de Bristol," the poetic voice articulates the excitement of her sea travel within an initial and concluding exclamatory frame:

> ¡Canal de Bristol un día
> a bordo de aquel mercante! . . .
> —novia del mar me sentía
> novia del mar, o su amante—
> Subida al palo trinquete,
> bañada en viento marino.
> Mi alma, moreno grumete.
> Proa frente a mi destino
> por el azul navegaba
> a bordo de aquel mercante.
> Y el corazón me gritaba:
> ¡adelante y adelante! . . .
>
> (49–50)

[The Bristol channel
aboard that merchant ship! . . .
—I felt like the bride of the sea
the bride of the sea, or its lover—
    Atop the foremast
bathed in the sea breeze.
My soul, a tanned cabin boy.
    A prow facing my destiny
I sailed the blue
aboard that merchant ship.
And my heart shouted:
forward and forward!]

The ellipses at the end of these sets of lines reflect the speaker's insistence on continuance and her poem's refusal to close. Between the poem's introductory terse description and its final imperative, an intensification of movement and self-awareness takes place. The poetic speaker sees herself at first united to the sea in a loving relationship as "novia," but quickly changes her role to the less decorous one of "amante." Any passive, recumbent pose suggested in either label is adjusted by her repositioning herself on the boat's foremast; and the sea wind striking her body begins to add movement to an otherwise static scene. The metaphor of the speaker's soul as a tanned ship's boy, while implying a dependence on the ship, also evokes an image of physical activity in the open air. In the last stanza the speaker takes possession of herself as well as of the sea. No longer fused with the sea, she becomes the boat with a prow cutting through its waters and her inner yearnings, personified by a voice of authority, directing the boat's movement.

Travel is an experience of expansion and freedom for Méndez. In verses not quite as brash as those of Espronceda's pirate, but comparably exuberant, her poetic persona declares: "No me pidáis pasaporte / porque no soy extranjera, / que las puertas de mi casa / son las de cada frontera" (89) [Don't ask for my passport / because I am not a foreigner, / for the doors of my house / open onto every border]. Renouncing regulations and barriers, she envisions free and fluid access to the world around her. Not all, however, is assertion and dominion in *Canciones*. In the poem "Trasatlántico" [Ocean liner], a setting of coldness, darkness, and death in the first stanza establishes a mood of ambivalence:

Llegaba un frío de adioses
de la noche de los puertos.
Aires vírgenes llevaban
a enterrar planetas muertos.

Y yo en el puente alto,
en el puente de mando,
sin mando,
quieta,
inquieta
—creo que el mar tenía
el alma violeta—
Y yo en el puente alto
    del trasatlántico
(No me conocía nadie)
                    (87–88)

[A coldness of night farewells
bidden in ports was approaching.
Virgin breezes were coming
to bury dead planets.
    And I upon the high bridge
up on the bridge
without any command
motionless
restless
—I think the sea had
a violet soul—
and I upon the high bridge
    of the ocean liner
(No one recognized me)]

The speaker finds herself on the bridge in command yet "sin mando"; she sees herself as "quieta" and immediately "inquieta." This double subversion of control and tranquility coupled with the contrast at the end of the poem between her conspicuousness and the lack of recognition of her by others creates an emotional turmoil the poem never completely resolves. The isolated last line of the poem affirms solitude, but its parenthetical construction softens its negative impact and reverts attention back to the image of the speaker on the bridge, literally above it all, in the poem's only repeated line: "Y yo en el puente alto."

The placement of the poetic speaker on the foremast in "¡Canal de Bristol un día . . ." [Bristol channel one day] and on the bridge in "Trasatlántico" serves to underscore the significance of the images of verticality that reappear in *Canciones*. Verticality, as an archetypal symbol, has been associated with positive meanings. As Philip Wheelwright explains, "Physically all men are subject to the law of gravitation, for which reason *up* is normally a more difficult direction in which to go than *down*; and this makes it natural enough that the idea of going up would associate itself with the idea of achievement, and that various images connoting loftiness or ascent should associate themselves with the idea of excellence, and often of regality and command."[40] Physically, all women are also subject to the laws of gravitation; but within our conventional system of symbols, verticality and its metonymic attributes are identified with masculinity while the horizontal with its chain of associations of submission, inactivity, and death are identified with femininity. This discrepancy is explained by the fact that metaphors both reflect and shape our world. As George Lakoff and Mark Johnson convincingly argue, our ordinary human concepts, metaphorical at their core, "structure what we perceive, how we get around in the world, and how we relate to other people."[41] Thus the metaphors we use are grounded in our interaction with our physical environment, but once formed, they precondition subsequent thought patterns that come to be viewed as natural conclusions rather than unconsciously perpetuated interpretations.

In this way, over the centuries, male-generated mythologies, both sacred and secular, have justified the association between men and the privileged vertical position while assigning women to the devalued horizontal state. Alicia Suskin Ostriker explains that from Plato to St. Paul and from St. Paul to Freud, the transcendence of all that is considered base has been tied to vertical mobility and masculinity; and woman, by virtue of her conspicious physical role in procreation, *is* flesh, inferior matter that must be despised or surpassed.[42] When not renounced as base, woman is reduced to a passive, compliant Sleeping Beauty, whose place is, in the words of Hélène Cixous, "in bed and asleep—'laid (out).'"[43] Or as Madonna Kolbenschlag says,"[A]t the universal level of meaning, Sleeping Beauty is most of all a symbol of *passivity*, and by extension a metaphoric spiritual condition of women—cut off from autonomy and transcendence, from self-actualization and ethical capacity in a male-dominated milieu."[44]

The appropriation of verticality by a woman can be considered an accidental exception or a voluntary rejection of the traditional distinction between transcendence and immanence. The interpretations of deviations from the norm in poets have been complicated by the findings of recent critics of literature by women. Throughout her book on contemporary American women poets, Ostriker discerns not only a persistent male representation of women as horizontal, "at rest," and passive, but a lasting aversion to verticality among women writers.[45] If verticality and a desire for transcendence in Méndez are not only a denial of the destiny deemed appropriate to women by male thinkers, but also a contradiction of the posture defined as characteristic of them by female theorists, then her early poetry must be seen as a double subversion, a subversion of male as well as female crafted paradigms. Beyond this rebellion against gender-bound conventions, Méndez's response to metaphors also reflects the youthfulness that colors her poetry before it acquires a more somber tonality in later collections.

In *Canciones de mar y tierra* the prevailing direction is up. The poetic persona invariably finds herself seated on top of a vertical pole of some sort or climbing upward. She climbs mountain peaks and sails to the moon. When not on the "puente alto" or "subida al palo trinquete," we find her identified as an "atalayo," focused on the highest mast of her ship or situated in a tower as a lookout. The poem "Escalas" [Ladders] can serve as a clear illustration of the force that verticality holds within these poems:

> Escalas.
> Más escalas.
> Unas, que suban a los cielos.
> Otras, que bajen a las aguas.
> A las profundidades
> más altas y más bajas.
> A desentrañar misterios azules
> Almas
> de misterios azules.
> Escalas.
> Más escalas.
> Unas, que bajen a los cielos.
> Otras, que suban a las aguas.
> ¡Qué importa!
>   (91–92)

> [Ladders.
> More ladders.
> Some, let them go to the heavens.
> Others, let them go down to the seas.
> To the highest
> and lowest depths.
> To expose the blue mysteries
> Soul
> of blue mysteries.
> Ladders.
> More ladders.
> Some, let them go down to the heavens.
> Others, let them go up to the seas.
> What's the difference!]

Through poetic transformation and hyperbole, ladders reach both the sky and the bottom of the sea, functioning as vehicles of movement rather than merely as images of an upright position. By attributing fanciful qualities to the object "ladders" without the superposition inherent in the metaphor, the poet creates what Carlos Bousoño terms "visión," an irrational expression which nonetheless communicates the spiritual aspirations of the

speaker.[46] The picture in "Escalas" of cosmic expanse and inclusive movement incarnates the sense of exaltation and possession that obsesses the
speaker. The distant and intangible—sea and sky—are given a tangible
presence through the concrete link of the ladder. The absence of any independent main verb erases temporality in favor of spatial immutability, but
the implicit requests in the phrases "que suban a los cielos" and "que bajen
a las aguas" contain dependent subjunctive verbs pointing to a potential
future realization. In addition, through repetitions, contrapositioning, and
parallelisms, the poet creates a series of structural vibrations that evoke
movement without assigning a time frame. Each line, except the last one,
forms part of a chain of repetitions with variations. After line two, a contrast of directions begins and in line seven, literal references are transformed
into abstractions as the blue of the sky and the sea is displaced from organic matter to "almas." This displacement serves as a transition for the
more radical transposition of expectation in the lines "Unas, que bajen a
los cielos, / Otras, que suban a las aguas" [Some, let them go down to the
heavens, / Others, let them go up to the seas], lines that repeat lines three
and four with a significant inversion. Now outside the realm of reality, ladders symbolize the speaker's ambition to preclude descent and to disrupt
fixed relationships. The impossible interchange between the sky and the
sea animates her poetic universe with a sense of playful restlessness. The
playfulness of the upheaval created is reaffirmed by the flip exclamation at
the end of the poem.

The playfulness hinted at in "Escalas" is more pronounced in "Dancing." An animated and personified nocturnal landscape takes on the festive, frolicsome air of a high-society party of the twenties. The night dresses
in tails; a star and a comet dance a fox trot; and three stars, drunk on cham-
pagne, stumble along the firmament. Both superposition of human attributes
on the cosmic sphere and the modern motifs attest to Méndez's responsiveness to the spirit of the age. She often incorporates references to sports,
jazz, and technological advances. The wind, for example, is associated with
telegrams, mail, and cablegrams. By making motifs from contemporary
popular culture the vehicle of metaphoric transformation, she affirms their
legitimacy as poetic tools, or as Dámaso Alonso says of her male counterparts, she achieves "el ennoblecimiento del humor, mejor dicho, de cierta
alegría deportiva y despreocupada" [the ennoblement of humor, or rather,
of a certain sportive and carefree joy].[47] Beyond dignifying frivolity, Méndez's
reversal of expected analogies, her sublimation of mundane motifs, and
the general commotion in a poem like "Dancing" help sustain the element
of motion throughout *Canciones*.

The use of verticality easily leads to the inclusion of flight. If enclosure
has been a consistent feminine condition, then flying becomes, as Cixous
says, a "woman's gesture," a distinctly female dream with literal as well as

metaphorical implications of escape or change.[48] Although literary expressions of flight reflect a real-life counterpart of confinement for women, as symbol, flight is also a long-standing, comprehensive archetype of transgression and transcendence in masculine texts. As Cirlot explains, flying implies raising oneself, and is therefore closely connected with such qualities as power or strength.[49]

The yearning for escape, travel, and adventure that underlies Méndez's early poetry is represented by a whole array of images of flight in *Canciones*. Méndez uses the verb "volar" [to fly] and incorporates sea gulls, dragonflies, leaves, wind, airplanes, and trains into her poems repeatedly. People, animals, and things all acquire wings. Autumn leaves, for example, become "alas de oro" [wings of gold], canceling any association with descent, gloom, or loss. If suggestions of descent occur in the book, they emerge most often in descriptions of the foggy, dim streets of London, and not in poems that translate personal moods. When, in the poem "Pampera" [the female inhabitant of the pampas], the horse that the speaker rides acquires wings, metaphor verges on myth as the fast running horse suggests a mythical steed.

In the poem "Patinadores" [Skiers], the poetic speaker urges skiers to follow her lead and fly to reach indefinite heights:

> La tarde sueña trineos.
> Y la nieve cascabeles.
> Y las montañas luceros.
>   ¿Las ramas del pino verde
> qué soñarán en sus sueños?
>   ¡Seguidme, patinadores,
> que llevo el alma y el traje
> encendidos de colores.
> Vamos a soñar alturas
> por entre la tarde gris,
> por vertientes y llanuras
> volando con los skis!
>
> (35)

> [The afternoon dreams of sleighs.
> And the snow of bells.
> And the mountains of stars.
>   What do the branches of the green pine
> dream of?
>   Skiers, follow me,
> for my soul and my suit
> are ablaze with colors.
> We shall dream of heights,

during the gray afternoon,
along the slopes and the plains
as we fly on our skis.]

The juxtaposition of bright colors with both soul and suit not only gives corporeality to "soul" but also transforms the palpable suit into part of a poetic entity. The tangible and the intangible, nature and the human figure share the same space and emotion. With the one verb "soñar" assigned to afternoon, snow, mountains, and pine, the skiers prepare to move within a sublimated landscape. In the last stanza of the poem, the central position of "soñar" [to dream] serves as an axis for the other verbs and melds the skiers with the dreaming natural elements clustered in the first half of the poem. In this way, the concrete is transformed into an abstraction in a unified vision of animation, expectation, and hope.

Not all the patterns of movement in *Canciones* are vertical and upward. The forward motions of running, roaming, and drifting also appear. Figures run across the land and the sea; and shadows of the night playfully roam the streets. Drifting, literally, forms part of the calm on the high seas ("Altamar" [High seas], 97) and, figuratively, defines the poet's life as it equates to freedom: "—¡Sola y a la deriva / por mi verdad: / por mi blanca bandera / de libertad! . . . —" (156) [Alone and drifting / for the sake of my truth / for the sake of my white flag / of freedom]. Physical extension can intersect with temporal prolongation, as occurs in "Dame la mano" [Give me your hand]:

> Dame la mano, que se me quite el miedo.
> Así pasaré el puente alto de las horas
> sin vértigo.
> E iré por caminos de soles
> hacia los mundos quietos,
> hacia los mundos presentidos,
> hacia los mundos nuevos.
> Dame tu mano,
> tu mano alargada de dedos inciertos
> con el último anillo de Saturno
> reluciente, reluciendo.
> Subiremos las cuestas imposibles
> hasta llegar arriba, a los tiempos.
> ¿No sabes dónde?
> Mira mis sienes.
>
> (67–68)

[Give me your hand to calm my fear.
So I will span the high bridge of time

without dizziness.
   And I will walk along sunny roads
toward still worlds,
toward expected worlds,
toward new worlds.
   Give me your hand,
your outstretched hand of nervous fingers
with the last ring of Saturn
shiny, shining.
We will climb impossible heights
until we reach time itself.
You don't know where?
Look at my temples.]

In the first two lines, space unfolds into time: the outstretched hand facilitates the passage over the high bridge of "hours." Immediately afterward, repetitions and parallelisms lead the speaker through the poem from fear to assertion. The future tense of the verbs of the second and fourth lines initiates the affirmative tone of the poem. The emphatic insistence on "mundos," in lines five, six, and seven, focuses attention on destination begun by the single mention of "caminos"; and the qualifiers "de soles," "quietos," "presentidos," and "nuevos" firmly establish a mood of confident expectation. In the second stanza, the real gives way to the mythical, as the ring placed on the companion's finger proves to be one of the unattainable rings of the planet Saturn. The verb forms "reluciente, reluciendo" of verse four confirm the poem's overlapping of space and time, the adjective suggesting essence while the gerund implies existence. At this juncture the vision of the speaker turns upward to underline the figurative implications of ascent. The shift from space to time seen in the initial lines of the poem is reconfirmed with the difference that now the more finite "horas" [hours] becomes "tiempos" [times], the transitory "pasar" is substituted by the finality of "llegar," and the goal is clearly defined as "cuestas imposibles." Thus even when centering on extension, Méndez turns the vantage point of her poem upward.

Occasionally a suggestion of circularity or a swaying motion infuses a calming note into the poetry of *Canciones*, but over all the movement created by its imagery, syntax, and lexicon, when not one of upwardness, is of advancement, acceleration, and passage. Negative emotions, for example, are generally converted into a material substance and then dismantled with a piercing gesture of some sort, as the following poem "Rumbos" [Direction] illustrates:

Si con rumbo a Escandinavia
ya los sueños se me van . . .

izen velas, leven anclas
y ¡avante! mi capitán.
　　Hacia las tierras polares,
surcando la soledad
sóla de los altamares.
　　Los paisajes de alabastro
esperándonos están.
Y su sol de media noche.
Y las horas que vendrán . . .
　　　　　　　　　　　　(139–40)

　　[I am bound for Scandinavia
my dreams leave me . . .
hoist sails, lift anchor
and, ahoy! my captain.
　　Toward the polar regions,
furrowing the lonely
solitude of the sigh seas.
　　Alabaster landscapes
are waiting for us.
And the midnight sun.
And the hours that will come.]

After affirming an inclination to begin through the imperatives "izen," "leven," and "avante," the poetic speaker points her vision forward from "hacia," the first word of the second strophe. The loneliness ("soledad") epitomized by the open sea is cast aside by the ship's furrowing through the water. Throughout the collection, a series of verbs, like "to furrow," connoting violent action generally associated with maleness, reinforces the leitmotif of forward movement and power that structurally sustains the book. The morning "lanza el disco" [throws the discus]; the sun "le pone rejones" "al torito de la aurora" [stabs the little bull of the dawn with lances]; a train "perfora la noche" [perforates the night]; and the poet harpoons hearts with her songs.

　　The dialectics of gender uncovers cultural associations between verticality and the male perspective, social mobility, and aggression, but the early poetry of Concha Méndez disregards the gender-bound distribution of spatial areas.[50] The sea and open spaces become Concha Méndez's symbols of desire and vehicles for the realization of dreams. Rarely does a suggestion of inner space arise in *Canciones de mar y tierra*. Seascapes, wide plains, and vistas of the sky predominate. These poems are fundamentally songs of free and expansive movements, movements upward or outward. An absence of the sense of enclosure often found in women's writing up to her time gives Méndez's poetry a distinct quality recognized already in her own day. In her preface to *Canciones*, Consuelo Berges remarks that the book is imbued with a "tácita protesta contra la mezcla y alternación de tagorismo, erotismo y ñoñismo que uniforma de gris a casi todas las poetas y poetisas hispanoamericanas" [a tacit protest against the mixture and alternation of Tagore style, eroticism and prudishness that clothes almost all of the Hispanic American women poets and poetesses in gray]; what surfaces instead, she says, is "un magnífico apetito de vivir, de actuar, de ser feliz" [a magnificent appetite for living, for doing, for being happy] that sets her apart from all the poets of the day. The predominance in *Canciones* of movement over stillness, of flight over descent, and of progression over withdrawal creates a vibrating presence which, by virtue of its inconclusiveness, only approximates fulfillment but still incorporates the potential for its realization.

VIDA A VIDA: AWAKENING FROM THE DREAM

The light, movement, and joy predominating in *Canciones de mar y tierra* slowly subside as shadows begin to cast increasingly darker tones upon Concha Méndez's poetic landscape. Shadows establish themselves as a living presence beginning in *Vida a vida* [Lives together], a brief collection of twenty poems published in 1932. What was previously jubilation, cheerfulness, and assertiveness becomes loneliness, somberness, and even nihilism. Emilio Miró points to the poems "Insomnio" [Insomnia] and "Silencio" [Silence] as explicit examples of this new tonality in lines such as "¡Y este infinito terror / al vacío de las horas! / ¡Y este ver como se va / lo que soy / para no ser más allá!" [And this infinite terror / of the emptiness of time! / And this seeing what I am / slip away / and disappear in the great beyond!] and "De piedra siento el silencio / sobre mi cuerpo y mi alma. / No sé qué hacer bajo el peso / de esta losa" [I feel a silence of stone / on my body and soul. / I do not know what to do beneath the weight / of this stone slab].[51]

The escape from confinement dramatized in her first three collections gives way in these poems to a metaphorical imprisonment in an iron jail facing a world of emptiness:

> ¡Qué angustiosa cárcel ésta
> de hierro por todas partes,
> con las ventanas al mundo
> a las sombras, a la nada!
> 　　　　　　(*Vida a vida*, 47)

> [What an agonizing prison of iron
> this is everywhere,

with windows to the world
to the shadows, to nothingness!]

The open vistas and the focus on distant, exciting geographical places of her early poetry are substituted by introspection and reflection. Words of disquiet like "alma," "angustia," and "nostalgia" [soul, anguish, and nostalgia] appear frequently; questions create an atmosphere of uncertainty; and repeated negations imply lack and even loss of identity. In the poem "Ultima cita" [Last encounter], for example, an absence of all light is counterpoised by pervasive silence as an apt scenario for impending separation:

Ni había sol, ni luna, ni noche, ni día.
Un silencio frío
nadaba en el tiempo.
Y tus ojos no eran tus ojos
y los míos no sé de quién eran.
Para no mirarnos miramos a un cielo,
faltaban estrellas.
. . . .
Porque era la última cita
no se vieron las lágrimas nuestras.

(*Vida a vida*, 49–50)

[There was no sun, nor moon, nor night, nor day.
A cold silence
swam through time.
And your eyes were not your eyes
and I don't know whose mine were.
Not to look at each other we looked at the sky,
stars were missing
. . . .
Because it was our last rendezvous
our tears were not to be seen.]

Love and desire can impose light, joy, and exaltation upon silence. As John C. Wilcox affirms, coitus provides Méndez with images to express fulfillment and personal ecstasy.[52] Love in this book is celebrated as both a transcendent and an erotically charged experience. Yet physical union creates a consciousness of shadows, of uneasiness; and it is the beloved who introduces the notion of shadow into this poetry. These first shadows in Méndez's poetry represent more a lingering than a loss, an intangible presence of a fleeting material union, as evidenced in "Recuerdo de sombras" [Memory of shadows], the initial poem of the collection:

Sobre la blanca almohada,
más allá del deseo,
sobre la blanca noche,
sobre el blanco silencio,
sobre nosotros mismos,
las almas en su encuentro.
Sobre mi frente erguido
el exacto momento,
dices que en una sombra
vives en mi recuerdo.
Síntesis de las horas.
Tú y yo en movimiento
luchando vida a vida,
gozando cuerpo a cuerpo.
Dices que en estas sombras
vives en mi recuerdo,
y son las mismas sombras
que están en mí viviendo.
                    (*Vida a vida*, 39)

[On the white pillow,
beyond desire,
on the white night,
on the white silence,
on ourselves,
our souls meet.
The exact moment
on my straight brow,
you say that in a shadow
you live in my memory.
A synthesis of hours.
You and I in movement
struggling one life against another,
delighting body to body.
You say that in these shadows
you live in my memory,
and they are the same shadows
that are living in me.]

As the singular "sombra" becomes plural "sombras," the "tú" and "yo" commingle on a sublimated, psychological level. The poetic persona who assumed male patterns of verticality, mobility, and openness begins to envision images more commonly associated with traditional feminine identity: immanence, containment, and stasis. She sees herself, or more precisely her memory, as a life-sustaining medium, an incubator to keep alive the "shadows" of reality. Formerly a skier, swimmer, and skipper, the speaker in

Méndez's poetry repositions herself in private spaces and re-identifies herself as an expectant consoler and a source of refuge: "Ven a mí que vas
herido / que en este lecho de sueños / podrás descansar conmigo" [Come
to me for you are wounded / and in this bed of dreams / you can rest with
me]. Rather than being an autonomous wanderer, she directs her movements toward the lover in function of his existence:

> Mandaré a mi alma
> que te dé consuelo
> hasta que esta mano
> que me ancla a la ausencia
> liberte mi cuerpo
> y vaya mi cuerpo
> a darte su vida.
>
> (*Vida a vida*, 51)

> [I will send my soul
> to give you comfort
> until this hand
> that anchors me to absence
> frees my body
> and my body
> gives you life.]

The discovery of the "other" causes her to redefine herself as a concomitant of another human being and to refocus her attention away from
the ideal and the imaginary toward more personal, more real, and therefore more troubling circumstances. James Valender considers the self-doubt
provoked by the presence of the other to be a dynamic tension that en-
riches Méndez's poetry and advances the poet's evolution from self-awareness to an acute recognition of the world around her.[53] This fall into reality,
however, has an ambivalent impact. Love awakens the soul to the fire of
passion ("Con el brillo de tu espada / las sienes se me encendieron;" "hecha
de fuego en el aire;" "Me parece estar contigo / en las entrañas del mundo")
[My temples were lit by the brilliance of your sword; made of fire in the air;
I seem to be with you / in the core of the world], but anguish also becomes
fiery ("Mi angustia se hace de fuego" [My anguish becomes fire] and "qué
cadena de fuego / me sujeta a este todo!") [what a chain of fire ties me to
all of this]. Life unfolds now, not as a limitless horizon and unbound gladness, but within more private, inner confines, and as a succession of both
happy and sad moments. In this rite of passage between the adolescent
dream state and the adult phase of experience, love serves as a mediator
between the ideal and the real and brings, along with the joy of fulfillment,
the pain of separation of the "última cita." As her "green world" of the sea

gives way to the world of human beings, the occasions for introspection and anguish will increase for the protagonist of Concha Méndez's poetry. What was before an unidentified dream of escape becomes a nebulous panorama of pain and lost freedom:

Todas las calles en sombra
por la ciudad donde paso.
La bandera del dolor
en ventanas y balcones.
Ni una voz que me distraiga
y me saque de mí misma.
                                        (*Vida a vida*, 45)

[All of the streets are dark
in the city where I walk.
The flag of pain
in the windows and on the balconies.
No voice to distract me
and take me out of myself.]

¡Qué perpetua cadena,
qué cadena de fuego
me sujeta a este todo!
Sin libertad posible,
¡cómo pesa en mis hombros!
                                        (*Vida a vida*, 46)

[What a perpetual chain,
what a chain of fire
ties me to all this!
Without any possible freedom,
How it weighs on my shoulders!]

Vida a vida is a pivotal, although extremely brief, moment in the tale of Concha Méndez's journey from open spaces to the realm of shadows. With the establishment of the presence of sexual desire, the concrete world of human experience supplants the realm of imagination; and the real replaces the ideal with all the somber consequences this shift away from dream space implies.

RETREAT INTO THE SHADOWS

The encroachment of the world of experience announced in *Vida a vida* intensified in the poetry Concha Méndez wrote after 1933. The discovery of the other awakened her poetic persona from the dream of emancipation to the reality of attachments, interdependence, and containment. In *Vida a vida* the potential for loss was only alluded to, but loss became soon afterwards an indelible reality that colored her verse with pervasive somber tones. The period between 1933 and 1944 was one of difficult years for Méndez—years of grief, multiple changes in residence, and economic hardships. In that decade her first child died, she went into exile, and her husband abandoned her in Mexico where they had settled after the civil war.[54] Physical and psychological estrangement interacted to create a multifaceted environment of exile with all its ramifications of horror, grief, nostalgia, uncertainty, loneliness, and despair. Although the poetic persona that emerged in her later poems is that of one who posseses a remarkable capacity for self-renewal, shadows and other forms of absence loom with relentless force.

The phenomenon of exile within the context of the poetry Méndez wrote from 1933 to 1944 comprises multiple implications of separation, alienation, and silence. Beyond its most common definition of absolute separation from one's homeland for political reasons, exile can also be experienced on ontological, social, and psychological levels of existence.[55] While Méndez suffered geographical exile along with hundreds of thousands of other Spaniards, it is in its other manifestations—of social exclusion, rupture in psychological bonds, and loss of a sense of self—that exile makes a lasting impact on her poetry and turns most of the second half of her literary production into, in the words of Biruté Ciplijauskaité, "a song to loss."[56] The pain of separation, absence, and silence associated with any kind of exile is often represented in poetic form as shadow along with its complementary motifs of darkness, emptiness, and negation.

The prominence of shadows in the poetry Méndez wrote after 1933 is announced in the very titles of her next three collections—*Niño y sombra* [Child and shadow] (1933), *Lluvias enlazadas* [Interlaced rains] (1939), and *Poemas. Sombras y sueños* [Poems. Shadows and dreams] (1944). Shadows flood this poetry, as Emilio Miró observes: "El desarraigo de la ausencia, la mordedura de la nostalgia, presentes y dolientes en casi todos los poetas 'del éxodo y del llanto,' son también en ella sombras y silencio, sombras y soledad, sueños y recuerdos. La luz, el mar, el viento, el alma . . . se irán oscureciendo, adentrándose en la noche, poblándose de sombras invasoras, crecientes. Y la esperanza se metamorfoseará en memoria" [The uprooting of absence, the bite of nostalgia, present and painful in almost all poets of 'the exodus and tears' are also in her shadows and silence, shadows and loneliness, dreams and memories. Light, sea, wind, soul . . . all get dark, penetrating the night, filling up with growing, invasive shadows. And hope is metamorphosed into memory].[57] Shadows dim the luminosity of her earlier poetry, convert hope into memory, and substitute presence with absence. The sense of presence generated in Méndez's early poetry by elements of visibility, audibility, and mobility cedes to a dismal reality of absence defined in terms of the indistinct, the silent, and the static. Shadow functions as a complex symbol of loss and as a unifying thread to interconnect the different varieties of exile that surface in the second half of Méndez's literary production.

The image of the shadow becomes a fitting vehicle, not only to document present pain but to communicate the sense of emptiness that has been infused into the past and the feelings of despair that extend into the future. Because Méndez, as often happens with women, did not have first-hand knowledge of the horrific scenes of death and destruction that surrounded the civil war, images of blood make a briefer appearance in her poetry than in that of her male compatriots.[58] When the shadow appears in connection with war in Méndez's poetry, it is generally an image for loneliness. The loneliness provoked by the nostalgia of the exile, as Ciplijauskaité affirms, not only creates a gap in the existence of that person, but the land itself, left behind, suffers from the absence of those who have gone.[59] The homeland can only be evoked through the indistinctness and intangibility of memory; and once evoked, the recreated landscapes prove to have been transformed by war into a shadow of their former reality. Thus shadows define the situation of separation between exile and homeland as well as the changed essence of both. Méndez evokes the Manzanares River, but sees it changed by war: "Pequeño río de un cuento, / hoy con la guerra, más chico, / todo enfangado y sangriento" (*Poemas*, 38) [Small river of a story, / smaller today because of the war, / all muddy and bloody]. In this way, nostalgia serves as an avenue to a consoling refuge in the past, to a dissipation of the shadows created by the distance between the exile and her home, but at the same time darkens the present with its reconfirmation of that same distance.

In Méndez's poetry more than as the blurred presence of a lost past, shadows emerge as a metaphor for the uncertainty, ambiguity, and confusion of life, for existential vacuousness, for the nothingness of being. This element of erasure is converted, through metaphorical transformation, into a palpable environment of darkness punctuated with shadings of murkiness and gloom:

> Entre turbias lagunas bogar veo la Vida.
> Deja estelas de fango, al pasar, cada cosa . . .

. . . .
No despierto a una hora que no traiga consigo,
en un sordo silencio, una queja enganchada.
Tiene el alma un oído que la escucha y la siente
y recibe esta queja con la pena doblada . . .

(*Lluvias*, 56)

[I see life sail through the murky lagoons.
Everything leaves a wake of mud as it passes . . .

. . . .
There is not an hour in which I wake that does not bring
a snarled complaint, in a deaf silence.
The soul has an ear that hears and feels it
and receives this complaint with doubled grief . . .]

Disorientation, upheaval, and stagnation have replaced the mobility and the sense of focus and purpose that characterized the first half of her work.

For the exile, the painful present is irreconcilably disconnected from the lost past; and the present self, uprooted from its former attachments, becomes a mere shadow, a faint and inadequate double for a distant wholeness. While occasionally resorting to antithesis to communicate the psychic polarization experienced by the exile, Méndez prefers to exploit instead the implications of ambivalence inherent in the notion of shadow. Within the shadowy confines of her spiritual reality, this metaphorical traveler loses her sense of existential direction, becomes confused, and remains suspended in a silent vacuum. The present is uncertain ("Camina sin saber adonde / acompañada sólo de los vientos" [It walks without knowing where / accompanied only by the winds]), as is the future. The radical rupture in their lives that exiles suffer compels them to question the authenticity of life.[60] To express broken progression and uncertainty, Méndez turns not to the motif of the road but to that of the labyrinth for a strong composite image of darkness, confusion, enclosure, and arrested movement:

De distintos puntos que yo no conozco,
oigo que me llaman voces que no entiendo;
y me desespera el no entender nada
y me desanima verlo todo incierto.
A veces pregunto: ¿por qué habré venido
a este laberinto de las soledades . . .

(*Lluvias*, 62)

[From different points unknown to me,
I hear voices I do not understand calling me;
and not understanding makes me despair
and seeing everything with uncertainty depresses me.

Sometimes I ask, Why have I come
to this labyrinth of loneliness?]

Both the poetic protagonist and her life sustain the weight of a comparable
distress. Metaphorically the difficulties of life are burdens, but if one conceives of life as one constant, relentless difficulty, then it is possible to think
of the whole of life as a burden.[61] In this way, life passes from arduous
journey to the state of fruitless bewilderment and limited movement that
the labyrinth metaphor expresses. As a dark and intricate passageway, the
labyrinth twists and negates the flow of life, converting it into the gloomy
stagnation of the "turbias lagunas" in the lines quoted earlier. Thus the
shadow motif expands from a metaphor for the grief brought about by
exile to a broad representation of life itself.

Shadow signifies not only the absence of light; but in its connotations of
weak, faint, or oblique representation, it conveys the idea of lack of substance. Surrounded by a "silencio sordo" relieved only by a "queja
enganchada," the poetic speaker in Méndez's poetry falls into a closed and
confusing existential maze. This position instills a nihilism in her that shifts
her vision of life from one of disorientation within a shadowy environment
to that of anguish within gaping nothingness. Humans and their realm are
merely shadows: "Se mueve el mundo silenciosamente; / en él no somos
sino una sombra; / es nuestro clima: soledad y descanso; / es el misterio el
que nos da la forma" (*Poemas,* 24) [The world moves silently; / in it we are
nothing but a shadow / our climate is: solitude and repose; / mystery is
what gives us form]. Although not completely losing her ability to give
corporality and even color and texture to grief, Méndez's later poetry rests
on pronouncements of negation, absence, and emptiness. These themes
are reflected in the frequent use of words like "sin," "ni," "no," and "nadie"
[without, nor, no, no one] and of images that connote coldness or emptiness, such as "desierto," "frío," "escarcha," "nieves," "eco," "sombra,"
"ceniza," "niebla" [desert, cold, frost, snows, echo, shadow, ash, fog]. The
loss of interest in life breeds an indifference that makes her declare, "Nada
me importa. Hasta aquí he llegado / importándome todo en demasía"
[Nothing matters to me. I have come this far / letting things matter too
much to me]. It produces a bitter cynicism that makes her seek out lies,
masks, and oblivion. Life has become a shadow of all that has been lost, is
absent, and does not exist.

Split between two places and two time frames, the exile's existence is
broken and ambiguous. One way to resolve this inner trauma and reconcile the divisions between the past and the present is to find links with past
literary masters. To satisfy this need for connection and continuity, Méndez
looks back to a female precedessor, the poet Rosalía de Castro, for sympathy, consolation, and companionship. Although she does not seek out this

female model to "legitimize her own rebellious endeavors," as Gilbert and Gubar discover in English-language writers,[62] she begins to engage in the "double-voiced discourse" that characterizes many of them. She begins to participate in the female literary tradition without losing consciousness of the canonical, male voices that have nurtured her literary development. Therefore her configurations of the nothingness of life rely primarily on the conceptions of the baroque writers Francisco de Quevedo and, especially, Luis de Góngora. The sense of temporality, disillusion, and descent in Góngora's famous line "en tierra, en humo, en polvo, en sombra, en nada" [in earth, in smoke, in dust, in shadow, in nothing] surfaces in the line "una luz, una pausa, un suspiro, una sombra" [a light, a pause, a sign, a shadow]. She glosses Góngora's verses, defining life as painful and ephemeral; but she magnifies the somberness of the inserted intertext by infusing into them touches of bitter fatalism. Góngora's lines "La vida es ciervo herido / que las flechas le dan alas" [Life is a wounded deer / given wings by arrows] become in Méndez's hands "la vida es ciervo herido sin remedio / que las flechas le dan veneno y alas" (*Lluvias*, 58) [life is a hopelessly wounded deer given poison and wings by arrows]. Whereas her seventeenth-century model reflected stoic endurance before the imperfections of life, Méndez embraces negation with melodramatic fervor.

Although the opposition between shadow and dream, darkness and light, made an appearance in 1932 in *Vida a vida*, it becomes more pronounced once Méndez's poems begin to reflect more directly the negative circumstances of her life. Death, exile, and divorce follow one another in rapid succession and project themselves as an oppressive shadow over most of the rest of her poetic production. The opposition between the negative and the positive at times produces a balanced alternation between extremes, but more often it translates into irresolvable inner conflict and despair. A dense shadow spreads across the poems of *Niño y sombra* and especially *Lluvias enlazadas*, extinguishing all glimmers of light. Images of darkness—night, mist, fog—combine with others of silence and coldness to create a desolate emotional landscape. Silence pierces the human body, exceeding its quality of absence of sound to include physiological dimensions: "Que vacío dejaste, / al partir, en mis manos! / ¡Qué silencio en mi sangre!" (*Lluvias*, 13) [What emptiness you left in my hands when you went away! / What silence in my blood!]. The shadow acquires multiple qualities: as a perceptible attribute, it darkens, weighs, and turns cold and as an abstraction, it represents human experience and essence. The mother feels herself to be a shadow and the lost child is seen as an impalpable, unreachable shade, while life is defined as a parenthetical emptiness within dark boundaries. The poet declares: "De lo oscuro venimos y vamos / a otra noche pulsando caminos. / Y la luz de la vida no sirve" (*Lluvias*, 24) [We come and go from the darkness / to another night feeling the roads. / The light of life is of no help]. As with her poems on exile, in those dedicated to her dead son the shadow is an external presence that becomes a vital force, but here the feelings of loneliness, distance, and loss derive from a separation from a person, not a place. A sense of inner emotional exile is created that cannot be reconciled in any way by a physical, exterior setting.

This emotional exile, this destruction of the self as an interconnected unity with an other, was repeated a decade later when Méndez's husband left her. Motifs of physical, collective exile, and emotional, private exile intertwine in *Poemas. Sombras y sueños* to form a dark weave of only occasional bright threads of self-affirmation. The dominance of shadows in this collection is openly announced in the poem appropriately entitled "Sombras" [Shadows]:

> Las sombras bajan, se esconden
> por los troncos, por la yedra,
> entre los altos ramajes;
> otras por el suelo quedan
> como fantasmas tendidos
> bien pegados a la tierra.
>
> (*Poemas*, 13)

> [The shadows fall, they hide
> in the trunks, in the ivy,
> among the branches;
> others stay on the ground
> like stretched phantoms
> well-glued to the earth.]

The poetic speaker fuses herself externally and internally with this gloomy substance, calling herself first "otra sombra" [another shadow] and then referring to her anguish as "la noche de mí misma" [the night of myself]. The monochromatic representation used up to this point to depict pain proves insufficient for an accumulation of woes differing in magnitude and intensity. They now take on all hues—white, yellow, blue, red, gray, green—including the customary black; but contrary to what might be expected, color complements, rather than contradicts, shadow. Opacity cedes to a certain extent to light, establishing an alternation between spiritual defeat and hope. At one moment, the poetic speaker feels "perdida del todo / por terrible tempestad" [completely lost / because of the terrible storm] and at another, she sees her soul moving along the sea "camino de algún lugar" [in the direction of some place]. The absolute despair of *Niño y sombra* gives way in *Sombras y sueños* to occasions of struggle. Located in the middle of the dark forces of evil and the luminous ones of good, the protagonist of this interior battle resists defeat and catches glimpses of light filtering through her dark psychic landscapes. The "fantasmas de hielo y sombra" [phantoms of ice and shadow] that pursue her do not succeed in intimidating her since she still can affirm, "al hielo que me oponen / les pongo fuego y llama" [I use fire and flame / in the face of the ice pitted against me]. Exiles of all types impose themselves upon her from the outside, but within she feels free and triumphant:

> Para que yo me sienta desterrada,
> Desterrada de mí debo sentirme,
> y fuera de mi ser y aniquilada,
> sin alma y sin amor de que servirme.
> Pero me miro adentro, estoy intacta,
> mi paisaje interior me pertenece,
> ninguna de mis fuentes echo en falta.
> Todo en mí se mantiene y reverdece.
>
> *(Poemas*, 71)

> [For me to feel exiled,
> I have to feel exiled from myself,
> and annihilated and outside my very self,
> without a soul and without love to resort to.
> But I look inside myself, I am intact,
> my interior landscape belongs to me,
> none of my inner fountains is missing.
> Everything inside me is sustained and grows again.]

Méndez's introspective turn has been interpreted by critics in contrasting fashion as both unproductive and fruitful. Ciplijauskaité sees only regression, repetition, and an "apparent anachronism" in Méndez's postwar poetry, while for Emilio Miró, *Poemas. Sombras y sueños* represents poetic maturity.[63] Whether the predominance of nostalgia in her poetry signifies a limiting of poetic horizons or the full realization of an enduring poetic impulse depends on differing expectations of critics. Nevertheless, it is evident that shadows provide Méndez an apt metaphor for the diffuse presence, the sense of darkness, and the oppressiveness created by feelings of absence, uncertainty, and emptiness. Diverting the pain caused by exterior circumstances through a retreat into the private, intangible confines of her own psyche, Méndez multiplies the dimensions of the shadows that absorb her existence and pervade her verses. Although pervasive, shadows do not obliterate her sense of self or her impulse to write. After *Poemas. Sombras y sueños*, Méndez wrote less than she wrote during her period of intense poetic production, between 1926 and 1946, but she continued to write, publishing an anthology of her work in 1976, a book combining *Vida o río* with her earlier *Vida a vida* in 1979, and *Entre el soñar y el vivir* in 1981. In her later works, self-referentiality closed her off within a detached private sphere, but it also functioned as an opportunity to exploit those inner resources that heal psychic fragmentation.

Qualitative evaluations aside, Méndez's focus on inner, private sentiments implies a shift in perspective of her poetic world from a subversive masculine discourse emphasizing spatial intrusion, physical mobility, and carefree bravado to a more traditional feminine mode of expression in which enclosure, intimate sentiments, and melancholy prevail. The specific way she lodges herself in the feminine tradition, in her poetry of exile, surfaces in the poems she dedicates to her daughter and then in those written in memory of her mother.[64] Not only does the consoling presence of her daughter temper the effects of the shadows surrounding her, it confirms for her the conditions of sameness, continuity, and identification that many feminist theorists designate as the characteristic features of the female sense of self.[65] The literal, corporal unity between Méndez and her daughter before birth anticipates the affective attachment and existential indistinguishability between both during life. Méndez describes the relationship between her daughter and herself as the simultaneity of separateness and fusion, of singularity and multiplicity that Kathryn Allen Rabuzzi calls a "binary-unity."[66] Besides evidence of the fluidity critical to female identity and its corollaries of continuity and expansion, in her poems to her daughter Méndez also reveals the emphasis on the body that Hélène Cixous insists is essential to woman's self-awareness and pleasure.[67] Méndez sees birth as a woman's active transformation of potential life into human form, and she depicts motherhood as a creative, life-sustaining process. For this portrayal she relies strongly on the image of blood as a physically shared substance and a figurative representation of union. This vision implies the confirmation of female power that inspires feelings of existential renewal, fullness, and vitality in the poetic speaker of her poems of exile. Corporal and spiritual fluidity between mother and child engenders a sense of plenitude that counteracts the disjunction and darkness of reality.

In her elegiac poems to her mother, Méndez is even more direct in her depiction of maternal blood as the origin of the child's existence.[68] Through an affirmation of physical connection, she attempts to bridge the gap that death has created between the two.[69] She also establishes connections between the daughter and her dead mother through temporal fusion and suggestions of existential indivisibility. Devastating grief over her loss drives her to seek ways to cancel what Adrienne Rich has called the "essential female tragedy," the wrenching psychic disruption that the death of a mother represents.[70] The mother-daughter bond lifts the poet to the height of joy, while a break in the bond between daughter and mother brings her to the abyss of despair. Absence still compels Méndez in her later poetry to create a poetic environment of reassuring presence. Although her goal remains the same as in her early works, in her poetry of exile Méndez seeks presence from a female perspective—through unity, attachment, and wholeness—and through "woman's writing," which stresses introspection, inner spaces, intimate feeling, and the creative implications of the female body.

Before the civil war, Méndez had been a recognized poet and a participant within the cultural circles of her day as publisher, friend, and colleague of the close-knit group of the Generation of 27. Margery Resnick, in summarizing Méndez's biography, has called her "una de las vidas más activas, excitantes y productivas de este siglo. Su curiosidad e inteligencia le dejaba gozar el contacto diario con las imaginaciones más intensas de nuestra época. Entró en círculos donde pocas mujeres participaron" [one of the most active, exciting, and productive lives in this century. Her curiosity and intelligence allowed her to enjoy daily contact with the most imaginative minds of our times. She entered circles in which few women participated].[71] Méndez's early assertive stance in both her life and her poetry won the passing notice of critics and the bewildered admiration of her fellow male poets. Her poetic persona assumed the pose of a liberated woman full of exuberance and self-confidence, who moved freely in all directions in open exterior spaces. As she awoke from this dream state of youthful carefreeness into the realm of adult experience, the poetic protagonist of Méndez's early poetry forfeited presence for absence. Multiple lessons in loss compelled her to withdraw into the shadowy zones of the inner world of emotion. Haunted by the shadows of those who had disappeared from her life and surrounded by the darkness of an existence dominated by loss, the poetic persona in the verse Méndez wrote between 1933 and 1944 became a shadow, both metaphorically and socially. Exile divorced her from her cultural milieu and supportive literary environment, and the poet herself withdrew into the hazy realm of memory. Separation from Spain and regression from the present helped guarantee the oblivion to which her works were relegated.

With *Poemas. Sombras y sueños*, Méndez lodges her poetic persona indefinitely within the realm of shadows. The spirited, self-affirming speaker of her earlier verses develops a mournful voice that can still pronounce declarations of inner strength, but now turns inward to speak most often in subdued tones. Valender finds these poems and particularly those that follow this collection to be an evasion of reality and a return to the poet's initial poetic forms and self-centeredness.[72] Méndez may return to the simplicity of form of her first poetry, but she can never recuperate her original spirit because nostalgia, repetition, and experience nullify its youthful sense of verve and adventure. She cannot retrace her steps back to her initial open climes. However, during a brief period before the civil war, when Spanish poetry tolerated minimal notes of female plenitude and joy, Concha Méndez articulated a rare voice of freedom for women.

4

Josefina de la Torre: The Unraveling of Presence

The poetry that Josefina de la Torre wrote during the twenties and thirties follows a path similar to that of Concha Méndez. Its initial patterns of presence, physical delight, and assertiveness unravel when absence, melancholy, and a consciousness of time overwhelm the poetic speaker. Like Ernestina de Champourcin, de la Torre articulated a noteworthy discourse of female desire in terms of traditional gender differences. In her poetry, de la Torre reconfirmed the complex reactions to patriarchy of many of her contemporary female poets. She subverted the notion of women's lack of creative voice, but she did not challenge the concept of woman as subordinate lover. Similarly, her relationship with her male counterparts was an ambivalent combination of marginalization and illusory moral support.

Virginia Woolf presupposed that if Shakespeare had had a "wonderfully gifted sister," the impossibility of her practicing her craft would have driven her to suicide.[1] But, as Sandra M. Gilbert and Susan Gubar affirm, "of course Shakespeare did—and does—have many sisters."[2] In Spain in the twenties, not only were Lope's sisters, to translate the metaphor, participating tangentially, at least, in avant-garde trends, one was literally the sister of an award-winning male writer of the day, Claudio de la Torre.[3] Unlike the hypothetical Judith Shakespeare, Josefina de la Torre enjoyed her brother's support in all of her literary activities. Within the small, closely knit cultural circle of her provincial city of Las Palmas de Gran Canaria, Josefina de la Torre received widespread encouragement in her artistic endeavors and by the time she was ten her precociousness as a poet was celebrated in print.[4] Despite her supportive environment and early development as a poet, de la Torre's career in poetry was brief, spanning basically only the fifteen years between 1920, when she began to publish in the leading magazines of the Generation of 27, and 1936, when she had finished most of *Marzo incompleto* [Unfinished March].[5] Honored in her times by being included as one of two women poets in Gerardo Diego's landmark 1934 anthology of poetry, Josefina de la Torre has today virtually disappeared from the annals of Spanish poetry, partly because of the traditional

84

resistance of the literary canon to affording women permanent stature as writers, but also because she shifted her career emphasis from poetry to singing and acting.[6] She abandoned poetic scripts of her own confection for the recitation of lyrics and stories crafted by others.

The trajectory of her poetic career from brilliant beginning to a quiet fading duplicates the evolution of the inflection of her poetry itself. An initial phase of vibrant material presence slowly unravels as feelings of absence and nostalgia predominate and the tone of her poetic voice grows increasingly somber. Lázaro Santana calls de la Torre's poetry ahistorical, a poetry that refers to immutable constants—grief, death, love, childhood, melancholy, time, friends, the seashore—in a language that is timeless.[7] Although it is true that certain universal themes reappear throughout her poetry and her preference for short, unrhymed lines remains constant, her three published collections are far from uniform. With similar notes, de la Torre intones three different melodies varying in tone, pitch, and focus. Emotions encroach upon her impersonal, often sun-drenched maritime scenes. Description gives way to colorless reflection as playful gaiety surrenders to melancholy. Time, although always insinuated, becomes an overt burden in her third collection.

De la Torre's declaration of enthusiasm for cars and sports in Diego's anthology, as Santana accurately discerns, seems to sketch an image of the ideal modern woman of the twenties as conceived by male avant-garde writers and embraced by some of the bolder women of the period.[8] However, the poetic persona profiled in de la Torre's poetry is less daring, affirmative, and defiant than that painted, for example, by her contemporary Concha Méndez. In her first collection, *Versos y estampas* [Verses and vignettes], de la Torre coincides with a number of her contemporaries, both male and female, by keeping the poetic voice fundamentally off stage and depersonalized. She also shares with them some of her choices of words, her use of disjointed strings of images, and the playful, amusing, and even magical tones she creates; but her lively surface does not project an underlying drive for artistic or existential freedom. When the poetic voice begins to speak more openly in *Poemas de la isla* [Island poems], the self struggles to establish her presence through words, but the assertive "I" fails to sustain itself, slipping instead into the posture of the suppliant, abandoned other. Gilbert and Gubar have explained that the lyric poem requires a strong and assertive "I" and the lyric poet herself must be "assertive, authoritative, radiant with powerful feelings while at the same time absorbed in her own consciousness—and hence, by definition, profoundly 'unwomanly,' even freakish,"[9] but in de la Torre's case the poetic "I" disappears and the lyric poet cedes to the crowd-pleasing performer.

Josefina de la Torre was not hindered by family and friends from developing her artistic talents, and therefore was seemingly exempt from the "double bind," from the inner conflict between vocation and society's view of gender roles that critics like Suzanne Juhasz identify as characteristic of the woman poet's situation.[10] But her example illustrates that despite favorable support from those closest to her, a woman can internalize sufficiently the image of woman fostered by prevailing societal values so that the poetic persona she molds in her poetry still conforms to the conventional conception of woman as passive, pretty, and pure. Although free to write, Josefina de la Torre did not write of freedom.[11] While some of her sister poets turned their backs on the sentimental feminine tradition in favor of the past and emerging masculine traditions as an inspiring avenue of escape from the artistic and psychological restrictions placed on their gender, Josefina de la Torre not only spoke of woman in more traditional terms as a neglected being, trapped between a desire for presence and the reality of absence, she also feminized her poetic discourse. The poetic speaker in her poems does not confront society but speaks instead in private, with subdued tones. Any tension that emerges in her poetry derives from interpersonal discord and existential anguish as the self seeks out the other only to find silence, as the mortal faces the inevitability of the passage of time, and as the edenic presence embodied by nature unravels with the encroachment of human emotion.

THE LANDSCAPE OF PRESENCE

Josefina de la Torre's first book of poetry is *Versos y estampas*, a short volume dedicated to her brother Claudio de la Torre and with a prologue by Pedro Salinas. The poet alternates sixteen prose sketches with an equal number of poems, places a poetic composition titled "Romance del buen guiar" [Ballad of good guidance] at the middle of the book in a section labelled "intermedio" [interval], and ends the collection with an additional poem. Except for the "Romance," all the poems are untitled; the poems are numbered with Arabic numerals and the prose vignettes with Roman ones. In *Versos y estampas* (1927), nature, in the form of water of all kinds (sea, rain, and pools), trees, sky, and wind, either constitutes pictures of sensuous or playful delight or represents peaceful moments of calming repetition. Somber allusions to death are restricted to one poem, and all reflection is restrained. As if to prevent any penetration of the quiet surfaces that prevail in the collection, one poem issues a warning against a contemplation of the depths of the water:

> . . . No te acerques
> al estanque:

tendrás el pecho hondo y frío
y tembloroso del agua.

[. . . Don't go near
the pond:
your chest will be deep and cold
and trembling from the water.][12]

and self-reflection is confined to a self-mocking parenthetical remark:

Yo, que contemplo la noche,
también lloro, infinitas, mis lágrimas.
(Pero al dejar la noche he sonreído:
"es la lluvia", le he dicho a mi alma).

(49)

[I, who contemplate the night,
also cry countless tears.
(But after the night, I smiled:
"it's the rain," I told my soul).]

Without the intrusive appearance of the human voice, nature exists resplendent in edenic and timeless unity. The realm of bliss depicted by de la Torre is devoid of turmoil and temporal perspective, but the appearance of the human subject initiates the possibility for a clash with the unresponsive and deceitful other. Nature's arrested presence in de la Torre's poetry succumbs to the irresolvable discrepancy between desire and loss.

Versos y estampas unveils a world primarily of unity and timelessness. These qualities are found in the realm of nature where human presence is usually secondary or only suggested. In the second poem of the collection, the entrance of the sea into the house creates a meeting of organic and inanimate essences intensified by a commingling of the senses of hearing, smell, sight, and touch. The human domain of the room has no inhabitant to perceive the sensorial stimuli of the sea:

El murmullo de la playa
entra a oscuras
por la ventana cerrada,
entre las maderas
verdes, apretadas.
Y se llena la estancia
de olor de arena húmeda,
de mar y de luna blanca.

(33)

[The murmur of the shore
enters during darkness
through the closed window,
between the tight,
green planks.
And the room is filled
with the smell of wet sand,
sea, and white moon.]

In the fourth poem, the sun and then a cloud come in contact with both the sea and the human faces hidden under sunshades:

El sol en la playa tiene
juegos de niño pequeño
con el mar y las sombrillas.
. . . .
Y una nube que pasa, blanca,
para dar sombra a la playa
dormida
y apagar el azul y el rojo
de las caras
bajo la cretona de la sombrilla.

(36–37)

[The sun on the beach
plays little children's games
with the sea and the parasols.
. . . .
A white cloud that passes,
to shade the sleeping
shore
and to dim the blue and red
of the faces
beneath the cretonne of the parasol.]

The unity between the natural and the human is achieved more subtly in another poem:

El hilo de agua, rizado,
sube y se abre en lo alto;
luego se pierde en el agua
tembloroso y blanco.
El pecho se alza. Un suspiro
todo luz se va en el aire.
Vivo, el ciprés se ilumina
entre los rosales blancos.

(51)

[A curled thread of water,
rises and opens on high;
and then is lost in the water,
tremulous and white.
The breast rises. A sigh
full of light disappears into the air.
Alive, a cypress is illuminated
among the white rose bushes.]

The rise and fall of the waterspout is repeated in the movement of the human breast. Besides a synesthetic confusion of two senses, the sigh of light endows the living being with a property peculiar to nature. At the end of the short poem, the cypress unifies both the natural and human orders by embodying the light that emanates from both. Like the human breathing at the center of the poem, the cypress is alive and like the water, it is associated with white. In this poem the union of the human and the natural world occurs on an abstract level of generalized perfection and pristine verbal expression. The poetic voice expresses her desire to unite with nature in a more direct fashion in the following poem:

Agua clara del estanque.
Era un espejo del chopo
y alfombra verde del cielo
con reflejos de los árboles.
¡Oh, si yo hubiera podido
entrar con los pies descalzos
y ser el viento en el agua
y hacer agitar el chopo!

(40)

[Clear water of the pond.
It was a mirror for the black poplar
and a green carpet for the sky
with reflections of the trees.
Oh, would that I could have
gone barefoot
and been wind on the water
and made the poplar stir!]

Water and tree reflect one another, with the first becoming the mirror of the second, and the latter lending its color to the former. In this poem the human entry into nature remains only on the level of the unfulfilled wish of the poetic voice.

The influence of Juan Ramón Jiménez may have played a part in Josefina de la Torre's formulation of harmony with nature; but his early poetry has a melancholy, almost maudlin quality absent in de la Torre, and when he opens up his claustrophobic garden for more expansive spaces, he sees sunny Andalusian fields or a grandiose sea whose power he assumes. De la Torre's relationship is less presumptuous and more intimate. A more likely reason for her rapport with her natural environment is her island origin. Santana finds in her discreet use of metaphor and her linguistic simplicity a greater kinship to the poetry of her Canary compatriots than to that of the mainland poets usually cited as her models.[13] It must be remembered that the Canary Islands in the twenties and early thirties were the site of significant cultural activity that culminated in the work of Eduardo Westerdahl and his surrealist magazine, *Gaceta del Arte*.[14] This fertile cultural environment provided de la Torre a favorable context for the writing of poetry; and daily exposure to the lush nature, especially the sea, around her gave her concrete raw materials for forming a vision of unity within nature.[15]

Time does not mar this landscape of united essences. De la Torre constructed the poems of *Versos y estampas* on the basis primarily of the present tense and tenses that support a sense of present: the present perfect, the future, and the past subjunctive used for polite assertions ("Yo no quisiera tener / el corazón tan incierto" [I would not like to have / such a doubting heart]). In much the same way, she relegated self-reflection in her eighth poem to enclosure within parentheses; and she conspicuously separated the past from the present by assigning the evocation of her personal past to the prose vignettes, "estampas," alternated with her poems, "versos." The prose vignettes evoke childhood memories—scenes, games, playmates, and local social outcasts—that resurrect the joy and the melancholy of the past. The division of temporal perspective as well as the separation of narration from description and the personal from the objective makes the poetry undergo a purification process.[16] Because they seem to be implicitly inspired by the paragraphs that precede them, the poems, in the first part of the collection at least, stand by virtue of their temporal contrast as a blissful escape from the nostalgia that permeates the prose. For example, her second prose sketch recalls the day she looked out the window at the big, black dog that terrorized her and her playmates. The image of the window forms a link with the poem that follows and its allusion to window. By focusing on an object, the poet located her poem in the sensorial world, the world of immediate experience away from the subject, the subjective, and the sentimental. Thus, through detachment and concentration, the poet created a temporary illusion of timeless presence within her poetic world.

ACTUALIZATION OF THE WORD

In de la Torre's second collection, *Poemas de la isla*, the Canary Islands still provide the sunny scenery for her descriptions. Nature continues to provide sensuous richness and a joyful atmosphere. Water and light, in particular, offer qualities to delight the five senses. The rain singing the happy song of a betrothed offers a resplendent gift of light and moisture: "Regalo de la mañana / sobre mi frente prendida / en un acorde brillante / y húmedo, de medio día" (89) [Morning's gift / fastened on my forehead / in a bright and moist chord, / of noon]. The merry music of the rain is replicated in the musicality generated by the rhythms and structures of the verses themselves. With their free verse of short lines and interspersed assonant rhyme, these poems generate a lilting cadence that is accentuated by the use of repetitions, structural pairings, and series of three elements:

> Remolinos del aire,
> del viento,
> del momento.
> va y viene,
> viene y va.
> Alrededor de mi frente,
> delante de mis ojos,
> por mis oídos.
> . . . .
> Y viene, y va.
>
> (81)

> [Whirls of air,
> of wind,
> of the moment.
> it comes and goes,
> it goes and comes.
> Around my brow,
> in front of my eyes,
> through my ears.
> . . . .
> And it comes, and it goes.]

In another poem rain, light, and the sea intermingle, forming a synesthetic mosaic of sensations:

> ¡Rómpete por el aire,
> rueda de cristal!
> Que me lluevan en los ojos

> luces y luces,
> arco iris
> de sal.
> Hielo del sol,
> azúcar de la mar,
> hilito de la tarde
> para bordar.
>
> (79–80)

> [Break, in the air,
> glass wheel!
> May many lights
> and a salty
> rainbow
> rain down on my eyes.
> The ice of the sun,
> the sugar of the sea,
> the little thread of afternoon
> for embroidering.]

Water turns into a round piece of glass, the rain becomes light, and light assumes the salty flavor of the sea while the sea acquires an unexpected sweetness and the sun, under the force of an oxymoronic combination, is associated with ice. This poem also illustrates de la Torre's frequent perception of round and circular forms in nature. In the following poem, the sea is reified by roundness and then, through metaphor, transformed into a white ring and the "curva salada" of a bride's waist:

> Mar redondo, desvelado,
> sortija blanca,
> novio enamorado.
> Desde el balcón,
> por la orilla, rizando
> va mi canción.
> Mar de siete colores,
> curva salada,
> cinturón de novia enamorada.
>
> (78–79)

> [The round, sleepless sea,
> a white ring,
> a boyfriend in love.
> From the balcony,
> along the shore,
> my song curls.
> Sea of seven colors,

salty curve,
a sash for the girlfriend in love.]

This tendency to convert the detached splendors of nature into concrete, palpable substances becomes more pronounced in the poem that
begins "Quisiera tener sujeta / la naranja de la tarde / así entre las manos,
fresca" [I would like to hold / the fresh orange of the afternoon, / like this
in my hands]. Here the intangible light of the afternoon solidifies into a
round, fresh, and succulent orange that imparts its flavor to the sea, the
sand, and the air, and which the night will gobble up at the golden boundaries between light and darkness from its "ventanal de cobre" [copper win-
dow]. The roundness, circles, and cycles of nature suggest a sense of continuance, serenity, and perfection; nature survives and continues:

> Hoy, mañana, y siempre más.
> Arenas, vientos y mares,
> cuerdas, brisas y resoles.
> Cintura, curva consciente,
> brazos y perfil. Compás
> de la mirada, dos, tres,
> parpadeo desigual.
> . . . .
> Y más. Por la mañanita
> niño pequeño, dormido.
> A la tarde niño malo.
> A la noche despertar.
> Hoy, mañana, y siempre libres
> caminitos de la mar.
>
> (93)

> [Today, tomorrow, and always.
> Sands, winds, and seas,
> ropes, breezes, and reflected sunlight.
> Waist, conscious curve,
> arms, and profile. The rhythm
> of the gaze, two, three,
> unequal blinking.
> . . . .
> And more. In the early morning
> a small child asleep.
> In the afternoon a bad little boy.
> At night awake.
> Today, tomorrow, and always, free
> the little pathways of the sea.]

The sea, the sand, the wind, and the sun last forever—today, tomorrow, and "siempre más." Without modifying adjectives, the elements of nature stand as abstract entities free from the changes in man's existence, implied here by the child's different circumstances over the course of the day. The alliteration in the third and fourth lines seems to coordinate the human and natural spheres in a similar state of repetition; but the word "consciente" hints at a cognitive value that nature does not share and the "parpadeo desigual" marks a discrepancy in the cycles of the two realms.

While the minimization of the human voice in *Versos y estampas* helps create a natural paradise, a world perceived by the five senses, but unencumbered by human sentiment, in *Poemas de la isla* with the appearance of human subjects, chords of disquiet begin to resonate. In Josefina de la Torre's second collection, nature shares the poet's attention with a consideration of ideas and human feelings. The human voice echoes throughout the book with varying emotional tones, and the word itself gains prominence. Specifically what concerns the poet is language and love and the potential for communication possible in the interrelation between the two. The capacity of language to create presence and the failure of love to sustain it bring about a delicate balance, if not an implicit tension, between potentiality and plenitude, psychological dependence and self-identity, and absence and presence.

Because the relation of women to language, particularly written language, has been problematic, de la Torre's appropriation of the word and her confrontation with the other through written language makes these poems noteworthy. The word is power. The power of the word derives from its dynamic nature, from its identity with positive movement and masterful creation. God is the Word, and humanity but the subsequent and dependent articulation of that Word. The projection of this hierarchical relationship between God and man upon all social, cultural, and personal arrangements within the patriarchal system casts women into the role of the silent and immobile object of male creation. This age-old theological base for the subordination of women was perpetuated in Western philosophy up to modern times in the ideas of Hegel on the master-slave relationship and the existential concepts of the relation between the subject and the other in the works of Heidegger and Sartre. It was precisely as a response to the inequality inherent in this opposition between the transcendent, observing, male subject and the fixed, observed, female object that Simone de Beauvoir in *The Second Sex* (1949) began the modern-day feminist discussion on the status of women in society. The reduction of woman to other had negative effects on a variety of aspects of women's lives. For example, women were systematically excluded from public discourse, and, as Adrienne Rich affirms, even succumbed to lying when they did speak.[17] Literary production, the most artistic form of public discourse, represented a forbidden territory for women which, if entered, aroused the censure of a public that equated female writing with sexual immorality and provoked inner anxiety in the female trespasser herself.[18] Women's writing, as Mary Jacobus puts it, becomes the site of "challenge and otherness."[19] When beginning to speak, one initiates a process that leads to dominion. As Monique Wittig explains: "when starting to speak, one becomes "I." This act—the becoming of *the* subject through the exercise of language and through locution—implies that the locutor be an absolute subject."[20]

While de la Torre dares to speak, her challenge rests on the symbolic value of her gesture more than the content of her words. What she says is neither radical nor harsh; she does not explore the implications of gender difference to raise a protest against social norms. Her focus remains fixed on personal sentiment, on the emotional distress produced on the poetic speaker. While she breaks the traditional female pose of silent, inactive object, she does not often collapse the patriarchal assignment of roles of action to the male and of reaction to the female. Yet by expressing her desire for communication and her frustration over her failure to be heard, she highlights the question of female silence and indirectly contradicts its inevitability.

De la Torre is capable of making a forceful declaration of her desire to speak. In the third poem of *Poemas de la isla,* assertive statements divide the composition structurally into four quatrains and a concluding pronounce-ment of self-assertion. She writes "Déjame que te lo diga" [let me tell you] and "Te lo voy a decir todo" [I am going to tell you everything] twice and ends with "Mi palabra nada más." She dares to speak up despite the conse-quences: "aunque después se desprenda / aquel amor presumido / y se me duerma en los ojos" (70) [even though that vain love / may later work loose / and lodge itself in my eyes]. Shedding all its veils of distracting beauty, her bare word stands boldly audible at the close of the poem. This distilla-tion of the word, achieved through repeated negations, is intensified fur-ther by the use of anaphora:

> Ni las olas, ni los barcos,
> ni la estrellita perdida,
> ni el aire que riza el viento.
> Mi palabra nada más.
>
>   (70)

> [Neither waves, nor boats,
> nor the lost star,
> nor the air that the wind curls.
> Only my word.]

More often, however, she speaks of her inaudibility. It is not that she cannot speak, but that she is not heard. Much like the invisibility that Alicia Suskin Ostrisker finds to be part of a set of universal images in women's poetry, her inaudibility registers her condition of marginality and incomplete existence. As Ostriker says, in women's poems of both invisibility and muteness, there is usually a sexual script. To love a man presupposes a dependency that calls for silence.[21] Also, when she does speak, the sexual politics underpinning patriarchy denies the female word authenticity and authority. Her words fall on deaf ears. The disillusioned poetic persona in de la Torre's poetry laments her frustration through the repeated use of negatives that erase her word and an absence of figurative language that underscores its loss of power:

> Tú, inmóvil, escuchándome
> sin escuchar.
> ¡Qué desilusión mía
> en mi afán,
> sin palabras
> ni gesto
> ni réplica
> que alzar!
>
> (84)

> [You, motionless, listening to me
> without listening.
> What a disappointment
> in my zeal,
> without words
> or gesture
> or reply
> to raise!]

De la Torre defines the love relationship as an exchange not only of words but of silences; to love is to lose the self in the other, and the self incarnate in the word is retrievable only when that other remains silent: "Cuando tu presencia—forma— / dejó vacío el momento, / encontré aquella palabra / entre los labios, dormida" (78) [When your presence—form— / left the moment empty / I found that word / between my lips, asleep]. She is quick to strike the conventional pose of the dependent, female supplicant: "Dime tu palabra intacta / de luz repetida y libre. / Pero no me dejes sola" (84) [Give me your whole word / full of light and free. / But don't leave me alone]. She fears the silence and absence that the other controls. De la Torre's poetry shows that breaking the code of silence by speaking through the written word does not eliminate the problem of silence from women's writing. In addition to the external social silence that has inhibited women from speaking, there is within their discourse an internal textual silence that manifests itself in the configurations of their writings.[22] When de la Torre attempts to express her desire for love and assert her audible presence, the indifference of the other presses her into a silence she logically records in her verses.

In de la Torre's poetry power does not lie within the person, but in the word. The word clearly emerges as the generator of presence. That presence need not entail the physical appearance of a person, for the metonymic representation of the other through a name alone suffices in the poem "Tu nombre ya me lo han dicho" [They have already told me your name]. For de la Torre the presence that the word of the other creates transcends all earthly qualities of time, movement, and progression:

> No es presencia ni vaivén
> ni caminito seguro
> ni ruedecitas del aire
> ni luz, ni sol, ni mañana.
> Es un presente, constante,
> aquí, cerca, más, despierto,
> vivo, alerta, repetido,
> único instinto posible.
>
> (84)

> [It is not presence or oscillation
> nor a sure little path
> nor little air wheels
> nor light, nor sun, nor morning.
> It is a constant presence,
> here, near, more, awake,
> alive, alert, repeated,
> the only possible instinct.]

More than a presence, the word creates a consolidated, integral, and present moment of existence. Once again the poet resorts to negation and anaphora to peel away worldly impurities. Then after attempting to describe the present through the accumulation of adjectives and adverbs connoting presence, she reaches her conclusion: that the word is the essence of existence, the "único instinto posible" [only possible instinct].

The word in de la Torre's poetry is to a great extent an abstraction and a vehicle for fixing ephemeral human existence in a brief but splendid moment of plenitude, in a "Seguro instante de sorpresas," as she writes:

> Cerca. Palabra inútil.
> Yo te busco

por donde llega mi distancia.
Cerca.
Seguro instante de sorpresas.
Dormido vuelo alzado
de mí, por mí.
Cerca.
Donde mi corazón te sienta:
pulso del mar,
tictac de la ausencia,
caminito seguro,
vaivén.
Cerca.
Donde la indecisión no deje
huella.
Donde palabra,
vuelta,
marque un signo seguro.
Cerca.

(85)

[Near. Useless word.
I seek you
where my distance reaches.
Near.
Secure instant of surprises.
A sleeping flight taken
from me, by me.
Near.
Where my heart feels you:
sea pulse,
ticktock of absence,
safe little path,
oscillation.
Near.
Where indecision doesn't leave
a trace.
Where the word,
returned,
records a sure sign.
Near.]

In a paradoxical conjunction of distance and nearness, absence and presence, indecision and certainty, she gives substance, constancy, and visibility to the abstract, the fleeting, and the impalpable. Much like Pedro Salinas and his pursuit of the "seguro azar" [sure chance], she tries to turn the intangible into something more concrete, in her case into "un signo seguro" [a sure sign], a solid representation of nearness as an abstraction, not a spatial phenomenon. The gap between the two elliptic statements in the first line can be seen as designating a relation of equivalency and therefore suggesting the incapacity of the word to create nearness, but the rest of the poem subverts this initial impression. The inclusion of four adverbial clauses beginning with "donde" [where] endows "cerca" [near] with a certain contiguity and implies its future realization. The placement of the word "cerca" alone as a line in itself four times anchors that pending materialization in a firm structural presence that contradicts the phrase "Palabra inútil." In a similar fashion, the poet joins the word "seguro" three times with a word of antithetical connotation to neutralize the implications of instability, be they the temporal "instante," the spatial "caminito," or the linguistic "signo."

A consistent ambivalence in her poetry toward her own identity accounts for her fluctuation in her posture as subject; sometimes she describes herself as the creator of presence and other times as the object of the other's discourse. In one poem, the word is a generous gift, a projection of the other upon her, with a subtle suggestion of penetration, gratification, withdrawal, and memory that makes the word a sublimated metaphor for the sexual act. Although she initiates the encounter and the "I" stands conspicuously at the beginning of the poem, the female persona is cast in the role of recipient of male speech:

> Yo te busqué la palabra
> con una mirada sola
> y tú me la diste intacta
> por el círculo de luz.
> Se quedó en el aire inmóvil
> el hueco azul de tu voz
> y dentro de mí, cantando
> la antena por los oídos.
>
> . . . .
> Y me quedó entre las sienes
> presencia limpia y segura
> de oculta palabra cierta.
>
>   (73–74)

> [I sought the word from you
> with a single gaze
> and you gave it to me whole
> through the circle of light.
> The blue hollow of your voice
> stayed in the motionless air
> and, within me, with its aerial
> singing in my ears.

. . . .
It stayed in my temples
as a secure and clean presence
of a hidden and sure word.]

The word, the powerful force in this interchange, creates a connection between the two partners and remains afterwards an autonomous and lasting
presence. In contrast, in the next poem in the collection, the woman assumes the posture of speaker and the other that of self-absorbed observer:
"Tú te quedaste absorto / contemplándola" (74) [You were absorbed /
contemplating it]. However, as with the former poem, the word remains an
autonomous entity: "segura," "clara," and "libre" [sure, clear, free].

The human players in her poetic drama may not be able to synchronize
their desires, and love may appear most often in *Poemas de la isla* as a distant,
past, or imperfect experience; but the word as an abstraction detached from
human verbalization is secure, constant, and free. The poet may call certain words useless, but their potential for rendering the abstract concrete
gives them considerable power. As the generator of presence, the word is
the prelude to existence and when placed within the hands of the female
poet, the word makes possible a godlike gesture of transubstantiation. *Poemas
de la isla* celebrates the presence created by nature, love, and the word, but
because the open and free access to the word has traditionally been pre-
cluded for women, de la Torre's consideration of the potential of the word
and of speaking becomes significant within the history of the self-realization of Spanish women writers. Josefina de la Torre belongs to a middle
ground of ambivalence and hesitation between the frustrated exploration
of the feminine self that Susan Kirkpatrick exposes among nineteenth-
century Spanish women writers and the more successful articulation of
protest and of a strictly female perspective that Sharon Keefe Ugalde studies among contemporary women poets of Spain.[23] In de la Torre's poetry,
when enclosed within personal experience, the word, although a presence
in itself, usually fails to produce sustained communication. Only as an abstraction, as an end unto itself, does the word create a state of arrested
presence. In the same way, desire signifies harmony only as a concept not
an experience, as an internalized abstraction not an external phenomenon:

Qué repetido deseo,
todo igual y siempre el mismo,
distinto y otro, inconsciente,
confundido y tan preciso,
se me va quedando dentro
escondido y dueño solo,
perdido y presente siempre.

(76)

[What a repeated desire,
everything the same and always the same,
distinct and something else, unconscious,
confused and yet so precise,
it stays within me more and more
hidden and self-possessed,
lost and always present.]

THE VOICE OF ABSENCE

The successful exclusion of most of the effects of the passage of time from her first collection breaks down in *Poemas de la isla*. Just as the presence of human interaction introduces an element of tension among the descriptions of the sunny landscapes of the Canary Islands, so it also brings a temporal dimension of change and loss. The clock, which in *Versos y estampas* is a metaphor for life, for the beating of the heart, becomes a symbol of time in *Poemas de la isla*. The clock is a surprising and complex configuration of union and discord, of repetition and immobility that triggers spontaneous moments of joy:

> cuando te vea múltiple
> complicado y distinto,
> con cada gesto único
> desordenado y rítmico,
> ¡qué sensaciones nuevas
> de sorpresas y olvidos
> surgirán en el recto
> espacio del instinto!
>
> (72)

> [when I see you multiple
> complicated and distinct,
> with each unique gesture
> irregular and rhythmical,
> What new sensations
> of surprise and oblivion
> will emerge in the linear space of instinct!]

But only as this self-contained abstraction, as a "seguro círculo," embodied in the concrete object of the clock can time represent harmony. As a living succession of human events, time signifies negation and loss. Recuperation of the past is only temporary ("Como el viento, tu recuerdo / viene y va sobre mi frente," 75 [Like the wind, your memory / comes and goes over my brow]), and memory at times is best rejected because it brings solitude, not consolation ("No quiero mirar la orilla, / no quiero mirar el mar, / que me voy quedando sola / con las dos manos vacías," 72 [I do not want to look at the shore, / I do not want to look at the sea, / for I am left more and more alone / with my two hands empty]). Space intensifies the negative effects of time by giving shape to vacuousness. The window, which in *Versos y estampas* constitutes the metaphorical entryway for the sea into the human realm, casts a dark shadow on the outside world in *Poemas de la isla* and opens up a scene of lost moments lingering only in their trail of negation:

> Altas ventanas abiertas
> dejaron sombras de luces
> disparadas en la arena.
> . . . .
> Una vez cerca. El espacio
> vacío, libre, perdido
> a lo largo de los brazos.
> Y qué lejos el momento,
> cuatro paredes baratas
> imágenes del espejo.
> Ni tú ni yo. Las ventanas
> altas, abiertas, desnudas,
> suicidas de madrugada.
>
> (71)

> [Tall open windows
> left shadows of light
> hurled on the sand.
> . . . .
> Once near. The empty,
> free space lost
> along my arms.
> And the moment is so far away,
> four cheap walls
> mirrored images.
> Neither you nor I. The tall,
> open, bare windows,
> suicides at dawn.]

Notes of disquiet occasionally filter through the predominantly affirmative atmosphere of *Poemas de la isla*, but in de la Torre's third collection, *Marzo incompleto*, absence and loss predominate. A sober book combining a retrospective wistfulness for the past with a stoic recognition of the present, *Marzo incompleto* forfeits the poet's former contemplation of the external, natural world and a conceptualization of language for a reflection on private experiences with love, time, and death. The poet nostalgically looks back at an earlier incomplete spring, while recognizing the completion of life. The incompletion announced in the book's title is defined in its first poem as the potential for youth, growth, and joy. In that lost March, existence was an endless, "incomplete" presence centered within a timeless circle: "No tenía principio / ni fin. Era mitad, / centro predestinado, / eje de un solo sueño" (101) [It didn't have a beginning / or an end. It was half / a preordained center, / the axis of a single dream]. The poet at that time possessed her own "voices," but now temporal progression and silence surround her, obliging her to reflect in the rest of the book upon her alienation, unfulfilled love, childlessness, temporality, and death. As Joy Buckles Landeira writes, "technically naked" these "seemingly cathartic verses undress the emotions, baring suffering, alienation, sadness, and desolation."[24]

As March has given way to the April and May of life, the poetic speaker has fallen into time; she has stepped onto the moving walkway of life leaving behind people, places, and dreams of the past. Through her verses she temporarily evokes them—her school days, a lover long gone, and the son she never had. The absences of the past, be they what once was or what never could be, are given shape by her words, but she realizes that living in time brings forgetting and forgetting carries memories away. Time and wind, as a symbol of the passage of time, impose their power upon human reality:

> ¡Ah, si todo eso fuera . . .
> yo no me olvidaría
> de una vez que en los ojos,
> de otra vez que en el pelo,
> de otra que en la garganta . . . !
> ¡Pero el viento y el tiempo . . . !
>
> (106)

> [Oh, if all of that were . . .
> I would not forget
> once and for all that in the eyes,
> once and for all that in the hair,
> and again that in the throat . . . !
> But the wind and time . . . !]

The futility of memory is even more pronounced in the following poem, where images evoked from the past are deemed distant, inert, and dead:

> Soñar contigo
> es como soñar con los muertos.
> . . . .

Así tú, imagen resucitada
del tiempo vivo del recuerdo,
lejana, en un mundo invisible
a través de un mar de silencio . . .

(112)

[To dream of you
is like dreaming of the dead.
. . . .
That's the way you are, a resurrected
image of the living time of memory,
distant, in an invisible world
across a sea of silence.]

The absence alluded to in these poems constitutes an emotional loss of
material or potentially material experience, but another type of absence
preoccupies the poet also, an ontological absence that involves the loss of
the self and the meaning of existence. This kind of absence is metaphorically embodied in the empty room. In the third poem of the collection, the
poetic voice finds herself forgotten, alone, and enclosed within four walls:

Me olvidan sola, en la ausencia
y me cierran las paredes
a oscuras, con cuatro puertas.
Nadie me ve ni me oye.
Nadie sabe de mis voces.
Ni de mi cuello inclinado,
ni de mis brazos ceñidos,
ni de estos mis pies descalzos.

(104)

[I have been left behind, alone, in absence
and the walls have been closed on me
with four doors, in the dark.
No one knows about my voices.
Nor about my inclined neck,
nor about my crossed arms,
nor about these bare feet.]

Insistent negations intensify her alienation from others and her enclosure
within anxiety. In a later poem the distinction between the self and her
environment is collapsed as the poetic persona becomes the room itself:

Me busco y no me encuentro.
Rondo por las oscuras paredes de mí misma,
interrogo al silencio y a este torpe vacío

y no acierto en el eco de mis incertidumbres.
. . . .
Y no pude ser tierra, ni esencia, ni armonía,
que son fruto, sonido, creación, universo.

(121)

[I look for myself and don't find myself.
I patrol the dark walls of my inner self,
I question silence and this awkward emptiness
and I do not get answers from the echo of my uncertainties.
. . . .
I could not be earth, nor essence, nor harmony,
for they are fruit, sound, creation, universe.]

She has lost her sense of substance ("tierra"), essence ("esencia") and spirituality ("armonía") and with them self-realization, dynamic existence, and transcendence.

It has been common among feminist critics to see in images of enclosure, like that of the room, significant implications for female subjectivity.[25] Physically restrained by patriarchal social conventions, linguistically marked by gender as difference, and conceived by philosophy as static and subordinate, women have been seen by others and by themselves as circumscribed, limited, and enclosed. From this vantage point, women writers have tended not only to favor domestic imagery but to use that imagery, as Gilbert and Gubar argue, to reflect the literal reality of their personal experience more than elaborating metaphorical and metaphysical visions that presume to embrace the universal, human condition.[26] In keeping with this tradition, de la Torre speaks of no one other than herself and extrapolates no collective lessons from her own personal experience. However, at the same time she purges her verses of any specific, literal references, and in doing so, the doubts and insecurities she expresses in her poems, while at bottom perhaps projecting woman's traditional exclusion from self-definition, on the surface reveal generic vulnerability in the face of human destiny.

As a lyric poet, de la Torre concentrates on emotional consequences rather than on reasons and rationales. Doubt invades her, leaving her unable to understand herself ("Y hoy no sé qué me pasa . . . " 105 [And today I do not know what is happening to me]), the other ("No saber si por tus ojos / una verdad se me ofrece," 106 [Not knowing if your eyes / offer me a truth]), or existence ("No sé por qué voy y vengo / de la sombra a la pared," 104 [I do not know why I come and go / from the shadow on the wall]). An undefined, unspecified uncertainty manifests itself not only in these overt declarations of ignorance but through the frequent use of the subjunctive mood. In *Marzo incompleto* de la Torre speaks of dreams not reality, of wishing not possession, and of possibilities not actuality. She would

like to be in another time span ("Quisiera que en lugar / de este Abril y este
mayo . . . fuera . . . aquel Marzo incompleto," 101 [I would like that in
place / of this April and this May . . . it were . . . that unfinished March])
or be of another temperament ("Si yo pudiera, amor, / engañarme a mí
misma," 107 [If I could, love, / deceive myself]). The subjunctive can also
reveal, through uncorroborated conjecture, a regret over the verifiable reality of her childlessness: "Hoy nuestros hijos ya serían hombres . . . Jamás
el mar hubiérase apartado / de mi contemplación, hija de la isla" (113)
[Today our children would be men . . . the sea would never have separated
me, / daughter of the island / from my reflections]. These notes of doubt
and speculation give way in the final poems of the collection to the certainty and the glad anticipation of death, as her attention shifts from worldly
to religious themes.

Between the strains of nostalgia of the first poem and of anxiety of the
last ones of the collection, there emerges a third kind of absence, a psychological absence associated with love and arising from the gap within the self
when the other is beyond reach. María Zambrano, a philosopher contemporary to de la Torre, explains that absence is inherent in love because love
signifies the persistent search for the discrete and elusive other.[27] In her
characteristic ambivalence between tenuous, but positive, self-assertion and
passive dependence, de la Torre sees intangible love as both a source and
antidote to pain. Before concluding that the search for the other has been a
vain venture that has left her blind and lost ("ciega, perdida, / con esta vida
inútil en tu busca," 123 [blind, lost, / with useless life in search of you]), she
describes the unidentified "you" of her poetry as a source of light and
inner presence accessible only within a sightless dream state:

> No quise abrir los ojos
> porque encerraba dentro de mí la luz.
> Estabas allí, sobre mi sueño,
> limpia aún tu presencia.
>
>   (111)

> [I did not want to open my eyes
> because light was locked inside me.
> You were there, in my dream,
> your presence still pure.]

When configured as a human body, the other brings ephemeral tokens of
hope:

> Todo tú
> venías en mi busca
> y no pude reconocerte.

¡Arena blanca, compás de espera, espuma blanca!
¡Inquieto sueño de la verde orilla,
rizado de preguntas . . . !

(109)

[All of you
came in search of me
and I could not recognize you.
White sand, the rhythm of waiting, white foam!
Restless dream of the green shore,
rippled with questions . . . !]

Her sense of self depends on the presence of the absent other, who can conceivably in a different space, other circumstances, and a future time become the means of her recuperation of self:

frente a frente,
yo buscaré detrás de tu mirada
la imagen de mi imagen,
y todo
lo que ahora he perdido
lo volveré a encontrar.

(110)

[face to face,
I will look behind your gaze
the image of my image,
and everything
that I have now lost
I will find again.]

Her posture is more active in the poem beginning "Encontrarte / por las abiertas mariposas de la noche" [Finding you / in the open night butterflies]. Four verbs—"encontrarte" [to find you], "descubrirte" [to discover you], "sorprenderte" [to surprise you], and "hacer de ti la luz" [make light from you]—cast the female subject in the role of the pursuer, the beholder, and the one with the power to transform the beloved. This energetic stance is easily compromised, however. The following poem again begins with a verb, a verb of action coupled with the substantive "alas", predicting free movement and subsequent accomplishment, but the image of the kneeling figure embedded within the poem and the concluding one of the "pies esclavos" channel the initial movement toward subordination:

Llegar sobre las alas de mis pies
hasta tu ausencia.

Quedarme así, sobre tu imagen,
y apoyar la rodilla
en el borde de tu abandono.
Quisiera,
en la paz de ese absurdo que inventamos
para que todos lo dudaran
y tan sólo tú y yo
en él creyéramos,
alzar la vida sobre el mundo.
¡Si yo pudiera llegar así
y sorprenderte,
sobre las alas de mis pies esclavos!

(110–11)

[Arriving at your absence
on the wings of my feet.
Staying like that, on your image,
and resting my knee
on the edge of your abandonment.
I would like,
in the peace of this absurdity
that we invent
so that everyone can doubt it
and only you and I
can believe in it,
to lift up life over the world.
If I would arrive like that
and surprise you
on the wings of my slave feet!]

Speaking of Marina Romero, a contemporary of de la Torre, Noël Valis reaches a conclusion that aptly summarizes the ambivalence reflected in the poetry of Josefina de la Torre: "Slave and owner are one in much of women's writing: the inner luxury of self that women possess is, in turn, possessed by someone else, the trace of otherness informing memory and word."[28] Practicing a "diction of reticence,"[29] like many other women poets, de la Torre expresses self-assertion through a delicate interplay of dependency and vigor. Her poetic "I" may show reverence and subordination to the unnamed "you," but at the same time she senses a power within her to bridge the gap of absence and envisions, for both of them, a personal victory over the incredulous world.

FEMINIZATION OF THE POETIC IMAGE

Ambivalence surfaces not only in de la Torre's posture before the other but also in the bi-directionality of her relationship with the emerging vanguard canon. In her first two collections, Josefina de la Torre incorporates features of the Spanish poetry tradition, especially of the "romances," but her name has most regularly been linked with masculine poets of her own time, in particular with Pedro Salinas, who wrote the prologue to *Versos y estampas*. This connection was firmly fixed in an early history of the Generation of 27 by Angel Valbuena Prat, who in 1930 described her as "fina, depurada, al estilo de Pedro Salinas" [refined, pure, in the style of Pedro Salinas].[30] While it is true that her poetry shares with his an inclusion of an unidentified "you," an interplay between absence and presence, and a certain tendency to focus on the intangible, her poetic speaker does not aspire to use the other as a platonic instrument for transcendence nor does she flee to her inner self to enjoy a refuge of precision, perfection, and plenitude. Unlike Salinas, she neither possesses the beloved nor displays his self-assurance. Similarly her poetic persona lacks the self-absorption of Juan Ramón Jiménez despite the apparent coincidences between their poetry: the frequent use of light, conspicuous appeals to the other senses, and a preference for subtle musicality—assonance, alliteration, and short verse. Another name that comes to mind for some in the reading of de la Torre's poetry is Federico García Lorca, whose impact one writer discerns in her motifs of the moon, pools of water, and galloping horse.[31] However, apparent similarities mask essential differences in this case. Although sharing Lorca's appreciation for the fertile Spanish folk tradition of lullabies and children's songs, her poetic world does not manifest the destructive physical passion, the sense of impending doom, and the harsh imagery that distinguish his. The tendency of literary historians and critics to equate women poets like Josefina de la Torre exclusively with their male counterparts reflects an attempt not only to validate their poetic talents but to confer upon them a literary existence within a concrete temporal framework. The women poets of the twenties and thirties themselves abetted their inscription within the masculine canon by their whole-hearted adoption of the poetic modes embraced by their vanguard brethren.

De la Torre coincided with her female contemporaries in utilizing some of the themes and motifs—sports, cars, and movies—that captivated the masculine poets of the day, but she did not show for them the enthusiasm of Concha Méndez, the mastery of Ernestina de Champourcin, or the virtuosity of Rosa Chacel. Nonetheless, in her first two collections, she tended to construct poems in the manner of the *ultraístas* as disjointed, brief series of novel visual images. She also demonstrated their fondness for abstract shapes. She particularly delighted in the multiple manifestations of circularity:

La cintura para el brazo.
Brazo para la cintura.
Que naciste cinturón
y que naciste contorno.
Así, círculos del aire,
tiovivos del momento,
ruedecita de fortuna,
ondas de la superficie.
Brazo, cintura, paréntesis,
interrogación doblada.
Y no hay más. Cintura, brazos.
Resumen de geometría.

(94)

[The waist for the arm.
The arm for the waist.
For you were born to be a belt
and your were born to be a contour.
Thus, circles of air,
carousels of time,
little wheels of fortune,
waves on the surface.
Arms, waist, parenthesis,
a double question mark.
There is no more. Waist, arms.
A summary of geometry.]

Her poem represents an exuberant embrace of palpable objects. Semantic implications along with repetition of words, alliteration, and anadiplosis expand the "resumen de geometría" into a myriad of concrete examples. Her preference for juxtaposing fragments of visual images also links her to cubism; Santana calls her poem "Mi falda de tres volantes" [My skirt with three ruffles], "un grácil juego de recomposición cubista de la realidad según el 'objeto'" [a graceful play of cubist restructuring of reality according to the object].[32]

The parallels between de la Torre's poetry and that of some of her male contemporaries, although indisputable, cannot obscure one of her salient features: a tendency to femininize her poetic world. For example, in the first poem of her first collection, the sea images coalesce to form an intriguing picture of a geometric pattern in much the same way Ramón Gómez de la Serna merges metaphor and humor to create ingenious "greguerías." The novelty of the image calls attention to the cleverness of its creator as the *greguería* required, but beyond this immediate, provocative effect, the image evokes a long-standing female archetype of woman as weaver or sewer:

Sobre la superficie
del mar encandilado
de las seis de la tarde,
saltan algunos peces
que dejan sobre el agua,
al caer, una onda.
Así, a trechos, bordado
el mar por esta aguja
parece que sonríe:
sonrisas que se ensanchan
y cierran lentamente;
sonreír de la orilla,
encaje de la falda
azul y transparente.

(31–32)

[On the surface
of the high sea
at six in the afternoon,
some fish leap
leaving a wave on the water
as they fall.
Thus, here and there,
the sea, embroidered by this needle,
seems to smile:
smiles that expand
and close slowly;
the smile of the shore,
lace of the blue
and transparent skirt.]

The movement up and down of the fish simulates that of a needle and the wave they create becomes a watery thread that leaves the "mar bordado" and a lacy design upon the shore.

The figure of the weaver or sewer has come to symbolize the feminine and the empowerment of women. Gilbert and Gubar have written that "like Ariadne, Penelope and Philomela, women have used their loom, thread and needles both to defend themselves and silently to speak of themselves."[33] The power to weave, to design, to fabricate, and ultimately to create poses a threat to patriarchal control. For this reason, for Nancy K. Miller, Arachne becomes the archetype of the woman punished for her talent by being restricted to spinning outside of representation, beyond the locus of the self-possessed subject. For Miller, as well as for Patricia Klindienst Joplin, the "voice of the shuttle," the weaver, is the symbol of the proud woman silenced, also the paradigm of the subversive spider, the defiant speaker, and the assertive artist.[34] Weaving and sewing reveal women's relation with and within the dominant culture. They are instruments of subversion, avenues of self-expression, and the substances of their reality of confinement to the domestic sphere. They also focus women's artistry on manual dexterity and utilitarian production. Transferred to the literary works of women, the tradition of piecing, patchwork, and quilting, as Elaine Showalter has pointed out, has a referential value as well as consequences for the structures, genres, themes, and meanings of American women's writing.[35] The connections she discerns between quilting and American women's literature must, however, be translated for Spanish women writers to associations with embroidery.

Embroidery was a fundamental and obligatory skill for Spanish women of all classes. Turn-of-the-century lists of appropriate activities for the ideal woman did not deviate much from those of Fray Luis de León and Juan Luis Vives in the sixteenth century: "labores manuales, reposando, calcetando, planchando, bordando a bastidor o haciendo dulce de conserva; zurciendo" [manual labor, resting, knitting, ironing, embroidery, or making sweet preserves, darning].[36] Even when girls of the middle and upper classes began to receive rudimentary schooling, be it at home, in girls' schools, or in religious institutions, the educational goal established for them was the acquisition of a "cultura de adorno" [culture of adornment] through a curriculum of painting, French, music, and embroidery.[37] In 1920, Gregorio Martínez Sierra, a male who prided himself on supporting the education of women, noted the Spanish obsession with teaching embroidery to females: "Desde que . . . levantan media vara del suelo, la madre las sienta a su lado y les pone una aguja en la mano. Antes de aprender a leer, aprenden a hacer vainica . . . Las escuelas, los colegios . . . siguen . . . este impulso familiar: dos, tres, cuatro horas diarias se consagran . . . al cosido, al bordado, a las . . . labores de adorno" [From the time they are two feet tall, their mother sits them down alongside her and puts a needle in their hands. Before learning to read, they learn to do hem stitching . . . the schools continue this push by the family: two, three, four hours are devoted to sewing, to embroidery . . . to hand work].[38] When, in the early twentieth century, education became the panacea for reforming the nation and superficial notions of history, art, geography, and mathematics were added to girls' programs of study, their education was still aimed at the creation of religious, socially gracious, and manually skillful women.[39] Formal schooling did not diminish this emphasis because the books girls read reinforced, rather than transformed, the pervasive conservative ideology. La buena Juanita [Good little Jane], the book with which thousands of Spanish girls learned to read during the first decades of the twentieth century, was an important instrument in the socialization of females to traditional gender roles. It presented boys as competitive and engaged in academic pursuits, while Juanita and her friends learned to embroider, play the piano, and dress well.[40]

It is not surprising, then, to find reflections of this socialization preserved in de la Torre, born in the remote outpost of the Canary Islands far from the few Spanish experiments in progressive and practical education carried out in mainland urban centers. Embroidery and images of traditional feminine attire find their way into her poetry. In one poem a young girl in love imagines embroidering herself a pretty white dress as she awaits her absent lover (¡Qué bonito vestido / transparente de lirios me bordara! . . . ¡Qué bonito vestido / vestidito, de niña enamorada!" 87 [What a pretty and filmy dress / covered with lilies I would embroider! . . . What a pretty dress / the little dress of a girl in love!]). Echoes of the conventional motifs of Spanish folk poetry aside, the adoption of the voice of the embroiderer by the poetic speaker situates de la Torre's protagonist within a long social tradition for women. The poet herself stitched her poetic cloth with metaphoric threads originating in embroidery terminology. This same poem begins with the notion of "threading" as a figurative vehicle for the permanent distance between lovers: "Sobre las hojas blancas / los números enhebran las distancias" (87) [On white leaves / numbers thread distances]. In another poem, the ability to embroider is mapped upon nature and its potential for creating beautiful afternoons:

> Hielo del sol
> azúcar de la mar,
> hilito de la tarde
> para bordar.
> Bórdame corazoncitos azules
> para regalar,
> que hoy es fiesta . . .
>
> (80)

> [Ice from the sun
> sugar from the sea,
> a fine thread from the afternoon
> for embroidering.
> Embroider me little blue hearts
> that I can give away,
> because today is a holiday . . .]

She continues the feminization of the word by personifying the sea as a little girl with a "Delantal / de los picos de encaje" [apron / with lace corners] or as a glittering gypsy: "El mar hace lentejuelas / en su pandero amarillo. / Nada se quedó olvidado: / ni un pañolito de seda" (65) [The sea puts sequins on its yellow tambourine. / Nothing is left unforgotten: / not even a silk handkerchief].

The sensuality of the attractively dressed female becomes more evident in her second collection where the poetic personae seem more directly related to the poet herself. She becomes both the subject and object of contemplation; in a narcissistic flourish of self-satisfaction, she looks at her own voluptuous image in the reflecting glass of a shop window with unabashed approval: "¡Qué bien me veo pasar / remolino de las brisas / pequeña y grande, confusa / huella blanca en el asfalto" (95) [I look so good passing / like a breeze whirlwind / little and big, a blurred / white imprint on the asphalt]. Her blouse is open, but her skirt is a frilly three-ruffled dress. Despite her outburst of sexual self-awareness, the female protagonist of her poetry is in a traditional, feminine dress typical of an innocent young provincial girl and radically different from the masculinized garçonne look of the daring flappers. While her contemporary Concha Méndez portrays herself as skier, pilot, and champion swimmer, De la Torre depicts a poetic persona clad in pinafores of embroidery and lace. While Méndez's donning of athletic garb illustrates a trend in modern literature by women that Sandra M. Gilbert interprets as a desire to collapse fixed gender identity enforced through costume, de la Torre's perpetuation of feminine attire reflects conformity with traditional gender distinctions associated with clothing.[41] De la Torre paints herself as dressed "en el encaje bordado / de mi traje azul y blanco" (77) [in a blue and white dress / of embroidered lace] and standing with "las manos dobladas / sobre el delantal bordado" (76) [hands folded on her embroidered apron]. The fascination with comfortable, modern attire that manifested itself in the capital did not seem to leave a strong imprint upon the poetry of this writer from the periphery.

De la Torre projects an ambivalence toward the world around her, complicating the design of her poetic surface. The accumulation of varying and even contrasting stitches, which at close range give the impression of confusion, from a distance reveal a blended overall pattern. Even though it might confound a reader expecting simple, smooth, textual designs, this ambivalence between contradiction and unity, between the specific and the general, gives the poetry of de la Torre its richness. Also by sewing into her text many of the motifs of traditional Spanish womanhood, she helped embroider her gender upon the cultural tapestry of her day. Some of the insightful observations that Amy Katz Kaminsky makes regarding the fiction of the seventeenth-century María Zayas and clothing are relevant to the present discussion. Kaminsky writes that "Zayas's transformation of feminine culture into literature is an implicit feminist act. By deeming it worthy of codification in art, Zayas validates and values women's realm of experience and knowledge." Kaminsky points out that the designation of clothing as primarily a feminine concern has rendered women's descriptions of clothing unreadable to male critics as anything but a sign of women's concentration on trivial ornamentation. She warns that this reliance on culturally determined notions of femininity can obscure the rhetorical, textual function of clothing, striping a woman of subjectivity as a writer, and deprive her art of significance beyond historical accuracy. Therefore, care should be taken to see in the use of clothing by a writer like de la Torre not just literal documentation, but a poetic device that created a feminine presence within her poetic environment.[42]

When it comes to the presentation of the self in her verses, de la Torre basted together contrasting tones. At first glance she seems to have grounded her poetry in the feminine experience of absent love. She regularly projected the patriarchal view of woman cherished by the vast majority of Spanish society—both male and female—as natural and appropriate, the image of woman as passive, observed object rather than as active subject or observer. At times with regret and resentment, but never with defiance, the female speaker in de la Torre's text stands passively waiting, abandoned or somehow frustrated by her lover. The woman in her poems waits on shore for the boats to return; she waits in the morning fog; and at night, like some modern-day Sleeping Beauty, she awaits the magical touch of the other: "Tu presencia lejana / deja sobre mi frente / la mano que despierta / mi sueño, poco a poco" (70) [Your distant presence / leaves on my brow / a hand that awakens / my dream gradually]. Despite an occasional exhibition of self-contemplation or a display of erotic arousal ("¡Cómo temblaban mis labios / a la sombra de mi sueño!" (73) [How my lips trembled / under the spell of my dream!]), her poetic persona usually finds herself enclosed and even trapped, especially in *Marzo incompleto*, where the circles of timeless presence of the previous collections unravel into the tangled shreds of past joys. The speaker portrays herself as the trapped victim of a callous collector of butterflies:

Estoy clavada en el espacio, inmóvil
como una mariposa prisionera.
Coleccionista ciego no dudaste
en dejar a los aires sin adioses.

(122)

[I am nailed to the air, motionless
like a trapped butterfly.
Blind collector you did not hesitate
to leave the air without farewells.]

Just when it seems clear that de la Torre accommodated her self-presentation to the traditional, indeed stereotypical, portrayal of the feminine as enclosed and immobilized by the male possessor, by the collector with his "mariposa prisionera," a closer examination of other poems uncovers a desirous female scrutinizing a masculine body. The role of spectator of sensual beauty has long been considered a masculine posture because of its implications of sexual arousal and control over the object of contemplation. Traditionally the female gaze has been associated with cupidity, seduction, aggressivity, and transgression, qualities strongly restricted and condemned in women. Therefore, within the context of a society that idealized demure "señoritas" and feared the malevolent force of the female "mal de ojo" [evil eye], the pleasure de la Torre took in looking at young male bodies introduced into her otherwise decorous verses a noteworthy suggestion of sensuality and a note of subversive disregard for traditional gender-defined demeanors.[43] The poet of seascapes holds within her gaze the robust frame of tanned sailors whose strength merges with that of the sea:

> ¡Qué bien sobre el mar tus brazos
> morenos, fuertes, seguros
> como dos remos, salados!
>
> . . . .
>
> ¡Que eres de mar, no de tierra,
> remero de tus dos brazos
> salados, color de arena!

(92)

> [How wonderful your tanned,
> strong, firm arms,
> over the sea, like two oars, salty!
>
> . . . .
>
> You are made of sea, not land,
> oarsman with your two
> salty arms, the color of sand!]

"Seguros," with its composite connotations of solid, steady, and sturdy, is the qualifier she invariably attaches to the male body: "brazos / morenos, fuertes, seguros," "la curva constante de tu brazo . . . segura y presente en su dominio" [the constant curve of your arm . . . assured and present in its control], "línea pura de sus manos / seguras" [the pure line of your firm hands].

The virginal child dressed in lace gives way to the sexual being who emulates masculine dominion with her own brand of visual possession. One afternoon, she writes, she held but briefly under her control a set of bronzed and electrifying hands:

> Manos que me estremecían
> de ese miedo de encontrarse
> y al borde de mis anillos
> daban un filo cortante.

Yo las tuve en mis pupilias,
viril triunfo de su imagen
prisioneras de mis sienes,
mías, una sola tarde.

(90)

[Hands that made me tremble
from the fear of our meeting
and they made a sharp ridge
at the edge of my rings.
I held them within the pupils of my eyes
manly triumph of their image
prisoners of my temples,
mine, for a single afternoon.]

Discreet, if not timid, in her allusions to the body, whether it be male or female, de la Torre refers primarily to hands and arms, the instruments of the caress. A far cry from the contemporary Spanish poet Ana Rossetti, who speaks freely of heterosexual as well as homosexual love and ventures an inclusion of underdrawers as readily as an allusion to masturbation, de la Torre still possesses that inhibition toward anatomical references that Ostriker finds to be an important distinguishing feature of the "poetess," as opposed to the female "poet."[44] This inhibition tempers, to be sure, the erotic quality of her verses, but her poetry nonetheless is imbued with a tactile physicality and a strong sense of connection between the self and the other.

This connection is, however, more often suggested than realized and not infrequently presented through its absence, as the memory of the other materialized into a hand upon her forehead or as an illusory ghost of "unos brazos amigos" [friendly arms]. Hands can potentially hold within their grasp the greatest human joys—the touch of the other and the warmth, the "moneda de oro" [gold coin], of nature—but when empty, they signify supreme loss. For that reason, de la Torre captures the grief of absent motherhood with the image of empty hands:

Cuando he visto
otras madres que guardan su silencio
sobre pequeñas frentes,
he comprendido el torpe desamparo
de mis manos vacías . . .

(115)

[When I have seen
other mothers who keep quiet
over little brows,
I have understood the awkward helplessness
of my empty hands . . .]

In *Marzo incompleto*, as her grief intensifies, and its precise causes become more indistinct, de la Torre resorts to hands and arms to portray graphically the absence of tactile presence. Twice, empty outstretched arms suggest the physical position of crucifixion and the metaphoric pose of depleted existence; and the book concludes with these lines of desperation: "y de este gran amor que voy perdida / ya nadie más podrá juntar los brazos" (124) [no one can ever join the arms of this great love that I have lost]. If life and love are felt through physical contact with others enacted in the embrace, then the loss of these vital emotions is aptly represented with the loss of limbs. According to Hélène Cixous the greatest tragedy for women is decapitation, but for Josefina de la Torre it is amputation, the loss of hands or arms, the conduits for physical contact with the other.

> Pez frío de mi cuerpo
> que resbalas por la humedad en sombra
> de la angustia.
> . . . .
> ¡Cuerpo mío, perdido,
> sin brazos que lo alcancen
> al final del olvido!
> Carpa dormida entre las aguas quietas,
> eternamente viva.
>
> (120–21)

> [The cold fish of my body
> you who slip through the dark dampness
> of my anguish.
> . . . .
> My body, lost,
> without arms to reach out to it
> at the edge of oblivion!
> A sleeping carp, perpetually
> alive, among still waters.

Unlike the French theorist, the Spanish poet does not seek the liberation of a female sexual economy that makes a gift out of departure and asserts itself as a transgressive disruption of masculine-oriented binarism; on the contrary, she laments the separation from the other and the loss of her ability to define and detect the other physically, and to sense duality.[45]

Where Josefina de la Torre did anticipate recommendations like those of Cixous was in her pursuit of physical contact and in her refusal to keep silent. She authorized herself to speak and thereby created a speaking female subject. When she spoke, she did not waver in her focus, describing the beauties of nature or telling of the emotions within her; but the tone of her voice alternated between contrasting accents that reflect traditional gender differences. She affirmed her need to be heard, but presented the self most often as abandoned or in some way subordinated to the unidentified "you" in her poems; she celebrated the strength of the masculine body at the same time she took delight in her own feminine appearance; and she subtly incorporated the expressions and structures of the male canon into her poetry while conspicuously infusing into them images and perspectives associated with female experience. Seemingly ambivalent in its stance, de la Torre's poetry nonetheless follows a steady course from presence to absence and from potential speech to solitary voice. In *Versos y estampas* the unobtrusive poetic persona allows nature to establish its splendid and autonomous presence; but as the human speaker assumes prominence, the tones of the voice change, becoming increasingly reflective, subjective, and internalized. *Poemas de la isla* still records moments of plenitude and the possible definition of the self through the other, but by *Marzo incompleto* the vibrant presence of nature disappears and the fulfilling presence of the other becomes problematic. The fabric of the speaker's world unravels into the stands of an empty existence.

5

Rosa Chacel: Masking the Authoritative Voice

Absence in the early poetry of Rosa Chacel is relevant to her attitude toward female creativity, her expression of her own subjectivity, and her relation with her general cultural community rather than to a textualization of sentiments of loss. This inner, emotional type of absence manifests itself in her poetry written in exile, when overtones of alienation, a disclosure of existential distress, and references to the passage of time, to the dehumanizing effects of the city, and to the fear of oblivion make their way into her verse. As Dona M. Kercher indicates, a heartfelt gratitude for friendship, reflections on frustration with life, and intellectual questioning characterize the poems Chacel wrote after 1940.[1] In the poetry she wrote before the civil war, she is more self-protective; she consistently excludes her personal feelings from her poems and shuns autobiographical revelations in favor of biographic portraits. By eschewing the autobiographical in her poetry, she becomes a notable example of the rejection of the spent female tradition of sentimental poetry she and her female contemporaries inherited. Without the weight of that heritage, Chacel can presumably forge a female persona rooted in intellectual and linguistic control. But as a woman of her times, to achieve this power Chacel must engage herself in ambivalent postures of masking. She masks her emotions, her intellect, and her reactive authority. She hides her compelling presence as a creative woman behind a self-effacing facade of absence. In her relationship both to her readers and to her work, she masks her sense of creative authority with protective mechanisms of self-censure and deferential gestures of conformity. With the help of a double-voiced discourse that overlays an adherence to norms on a disregard for customary expectations, she can maneuver among her predominantly masculine readership. By covering non-conventionality with her adoption of canonical practices, she validates herself as a master of respected art forms; by denying gender differentiation in artistic creation, she defers to patriarchal dominion in a gesture of accommodation that reinforces the traditional notion of women's artistic inferiority.

In Chacel's ambivalent relationship to poetry, there lies an implicit confrontation with the all-encompassing, ontological absence to which all members of her gender have been confined. She adamantly denies throughout her life the existence of absence as a factor in the marginalization of woman from culture. By refusing to recognize the concept of woman as absence or lack, Chacel attempts to escape the possibility of questioning the legitimacy of her role as writer, while at the same time unconsciously avoiding an overt challenge to patriarchal ideology. Despite her continual denial of the existence of gender difference in art, what she writes unveils the reality of what she rejects. Her rapport with her poetry discloses the problematics characteristic of the woman writer of her time: a need to temper feelings that could be construed as feminine frailty and a hesitancy to exhibit openly masterful authorship as well as intellectual prowess. The first problem creates in her a discomfort with self-revelation, and the second drives her to mask her creative authority. In the end, Chacel grapples in her own distinctive way with the dilemma she says does not exist. Chacel's poetry of the thirties does not incorporate the same female iconography found in the other female poets studied in this book, but she shares with them a desire, carefully disguised in her case, to create a personal presence. All her self-effacement, self-censorship, deference to patriarchy, and displacement of the personal prove to be a mask concealing an authoritative voice and a commanding female presence.

This implicit affirmation of the self demands attention, not so much by its extensiveness as by its intensity. Although known primarily as a novelist, Chacel also wrote poetry.[2] She restricted her poetry-writing while concentrating on prose somewhat like Ernestina de Champourcin, who abandoned prose quickly while continuing to find pleasure in poetry.[3] Chacel's poetic output is very small in comparison to Champourcin's, but it nonetheless tells a great deal about both her creative disposition and about the situation of the female writer of her generation. Rosa Chacel's career spans more than sixty years from 1930, the date of the publication of her first novel, through a period of exile divided between Argentina and Brazil, to the years after her permanent return to Spain in 1974, when she began to enjoy a certain amount of overdue recognition as a novelist, and finally to 1994, the year of her death.[4] Her poetry, however, has escaped critical scrutiny, and she herself disavowed it. Most of the poetry Chacel wrote before 1940 is highly imitative, a conscious superimposition of avant-garde elements upon a grid of the most classical verse forms, of an irrational veneer upon a highly rational base. This indisputable appearance of imitation conceals, however, a creative posture that is at bottom articulate, authoritative, and assertive. The interplay, in Chacel's limited poetic production, between assimilation of progressive, male-initiated norms and the assertion of individual identity enacts the broader struggle for a certain sense of personal freedom, poetic legitimacy, and creative self-assertion that is found in the textual reality of her female counterparts. Thus, a consideration of Chacel's neglected and rejected poetry uncovers significant features of the creative process in her and indirectly reveals some of the possible ways in which a woman writer of her day could craft her words if she was to offset unresponsiveness to female writing and to exert her own creative energy.

Although she began composing poetry as a child, Chacel regarded poetry a game, merely a mental diversion and an embarrassment to be concealed. She recounts that she wrote most of her poetry casually walking down the street or riding on street cars and that she wrote most of her sonnets during intervals of rest from the writing of her novel *Teresa*.[5] She never saw her poetry as part of her intellectual or literary development: "Yo no creí nunca en mis versos, no los tomé como camino de mis poderes intelectuales, no los vi proyectados en el porvenir" [I never believed in my poetry, I did not take it as an avenue for my intellectual power, I did not see it projected into the future].[6] This view of her poetry as separate from and implicitly inferior to her authentic literary production accounts for her refusal to publish any poetry between 1937 and 1978. When she did publish the poetry of that period, she aptly titled it *Versos prohibidos* [Forbidden verses]. In the prologue, self-censorship cedes only to severe negative self-appraisal; she calls her attempt to combine fixed classical verse forms with free, irrational surrealist images in the sonnets of *A la orilla de un pozo* [On the edge of a well] (1936), "el mayor disparate, el más *desaforado* sinsentido" [the silliest thing, the most outrageous nonsense].[7]

Within this censorious recognition of the apparent feebleness of her poetry lies a concealed assertion of her power of discrimination and of her control over her image as a writer. A similar observation is made by Peter S. Temes in his discussion of the ban that Laura (Riding) Jackson placed on the publication of her poetry as a strategy to eschew the role of object and to win instead a kind of authority over critics and interpreters. She eventually modified the ban, allowing her poems to be published with a note by her on her renunciation of her poetry, turning silence into a public gesture of self-rejection, much in the same way Chacel did through self-censorship in her *Versos prohibidos* and her comprehensive collection *Poesías (1931–1991)*.[8] Temes writes that "(Riding) Jackson achieved a certain authority through her rejection, casting out along with her poems the vulnerability that attends statement, refusing the risk of becoming the object of someone else's interpretation. By disavowing her poetry, she also disavowed, implicitly, all who would attempt to interpret it for they would have to begin by assuming that in it lay at least some value."[9] Unlike (Riding) Jackson, Chacel did not face adverse criticism; in fact Angel Crespo has called her sonnets "uno de los mejores libros compuestos en el ámbito y el clima de la denominada generación del 27" [one of the best books written within the boundaries and climate of the so-called Generation of 27].[10] Nonetheless, through self-censorship she also protected her poetic speaker from possible reproach, from a subjection to "the vulnerability that attends statement."

Chacel's reluctance to publish poetry seems to parallel her self-consciousness regarding aspects of her person she considered weak, but the lack of stature of her poems, unlike her lack of physical stature, could effectively be eradicated through silence.[11] However, while her adoption of the role of critical evaluator of her own poetry may appear at first to be a gesture of self-effacement, it proves to be the appropriation of authority over the destiny and meaning of her poems, for her silence served as much as a self-defense mechanism to protect her poetic inadequacy as a technique for controlling her image as a writer. Chacel's ban on the publication of her poems guaranteed the insignificance she firmly believed characterized them. Poets understandably fear that critics' interpretation might distort, corrupt, or somehow minimize their work, but what caused apprehension in Chacel was that her poems would be seen not for less but for more than they are. In addition, by withholding her poetry, she not only made its public fate coincide with her private opinion, she renounced the very role of poet itself and by extension could enhance her image as a novelist.[12]

Like the other female poets of the Generation of 27, Chacel rejected the prevailing feminine poetic tradition with its image of the female poetic voice as sentimental, sad, and sensitive and turned instead to her male contemporaries who championed liberation from the literary past and promised a freedom of spirit favorable to youthful optimism and artistic innovation. The female poets of Chacel's generation welcomed the new avant-garde movements because they offered possibilities for writing and a sense of creative freedom not available from their female predecessors. Thus Chacel's subscription to the tenets of modernism defended by José Ortega y Gasset and her enthusiasm for writers such as James Joyce allowed her to break away from the limited and limiting feminine past and to participate, albeit tangentially, in the vitalizing trends of her own times. The willingness of women poets to discard literary constrictions of the past and to adopt new artistic modes was a part of the broader reality of social change beginning to affect Spanish women. Although not practicing the extreme defiance of established codes of female dress and behavior of the flapper in the Anglo-Saxon world, the "new" woman emerging in Spain did break with certain conventions of decorum and inactivity. Chacel, for her part, besides attending the prestigious art school of San Fernando, was known for her sense of independence. Even in her nineties, she indulged in a pipe and a whiskey a day.[13] If she adopted masculine mannerisms, it should not surprise that she imitated their writing.

Rosa Chacel does not find the imitation of masculine modes problematic for the female writer. Seeing culture as male-generated, she finds no other option for women who want to participate in it than to follow the male lead: "La mujer . . . sigue la historia de la cultura, no se pone aparte" [Women . . . follow the history of culture, they don't stand apart from it]. She firmly believes that this masculine phenomenon has not excluded women: "tratar de indicar que las mujeres quedaron excluidas o que si hubiera sido hecha por ellas sería de otra forma, es una tontería. . . . La mujer, en general, no niega la cultura que recibe porque normalmente se siente copartícipe de ella" [to try to show that women have been excluded or that if it (culture) had been made by them, it would be different is foolishness . . . women, in general, do not reject the culture they receive because normally they feel themselves to be co-participants in it].[14] She consistently rejected the existence of a separate feminine literature and ridiculed those women who refused to join the boys' "club" of literature: "las mujeres que no quieren ingresar en eso . . . están fritas, para mí son inexistentes. La cultura está hecha por los hombres y las que quieran entrar, que entren" [the women who don't want to enter there . . . are cooked. As far as I am concerned, they are nonexistent. Culture is made by men and those women who want to enter let them do so].[15] Chacel intuitively understood the discoveries articulated by current theorists regarding the survival of female writers within the context of public discourse: only by following the gender-defined norm could a female writer speak with an authoritative voice. Sidonie Smith has made important observations on the dilemma of female writers: "When a woman chooses to leave behind cultural silence . . . she chooses to enter the public arena. But she can speak with authority only insofar as she tells a story that her audience will read." To speak with intentional authority, many women reject "the realm of the mother for the realm of the father," because only to the extent that woman gives her allegiance to male-defined culture, does she gain cultural recognition. But in this way, she perpetuates the political, social, and textual disempowerment of mothers and daughters.[16] This rejection and its consequence characterize Chacel's work.

Despite her adamant repudiation of feminism, Chacel repeatedly addressed the question of the relationship between women and culture, while consistently refusing to equate restrictions with marginalization. Chacel began her public discussion of women in a lecture delivered in her early twenties at the Ateneo. Then in 1931 she refuted the essentialist views on women that had been aired since Ortega published the theories of Georg Simmel in *Revista de Occidente* in 1923. In her article she called these sociopsychological ideas "la falsa y efímera norma que constituye la desorientación y desconcierto íntimo de nuestra época" [the false and ephemeral norm that constitutes the inner disorientation and uneasiness of our era].[17] Later, in her 1972 *Saturnal* [Saturnalia], a book on the philosophy of eroticism, she delved into the question of the masculine and the feminine, feminization, and the drive to union, and she proclaimed her steadfast belief that to be a Man is to be human and to be a "Man" therefore includes both man and woman. Distinguishing between marginalization and enslavement, Chacel recognizes that women have been deprived of culture and freedom, but she insists they have never been marginalized: "Yo afirmo que *nunca* fue *marginada,* sino que fue *siempre*—hasta muy poco— esclavizada" [I affirm that they (women) were never marginalized, but that they were always—until very recently—enslaved.].[18]

As Teresa Bordons and Susan Kirkpatrick have already noted, her affirmations underscore her engagement in double-voiced discourse, for while feeling obliged to voice her disagreements with Ortega's concept of the nature of women, Chacel wrote her novel *Teresa* in accordance with his and others' views on the "natural" subordinate nature of women.[19] Likewise, Chacel does not discern any contradiction between her stated beliefs and the marginalization from the canon she experienced throughout most of her career nor between her open affirmation of the literary possibilities for women and her masking of the female voice of authority in her poetry.

Chacel frequented some of the "boys' clubs" of the day: the Escuela de Bellas Artes de San Fernando [The school of fine arts of St. Ferdinand], the Ateneo, and various "tertulias" [café groups] of the vanguard writers; and she contributed to the prestigious journals *La Gaceta Literaria* and *Revista de Occidente.* A series of male friends and mentors, particularly José Ortega y Gasset, were decisive in the evolution of her literary career. Repeatedly declaring herself a faithful disciple of Ortega, Chacel reaffirmed over the years her indebtedness to his ideas on the avant-garde novel and her admiration for the values he represented.[20] The impact of Ortega's promotion, in his *Ideas sobre la novela* [Ideas on the novel] and *Deshumanización del arte* [Dehumanization of art], of the evasion of realism in fiction and of sentiment in poetry, along with Chacel's own inclination to open the avenues of her intellectual power, conspired to direct her interest away from the lyrical potential of poetry and toward its formalistic or philosophical possibilities. When she did overcome her resistance to publish poetry, the literary persona emerging in those verses is that of a figure of intelligence and intellect rather than of sentiment and sentimentality.

Chacel published a handful of poems scattered throughout periodicals of the day in the twenties and thirties.[21] However, the only volume she published before 1940 was *A la orilla de un pozo* (1936), thirty sonnets dedicated to different friends of hers and written shortly after the experiment in extemporaneous poetry composition that she and Rafael Alberti performed in 1933 at a Berlin café. The collection combines the incongruous, irrational imagery adopted by her avant-garde contemporaries with the rigid formula prescribed by the sonnet. Disclaiming any significance or autobiographical impact in her poems, she insists that the book aspires to no other interpretation than that of "una franca acogida en su total condición de extemporáneo" [a candid accumulation of its overall extemporaneous impulses].[22] However, as often happens in Chacel, beneath her disavowals lie noteworthy implications about her relation to her art. For example, in her novels, which are highly autobiographical, Chacel circumvents clear self-revelation; but Shirley Mangini suggests that her creation of a *doppelgänger* relationship between the male and female characters in her first novel *Estación. Ida y vuelta* [Station. Round-trip], written about the same time as these sonnets, blurs gender identification and serves as a "method for masking her feminine 'weaknesses' vis-à-vis her male contemporaries."[23] Masking is also found at the very heart of her sonnets. Chacel herself admits that her sonnets entail masking; they disguise no confidential personality trait but their content masks her preference for academic rigor; they are "sonetos que envolvían o enmascaraban la corrección académica de su forma en el delirante surrealismo de su contenido" [sonnets that wrapped or masked the academic correctness of their form in the wild surrealism of their content].[24]

The concealment of the personal self has been common among women attempting to enter the canon. Alicia Suskin Ostriker writes that with the advent of modernism, many American women poets strove to escape the ghetto of feminine poetry by standing on "the provocative edge of the avant-garde"; yet despite being "analytical, cosmopolitan, erudite, brilliant. . . . At the same time they remain masked women."[25] What is noteworthy about the masking process in Chacel's sonnets is that it works in two directions, for not only does classical versification restrict the free explosion of personal feelings nurtured by surrealist writing, the presence of avant-garde motifs corroborates her comparable hesitation to reveal her "amor secreto" [secret love] for a highly intellectualized form. Surrealism was for her not a cathartic experience of release of subconscious turmoil, but a technical exercise in linguistic manipulation. Any hint of surrealism in these poems does not reveal the psychosocial liberation that poets like Cernuda and Lorca found, but suggests an attempt to create a discourse acceptable to her male colleagues with which to disguise her enthusiasm for its antithesis. She masks not only any disclosure of private sentiment that might identify her with feminine poetry but also the exposition of formal features not popular among her male contemporaries. Chacel confesses that her personal aesthetic formula was a passion for form, since she professed faith in the cult of Apollo at the age of eight. In *Desde el amanecer* [From dawn], the autobiography of her first ten years, she recounts that she declared herself a classicist the moment she saw the enormous reproduction of Apollo in the vestibule of the Escuela de Artes y Oficios [School of Arts and Crafts], in Madrid. She blames her obsession with form for her early abandonment of sculpture, her field of professional training, and for her failure to convert her love for classic elements into a modern personalized expression.[26] Although Chacel contends that the dominion that form held over her did not allow her to evolve as a poet, the dilemma of self-exposure for female poets of the time also seems likely to have made poetry an objectionable genre for her. She eludes the effusion of sentiment that long has been censured in poetry by women while at the same time shying away from undisguised intelligence. A genre given to the immediate and unmediated exposure of private emotions and thoughts, poetry requires a degree of self-revelation Chacel was not prepared to make.

Without the Oedipal gesture of rebellion that Harold Bloom finds essential to the fulfillment of the creative impulse in male writers, Chacel embraces the possibilities of imitation. Openly recognizing the impact of assimilation on her essays, she says: "es muy poca la filosofía que conozco y mi filosofía consiste en la asimiliación" [I know very little philosophy and my philosophy consists of assimilation].[27] While free of the male "anxiety of influence," she also eschews any similarity with the sentimentality, the tenderness, and passivity associated with "feminine" poetry. Instead, she adopts both established and emerging canons, following the example of her male contemporaries in their use of subjective, irrational metaphors with lines like "La ilusión puso un huevo blanco y puro" [illusion laid a pure, white egg], reminiscent of Lorca's "la muerte puso huevos en la herida" [death laid eggs in the wound], while also incorporating the fixed meters and classical erudition of traditional patriarchal literature. Despite the reticence, the denials, and the masking in her posture in the face of the poetic enterprise, an examination of the poems of *A la orilla de un pozo* discloses an authoritative voice inconsistent with her apparent modesty.

She freely flaunts her mastery of two essential components of high culture: the venerable sonnet and classical erudition even exceeding the challenge of the rigor inherent in the sonnet by making all but three of her thirty poems conform to the same traditional rhyme scheme: ABBA:ABBA:CDE:CDE. Her inclination to follow sanctioned poetic forms is reconfirmed by the fact that the sonnet rhyme scheme she chooses is one of the two most common in Spanish poetry as well as the one favored by the poets of her period like Jorge Guillén, Vicente Aleixandre, Dámaso Alonso, and Rafael Alberti.[28] Chacel displays her erudition in allusions that range from mythical to biblical references, from Aphrodite to Esther, from Minerva to Rebecca. Although Chacel claims to fill the traditional sonnet with contemporary images, her poems are laden with learned words and classical motifs. She uses "poma" [apple] instead of "manzana" [apple] and includes words like "ebúrneo" [eburean], "mélico" [melic], "ínclito" [illustrious], "almo" [sacred]. Similarly the classical motifs of acanthus, olive and laurel trees, and doves stand out in these poems as do certain metaphors that recall the poetry of the Siglo de Oro: "en sus perlas de amor claros abriles / hervirán al compás de tu mirada" (14) [in its pearls of love bright Aprils / will boil to the beat of your gaze].[29]

As easily as she wields the ingredients of Spain's esteemed literary heritage, she creates provocative comparisons and suggestive juxtapositions like those used by avant-garde poets. Alongside her refined lexicon, she places words such as "corsé" and "wagon-lit," and alongside traditional metaphors, she places those that conform to the "imágenes visionarias" [visionary images] that Carlos Bousoño defines. In the poem to Paz González, she includes a traditional, sober metaphor, "el cáliz de la noche umbría" [the chalice of the shadowy night], and a novel, rather humorous metaphor, "En un corsé de cálidas entrañas / duerme una estrella" [A star sleeps in a corset, of warm innards]. In the latter metaphor, although unexpected, the vehicle "corsé" still conveys a sense of circular enclosure in a fairly logical fashion. More perplexing is the irrational coupling of silence and alligator in a poem with the lines "Llora y tiembla al pensar en la irrisoria / ternura que retó al caimán impuro" (16) [It cries and trembles when it thinks about the absurd / tenderness that challenged the impure alligator]. The syntax of her poems also partakes in both the classical and the vanguard traditions. On the one hand, she makes ample use of the hyperbaton common in seventeenth-century sonnets, and on the other hand, she produces loose, random series of words and phrases typical of the fragmentation of vanguard poetry. For example, the lines "y cien aulas con libros amarillos / y nieve y sangre y barro por el suelo" (25) [and one hundred schoolrooms with yellow books / and snow and blood and mud on the floor] may faintly echo the syntax of lines like Góngora's famous "en tierra, en humo, en polvo, en sombra, en nada," but they sound semantic chords that provoke emotional responses rather than rational associations.[30]

Chacel's quick assimilation of vanguard techniques can be seen in the poem dedicated to Gregorio Prieto, a composition in which she reproduces several of the traits characteristic of Vicente Aleixandre's surrealist poetry: the use of the conjunction "o" [or] as a marker of identification rather than of disjunction, the coupling of the erotic with bestial destruction, reification, and the creation of what Bousoño calls a "visión":

> Va el pensamiento oculto en la certera
> delicia o flecha, hundida y enconada
> en la impasible estatua, descuidada,
> que ignora el beso y garra de la fiera.
> En un vaso de sol que el sol destila,
> un alcohol de deseo se dibuja
> y se evapora en la excelsa lumbre.
>
> (35)

[Thought lies hidden in the certain
delight or arrow, embittered and embedded
within the impassive and neglectful statue
that knows not of the kiss and claw of the wild beast.
In a glass of sunlight that the sun distills,
an alcohol of desire is sketched
and disappears in the sublime fire.]

Intellectual delight becomes an arrow embedded in the impassive statue, who overlooks the passionate connection between the kiss and the claw. Although the intellect gains the solidity of matter, desire, metaphorically transformed into alcohol, quickly losses its liquidity in this poem of fanciful cosmic disarray.

Successful, even by her own admission, is the sonnet she dedicated to María Teresa León, an ekphrastic composition inspired by the collages of Max Ernst:

Si el alcotán anida en tus cabellos
y el Nilo azul se esconde en tu garganta,
si ves crecer del zinc la humilde planta
junto a tus senos o a tus ojos bellos,
no cierres el ocaso con los sellos
que el Occidente en su testuz aguanta:
tiembla ante el cierzo y el nublado espanta.
Si oyes jazmines corre a través de ellos.
Yo sé bien que te escondes donde siguen
los hongos del delirio, impenitentes,
y que al cruzar su senda de delicias
mariposas nocturnas te persiguen,
se abren bajo tus pies simas ardientes
donde lloran cautivas tus caricias.

                                                        (13)

[If the falcon nests in your hair
and the blue Nile hides in your throat,
if you see a humble plant grow out of the zinc
near your breasts or your beautiful eyes,
don't close the sunset with the imprints
that the West sustains on its brow:
tremble before the north wind
and frighten away the storm cloud.
If you hear the jasmine, run through them.
I know very well that you are hiding where
unrepentant mushrooms of delirium grow,
and that when you cross their path of delights
nocturnal butterflies pursue you,

beneath your feet burning abysses open up
where your imprisoned caresses cry.]

Essential to ekphrasis is the description of visual motifs of the first stanza.
In the surrealist manner, the poet juxtaposes and fuses, as Ernst does, the
material and the organic (cold metal zinc with the humble plant), and the
human and the animal orders converge in the dehumanized image of the
woman's hair as a nest. Once the encounter between incongruous elements
changes things from their original form into new creatures, a series of transformations can be enacted with the smoothness of a dream sequence. Thus,
once the woman is turned into a tree-like object, the blood of her veins
can, metaphorically, become the river Nile. The bright Nile blue identifies
the spectral color characteristic of many surrealist paintings. Beyond this
visual overlaying, the poem displays multiple other mergers, those of the
senses in the synesthetic union explicit in the line "Si oyes jazmines corre a
través de ellos" as well as of attributes, of the material with the emotional
("los hongos del delirio, penitentes"). Also conceptual associations convert
literal, visual images ("mariposas") into symbols, and metonymic substitu-
tions extend the qualities of a subject to its gestures ("caricias") as occurs in
the lines "mariposas nocturnas te persiguen, / se abren bajo tus pies simas
ardientes / donde lloran cautivas tus caricias."

While indulging in the elements of playfulness, randomness, and lack of
transcendence that characterize some of the avant-garde poetry in Spain,
Chacel did not create an aesthetic out of the meaninglessness of art nor
did she incorporate private emotions, sensations, or thoughts into her poetry. Avant-garde practices—be they "visión," "la imagen visionaria," or
the objective correlative—remain in Chacel's poetry disconnected, imitative gestures. Imitation, however, produces resemblance not identicalness
and, as Noël Valis has shown, although readily suggesting passive subservience, copying implicitly possesses authority because it is also writing.[31] For
all her conscious admiration for her male mentors and her willing acceptance of male influence, Chacel projects a voice of firmness, self-confidence,
and intellectual strength.

One reviewer discerns in *A la orilla de un pozo* a "tono de incertidumbre en
el intento lírico de autodefinirse en su esencial humanidad" [a tone of uncertainty in her lyric attempt to define herself in her essential humanity].[32]
Although it is true that in her first poem, Chacel contrasts Concha Albornoz's
noble detachment from the crowd, the "turba impura" [impure crowd], to
her own anguish before the world ("Yo, en tanto, mientras la sangrienta,
oscura / trepadora mis muros amenaza, / piso el fantasma que arde en mis
desvelos" [I, meanwhile, while the dark / bloody vine threatens my walls /
I tread upon the phantom that burns within my anxieties]), in most of
these poems she energizes the speaking "I," displacing the uncertainty of

self-reflection with a confident posture of power over others. She places her poetic objects—the writers, painters, and friends to whom she dedicates each sonnet—in different landscapes reflecting their particular lives but then invariably defines, reassures, or prods them. The self-assurance of the poetic speaker is reflected in the prevalence of the imperative, used in nearly half of the of the poems. The speaker commands her subjects for the sake of caution ("aguarda ¡por tu vida!" [wait, for the sake of your life!]), of consolation ("No temas, el olivo es justiciero" [Do not fear, the olive tree is just]), of encouragement ("Busca en tu antigua selva esa viviente / fe que se esconde . . . " [Look in your ancient forest for that living / faith that eludes you]) or of instruction ("Mira el error que, apenas si dibuja" [Look at the error that it barely draws]). Whether motivated by a desire to soothe or to advise, the consistent appearance of the imperative in *A la orilla de un pozo* reflects the resolute will of the speaker to impose herself upon the addressee of her poems.

Beyond the disposition of her verb forms, Chacel inscribes the assertiveness of her stance in her poems by coupling the emphatic first-person pronoun to its inflected verb form ("Yo sé"; "Yo veo"; "Yo me encontré" [I know, I see, I found myself]) in the conspicuous position at the beginning of lines. The authoritative stance she appropriates from her male predecessors and peers creates an environment that makes confident pronouncements possible. Her poetic speaker, for example, presumes an access to knowledge when she defines Pablo Neruda's life ("el placer del martirio es tu camino" [the pleasure of martyrdom is your destiny]) and to moral judgment when she evaluates Jesús Prados's talent ("Tu genio . . . camina / hacia la excelsa exactitud del Todo [Your genius directs itself toward the sublime exactness of the grand Whole]). The sense of mastery over words, of ownership of truth, and of influence over others that identifies the creative subject as powerful can easily be summarized in Chacel's poem to a female contemporary, the poet Concha Méndez. Although focusing on the "tú," the poem reveals the poet's ability to synthesize the life of another and demonstrates the presumption of advantage that the reliance on the imperative form implies:

> Tú que fuiste sirena y golondrina,
> Tú que escondiste cielos en tu alcoba,
> Tú que oíste la música que roba
> su sueño al pez y la borrasca empina,
> sal de esa oscura gruta, mortecina
> como caverna de medrosa loba,
> y al sol embalsamado que te arroba,
> sembrado por tu mano, sé vecina.

(33)

[You who were siren and swallow,
You who hid skies in your bedroom,
You who heard the music that robs
fish of its sleep and lifts the storm,
come out of that dark, dim grotto
like a cave of the fearful she-wolf,
be a neighbor of the hoisted sun that enchants you
and was sown by your own hand.]

The first quatrain lists the past attributes of its subject, but the implicit contrast between positive references of the first strophe and the gloomy images in the second attach a tone of admonition on its two imperatives. Méndez is ordered to come out of her doldrums into the sunlight.

The implications of dominion in her forthright instructions to many of the addressees of her poems reflect as much a drive to authority as an expression of affection. Love, be it sexual or affectional emotion, involves connections with an "other" that activate the interpersonal dynamics of dependency and possession. While arising from a need for merger, love of any kind involves the extension, if not the imposition, of the self upon another. The desire to make the other part of one's own self constitutes an impulse to possess that other, eradicate its separateness, and exercise one's own will over it. In this way, an attempt to transcend the self becomes closely linked with a drive for power. The drama of dependency and dominion basic to relationships of love is enacted in occasional poetry within its dual objectives of generous tribute and eager possessiveness. The object of attention becomes the poet's prevailing sphere of reference and predetermined point of departure, but within these bounds she can subject another human being to her own initiatives and interpretations. A large portion of the poems Chacel published throughout her career falls within this genre; in addition to the thirty sonnets of *A la orilla de un pozo*, nearly half of the poems included in *Versos prohibidos* are grouped as "Sonetos de circunstancia" [Circumstantial sonnets], a series of poems to beloved people and things.

Chacel herself recognized the role possession plays in circumstantial poetry. In a commentary on Sor Juana Inés de la Cruz's obsession with clarifying her use of the possessive pronoun "my," Chacel explains that the element of possession in the seventeenth-century poet reflects humble admiration, not arrogance, and supports a reverent distance between herself and her object of attention. For Chacel, Sor Juana's stance coincides with Ortega's sense of "delimitación," of boundaries, of distinction between the self and its world or circumstances as opposed to Unamuno's search for "confusión," fusion and mutual recognition.[33] Chacel believes she adheres to the second posture. Although Chacel takes possession of her subjects, her poetry lacks the anxiety over ontological union characteristic of

Unamuno. Her poetry does not display the deferential subjugation evident in Sor Juana either. Despite her overt affirmations of similarity to Unamuno, she seems to coincide more with Ortega's concepts of differentiation. In this she differs significantly from the other women poets of this study who repeatedly display a tendency to erase ego boundaries and surrender the autonomy of the self to the other. Without calling any of the subjects of her poetic tributes "mine" nor showing signs of forfeiting her individuality, Chacel establishes congenial bonds between peers in her poems. She maintains a posture of moral imperative with admonishments such as "¡La vida es gracia y el reír no cuesta" [Life is funny and it costs nothing to laugh] or a more subdued stance of nostalgic remembrance: "Bien recuerdo aquel día en que me diste / tu corazón de niño desvelado" [I remember well the day you gave me / your wakeful, childlike heart]. Indications of psychological unity surface only occasionally as for example, understandably, in the poem dedicated to her husband:

> ¡Ay! recuerda los monstruos y tesoros
> que alcanzó a contemplar nuestra ventura,
> al filo del abismo o de la gloria.
>
> (40)

> [Oh! remember the monsters and treasures
> that our fate managed to see
> at the edge of the abyss or of glory.]

Closeness and distance, love and possession are the essence of these poems honoring her friends. The interrelationship between writer and text duplicates the same duality inherent in love. Writing is an erotic act, says Chacel. Inspiration, she affirms, sets in motion a desire to reach, capture, hold its originating stimulus: "Toda obra es un acto erótico. . . . Mis ideas suelen ser ideas fijas. Entonces, voy hacia ellas. Y ese *ir* es un deseo de posesión. Un deseo erótico, por supuesto. . . . Mejor que posesión podríamos decir identificación. Por eso es idéntico el movimiento erótico hacia la obra y el movimiento erótico hacia Dios. Porque no se trata de poseer/agarrar, se trata de poseer esencialmente, de identificarse con la cosa, con el objeto del deseo" [Every work is an erotic act. . . . My ideas are usually fixed ideas. Then, I go toward them. That going is a desire for possession. An erotic desire, of course. . . . More than possession we could say identification. For that reason the erotic movement toward one's work is identical to the erotic movement toward God. Because it not a question of possessing/seizing, it is a question of possessing essentially, of identifying oneself with the thing, with the object of desire]. [34] For Chacel, the vital force that informs all that is human is Eros, a phenomenon she characterizes in *Saturnal*, her metaphysical study on love, as a need to engender, to transcend the self propelled by "lo genésico" [the genetic]. Love, poetry, and life itself coincide in their shared desire for movement, for possession, and for identification with the other.

Writing as an erotic act is a process of desire, motion, and contact, a reaching out to the other that solidifies, more than dilutes identity; it is, in short, the will to live. The urge to seek self-affirmation in an other manifests itself with great intensity early in Chacel's works. Her first novel, *Estación. Ida y vuelta*, incorporates multiple levels of doubling—between the protagonist and his feminine counterpart, between him and his inner self, and between the author and her creative self.[35] Although the poems of *A la orilla de un pozo* lack the sense of fluid identity, philosophical meditation, or autobiography of this novel, they nonetheless project, in their focus on other people, the same need to capture the essence over the intrigue of life and to perpetuate human existence through protagonists of her own confection. People like her sister Blanca, her good friend Concha Albornoz, and poets Luis Cernuda and Manuel Altolaguirre become fixed through language in a gallery of poetic portraits that remain the poet's lasting possessions. The living, human quality in her poems is accentuated further by a liberal use of personification. The physical and emotional agitation of the sea seems an apt metaphor for the movement, struggle, and grand force of the life process that Chacel endorses beneath the stable guise of her rigid sonnets:

> Ve con qué angustia y qué tesón enmienda
> sus ondas en la arena el Océano.
> Ve cómo borra su contorno vano.
> Rugiendo llora y sigue en su contienda.
>
> (28)

> [Look with what anguish and tenacity
> the Ocean alters its waves on the sand.
> Look how it erases its formless contour.
> It cries out with roars and continues its struggle.]

While Chacel's repudiation of her poetry may belie a sense of insecurity with the genre, the language she employs in her poems unmasks a confident voice. And that voice articulates celebratory pronouncements full of brilliance, vigor, and movement that reveal the same drive toward others underlying her definition of writing as an erotic act. She wholeheartedly celebrates the genius or excellence of her subjects. Her panegyric poem to Jesús Prados concludes with "tu genio . . . camina / hacia la excelsa exactitud del Todo," and in her poems to Concha Albornoz, Luis Cernuda, and Musia Sackhaina she spotlights their spiritual purity against the "turba impura," "muros de angustia y cerros de despojos" [the walls of anguish and hills of waste], and "infierno" of their surroundings. Even when treating silence or suffering, Chacel invariably finds possibilities for positive affirmation. She often counterpoises a final tercet of exhortation to a preceding outline of darker images. For example, to counteract the silence that roams "como un perro avieso" [like a sinister dog], she implores that Mariano R. Orgaz "pide a la verdad su blanco beso" [ask truth for its white kiss] and to compensate for the loss of love, she urges María Zambrano to weave the cloth of fame and drink the "néctar fiel de tu memoria" [faithful nectar of your memory]. Distant friends provoke an occasional nostalgic evocation, but any dark feeling is readily dispelled by memory, which soothes like a chirping bird from a "nido secreto" [secret nest] or endures like a "paciente perla que al dolor persiste" [patient pearl that resists pain]. Even when offering death as a relief from the painful, steady passage of time, she recommends that the intensity of faith, hope, and love be embraced. In a series of forceful commands to Arturo Serrano Plaja, she entreats him to pursue life even as death is sought. She advises him to seek union with God in the face of danger, to pursue love as an antidote to despair, to enjoy the sweet fruits of life, and to find the faith that ultimately leads to death:

> Hoy te ofrezco esta copa envenenada
> porque el tiempo es fugaz y el alma pena.
> Si te persigue, inmunda, la ballena
> piérdete en la divina encrucijada.
> Húndete en la corriente enamorada
> . . . .
> No comas frutos sin la sangre hirviente
> . . . .
> Busca en tu antigua selva esa viviente
> fe que se esconde y quiere serte esquiva
> y a la muerte, por ella, ve derecho.
>
>   (20)

> [Today I offer you this poisoned goblet
> because time is fleeting and the soul suffers.
> If the foul whale pursues you
> lose yourself in the divine crossroads.
> Sink into the amorous current
> . . . .
> Don't eat fruit without its boiling blood
> . . . .
> Look in your ancient forest for that living
> faith that hides itself and wants to elude you
> and through it head directly for death.]

The intense energy that confirms life as an erotic impulse manifests itself in Chacel's poetry in her frequent recourse to images of fire and burning and of light and brilliance. Her handling of light is thoroughly
traditional. Except in the first poem, in which the dyad of light and dark
represents the contrast between the corrupt light of the material world and
the dark, hidden integrity of her subject, darkness translates sadness and
suffering, while light regularly corresponds to the sublime qualities of beauty,
truth, and immortality. It is not surprising that Chacel, a writer with a strong
intellectual bent, should single out the Sybil, that mythical prophetess of
mysterious truths, to inspire patience. For Chacel, the Sybil is light and
foresees nothing but light:

> La sibila que alumbra con su frente,
> con su linterna de implacable brillo,
> . . . .
> Vio una aurora de líneas, sonriente,
> sobre la espuma del vivir sencillo
> y vio, partiendo de dorado ovillo,
> la bondad de un estambre refulgente.
>
> (14)

> [The Sybil who lights up your brow,
> with her relentlessly bright lantern,
> . . . .
> She saw a smiling dawn of lines,
> upon the foam of the simple life
> and she saw, coming out from the golden ball of yarn,
> the goodness of a brilliant worsted.]

The visual acumen of the Sybil in this poem cedes to the intellectual abstraction of numbers and divine perfection in her poem to Jesús Prados.
The sacred light of numbers touches Prados's forehead (a metonym for the
mind) with its perfect truth ("la marmórea verdad"):

> De la luz de los números, sagrada,
> con su impecable huella y su blancura,
> como un dintel, sobre tu frente pura
> la marmórea verdad edificada.
>
> (26)

> [The marmoreal truth built,
> from the sacred light of numbers,
> with its impeccable imprint and its whiteness
> like a lintel, on your pure brow.]

The associations between light and the Deity have formed a lasting composite image deeply ingrained, in both mythology as well as Christian theology.[36] Following this tradition, Chacel incorporates references to the Sybil and other mythological figures along with images and symbols of Christianity. In keeping with the underlying compulsion in the collection to combine divergent modalities, in two poems Christian symbolism meets mythological emblems of sexuality (the Minotaur) and love (Aphrodite). In both of these poems she refers to love in its manifestations of lust with allusions to the story of the Garden of Eden. In one of them, poem twenty-four, dedicated to Manuel Altolaguirre, she writes of the desire that escapes the "encendida poma" [fiery apple] and consumes itself in flame. In the other, poem twenty-two, dedicated to Angel Rosemblat, the garden of Genesis acquires an untamed aspect becoming a lusher, more exuberant jungle suggestive of fantastic, surreal landscapes. The burning edenic jungle is identified as the place of temptation as well as the site of the essential manifestations of life. Physical perception of sound ("susurros") [whispers], elements of propagation ("gérmenes") [germs], and emotions ("anhelos") [longings] fill the place and reconfirm existence:

> ¿Dónde vas tú por esa selva, llena
> de susurros, de gérmenes y anhelos,
> que ardiendo en perennales, sacros celos
> toda de arrullos traspasada suena?
> . . . .
> ¡Lugar de tentación! Su loco ejemplo,
> su prurito y poder copulativo
> van a inflamarte con su ardor profundo.
> La Afrodita Semántica, en su templo
> de vivo enigma, te imbuirá cautivo,
> filológico afán, tesón fecundo.
>
> (32)

[Where are you going through that forest full of
whispers, seeds, and yearnings,
that, burning within its everlasting, sacred zeal
resounds with piercing coos?
. . . .
A place of temptation! Its wild example,
its urges and copulative power
are going to inflame you with its deep ardor.
The Semantic Aphrodite, in her temple
of living enigma, will imbue you, her captive,
with philological eagerness and fecund tenacity.]

Chacel may incorporate motifs from the scriptures into her poetry, but her poems are not religious nor moralistic. They are recommendatory with appeals that spur her subject to action, hope, or a conscious sense of life. Although she speaks of "copulative power" and the arousal of passion, the erotic impulse in its narrow implications of physical desire serves as a metaphor for intellectual desire ("La Afrodita Semántica"), pleasure ("filológico afán") and generation ("tesón fecundo"). Chacel differs from her contemporary women poets in this omission of the physical aspects of desire, but she also diverges from her female antecedents in her intellectualized perspective as well as her non-sentimental tone.

Chacel celebrates the erotic impulse in its broadest terms as a drive or will to live. The predominance of fire with its concomitant images of burning, flame, and the color red reveals an underlying affirmation of the process and power of life. Occasionally fire signifies danger or pain, but the components of triumph and destruction in the image of fire are common complementary aspects of the sun that inform the poetic associations between fire and life. Just as widespread throughout a variety of times and places are the parallel images of fire as representing eroticism, solar heat, and physical energy on one hand, and mysticism, purification, and spiritual energy, on the other.[37] Thus in the same way that religious heritage prompted Chacel to link fire with passion and temptation, broader literary traditions led her to assign it the qualities of purity and joy. Fire can be the griffin's precious treasure ("En su escondido sésamo seguro / custodia el grifo de la fantasía / de hirviente manantial el fuego puro" [In its hidden, safe sesame / the griffin of fantasy watches / over the pure fire of a boiling spring]), and boiling can signal joyful fruition ("y en sus perlas de amor claros abriles / hervirán al compás de tu mirada" [and in its pearls of love, clear Aprils / will boil to the beat of your gaze]). Whether "polvo de tu fuego" [dust of your fire] or "invicta llama" [unconquered flame], the force that propels life is a fire. But because flames and fires go out, their extinction serves as a logical metaphor for death.[38] Thus, death appears in Chacel's poetry as a destruction by bonfire at the very edge of existence: "El confín de la vida arde en la hoguera / de implume mariposas abrasadas" [the edge of life burns in the bonfire / of burned, featherless butterflies].

During the 1930s Rosa Chacel published two poems in response to the conflictive events of the Spanish Civil War that reveal a poetic disposition similar to the one found in her more serene sonnets. The first of these poems, "¡Alarma!" [Alarm!], was published in the leftist journal *El Mono Azul* in October of 1936. It registers the collective fear provoked by night sirens in rather apocalyptic yet non-partisan terms. She personifies the siren as a wrathful god who unleashes a horde of deafening angels with blazing swords:

Sus fragorosos alientos
con ira pasando zumban.
Lanzas de fuego se arrojan,
que encendidas se entrecruzan

(180)

[Their deafening breathing
buzzes by with ire.
They throw fiery lances,
that all ablaze interlock]

Once again she resorts to metaphors of fire to represent a clash between destruction and triumph, death and life. After its flame attacks the living, the sinister flock ("la negra bandada" [the black flock]) retreats giving way to the birds of triumph—the peace and security that settles over the city when the sirens subside. The other poem, "Epístola moral a Sérpula" [Moral epistle to Sérpula], published in the primary journal of the Republican government, *Hora de España*, in June of 1937, conforms more closely to the prevailing nature of Chacel's poetry. Under the guise of imitation and beneath the classical, biblical, and religious allusions, lie a reflective mind and a sense of ethics which the poetic speaker does not hesitate to project in confident and moralistic pronouncements. In her introductory remarks to *Versos prohibidos*, Chacel confesses her personal preference for the "Epístola moral a Fabio" [Moral epistle to Fabio] by the seventeenth-century poet Andrés Fernández de Andrada and comments on the significance particularly of its last four lines for those, like her, who observed the confusion of events threatening the Republic without becoming physically involved in them. She maintains that reserve and reflection can constitute an optimistic attitude and an enriching dependency. Her defense of the contemplative posture in the face of turbulent political events also suggests a more generalized apology for her perennial disposition before life and art.

To a certain extent the tone and fundamental themes of her epistle are predetermined by her literary model, a lengthy poem that exposes the corruption, deceit, and transitoriness of the material world and extols the stoic acceptance of adversity, the willful withdrawal from public life, and the properties of the spirit. Although Chacel's poem remains faithful to the underlying intent of her literary forefather, notable variances surface. Living in an age less prone to stoic resignation and demonstrating a personal inclination to the erotic in its sense of life affirmation, Chacel does not exclude all possibility of hope from her solemn view of reality. Her poem calls for the return to the authenticity of life rather than ending with an entreaty to death as her model did. Alongside the themes of evil and time that Mercedes Acillona has already singled out,[39] life emerges as a central focus. Chacel defines life as a living intersection of both memory and hope, of past and future: "Esperanza y recuerdo, nudo vivo, / broche continuo, larva comedora / del anhelo entrañable sustentada" [Hope and memory, a living knot, / a continual brooch, a gluttonous larva / of sustained, intimate longing]. She ends her epistle with this stanza:

> Busca sólo en el centro de tu pecho
> ese lugar o nido preparado
> para mecer al sueño de la vida
> la dulce sien del hijo o del amante,
> ese lugar o abismo en que está escrito
> el sagrado secreto que escuchaste
> dentro del seno donde amaneciste.
>
> (49)

> [Look only into the center of your breast,
> that prepared place or nest,
> to rock the sweet temple
> of your child or your lover
> in the dream of life,
> that place or abyss where there lies written
> the sacred secret you heard
> inside the bosom from which you sprung.]

Her concluding image of inner peace regained as a return to the maternal bosom reshapes lines at the beginning of the poem in which mother's milk, called beloved liqueur and white tears, nurtures a bitter vision of truth.

Only in small ways such as this passing recourse to female iconography does Chacel come close to "stealing the language," in Alicia Suskin Ostriker's terms of adapting the images and myths perpetuated by male writers to a female-generated definition of reality. On the whole, however, she adopts, more than she adapts, canonical textual strategies. In her evocation of "those innocent days," of the edenic period predating the chaos, the dangers, and the evil of the present moment, Chacel comes close to incorporating emotional absence and autobiography into her poetry. Revelations of loss, anguish, and indignation seem to infuse an emotional charge into the poem; and the interjection "ay," uttered twice, would indicate a cry of pain. But a focus on abstract concepts, the stylizations of expression effected by biblical metaphors, and the attitude of the speaker deflect any direct outpourings of personal feeling.

The cerebral and erudite elements of Chacel's poetry set her apart from the other women poets of her generation, but she, like them, attempted to navigate, the best she could, around the barriers placed by her society to prevent the integration of women writers into mainstream culture. Through her works she established a presence not so much for gynocentric concerns

and imagery, as for the talents and tendencies of one particular woman—
herself. Despite her disavowal of feminine subjectivity, when she spoke
through her poetry, she was still a woman and, as such, the timbre of that
voice becomes significant. Like the other women writing poetry in the twenties and thirties, she dared to speak as a poet; but where they spoke their
heart, she spoke her mind. What distinguishes her voice from that of her
female contemporaries is that beyond the fact of its mere existence, hers is
a commanding, authoritative one. The timid, mournful voice of traditional
female poetry is replaced by an assertive female persona who usurps the
male monopoly on moral and intellectual superiority. "Epístola moral a
Sérpula" and Chacel's other epistles are not part of the private, intimate
letter-writing practice considered typical of female culture, but rather a
continuation of the male convention by which poets publicly air their moral
and literary notions in a style that approximates the informal candor and
civility of conversation. Availing herself again of a factor of disguise, Chacel
uses a familiar canonical framework to legitimize her serious, intellectual
concerns and her stance as moral arbiter. She lodges her exposition of the
devastation that rocks her world at the center of her missive to her friend,
calling attention to the harsh reality of collapse and ruin:

> Por terrestre marea arrebatados
> los peldaños que fueron gradas áureas
> derivan sobre el lomo de la furia.
> Mira sus restos, sus murientes chispas
> contra negros taludes estrellarse.
>
> (46)

> [The steps that had been golden tiers
> torn away by a terrestrial tide
> drift mounted on the back of fury.
> Look at its remains, at its dying sparks
> smash against black banks.]

But the indignation of the poetic speaker is subtly highlighted by her distancing herself from those who have strayed. By addressing them in the
second person plural, she implicitly sets herself on a higher moral plane:

> Ay de los que cabalgan atrevidos
> sobre los hombros de estas formas tiernas,
> ay de los que pusisteis vuestro peso
> sobre el plumón naciente de sus alas
> si no sabéis cuidar la excelsa rosa
> que deshoja sus horas una a una . . .
>
> (47)

[Alas for those brave ones who
ride on the shoulders of these tender forms,
alas for those of you who put your weight
on the new down of their wings
if you do not know how to care for the sublime rose
that strips off its hours one by one . . .]

As in her sonnets, this poem rests on a series of instructions that lend an imperious tone to the speaker's voice and disclose her authoritative stance.

Although Chacel's poetry deflects the disclosure of personal feelings and autobiographical detail, an examination of the sonnets of *A orilla de un pozo* unmasks telling aspects of her relationship with her art and the world around her. Her resistance to self-exposure compels her to look outside herself for the fibers of her poetry; she turns to the classics for its versification and allusions, the avant-garde for a number of its images, and to the lives of others for its content. Her recourse to opposing literary traditions reflects as much her confessed desire to conceal her secret love for classical forms as her strong, hidden need to gain access, through imitation, to the masculine circle of modernist writers. To enter the scene of public culture Chacel not only had to accept male-defined cultural forms, but she also had to dispute gender difference and the cultural marginalization of women. Chacel instinctively understood that if a woman broke the code of silence and sentimentality excluding women from cultural participation, she could speak with authority within the canon only if she adopted the patriarchal conception of a unified, undifferentiated literature. Nevertheless, given the conservatism of her society, her acceptance of male culture implied an important, partial transgression of gender-defined boundaries. The traditional and imitative aspects of her poems may suggest a creative posture of timidity, but this facade of reticence masks a self-asserting poetic personality that establishes its control on every level—on the level of reception of her finished products, upon the subjects she chooses to convert into textual reality, and in the structures and language she uses to fabricate her individual compositions. Inclined toward narrative rather than poetry and toward the intellectual more than the lyrical, Chacel was unable to sustain the poetic impulse or develop a distinguishing accent in her poetry, but the decisive, authoritative voice that characterizes her poems creates a strong female presence.

6
Carmen Conde and *Brocal*: Speaking from the Center

Carmen Conde, unlike her sister poets, did not slip into the void of literary oblivion after the Spanish civil war. On the contrary, she is the only Spanish woman poet of the twentieth century to enjoy persistent acclaim. She has been enthusiastically praised not only as an exceptional woman poet but generically as an extraordinary poet. Dámaso Alonso placed her among the top ranks of contemporary Spanish poetry, and Joaquín de Entrambasaguas goes further, affirming that she is the equal of Lope de Vega as a human being.[1] The most obvious manifestation of Conde's acceptance by the patriarchs of Spanish culture occurred in 1978 when she was honored as the first woman elected to the Royal Academy of Language.[2] Despite this official promotion to codifier of the national language, Carmen Conde's integration into the Spanish literary canon has remained only partial. An illustration of this point is contained in the conclusions of Howard Mancing, who, after surveying a hundred anthologies, found that, although Carmen Conde is the only Spanish woman poet of the twentieth century regularly anthologized, she must be listed under the heading "other poets": she appears in between twelve and twenty-three anthologies and has no single poem anthologized at least twelve times.[3]

This measure of marginalization makes Conde share one feature in the situation of Spanish women writers of the first half of the twentieth century. Her birth date of 1907 makes a consideration of her poetry particularly germane to the study of the poetry of Méndez, de la Torre, Champourcin, and Chacel; and the disposition and tonality of the poetry she wrote in the twenties reveals an additional kinship with them. Her privileged position relative to the reception of her work makes her a notable exception among women poets. For one thing, she stands out among the other women poets who began writing in the twenties as the only one cred-

ited with changing the course of writing by women. José Albi credits her
with opening new possibilities for women by displacing sentimentality with
"el impulso de una fuerza poética que nace de las zonas más claras y
profundas de la sinceridad" [a tendency toward a poetic impulse that rises
from the clearest and deepest regions of sincerity].[4] Susana March, herself
a poet, affirms Conde's influence on her own poetry and by implication on
all poetry by women after her.[5]

Despite her beginnings in the twenties, Conde is generally associated by
critics with the Generation of 1936 and with the postwar generations of
poets.[6] She was able to achieve recognition within Spanish literature of
these later periods because her themes, perspectives, and style were compatible with the prevalent literary timbre of her time. Fundamental to the
marked difference between the fate of her poetry and that of her female
counterparts of the twenties and thirties was the fact that she continued to
live and write in Spain after the civil war.[7] Both the subject matter and
disposition of her poetry were in concert with the mood of the poetry of
her male compatriots in Spain. She wrote of the horrors inflicted and
sacrifices exacted by war. Concha Méndez had alluded to the civil war in
her poetry before retreating into the shadowy confines of her inner world
as did Ernestina de Champourcin before withdrawing into her poetic mono-
logues to God, but Conde confronted the reality and implications of war
directly and extensively in collections such as *Mientras los hombres mueren* [While
men die] (1952), *En un mundo de fugitivos* [In a world of fugitives] (1960), and
En la tierra de nadie [In no man's land] (1960). Conde succeeded in capturing
the sense of collective grief that gripped the national psyche in the first
decades after the war and in articulating publicly the anger and despair felt
by her compatriots. Even though not herself a mother, she identified with
the Spanish women who had lost husbands and children in the war and
became a spokesperson for their losses. Assuming the role of the wailful
female mourner, Conde fulfilled the function of the *mater dolorosa* [grieving
mother], the female image essential to Christian iconography and sanctioned by the conservative ideology that shaped Spanish postwar society.
For the Spanish critic Emilio Miró, Conde represents universal womanhood, the "gran Madre universal" [the great universal mother], who cries
for her suffering son and "se desgarra por el hijo muerto" [goes to pieces
over her dead son].[8] This traditional depiction legitimizes her as a poet for
the Spanish public. Thus, with its intermingling of personal, religious, and
existential emotions and its almost mystic search for transcendence balanced with a sorrowful contemplation of human suffering, Conde's poetry
fits well, as Andrew P. Debicki suggests, with that of male poets of her
generation.[9]

Personal circumstances also set Conde apart from the other women poets who began writing in the twenties. Unlike them, she was actively in-

volved in the public sphere. Conde and her husband Antonio Oliver Belmás both became respected members of the academic community in postwar Spain.[10] She nonetheless shunned specific political involvement and disavowed the use of poetry as a social tool, telling an interviewer once, "No creo en la poesía que aliente a un hombre a empuñar un arma, aun creyendo que con ella va a hacer justicia" [I don't believe in poetry that inspires a man to take up arms, even if he believes he will do justice with them].[11] Nevertheless, the compassion she expressed in her poetry for war victims and the less fortunate gave her work an element of social consciousness lacking in the other women poets studied here. Although not a political militant like her contemporaries Dolores Ibarruri or Margarita Nelken, Conde did speak out on the issue of improving education. As early as age twenty, she wrote articles in the press of Cartagena on the importance of education, particularly for the disadvantaged. The reverses in her family's economic situation that forced her to go to work after graduation from high school and later to study for a teaching degree might have instilled early in her a sympathy for and a solidarity with the poor. Her early sense of social commitment would motivate her later to found, with her husband, the Universidad Popular de Cartagena.[12] While the other women studied here struggled to gain access for themselves to the cultural arena of the capital, Carmen Conde grappled, in the provinces, with the limited access of workers to higher education.

The solidarity that drove Conde to be a spokesperson for her country's grief and to champion educational causes may in part explain her sense of fellowship toward other women poets. Her open defense of women's literature makes her attitude toward her art fundamentally different from that of her female contemporaries. It also places the genesis of a concern in Spain for legitimizing poetry by women within the life span of a female poet born early in the century and whose birth as a writer dates from the twenties. Conde concerned herself with ensuring that women writers, particularly poets, be recognized. She studied their work, published criticism on them, and collected their poems in four anthologies.[13] Her presence in the Real Academia also gave her the opportunity to address sexism in language.[14] Just as Ernestina de Champourcin in 1929 identified a new generation of bold and enthusiastic women poets (Conde among them), Conde herself celebrated Spanish women poets' coming into their own after centuries of imitation of male models. She saw the twentieth century as "una nueva edad media, un pasillo de luz hacia mayor luz" [a new Middle Ages, a passageway from light to greater light] for women.[15]

Carmen Conde steadfastly believed that women achieve authenticity as poets only if they speak with their own voice from their own experience. In stark contrast to Rosa Chacel, who adamantly rejected gender difference as a force in writing, Conde embraced it as an important factor in the ex-

pression of self-identity. Conde firmly believed that the elaboration of poetry is based on gender difference. She clarified her assertion by explaining
that this difference is one of content more than style, of variations in experience not spirituality, of differing emotions not forms of expression: "La
Poesía . . . no tiene sexo . . . Pero . . . sí hay poesía llamemos discriminada:
poesía de mujer y poesía de hombre" [Poetry . . . doesn't have a sex . . . but
. . . there is a poetry we might call discriminative: female poetry and male
poetry].[16] In words that predate the tenets of younger feminists, she insisted
that when women write from their own experience, they enrich the common culture: "No se trata de hacer una obra estrictamente femenina, sino
de enriquecer el común acervo con las aportaciones que sólo yo en mi
cualidad de mujer poeta puedo ofrecer para iluminar una vasta zona que
permanecía en el misterio" [It is not a matter of making a work strictly
feminine, but of enriching the common patrimony with contributions that
only I in my capacity as woman poet can offer in order to illuminate a vast
region that remains a mystery].[17] According to Conde, what women contribute is primarily their inner maternal essence. Whether or not a woman
poet is literally a mother, she affirmed that female creativity rises from the
maternal.[18] While Conde's works resonate with strains that were developed
by later, more radical feminists, like Hélène Cixous and Luce Irigaray, her
insistence on the essential maternal nature of women's literature presented
no threat to the perpetuation of the notion of the eternal feminine underlying the Francoist ideology.

Conde's lack of direct confrontation with the values of her society nonetheless had an indirect subversive effect. Her strong desire to allow women
to express themselves freely according to their own experiences was an important indicator that the beginning of the changes in perspective in women's
poetry that Champourcin first observed in 1929 were slowly proceeding in
Spain. Although the feeble alliance among the women poets of the twenties and thirties prevented the formation of a true female generation of
poets, Conde's work as disseminator of their poetry and that of later women
poets made her the first promoter of a female legacy within Spanish literature. In addition, her substantial presence in postwar poetry enhanced the
significance of her poetry of the twenties and invited a consideration of the
bonds she shared with the other women of the time.

Like Chacel, Champourcin, de la Torre, and Méndez, Conde was a
female anomaly in her time. She wrote her first poems in her early teens
and was publishing in local dailies from age seventeen. Like Josefina de la
Torre, her talents were recognized and nurtured by the male shapers of
culture in her provincial home city. She was well-integrated into the cultural life of Cartagena, publishing in a variety of newspapers and journals
and receiving positive critical commentary.[19] In much the same way that
the other female poets of the twenties learned their literary lessons from

their male contemporaries—Ortega y Gasset, Lorca, Alberti, Salinas—
Conde found inspiration and guidance in Gabriel Miró and Juan Ramón
Jiménez.[20]

Conde also displayed in her poetry concerns common to the other female poets studied here. Her expressions of sadness over the stillbirth of
her child and her tribute to her mother connect her to the poetry of Concha Méndez; her preoccupations with time, death, and mortality establish
parallels with the later poetry of Josefina de la Torre; and the emphasis she
placed on love and its implications for transcendence along with her religious interests, especially her appreciation of the mystic poet San Juan de
la Cruz, links her poetry to that of Ernestina de Champourcin. Conde's
poetry grows somber with the passage of time: darkness penetrates the light,
pain and bitterness disturb her initial atmosphere of joy, and loneliness
shatters the comfort of fulfillment, but a pronounced vitality that Dámaso
Alonso calls "pasión" remains the key to all of Conde's poetry.[21] It is not
coincidental that her second book is titled, *Júbilos* [Jubilation]. The regenerative passion that drove her to write at an unrestrained pace after 1945
and to embrace life in all its intensity may well be a personality trait of
Conde's, as José Luis Castillo Puche contends,[22] but its presence in her early
work also corroborates the jubilant and assertive tenor that characterizes
the poetry written by other Spanish women poets in the twenties and thirties.

After 1945, ample proof of textual or thematic absence can be found in
Conde's poetry. She writes then of grief, suffering, and sadness, and she
inevitably admits darkness, immobility, and coldness into her poetic world;
but these later works extend beyond the parameters of the twenties and
thirties chosen for this study. Between 1938 and 1941 Conde did, however,
write four collections that, with their evidence of absence, loss, and pain,
anticipate her more meditative and melancholy poetry of the post-civil war
years and which, in their acute social consciousness, set her apart from the
other women poets in this book. The first, *Sostenido ensueño* [Sustained day-
dream], written in 1938, dwells on the dark horse of death, ire, loneliness,
and discouragement. *Mientras los hombres mueren*, dating from 1938 to 1939,
springs from the intense pain and despair that the civil war's destruction
provoked in the poet. In it she mourns all the men victimized by the war
and grieves for the suffering mothers and children. Human agony is echoed in the violence befalling the earth, graphically described as burnt,
cracked, pierced, and bloodied. *El arcángel* [The archangel], from 1939,
poetizes the speaker's mystical longing for a fulfilling other, be he an idealized human lover or the incarnation of religious faith. Gone are the violent
images of the previous collections, but anticipation and unrealized dreams
still suggest absence. The last of these collections, *Mío* [Mine], composed in
1942, focuses on the solidarity and serenity of the earth and of El Escorial,

Philip II's monastery near Madrid. Attesting to the possibility of survival beyond the destruction of war, these poems correspond to the direction taken by Spanish poetry in the 1940s.

Not only are these four collections removed in theme and timbre from the poetry of the twenties, they remained unknown to the public until 1952, when *Mientras los hombres mueren* was published, and 1967, when all four were incorporated in Conde's *Obra poética* [Poetic works]. In addition, except for a small number of the compositions, these collections must be classified as prose, prose poetry to be sure, but nonetheless prose. Conde wrote another book before 1940: *Júbilos*. By virtue of its date of publication (1934) and the attitudes evinced in it, *Júbilos*, unlike the books she wrote in reaction to the civil war, would seem to belong to poetic modes of the twenties and thirties; but the length of its compositions and their anecdotal quality align it more with prose than poetry. This leaves *Brocal* [Well curb] (1929) as the only book Conde wrote before 1940 that can justifiably be considered consistently poetic.

Although a series of forty-nine brief prose vignettes and three longer prose poems, *Brocal* incorporates definite poetic qualities: condensation of expression, sensorial and chromatic effects, and the syntactical and semantic mechanisms of poetry.[23] *Brocal* projects the same youthful verve that underlies a book like *Canciones de mar y tierra* by Concha Méndez, *Verso y estampa* by Josefina de la Torre, or *Ahora* by Ernestina de Champourcin. Even though Conde later wrote *Mujer sin Edén* [Woman without Eden], *Brocal* represents that earlier stage in which the young poetic persona still dwells in an Eden of innocence and bliss. Desire for the female speaker is still only expectation and promise. Before her fall into experience, the persona still lives in paradisiacal harmony with the natural world, unaware of the pain and tragedies of life. She confidently locates herself at the center of her sheltered universe and joyfully affirms her own existence as well as celebrating the sensuous beauty of nature. She creates an environment of cohesion, presence, and wholeness through the acts of centering, anchoring, and fusing.

In *Brocal* Carmen Conde creates a strong female presence by the prominence she gives her speaking subject. Both the position from which the subject speaks and what she says connote presence, power, and plenitude. Women have traditionally been represented in literature as objects: objects of male desire, and objects of contemplation appropriated by and spoken to by the male subject. As Antónia Cabanilles writes, for many centuries woman *"ha sido hablada"* [has been spoken].[24] She has been alluded to but has, herself, for the most part, remained silent. When she does speak, she initially parrots masculine discourse, and even when inverting male models, she inevitably employs the dominant language and implicitly encodes its symbols. Conde herself recognized that when the woman poet began writing, her voice was totally mimetic and false: "impostaba su voz en tono ajeno, y por ajeno, falso" [she fraudulently put her voice in someone else's tone, and because it was someone else's, it was false].[25] Deferential, peripheral, or ancillary in its underlying disposition, the female voice must assert itself and actively seek self-definition if it is to begin to dislodge itself from canonical representations of women. In *Brocal*, the poetic speaker raises her voice conspicuously from the outset and articulates her own feelings of wonder. The first word she utters is "yo" [I]. From this first note of self-assertion, the poetic persona refers to herself consistently with confidence and verve.

Assuming the role of subject of her poetic universe, *Brocal*'s speaker significantly locates herself at the center of her world; she is the axis, the crossroad, and the center of the cosmos. The four cardinal points intersect at the very spot the female protagonist occupies: "Todas las tardes se sentaba en una de las cuatro esquinas" (29) [Every afternoon he sat down on one of the four corners]. This sense of convergence is reinforced by additional references to street corners and repeated allusions to weather vanes. From her vantage point, at the center of the natural world, the poetic persona acquires godlike powers that enable her to throw the cosmic light switch in the morning: "Del faro rojo, al faro verde. Del faro verde, al faro rojo. / ¡He abierto la madrugada, caminando de faro a faro!" (30) [From the red beacon, to the green beacon. From the green beacon, to the red beacon. / I have opened the dawn, walking from beacon to beacon!]. The lexical repetitions and the chiasmus in the first line impart a rhythmic motion into a verbless statement and create an image of sweeping extension into the distance. From her anchored position at the center of creation, the speaker reaches out in all directions, counteracting any impression of enclosure and stasis that the poet generates by placing her poetic protagonist in a stationary position and frequently referring to windows, terraces, and geometric shapes.

In her formation of an edenic existence for her young poetic persona, Carmen Conde creates beautiful and protective spaces conducive to peace and wholeness. In the two lines just quoted, the distant lights open the speaker's line of vision but keep her within the bounds of two lighthouses. Also, the first line establishes a material presence devoid of temporal dimension. This pattern of a stage set with articles that occupy space before any human figure does is reiterated throughout the book:

> Una esquina, al viento de los molinos que andan. Otra, al campo que tenía un horizonte rosa y sol. Las otras dos esquinas, atadas a los árboles de las sendas como dos perros blancos . . . (29)

> [One corner toward the wind of the moving windmills. Another one to-

ward the countryside with its pink horizon and sun. The other two corners, tied to the trees along the road, like two white dogs . . .]

Sur. A las tres letritas azules pintadas ondulando en los mapas dirigieron las veletas su persistente latido. (30)

[South. The weather vanes aimed their persistent beating toward the three little blue painted letters waving in the maps.]

In another poem, the sun and God, in their juxtaposition and syntactical inversion, implicitly suggest a close analogy between themselves, and together they form an immobile frame that cradles human action within a neutral embrace:

Sol, Dios.
Al mar, con brisas de gaviotas inmóviles, llevaremos esta alegría.
Dios, sol.

(36)

[Sun, God.
We will take this happiness to the sea with its motionless seagull breezes.
God, sun.]

The human activity that takes place between the first and last lines is minimal and nearly imperceptible. Borne on "the breezes of motionless gulls," the human lovers seem carried off on angels' wings more than by any means of transport of this world. Although this movement is unreal and contained within the mirrored images of the sun and God, standing over the lovers like watchful protectors, the emotion portrayed is that of happiness. Enclosure easily signifies the deprivation of freedom and acquires a particularly problematic character when applied to women, but in *Brocal* enclosed space implies the perfection of the circle and the happy isolation of two lovers from reality. From their position at the border ("orilla") of real life, emptiness and isolation represent a state of liberating bliss for the lovers.

Ya no hay casas en la ribera. Sólo quedó esa, donde tú y yo juntamos las sienes.
No están los arbolillos de la cuneta y el agua resbala, sin ellos, como una veta de luna caída del cuarto menguante.
¡Qué frescura tan dulce en esta marcha de todo!
¡Qué gran fragancia en esta soledad sellada!

(39)

[There are no longer any houses on the bank. The only one left is the one
    where you and I joined our temples.
The trees are not in the ditch, and the water trickles down, without them,
    like a streak of moon fallen from its last quarter.
What a sweet coolness in this passing of everything!
What a grand fragrance in this sealed solitude!]

For all the indications in *Brocal* of extension to one direction or another
and of the angular enclosure of houses and street corners, the prevailing
configuration is that of the circle. Within the specific context of Conde's
earliest lyric production, the circle serves primarily to convey the sense of
eternity and plenitude that engulfs the speaker. In the composition beginning "Sol, Dios," the circular structure of the poem itself underscores the
self-containment of the two lovers. In two poems the perpetual revolutions
of the mill suggest divinity: in one they evoke a beatific vision with a remi-
niscence of Dante's rose, and in the other, circularity empowers the self:
"Gira, molino! / Yo soy tu cielo" (36) [Twirl, windmill! / I am your sky].
    In the intervening space between woman and God, the world takes on
attributes of roundness ("Las mañanas, redondas y luminosas" [The round
and luminous mornings]) and circularity:

Formada estoy por molinos, balsas, torres, palomas, rosas . . .
En la rotación, lo primero se junta a lo último. Superposiciones simples. De
    la terraza a la luna, ¡cuántos kilómetros de estrellas!

(40)

[I am formed by windmills, rafts, towers, doves, roses . . .
In the rotation, first is joined to last. Simple superimpositions. From the ter-
    race to the moon, what a lot of kilometers of stars!]

In this poem, appropriately titled "Círculo máximo" [Greatest circle], the
natural world surrounding the speaker takes on the form of a circle, with
the beginning and the end joined together, and there is evidence only of
serene containment. In his examination of "felicitous space," Gaston
Bachelard concludes that being is round and that the round being propa-
gates its roundness, together with the calm of all roundness. He writes that,
when a thing becomes isolated, it becomes round and assumes a figure of
being that is concentrated on itself.[26] This inner cohesion gives the speaking subject in *Brocal* a sense of self that colors the way she views the other,
be it the human lover or the natural order, and that corroborates the feeling
of wholeness that permeates the entire book. Beyond the implications of
physical repose and emotional calm to which Bachelard refers, circularity
symbolizes spiritual salvation or bliss. The very title of the collection fore-
casts the significance that circularity and centering have in the ensuing po-

ems. The symbolism of the well combines the notion of sublime spiritual aspirations, of the "silver cord" that attaches the human being to the function of the Center with the attributes of things feminine.[27] The female speaker in *Brocal* looks from the earthly center, at the edge of the well, the "brocal," not into the waters of the well but out to the plenitude of existence and the unity of the universe. But as if in a mirrored image of the well curb, cosmic wonders are circumscribed within the perfection of a circle: "Mi corazón irguió sus lirios y detuvo a los vientos que venían en grandes barcas. Quedó un aro fresco flotando en el cielo" (32) [My heart raised its lilies and stopped the winds that were coming in big boats. A cool ring was left floating in the sky].

These poems are hymns of joy. "Alegría" [Happiness], as already seen, is the emotion with which God and the sun embrace the lovers. Church bells resonate throughout the poems, freeing themselves from the confinement of the afternoon ("De la cándida tarde se desprendieron las campanas" 30 [Bells were loosened from the innocent afternoon]) and then spilling over across the countryside ("Se derramaron las campanas por el campo" 34 [Bells spilled over the fields]). They reverberate, in the poem titled simply with the number "4," in thundering strokes of exaltation: "¡Qué júbilo el de la Torre, toda volada en giros locos, en aires dispersos, en palomas desbandadas" (43) [What jubilation of the Tower, flying in wild gyrations, in scattered winds, in freed doves]. This poem commemorates a significant moment in the poet's life, but any hint of the anecdotal has been absorbed in the textualization of the autobiographical through what Rosario Hiriart calls "una adecuada manipulación artística" [an appropriate artistic manipulation].[28] The book springs from the poet's love for Antonio Oliver, but what is transcribed in the book are emotions and sensations, not narrative details.[29]

Love in *Brocal* emerges as a process of tender reciprocity that promises a sublime union but does not yet deprive the female speaker of her own individual identity. The book opens with her surrender to the beloved:

> Yo no te pregunto adónde me llevas.
> Ni por qué.
> Ni para qué.
> ¿Tú quieres caminar?, pues yo te sigo.
>
>   (29)

> [I am not asking where you are taking me.
> Nor for what reason.
> Nor for what purpose.
> You want to go? Well, I will follow you.]

She unselfishly offers him the gifts of nature and her very being, itself but a variant of nature:

> El agua que correrá en tus ríos, seré yo.
> El alba que abrirá las claraboyas de tu día, seré yo.
>
> (34)

> [I will be the water that flows in your rivers.
> I will be the dawn that opens the skylights of your day.]

Her contribution is that of water and light, of nurturing and guidance, of both the earthly and celestial forces that sustain human existence. She stands poised before the lover more with expectant ardor than in passive submission. She calmly asks, "¿Me dejarás que descorra tus miradas?" (35) [Will you let me open up your gazes?]. The beloved, for his part, provides strength and protection, encircling her with his being: "Alrededor de mí, tú" (40) [Around me, you]. In their idyllic isolation at the "shore" of quotidian reality, the lovers revolve around each other. Together they are swept off, converging with one another in a sublime union with the cosmos:

> Fluye mi camino al tuyo, como un arroyo a un pino.
> El cielo, que sostiene mi agua, es el mismo que tú has izado.
> Nos reclinaremos juntos, cuando los vientos lluevan desde Dios.
>
> (35)

> [My road flows toward yours, like a stream toward a pine tree.
> The sky, which sustains my waters is the same one that you have raised.
> We will lie down together, when the winds rain down from God.]

The future tense of the verb "reclinar" in this poem and the frequent use of the future throughout the collection point to a consummation of love that is imminent, yet unrealized, for these poems textualize the awakening to love before the fall into experience and the intrusion of anguish into the realm of ecstasy. Love is a constant in Conde's poetry. Her display of eroticism and mystic surrender becomes more pronounced, but the sensuality of her poetic world continues to associate love, nature, and God; and her mysticism, similar to that of her contemporary Ernestina de Champourcin, coincides with a desire directed toward a human union of bodies rather than a true mystic fusion of the soul with God. *Brocal* represents a prelude to the vision that evolves in the rest of Conde's poetic production. As Hiriart writes, "Los cantos de este poemario no hablan de la unidad última a través del proceso místico o la vivencia erótica, se trata no del término sino de su principio" [The songs of this book of poems do not speak of the last union through the mystical process or the erotic experience, it is not about the end but about the beginning.].[30]

The female speaker in these poems is still a discrete being, not attached to the other and unencumbered by the weight of experience. She lives an edenic existence of freedom, of freedom not won by dint of a conscious struggle against her environment but enjoyed as an automatic consequence of her location at the center of a serene natural world. This element of autonomy, freedom, and self-containment links these poems of Conde to the early works of other Spanish women poets writing in the twenties. Like them, she articulates a celebration of the self, of its vitality and integrality. The poetic speaker secures her presence by declaring her desire with an uninhibited "I want":

> Quiero despertarme en el hombre de la noche
>
> (35)
>
> [I want to wake up in the man of the night]
>
> Por el agua alta, yo quiero ir descalza.
>
> (35)
>
> [I want to go barefoot through high water.]
>
> Quiero pasar entre la tarde y tus ojos.
>
> (37)
>
> [I want to pass through the afternoon and your eyes]

or by establishing her identity in simple equations between the first person pronoun, usually with the verb "to be," and a self-defining complement:

> ¡Yo seré de viento, de llama, de agua!
>
> (31)
>
> [I will be made out of wind, of flame, of water!]
>
> Yo soy tu cielo.
>
> (36)
>
> [I am your sky.]
>
> Yo soy más fuerte que tú
>
> (36)
>
> [I am stronger than you]

Yo era tan ágil como la ventolina

(38)

[I was as agile as a light wind]

She confidently defines herself as delicate, lissome, and joyous:

Yo, tan delgada como un horizonte, voy por este camino. Cantando. ¡Al
   viento mis cabellos ondulados, mis cabellos de mapa!
Llevo en las manos una rosa blanca llena de rocío.
Soy esbelta recóndita. Para llegar a mí hay que saltar cinco ríos y tres álamos.

(33)

[As thin as a horizon, I go along this road. Singing. My wavy hair, my map
   hair in the wind!
I carry a white rose wet with dew in my hands.
I am slim, hidden. To reach me you have to leap five rivers and three pop-
   lars]

These exhilarated assertions of the poetic ego are what release the passionate impulse that propelled all of Conde's poetry and which Emilio Miró
summarizes in this manner: "El *yo* de la escritora, brotando del paisaje, de
una realidad metaforizada en vuelo de fantasía y literatura, lo llena todo, lo
inunda en su lírico, arrebatado subjetivisimo. Pasión no sólo en el amor, en
las cosas, ante ellas y por ellas" [The writer's *I*, springing forth from the
landscape, from a metaphorized reality in a flight of fantasy and literature,
fills everything, drowns everything in her lyric, impetuous subjectivism. A
passion not only for love, for things, in their presence and through them]. [31]
   The female speaker characterizes herself as graceful, diaphanous, and
joyful, particularly in her equation between herself and the wind ("No, ¡no
era el viento! / Era Yo" 36 [No, it was not the wind! / It was I]). In her
brief comment on *Brocal*, Candelas Newton points out that because the
wind blowing through hair traditionally symbolizes vitality and joy of living, Conde's comparisons with the wind portray the participation of the
female figure in it creative powers.[32] The associations between the wind
and feminine grace recall creations like a Botticelli painting. Conde develops further the hint of elusiveness suggested in the word "recóndita" [hid-
den] of the lines cited above to a greater extent in her longer poem, "Círculo
máximo." The speaker locates herself "away from every thing" and defines
herself as innocently unaware of the contours of love: "Ni mi enteré del
color que tomó el cielo cuando cantabas" [I wasn't aware of the color the
sky turned when you were singing]. She is at first an angelic presence, immobile yet unapproachable: "Voy y vengo. Iré y vendré / Soy la pasajera
inmóvil de tus ríos" (40) [I come and go. I will come and go. I am a motion-

less passenger of your rivers]. But she soon acquires the solidity of "molinos, balsas, torres, palomas, rosas" [windmills, rafts, towers, doves, roses] to become a penetrating light that invades the beloved's inner landscapes assuming the corporal presence of "frente" [brow] and "hombros" [shoulders] only to evaporate into the luminous splendor of the morning sun:

> Mi luz recorre todo tu paisaje interior.
> Me veo en todo tú hecha mil *yos* chiquititas; yo, sólo perfil. Yo, sólo frente.
>   Yo, sólo hombros.
> Invado las galerías de tu silencio, descorro tus ventanas y sonrío . . .
> ¡Ríe tú, que mi sonrisa es toda la mañana descalza!
>
> (41)

> [My light goes through your interior landscape.
> In everything I see you made into a thousand little I's; I, only profile. I,
>   only brow. I, only shoulders.
> I invade the galleries of your silence, I open your windows and smile . . .
> Laugh, for my smile is the barefoot morning through and through!]

When not identifying herself as the wind, the female speaker defines herself as water. As she does in her rendition of wind in *Brocal*, Conde exploits that portion of the symbolization that can be associated with vitality and plenitude. She confers on water neither the fluid maternal values that Cixous exalts nor does she give water the quality of regenerative annihilation that underlies religious symbolism of baptism. In the early Conde, as Ostriker found in the modern American women poets, "water comes to mean security instead of dread."[33] Water as a metaphor in *Brocal* incarnates the undefined vital life force the female speaker feels flowing within her and conveys the sense of harmonious union she shares with nature. The moon, a proverbial feminine symbol, reaches down to earthly pools of water: "Así que la luna se baña en estas piscinas aéreas" (29) [As soon as the moon bathes itself in these elevated pools], and the human female asserts her erotic impulse in terms of water: "el agua que correrá en tus ríos, seré yo." The water with which she identifies is spiritualized and sublimated in "agua alta" [high water]. This young and inexperienced poetic persona does not feel herself earthbound. When she proclaims her self-affirming identification with the basic elements, she significantly excludes the earth ("Yo seré de viento, de llama, de agua," 31). She confidently declares herself to be a buoyant essence not yet confined within the stationary, inert earth.

This affirmation of spiritual freedom also explains Conde's reliance on images of light in *Brocal*. The rest of her poetic creation was a constant play of light and darkness. She published books with the titles *Sea la luz* [Let there be light] and *Iluminada tierra* [Illuminated earth], but also others called *En la tierra de nadie* [In no man's land] and *Su voz le doy a la noche* [I give the night its voice]. The light in her later works became a purifying element that frees the soul from anguish and material confines. It became, as Emilio Miró points out, the liberating light in the long, dark night reminiscent of the mystic liberation of San Juan de la Cruz as well as of the spiritual purification of Juan Ramón Jiménez.[34] In *Brocal,* light is still a physical phenomenon producing sensuous pleasure and confirming the corporeal presence of the speaker. Conde explained in an interview with Marie-Lise Gazarian Gautier her belief in the ancillary function of light in relation to the tangible substances: "If it weren't for the things in the world, light would not exist. Light has to have a reason to illuminate things. Without trees, or rivers, or sky, one cannot find light."[35] The landscapes she describes are bathed in light—in moonlight, blazing sunsets, and luminous dawns. The female speaker not only stands at the center of this luminescence, she joyfully celebrates her identification with light and its generative powers. A splendid display of fantasy makes her images incorporate her emotional state irrationally in the manner of the "visiones" that Carlos Bousoño defines.[36] The poetic speaker describes herself in cosmic terms of light: "Llevo luceros, luceros en la mano derecha. ¡Y llevo estrellas, estrellas, en la mano izquierda!" (29) [I carry morning stars, morning stars in my right hand. And I carry evening stars, evening stars, in my left hand!]. She likens herself to celestial light ("aquella luz mía que era cual otra luz del cielo" [that light of mine that was like another light of the sky]) and specifically to the nascent light of dawn ("El alba que abrirá las claraboyas de tu día, seré yo"). This identification with the morning reinforces the sense of awakening running through other images of the collection. Budding self-awareness brings with it the discovery of one's inner power. Thus the speaker can emphatically assert her control over light: "He abierto la madrugada."

The image of the poetic speaker reaching up and holding stars in her hands as well as the insistence in *Brocal* on verbs of motion such as "caminar," "ir," and "volar" [walk, go, fly] create a sense of broad movements. But just as the poet eschews the suggestion of enclosure in her configuration of space, in her use of kinetic imagery, she abstains from implying limitation. More than a projection of a desire to escape, the patterns of motion in *Brocal* translate feelings of transcendence and plenitude. Despite occasional allusions to walking and a number of metaphorical references to the self as a road or a river, the vertical predominates over the horizontal, making ascension prevail over advancement through space. Within the sheltered confines of her blissful state of young love and natural beauty, the protagonist of the poems of *Brocal* rises above the terrestrial plane, fixing her vision upward and feeling herself lifted to lofty heights. Most of the images in the book, whether natural phenomena (moon, stars, sky, wind) or man-made objects (roof, weather vane, bells, window, balcony), are situated high above the ground level. Even the human figures that traverse this poetic field acquire a decided verticality that stretches them upward. Young girls carrying water jugs become caryatid-like figures supporting the sky: "las muchachas de la huerta camino de la fuente . . . / La campana del cántaro, a la cabeza. Los brazos, sujetando el cielo" (31) [the girls from the vegetable fields on the way to the fountain . . . / The water jugs on their heads. Their arms holding up the sky]. Not only does the speaking subject of *Brocal* elevate her point of vision, but in her refusal to be earth-bound, she herself is swept upward in a movement suggestive of both physical and spiritual transcendence: "Balsa, ventana del panorama, ¡qué gran viaje hago a las estrellas cuando me asomo a ti, con esta altura de sienes volcada en tu agua honda!" (34) [Raft, panorama window, what a grand trip to the stars I make, when I look through you, from this height of temples emptied into your deep water!].

The last lines quoted suggest that in Conde's early poetry transcendence does not mean disconnection from the palpable world of natural phenomena as much as it reflects harmony and union with the cosmos. This interconnection with and reciprocity between woman and nature are the primary determinants of the impression of cohesion, presence, and wholeness that emerges from a reading of *Brocal*. Traditional cultural associations of women with nature confine them ontologically to organic matter and socially to the generative and nurturing sphere of children, home, and garden. *Brocal* predates Conde's adoption of the maternal as the natural gender-specific identification of woman and her later integration into the national culture. In *Brocal*, the protagonist of her created world still resides in the adolescent stage of female development, in the "green world" that Annis Pratt describes as a place in which a young woman enjoys a sense of oneness with the cosmos to one side of civilization. This early mystical experience provides the young woman with a sense of authentic selfhood and becomes a "kind of talisman that enables her to make her way through the alienations of male society."[37] In this initial moment in her evolution, Conde's poetic persona thrives within the blissful refuge of the self, away from society. It is not until later in Conde's development that nature becomes a vehicle for solidarity with the other and others, and an expression of her driving impulse to participate in life. According to Moraima de Semprún Donahue, when Conde wrote of nature, she wanted to become a part of the world that surrounded her in order to be eternally reborn in the landscape and, in this way, to be a witness of all humanity.[38]

The natural world acquired stronger referential values later, while in *Brocal*, despite the Mediterranean allusions, nature constitutes essentially a generic abstraction, an objective correlative of the edenic state the poetic persona enjoys. The feelings that the landscapes in *Brocal* arouse in the reader are those of freedom, joy, and plenitude. The scenes are expansive, resplendent, and charged with sensuous delights. They open before the reader in a vibrant display of light and sound:

De la cándida tarde se desprendieron las campanas . . .
¡Vuelo ancho de las ventanas con luna! ¡Cómo se entraba
a la noche honda del verano, todo quemado
  en ponientes de fragua!

(30)

[The bells were loosened from the innocent afternoons . . .
Wide flight of windows with moonlight. How one entered the deep night
  of summer, all burned in forge-like sunsets!]

The external ingredients result in a sensory experience that immediately sparks a sense of joy. Church bells reverberate throughout the sweeping expanse of a blazing sunset. The parallels between external and internal reality are strengthened by the bisemic qualities in the poem. The adjective "cándida," with its connotations of whiteness and purity, links the luminous scene to the unspoiled innocence of the poetic protagonist of the book. Likewise, the exclamations, while capturing visual splendor, also reflect human emotion. Conde uses church bells as a more elaborate objective correlative for the joyful awakening to love in the last poem of the collection, "4." Divided into seven sections, the poem narrates the successive climb by four men to the top of a bell tower and the repeated appearance of a variety of bells. Rising above a bountiful field of fruit-laden trees, the bell tower stands as the formula for the plenitude resonating through the entire collection. Although anecdotally textualizing the occasion of the poet's first kiss from her future husband, within the reality of the text the bells continue to connote a generalized celebration of bliss.

Conde believed that reality exists only when experienced. Just as light, for her, depended on the presence of objects, so the natural world is animated by the life imparted to it by the human subject. Conde's conviction echoed the philosophy of George Berkeley, for whom material objects only existed through being perceived.[39] The assumption of the position of percipient is particularly significant in the case of the female subject because she becomes the one whose gaze determines reality rather than being the object of the gaze of another, as her role has traditionally been. Conde identified woman not with the object perceived, but with divine perception. Rather than a product of nature or an object of God's contemplation, her female speaker emulates the Creator. Woman's exuberant presence is duplicated in the world surrounding her through Conde's frequent recourse to personification. She re-created the world in her own image. Inanimate objects became both animate and animated; terraces are likened to doves and, like stars, move far across the horizon. Mills are compared to roses, bells can kiss, and weather vanes have heartbeats. The elements of nature assume human qualities, becoming incarnations of human types; the moon is a bather and a boatman, the rain a slender maid, and a star a well-groomed, smiling, childlike figure. Conde saw no reason to presume that only humans have souls: "No vamos a admitir que solamente las personas, es decir, los seres humanos pensantes, tenemos almas. Hay muchas cosas también que, si no tienen un alma propia, la adquieren" [We are not going to accept that only people, that is, we thinking human beings, have souls. There are many things as well that, if they don't have their own soul, acquire one.]. [40]

As the counterpart to the humanizing process that nature undergoes, the human speaker defines herself in terms of nature. The elements of nature constitute the symbolic conduits for the verbal expression of the life force and of her youthful sense of self. In Dámaso Alonso's words, in Conde's poetry all forms of the world "se confunden, se trasmutan, se equivalen" [are merged, are transformed into one another, are made equivalent] but without negating human vitality.[41] She is water and wind, the lofty palm tree and the light in the sky. She is both a driving life-force, symbolized in the image of the river, and the luminous essence of dawn. The tree can be a stable comforting presence for the lover ("soy aquella palmera de tu huerto" 38 [I am that palm tree in your garden]) or a metaphor for erotic desire ("¡Estaba mi corazón en la lluvia, como una palma roja!" 38 [My heart was in the rain like a red palm tree!]). Destined to gain nuances of meaning in the section devoted to it in *Júbilos*, the wind in *Brocal* represents the gusts of sensuality that envelop her body and with which she compares herself ("¡Yo estaba en los álamos, como el viento, de la primavera!" 37 [I was in the poplars, like the wind, of Spring!]).[42] The poetic speaker absorbs the elements of nature, becoming indistinguishable from them. Calling the female body in *Brocal* resonating box, Newton writes: "La piel es el brocal o boca por donde el exterior es internalizado en la redondez del vientre femenino" [Skin is the well curb or mouth through which the exterior is internalized into to the roundness of the female belly].[43] The relationship between woman and nature is an intimate one that serves the poetic speaker as a key means of self-definition and of identity with God and his creation.

Neither a mere derivative of organic forces nor an inert natural substance, the female persona in *Brocal* is nature's double and co-creator. In her study of Conde's definition of herself as a creator in the prose poem "Autobiografía" [Autobiography], from *Sostenido ensueño*, Susana Cabello interprets Conde's identification with the generative powers of nature, specifically, the tree, as a manifestation of the archetype of the eternal feminine, of the Great Mother who bringing forth life from herself, is the mother of all vegetation. Cabello sees the tree/poet as uniting the chthonic values of instinct with the uranic values of logos. The poet, she says, searches through her roots, her instinctual forces, for greater understanding that can then be expressed in her poem.[44] What interests me is not the archetypal patterns evinced in the poet's relation with nature, but the precise psychological configuration of the poetic speaker and its implied advantage for the evolution of a young poet. The interconnection with nature manifested in *Brocal* is predicated on strength. By assuming an assertive position at the center of nature, the poetic speaker avoids the diffuseness that can be inferred from traditional associations made between women and nature. A consciousness of the self collapses the frequent identity of woman in masculine poetry with the absent other, and an infusion of sensual materiality into her affirmations subverts the negative implications for women of the elusive female presence characteristic of connections between women and nature in male poets.[45] The aspects of nature that the female protagonist of *Brocal* embodies are not its nurturing teluric nor its evaporative ethereal qualities, but rather its implications of existential vibrancy and sublimated sensuality.

The female speaker assumes cosmic features because she is part of the harmonious and exhilarating commingling of the natural and human orders that translates the pivotal sense of plenitude the poet attempts to textualize in *Brocal*. The human subject ascends skyward, acquiring cosmic dimensions. In her interaction with the stars, she becomes the possessor of light; and it, in turn, becomes a metonymn for her, with the result being the emergence of a transcendent female of fantastic proportions. In a correlative reversal of normal levels, aerial elements descend to earth and earthbound features rise in a reciprocal interchange of essence. The firmament reaches down, the night touching roof tops and the moon bathing in pools of water: "La noche estaba quieta, prendida a las veletas de las torres" (31) [The night was still, fastened to the weather vanes of the towers] and "Así que la luna se baña en estas piscinas aéreas" (29) [As soon as the moon bathes in these elevated pools]. Nature comes in contact with material substances:

> Por horizonte—¡aún!—, la ventana del puerto:
> Al fondo, en los cristales altos, el mar. En los cristales bajos, el mar.
>
> (31)

> [Along the horizon—still!—, the window of the port:
> In the background, in the high windows, the sea. In the low
>   windows, the sea.]

The different spheres of nature are mingled as, for instance, "almonds of the sea" and "blue branches" of the sky. The thoroughness with which the elements of nature assimilate to one another allows for the complete reversal of basic essences; in the subjective reality of *Brocal*, water is high and the sky is deep. The interconnection among the elements of nature and between them and the human speaker is both constant and multiple.

In one short poem, a chain of metaphors connects light to inanimate objects ("esquinas" [corners]), liquid substance ("lluvia" [rain]) and organic matter ("hojas" [leaves], "espigas" [spikes]):

> Me hice alta, alta . . . Caían en hojas de lluvia, diminutas esquinas de soles. Crecieron hacia abajo las espigas de luz de la tormenta, y de mi corazón fluyeron las cándidas barcas del amanecer. (34)

> [I became tall, tall . . . Diminutive corners of suns fell in leaves of rain. The spikes of light of the storm grew downward, and the white ships of dawn flowed from my heart.]

The speaker envelops the scene of sunlit rain. At the outset, before the light descends, she establishes her presence as an ascendant being, and at the end of the poem, she identifies herself in terms of water and light. The reciprocal fluid interchange of essences along with the counterpoint between upward and downward directions creates a permeating sense of unity and wholeness on a universal scale.

On the one hand, the ascension of the female persona sublimates human passion. On the other, the reification of intangible cosmic features anchors them in the materiality of the human world while the personification of the organic world infuses into the nonhuman an intimate kinship with the speaker. The descent of nature to a human level never signifies decline or diminishment; on the contrary, the coalescence of the natural and the human magnifies the grandeur of the former and sublimates the existence of the later. Furthermore, the contacts between the heavens and earth take place on the elevated plane of rooftops or from the grand vantage point of an expansive bird's eye perspective. The speaker is exhilarated by her interconnection with the world around her as her frequent use of exclamations and confident recourse to the imperative attest. Nonetheless, she never appears overwhelmed by the wondrous state of plenitude in which she is absorbed. She maintains a close, familiar rapport with the generic ingredients of nature. Creatures, both animal and human, emerged in Conde's next collection, but in *Brocal* the poetic protagonist lives in a pristine environment inhabited only by herself and her silent interlocutor. With open and almost childlike delight at the spectacle of felicitous union among all creation, the young speaker enjoys a relationship of warm congeniality with nature. She imagines almond branches caressing her temples and sky tiptoeing across her heart. These acts of endearment are enhanced by her frequent diminutives ("piedrecillas," "lavadito," "caminito," "borrequitos" [little stones, a quick wash, little roads, little burros]). Reciprocity engenders tender affection and blissful union in *Brocal*.

The anchoring of intangible cosmic phenomena in the precincts of concrete, human existence contributes to the formation of a poetic reality rich in sensorial sensations and sensual suggestions. Not only is the incorporeal rendered palpable through Conde's poetic vision, but material substances themselves stand as engaging objects of her ebullient gaze. The delights of the world stimulate the human viewer, infusing her with enthusiasm and passion and confirming her properties as a vital essence.

A strong sense of materiality and an interchange between nature and a person have been related by feminist theorists to a characteristically female way of thinking. Susan Griffin, for example, has explored women's feelings of connection to nature in contrast to the detachment and antagonism toward nature manifested in patriarchal thought. Equating nature and women, men have traditionally defined both as seductive, treacherous, and destructive. Griffin argues that once women separate themselves from the grasp of this view, they emerge from the darkness of night into an alternate vision of both themselves and nature.[46] From the female perspective, nature proves to be a fluid, pulsating presence, rather than a controlled object, and a life-sustaining energy, rather than a vehicle of death. In Carmen Conde, contact with nature does not signify the threat of a fall into the dark, mysterious abyss of the irrational but the potential for an advancement toward a bright horizon of emotional intensity. By substituting the negative connotations of the nature/woman equation of patriarchal thought with life-affirming possibilities, Conde resolves the equation's self-annihilating implication for women and she breaks the impasse of its denial of agency for the female creator. Within a relationship of complementarity, the speaker in Conde's poetry secures sensual pleasure, poetic impulse, and spiritual plenitude.

Conde's intense interconnection to the world of the senses has been linked by Hispanists to her regional roots. Born beside the Mediterranean, Carmen Conde was bred on images of sea, sun, and expansive vistas. In *Brocal*, she textualized those scenes with some of the same sense of ingenuousness and childlike wonderment that Rafael Alberti displayed in his initial collection, with the difference being that the seascapes of her youth are not those of an ocean and her verse appears more modern and spontaneous, more inspired by self-assurance and immediacy. With a sense of excitement and urgency, Conde's poems spring across the page in rapid succession accumulating positive sensations. If any intertext is to be singled out, it would have to be the works of Gabriel Miró. As Emilio Miró has already observed, "La riqueza y variedad cromática, el despliegue de elementos sensoriales, hablan de asimiladas lecturas de Miró especialmente" [the richness and chromatic variety, the display of sensorial elements, speak of reading assimilated from Miró, especially].[47] Carmen Conde herself has acknowledged her early debt to this novelist from Alicante. As she confessed, the reading of Juan Ramón Jiménez stimulated her lyric tendencies, but "con el incomparable Gabriel Miró habría de enlazarme la común mediterraneidad, gloriosa en él" [I would have to connect my common Mediterraneanness, so glorious in him, with the incomparable Gabriel Miró].[48]

Some of Conde's enthusiasm for physical reality is attributable also to the vanguard literary trends in fashion in Spain in the twenties. Little note has been taken of the possible manifestations of the avant-garde movement in Conde's poetry. In passing, César González Ruano points to her stylistic affinity to surrealism: "un surrrealismo moderado que no se olvida muchas veces de la rima e incluso de una profunda raíz española, pero que realza y cultiva con verdadera fortuna la imagen y las asociaciones simultáneas" [a moderate surrealism that does not often forget rhyme and even a deep Spanish heritage, but that highlights and cultivates the image and simultaneous association with true success].[49] And Bonnie M. Brown examines the coincidences with surrealistic images and motifs in a book Conde published in 1960, *En la tierra de nadie*.[50] The impressionistic quality of *Brocal* may well represent a tribute to the aesthetic spirit of Miró, but it also reflects the *ultraísta* mode of writing poetry. Following the lead established by her avant-garde contemporaries, in *Brocal* Conde eliminated the anecdotal, objectified natural phenomena, created poems as loose chains of juxtaposed visual images, and switched or reversed expected lexical relationships. In *Júbilos*, she exhibited the *ultraísta*'s enthusiastic attention to the prosaic machines of daily life; she dedicated poetic prose sketches to the "smiling" locomotive, the kite-like airplane, and the tired and rebellious typewriter. In contrast to this humanization of objects, in *Brocal*, traditionally sublime elements are objectified through equations with geometrical shapes. Stars become "poliedros diminutos de fuego" [small polyhedrons of fire], and the speaker finds herself on the diameter of the circumference of the heavens. Also reminiscent of the kinds of metaphors and images favored during the twenties are the occasional synesthesia ("cascabeles de aurora" [bells of dawn]) and the coupling of the novel comparison with a tinge of humor that characterizes the *greguería*: "los tejados sonríen con los labios rizados de sus tejas" (29) [the roofs smile with the curled lips of their tiles]. Where Conde showed her closest conformity to the aesthetic impulse of the vanguard spirit was in the verve with which she wielded the creative implications of the image. The creative power asserted in these poems came not so much from the referential potential of the individual images as from the accumulative effect of material existence that the mere verbal crafting of images produces. By virtue of naming, the poet brought into being all the basic elements of nature—sky, trees, water. She then placed them, usually without adjectival adornment, in close proximity to one another quickly passing from one item to the next as if compelled to embrace the whole world.

The poems of *Brocal* are verbal sketches, quick enumeration of images without transitions or reflection: "La noche estaba quieta, prendida a las veletas de las torres. Y la calle estaba muda, sola . . . ¡Un caballo negro la cruzó galopando!" (31) [The night was still, fastened to the weather vanes of the towers. And the street was quiet, alone . . . A black horse galloped across it!] or "En la noche grande, arraigó el lucero. / Ha girado el silencio y un viento leve juega con los pinares" (36) [A star took root in the grand night. / Silence has whirled around and a light wind plays with the pine trees]. Sometimes images are conjoined by a conjunction or by simple proximity. Metaphoric transformation creates links between different objects, resulting in a semantic compactness that allows falling rain to be seen as leaves which, once linguistically transformed, serve as a point of convergence for sunlight ("Caían, en hojas de lluvia, diminutas esquinas de soles," 34). At times one metaphor gives rise to another, forming a union between disparate orders of reality: "Sienes frescas de almendro, apoyadas en mis sienes como dos pájaros que cantan" (32) [The cool temples of the almond tree, resting on my temples like two singing birds]. The personification of the almond branch makes possible the loving union between nature and the speaker and likens both, in turn, to a third entity, the singing birds. The interweaving and expansion of metaphors can create more imaginary, fantastic effects: "Mi corazón irguió sus lirios y detuvo a los vientos que venían en grandes barcas. Quedó un aro fresco flotando en el cielo" (32). [My heart raised its lilies and stopped the winds that were coming in big boats. A cool ring was left floating in the sky]. Conde seemed to grasp the intent of Gerardo Diego's formula for the artistic process, which equates creation with the addition of "juego de relaciones, forma" [a play of relationships, form] to "idea."[51]

Although Carmen Conde showed some of the same enthusiasm as the *ultraístas* for constructing poems as a series of visual images, the interaction among them is less irrational or suggestive in her poetry. Her early poetry is filled with allusions to her familiar world of nature—fruit trees, flowers, gardens, and fields. The scenes she captured are both maritime and rural. Bell towers, lighthouses, and mills stand out against expansive skies and sweeping winds. Young girls carry water jugs to the fountain and old men dressed in black traverse her poetic stage. Although vaguely evocative of the scenery of her childhood, the images in *Brocal* remain generic annotations of physical settings. In her subsequent collection, *Júbilos*, children, as well as animals and places, are identified by their specific names.

This intersection between the generic and the specific in *Brocal* is seen particularly in Conde's poetization of the sea, which, despite its depiction in the book within generic contours, is her own sea—real, tangible, and accessible. The sea was decisive in both her life and work. She was born by the sea and it was through the sea, she says, that she entered into the lyric realm.[52] The sea saturated her very being. In the words of José Gerardo Manrique de Lara, "Carmen es una mujer mediterránea. Siente la influencia del mar, se satura de yodo, de libertad elemental, telúrica, edénica" [Carmen is a Mediterranean woman. She feels the influence of the sea, she is bathed in iodine, in elemental, telluric, edenic freedom].[53] Later in her career, as her lyric horizons broadened and her poetic sensitivity deepened, her treatment of the sea became richer in nuances and intensity. Semprún Donahue discerns multiple roles for the sea in Conde's poetry—a companion instilling hope and a sense of adventure in her as a child and later engendering nostalgia, a double with which she identified, a link to eternity, the source of life, a lover.[54] The shadow cast by war and human suffering darkened the appearance of the sea in Conde's later poetry, but in her first books the sea is pristine and peaceful. Although sketched in generalized terms, the sea provides the implicit backdrop for much of *Brocal*. The sea for Conde is visible, contiguous, and accessible. The sea is everywhere—above and below, situated far upon the horizon and anchored in the windows of the houses. In contrast to Concha Méndez, her female contemporary, the sea represents for Conde, not a vehicle for escape, but a confirmation of the existence of beauty and of her communion with its vital essence:

> Si yo derramase todas mis geometrías en el agua, cinco navíos descubrirían islas submarinas con ruedas de peces y sirenas.
>
> (36)

> [If I were to spill my geometries in the water, five ships would discover underwater islands with wheels of fish and mermaids.]

> Estaban cuajadas las almendras del mar. Finas ramas azules escalaban el cielo.
> Yo recogía vientos y frutas.
>
> (37)

> [The beach almonds were bursting. Thin blue branches scaled the sky.
> I gathered winds and fruits.]

Conde's drive to embrace all of the palpable world around her derived from her desire to experience the world fully as a rich physical reality and to become a part of its renewable energy. From the very beginning of her poetic creation, she established a strong sense of presence for herself and for things. Presence connotes not only existence in the world of phenomena but also interaction with concrete surroundings and the consciousness of that experience. From her position at the center of her subjective universe, the poetic speaker experiences landscape not as a distant observer but as one who touches and feels the natural world around her. She holds a white rose in her hand and jumps over rivers and trees. The poet herself affirmed that the sense of touch was of particular importance to her: "El tacto es una maravilla. Las manos nos acercan a todo. A veces no se necesita ver para saber tactar y el tacto es muy importante" [Touch is a marvel. Our hands bring us close to everything. Sometimes you do not need to see to know how to touch and touch is very important.].[55] In a later poem aptly titled "Tacto" [Touch], in *Iluminada tierra*, she wrote, "Tengo en mis manos, seguro, el secreto de las cosas / que no van a los labios ni a los ojos; / que tan sólo se tactan" (470) [In my hands, I hold securely the secret of things / that do not go to the lips or the eyes; / that are only touched]. Conde collapsed the spatial and emotional distance of the gaze, bridging differences between the disparate orders of reality through personal contact with the world around her and its vital forces. She experienced the world through all of her senses, and it was through the senses that she created her lyric world. Thematically as well as linguistically, her poetry is impregnated with a vibrant sensuality deriving as much from the landscapes inscribed within her poems as from the poet's renderings of her raw materials. This sensuality, as Leopoldo de Luis says, inevitably arouses readers, "llevándonos a un paisaje comunicativo y corporeizado: saboreamos la belleza frutal, nos llega la pulpa fresca de la mañana, las luces rojas de la cumbre, el aire salado del mar" [taking us to a communicative and materialized landscape: we savor the fruity beauty, the cool pulp of morning, the red lights of the summit, the salty air of the sea reaches us].[56]

The corporeality of nouns referring to buildings and elements of nature infuses Conde's text with a quality of bulk, of concreteness and timelessness. Most of the images she uses in *Brocal* represent things that can be experienced through the senses. In this, her first collection, the poet processes reality in all its physicality through her own body; she absorbs its sounds, smells, and colors. Perception is a prelude to possession. Assimilating the sensorial attributes of her surroundings, the speaking subject becomes one with them and their plenitude. The sounds she hears bridge the spaces of her open vistas. Water and church bells encompass nature and matter, the earth-bound and the lofty spheres. These samples of the organic and the spiritual realms nourish the poetic persona, filling her with their splendor. First, water offers its subtle, soothing sound:

¡Qué agua tan fresca, tan llena de quietudes, tan sobresaltada de cristales, bebimos todas!

(31)

[What water so cool, so full of stillness, so sparkling with crystals, we all drank!]

¡Qué transparencia tiene la lluvia en el huerto!
  Recta, afilada, continua . . .

(33)

[What transparency the rain in the orchard has!
  Straight, sharp, continuous . . .]

Then church bells unfold their glorious reverberations:

  De la cándida tarde se desprendieron las campanas . . .

(30)

  [The bells were loosened from the innocent afternoon . . .]

  Se derramaron las campanas por el campo . . .

(34)

  [The bells spilled over the field . . .]

Puestas en marcha las campanas grandes, unos mazos de hierro golpeaban a
las pequeñas; luego, a las pequeñitas; por último, la campanilla saltaba
descalza por el prado verde y fragante del cielo.
  ¡Qué júbilo el de la Torre, toda volada en giros locos, en aires dispersos,
en palomas desbandadas.
  Cuando todo terminó, graves, trascendidas de los siglos de la huerta,
cayeron las once campanadas del reloj. A la postrera quedó un hondo, ronco
vibrar en la Torre. Salió por las ventanas (¡de lejos la Torre era transparente!),
y no reposó ni en el agua del río. (43)

[After the big bells began, the iron mallets hit the small ones, then the very
smallest ones, finally the little bell jumped around barefoot through the green
and fragrant meadow of the sky.
  What jubilation in the Tower, taking flight in wild spins, in scattered winds,
in freed doves!
  When it all ended, the eleven strokes of the clock, full of centuries of
vegetable gardens, fell solemnly. A deep, hoarse vibration in the Tower was
left behind. It went out through the windows (from afar the Tower was transparent!) and it didn't even rest on the water of the river.]

The spectacular pealing of eleven strokes provides a dramatic accompani-
ment for the crescendo of human emotion underlying the text of this, the
last poem of the collection.
  The sensuality of these depictions is enhanced by an occasional allusion

to fresh fragrances but above all by the infusion of color and light. Carmen Conde is a colorist. Perhaps her love of color comes, as Rosario Hiriart suggests, from Conde's enthusiasm for painting.[57] Color is intense in *Brocal*. The glaring, unnuanced red and green lights emanating from lighthouses are reflected in the water ("En este caminito del agua, qué tibia el ala roja y verde de la luz!" 32 [In this little road of water, how tepid the red and green wing of the light!]) and repeated in young girls' ribbons ("Dos a dos. ¡Fila de lazos verdes y rojos!" 31 [Two by two. A row of red and green ribbons!]). The vividness of the colors red and green is accentuated by literal and figurative allusions to fire—the fiery sunset and the red palm tree that burn in the speaker's heart.

An occasional black horse crosses Conde's landscapes and the four mysterious men in the last poem of the collection dress in black, but any somber suggestion of death is dissipated by the radiance of the light that envelops the moving creatures in these poems. Regardless of their color, human figures represent only props on the stage on which nature and the speaker interact:

> Llenos de fruta los árboles. Azules y moradas las cordilleras.
> A la sombra de una casa en cuyo escudo amenazaban dos hombrones de
>   granito, reposaban unos bueyes.
> Ondulaban los trigos, mujeres blancas de cabellos negros, y los burrrillos
>   tiraban de las norias.
> ¡Alamos, ríos!
>
>   (44)
>
> [The trees full of fruit. Blue and purple mountain ranges.
> Two oxen rested in the shade of a house in whose coat of arms two big men
>   of granite peered out menacingly.
> The wheat, white women with black hair, rippled, and the little burros pulled
>   the water wheels.
> Poplars, rivers!]

The women, the roses, and the morning light are all white—luminous and undefined. Colors in *Brocal*, although descriptively accurate or metaphorically logical, do not create specific landscapes. Like the objects, places, and things in the book, they are used as a projection of the poet's passionate embrace of reality, of her creative urge, and of her joyful transcendence of the mundane.

Time envelops this generic world of the senses with an atmosphere of continuance and immediacy that tends to invalidate its sequential properties. The edenic world that encircles the speaking subject transcends the time barriers that divorce human creatures from the timelessness of the world of nature. The past exists in *Brocal*, not as a nostalgic evocation of lost experience, but rather as part of descriptive re-creations. For this reason, within the use of the past, the instances of the imperfect and present perfect tenses outnumber those of the preterit tense. What prevail, however, are the present, the future, and other techniques for arresting the passage of time. Without temporal dimension to threaten her assimilation of nature, the world seems within the grasp of the female speaker and her peaceful union with it becomes possible. Past participles engender stasis and the gerund produces duration. Adverbs also amplify this sense of temporal continuation. In one poem, the first line hinges on "aún" [still] and the last one revolves around "todavía" [still], both suggestive of arrested progression. What particularly makes the world stand still in *Brocal* is the ellipsis incorporated in many of the lines. Syntactical juxtaposition replaces temporal succession in this poetic universe of connections and cohesion.

In her first book, Carmen Conde's gaze was still fixed on the visual beauty of the Mediterranean coast, the purely sensual delights that she could experience, internalize, and make her own. As she became more reflective, she later turned her attention to the somber beauty of the Castilian plateaus, its inhabitants, and its implications of life and death. She gained a consciousness of the rest of humanity in all its splendor as well as its tragedy, but her initial poetic persona dwells in an isolated state of timeless harmony with nature and love. What remained throughout her literary production is her intimate relationship with nature. She fused with nature on an existential level in her explicit identification with a variety of its elements, on a creative level in her conception of creation as the channeling of instinctual, natural forces into words, and on the ethnic level, in her later concern for the national destiny as it was reflected in her country's landscape. From the palpable, sensorial, real world of natural phenomena, Conde created a sense of presence both tangible and cosmic, accessible yet transcendent. For Conde this resplendent world was not a discrete, self-contained field, but rather a potential force ready to be harnessed by the human spirit. For her, reality did not truly exist until experienced and engulfed by someone. Conde explicitly answered the philosophical tree-in-the-forest question by reconfirming the priority of human presence in the materialization of reality. Yet if a human must hear a tree fall to actualize sound, a tree must also be there for the ear to hear. Thus nature and the female speaker in Conde's poetry are dependent on one another for their own realization. What is particularly significant in *Brocal* is the early and firm sense of self-assertion that Conde's poetic speaker projects and her positioning of herself at the center and apex of creation. This initial posture might appear narcissistic, but it breeds the strong sense of self that characterizes Conde's poetry. This is a self that identifies with the world around her, experiences it, and embraces its beauty as well as its creative powers. Conde's poetic persona became more reflective, more profound, and more somber, but her initial poetic excursion brought a vitality that never left the poet. Bliss prevails in her first book; within the edenic precincts of dazzling light and first love, the female speaker exudes confidence and joy. Motivated by basic human emotions and using a simple, uncomplicated poetic discourse, Carmen Conde created in *Brocal* an uncommon vision of cohesion, materiality, and plenitude.

7

Ernestina de Champourcin:
Creating the Self through Transcendence

Men have been presumed to be the incarnation of transcendence, inventors and shapers of the future, capable of rising above reality and life itself, while women have been identified as immanence—a subordinate, sustaining, and immutable state of being. Woman, Simone de Beauvoir explains, "is defined and differentiated with reference to man and not he with reference to her; she is incidental, the unessential as opposed to the essential. He is the Subject, he is the Absolute—she is the other."[1] Women, traditionally, did not speak or write, gaze or depict; they only saw themselves through the reflections cast by the masculine imagination.

Thus, even if the woman writer does not criticize phallocentrism, she undermines its relegation of woman to object of desire, constructed sign, and inert matter because she herself becomes the agent of representation. Whether through imitation or difference, the woman poet, as the speaking subject, contradicts the pretended universality of masculine representation of both the Self and Other. When she constructs alternatives to the established conception of women, she subverts the epistemological system informing her culture. And when she reiterates traditional patterns of portrayal, her self-generated representation displaces the silence, the passivity, and the absence long assigned to women. The poet Ernestina de Champourcin exemplifies well the female writer who within a seemingly traditional configuration of woman as religious, spiritual, and loving delineates a nontraditional female self that is creative, passionate, and transcendent.

Recognized as the outstanding woman poet of the Generation of 1927, Champourcin published over fifteen books during her long lifetime. She is referred to by critics as either the only female poet of that generation or as one of the two women reluctantly included in Gerardo Diego's landmark anthology of poetry of 1934,[2] but, on the whole, she has disappeared from

the annals of literature. José Angel Ascunce, the editor of her complete
works, lists as reasons for the critical silence surrounding her work the circumstances of her gender, her preference for poetry of a personal nature
without a particular concern for theory, her work as a translator, her exile,
and her religious orientation.[3] To the condescending, sexist attitudes of
male critics, Andrew P. Debicki adds Champourcin's devotion to Juan
Ramón Jiménez as the prime reason for her exclusion from the group of
mainstream poets of the twenties, who by 1930 were looking to other poetic models for inspiration.[4] Joy B. Landeira attributes the critical neglect
of her poetry not only to the waning prestige of her mentor Juan Ramón
but to the pervasive influence over her life and poetry by another Juan, her
husband Juan José Domenchina.[5] Although Champourcin's poetry was
neglected for a variety of reasons after her exile from Spain in 1939, during
the period of the Generation of 27 she was surprisingly afforded the status
of poet. Couching his evaluation, to be sure, within the misogynistic separation between woman and poet, in 1932 Ernesto Salazar Chapela praises
Champourcin for her implied advancement from "poetess" to "poet." He
states, "Lo poético y lo femenino . . . se confunden . . . la poetisa no se
propone . . . transcribir emociones peculiares de su naturaleza femenina . .
. sino que quiere ser, ante todo, poeta" [The poetic and the feminine . . . are
blended together . . . the poetess does not propose to transcribe emotions
peculiar to her feminine nature . . . but rather she wants to be above all, a
poet].[6]

Champourcin obviously had to function within a society firmly grounded
on an uncompromising patriarchal ideology that denied women intellectual as well as artistic competence. She therefore understandably evinced a
certain "anxiety of authorship" in the modesty and self-effacement she
adopted before the task of poetry writing. She long maintained that she did
not see poetry as a career nor her own poems as the result of any special
artistry. She declined to define poetry in general or even her own, in both a
1928 interview and her introductory remarks for Diego's 1934 anthology.[7]
Sixty years later she continued to abstain from definitions, insisting that
poetry for her was a vocation, a gift, and not a profession or an obligation.[8]
Her demure detachment from poetic theory can be interpreted as a strategy for safely navigating the forbidden waters of male privilege. Her unas-
suming stance did not threaten the male prerogative of poetic genius while
it simultaneously deflected the impact of her bold intrusion into that very
realm. Equally duplicitous was her representation of sexuality; she writes
of desire and coitus with surprising clarity, but at the same time juxtaposes
or masks them with sublimating religious allusions. The words of Alicia
Suskin Ostriker aptly summarize Champourcin's situation: "the woman
writer throughout history has had to state her self-definitions in code, dis-
guising passion as piety, rebellion as obedience. . . . What the genteel tradi-

tion demanded of the ladies was that they bare their hearts, gracefully and without making an unseemly spectacle of themselves. They were not to reveal that they had heads, let alone loins."[9] Thus seemingly contradictory meanings co-exist with equal force in Champourcin's poetry. Eroticism and religiosity, self-assertion and denial of the self, innovation and tradition all go hand-in-hand in her poetry.

Despite Champourcin's repudiation of the notion of conscious artistic mastery and of the individual as a powerful creator, she delineates an active, creative, and transcendent self in search of self-expression, the fulfilling other, and spiritual plenitude. Her public unpretentiousness notwithstanding, poetry proves to be for her an ongoing means for the speaking subject of her verse to search, aspire, and sublimate. She asserts her own presence as an emotional being intent on self-fulfillment and plenitude through her interrelationship with a beloved, be he human or divine. In her expression of desire, the poetic persona of Champourcin's poems projects the gender dynamics in force during the poet's era; but at the same time her articulation of sexuality—the feelings and emotions connected with erotic desire—negates the alienation from pleasure imposed on women by patriarchal society and revises the masculine role as victor in the sexual act. For Champourcin, sexual desire is a means of self-expression and a way of reaching sublime love—an emotional yet transcendent attachment to the other. Thus in the poetry she published between 1926 and 1936, her poetic speaker presents herself as a self-aware, sexual being in search of love.

EN SILENCIO . . . : THE EMOTIONAL SELF IN LITERARY GARB

In 1926, Ernestina published her first collection of poems, *En silencio . . .* [In silence]. The titles of the four subsections—"Emociones," "Plegarias tristes," "Rimas sedientes" and "Acordes nocturnos" [Emotions, Sad prayers, Thirsty rhymes, Nocturnal chords]—overtly proclaim the romantic tonalities of the book.[10] Melancholic human sentiments encased in nocturnal settings punctuated with mournful sounds predominate. The hypersensitive poetic persona reacts emotionally to the world around her, and nature reflects back her moods in the romantic manner of pathetic fallacy. The tearful, emotional body in the collection is clothed in the recognizable garb of literary formulae that make the poems seem more an aping of conventional poetic paradigms than reflections of personal experience. This apparent lack of originality nonetheless reveals that the immature poet was a well-read practitioner of poetry capable of assimilating a number of prevalent literary trends.[11] Also her very exercises in stylistic manipulation indicate an enthusiasm for form and the beginning of the poet's development of technical dexterity. Ascunce, for example, discerns within her romantic and "modernista" tendencies evidence of artistry, particularly in her subtle manipulation of the acoustic elements of poetry such as interior rhyme, alliteration, and sonorous rhythm patterns.[12] Finally the book provides important signs of Champourcin's future thematic constant—the unending search for a love that transcends the terrestrial aspects of human love.

En silencio . . . can be discounted as a work of apprenticeship conspicuously imitative in its thematics and transparent in its absorption of influences. The author herself disavowed the book for many years, claiming it was an ingenuous, early attempt at poetry that should never have been published and that it only attracted attention because, by coincidence, in 1926, three young women poets published initial volumes of poetry.[13] Even though it was more of a publishing novelty than a poetic milestone, it was her book that received the best criticism during its day. It was praised for its originality, modernity, classicism, and reflections of the pure poetry espoused by Paul Valéry.[14] She was called the "aristocrática poetisa" [aristocratic poetess], the "promesa de los más hermosos frutos trasplantados del jardín de la Sinceridad" [promise of the most beautiful fruits transplanted from the garden of sincerity], and the "primera de nuestras musas contemporáneas" [the best of our contemporary muses].[15]

Traces can be found in *En silencio* . . . of many different poets—echoes of San Juan de la Cruz in her religious verses and strains of Maeterlink, Bécquer, Rubén Darío, and Juan Ramón Jiménez in the rest of the poems. Champourcin's early tribute to Juan Ramón was a conscious emulation of the poet she most admired and who would eventually become a cherished friend.[16] She remained among those who respected Juan Ramón as mentor and poetic leader, even after 1930, when Juan Ramón's conception of "pure poetry," of poetry as a world stripped of the impurities of quotidian concerns, was severely challenged by those who saw poetry as an instrument of social change.[17]

Her homage to JRJ is obvious in her poem, "A Platero." Like the early Juan Ramón, she senses a consonance between nature and her poetry. The sounds of nature and other sounds, recalling the poetry not only of Juan Ramón but also of his "modernista" predecessors, reverberate throughout *En silencio* . . . —sounds of pianos, sonatas, bells, and murmurs. Juan Ramón's preference for golden hues and the color mauve also surfaces as does his predilection for the use of synesthesia. In the poem "Nocturno" [Nocturne], for example, the romantic conception of love as the bond between diaphanous beings floating in a dream-like state is articulated through a linguistic festival of sensorial delights akin to the language in the first stages of Juan Ramón's long poetic career. Tactile sensations intermingle with sounds ("pasos de terciopelo" [velvet steps], and "un murmullo sedeño" [a silky murmur]), and fragrances, colors, and sounds overlap.

On the surface, Champourcin's deference to Juan Ramón Jiménez as her literary father and the ultimate poetic authority may seem to be a will-ful subjugation to masculine poetics and a concomitant sacrifice of female expression. But besides the practical benefits of a superb literary model, the poetry of Juan Ramón represented for Champourcin an expansion of her poetic horizon and an avenue to the validation of her poetry. Some-what like the American authors whom Sandra M. Gilbert and Susan Gubar found during this period "oscillating between their matrilineage and the patrilineage in an arduous process of self-definition,"[18] Champourcin re-jects her literary mothers, establishing an early allegiance to her literary fathers in an attempt to escape the confines of what was considered an inferior feminine mode of writing. When the critic Rafael Cansinos-Assens equates the "feminine" with emotion and concludes that Ernestina de Champourcin "acepta su abnegada misión de mujer" [accepts her self-sacrificing female mission],[19] it is evident that neither the female tradition nor critical discourse offered women writers more than a narrow gamut of poetic possibilities. In reaction against these limitations Champourcin feels compelled to discredit the "poetisas" of the past for their timidity and maud-lin verses.[20]

A poet like Champourcin did not feel "anxiety of influence" directed against paternal authority, which Harold Bloom identifies through mascu-line metaphors of competition and warfare as the characteristic experience of the male writers. Her anxiety was provoked by maternal figures of suf-fering, sacrifice, and asexuality. Unlike contemporary feminist critics, the Spanish women poets of the twenties and thirties did not envision female creativity as a process of loving rescue of maternal antecedents.[21] For them, contact with masculine models did not signify contentious opposition but a promise of artistic legitimacy and an opportunity to surpass the bound-aries that traditionally confined women poets to a limited range of registers and stances. Thus, deliberate mimicry exemplified a subversive act of in-trusion and an inviting vehicle for self-identity. Champourcin accomplished this, however, without abandoning altogether many of the elements of the feminine tradition. Disregarding the hierarchical nature of male literature, she constructs instead a relationship based on regard and proximity, on an intentional concession without apparent connotations of submission.[22]

Champourcin's obvious literary trappings do not obstruct the represen-tation of the tremulous emotional self who roams the book. Decidedly nega-tive in scope, her emotions include feelings of nostalgia, loneliness, loss, sadness, grief, anxiety, and languidness. An atmosphere of silence, dark-ness, and death hovers over the poems to create an all-encompassing effect of undefined and overwhelming melancholy. When not engulfed in a wel-comed silence, the poems are saturated with rain, tears, and unsubtle chiar-oscuro effects. Like a human sponge, the heart of the speaker willingly absorbs the sadness around her:

¡Llora, corazón mío, la desnudez enferma,
la mezquindad estrecha
que agobia a tus hermanos;
llora por su alma seca,
por los que te brindaron su vil indiferencia!
¡Deshoja tus sollozos, corazón mío, besa
con tus lágrimas puras
el haz de las miserias![23]

(79–80)

[Weep, my heart, for the sick nakedness,
the narrow meanness
that weighs upon your brothers;
cry for their dry soul,
for those that offer you their vile indifference!
Strip off your sobs, my heart, kiss
with your pure tears
the sheath of wretchedness!]

In addition to words like "silencio," "nocturno," and "triste" [silence, nocturnal, sad], the verb "deshojar" [to strip of leaves] appears frequently. The heart "drops" its sobs; the poet "strips" the flowers of her verses; the mind "unleashes" its caresses on the soul; and life itself metaphorically becomes a "shower of roses" whose petals the speaking subject removes to strew at Christ's feet. In these poems, the act of tearing off leaves carries with it more a sense of willful self-sacrifice than of inflicted destruction.

The poetic "I" dominates, establishing its presence through self-exposure and self-absorption. The emphasis on the first-person subject locates the female self at the center of this poetic universe, but it does not create a liberating situation because the feelings the protagonist speaks of are heavily cloaked in poetic conventions. Disconnected from the world beyond the boundaries of the self, the speaker seems restrained by the straitjacket of romantic introversion. As Ascunce accurately observes, when the poetic "I" is not unveiling her feeling, motifs from external reality are but a pretext to remember emotions or a stimulus for the expression of her own moods.[24] Even when she considers a distant, inanimate object like the cathedral of Bruges, she interjects herself into the scene through first-person references and imposes upon the city the whole array of melancholy moods that weigh upon her.

In true romantic fashion, she sensitizes nature; rain, snow, and the sun become the personification of human feeling. As a backdrop on which to project the materialization of intangible personal feelings, nature assumes the vitality forfeited by the self. Rather than securing a position conducive to self-affirmation, personification allocates to nature the role of active agent while the self stands as the recipient of the effects of nature. For example, in "Ocaso de otoño" [Autumn sunset], nature is the force that illuminates the soul's darkness and lovingly obliterates its disillusion ("Es que allí, en las cenizas del día que se marcha, / ha cuajado la escarcha / piadosa del olvido; / y entierra mis deseos y mis afanes rotos" [In the ashes of the day that passes / the pious frost of forgetfulness has congealed / and buries my broken desire and yearnings]). The apparent delight the speaker in these poems takes in the heaviness of being constitutes a sense of pleasurable masochism that corroborates the traditional depiction of the female as long-suffering, overwhelmed, and lethargic.

Equally traditional is her representation of the woman in love as weak, pale, and languid. Champourcin puts the female subject in these poems in the position of a static, virginal Sleeping Beauty who expectantly awaits the arrival of the beloved; but unlike the fairy tale character, this maiden will awake to suffering, not bliss:

> Yo sé que has de venir; te esperaré muy pálida,
> blanca como una estatua, en la paz matinal;
> y tenderé hacia ti mis dos manos tan lánguidas,
> que parecen vestigios de un místico vitral.
> . . . .
> Yo sé que pasarás, más rápido que un sueño,
> llevándote prendida mi alma de mujer,
> que ennublará el recuerdo mi rostro antes risueño,
> que volverás un día de la tarde al caer.
>
> (67–68)

> [I know you will come; I will wait for you, very pale,
> white like a statue, in the peace of the morning;
> and I will extend toward you my two very languid hands,
> that look like vestiges of a mystical stained-glass window.
> . . . .
> I know you will pass by quicker than a dream,
> taking away in your grasp my woman's heart,
> and memory will darken my once-smiling face
> and you will return some day at sundown.]

Although fleeting, painful, and chimerical, love remains her endless yearning. Her dependence on love is compared to the subjugated bird, and she resorts to the image of the flower as metaphor for herself. She wants to assume the beauty, delicacy, and purity of white lilacs in order to move the beloved:

> Quisiera ser un ramo
> de lilas blancas

y acariciar la sombra
    de tu mirada.
. . . .
Quiero ser un manojo
    de lilas blancas
y sembrar tus caminos
    de flores castas.

                (74)

[I wish I were a branch
    of white lilacs
and could caress the shadow
    of your gaze.
. . . .
I want to be a bouquet
    of white lilacs
and sow your paths
    with chaste flowers.]

The element of surrender to the other implicit in these references to the flower reappears in a later poem in the collection as a dream of her own deflowering: "Yo soñé que era flor y que tú me deshojabas" [I dreamed that I was a flower and you were deflowering me]. Rather than an object of contemplation and a symbol of otherness, as occurs in masculine poetry, the flower in Champourcin's poetry becomes a part of the speaking female subject's self-representation. Applicable to Champourcin's use of the flower is the conclusion Susan Kirkpatrick reaches regarding Carolina Coronado; unlike the male poet, who associates the flower with the female body as an erotic object, she establishes the figurative bond of woman and flower as a pathetic fallacy, the projection of subjectivity.[25] Also like Coronado's flowers, Champourcin's do not challenge the dominant ideology of gender, but they do transform the feminine in poetry by producing an image of woman as subject. The message is still one of receptivity and subordination to the other, but underneath its garb of romantic convention, the speaking subject is still female.

Although the female protagonist, in typical romantic fashion, is a pale, languid maiden who awaits the magical touch of the beloved, the male figure is not a dashing romantic hero. He is an elusive, aloof, or absent figure, a mere shadow evoked from the past as the "grim and bitter shadow" of memory or envisioned as an imminent shade. He approximates the qualities of unrealized love that causes pain and fades. The beloved, however, from the inception of Champourcin's literary career, constitutes only one half of the configuration of the other. Although not dominating the poet's attention, as occurred in the poetry she wrote after her exile to Mexico, God makes an appearance in this early collection.

In the five poems of "Plegarias tristes," she assumes before God the pose of the supplicant she adopts with the beloved. God, however, provides consolation and the means for transcendence beyond the world of unfulfilled yearnings, provoking the panegyric outpourings of a poem like "Magnificat." Also, the presence of God is more perceptible than that of the human figure. The meditation on the hands of Christ in "Manos divinas" [Divine hands] accumulates tactile sensations that not only bestow a corporal form upon the divinity but also afford the petitioner a vehicle for sensorial communication with Him. The prayers fall squarely within the religious tradition of renunciation of material existence ("Quiero cerrar los ojos y mirar hacia dentro / para verte, Señor" [I want to close my eyes and look inward / in order to see you, Lord]) and echo the oxymoronic phraseology of baroque literature on spiritual renewal in lines like "si es preciso, morir para llegar a la Vida" [if it is necessary, dying in order to attain Life]. The desire for withdrawal from the world of phenomena and the willingness to suffer in exchange for redemption conform to orthodox religious expression, but the declaration of almost masochistic pleasure in pain also corroborates the book's predominantly romantic tendencies binding the female self to a destiny of powerlessness, subordination, and dependency. Signs of a more dynamic or, at least, a more ambivalent relation with the other do not evolve until Champourcin's subsequent collections of poetry.

AHORA: THE MATURING SELF

Champourcin's second collection, Ahora [Now], continues to highlight personal feelings, but the tenor of these sentiments changes from dark, negative tones to expressions of delight, vital energy, and plenitude. Her poetry still reflects the influence of Juan Ramón Jiménez, but her initial superficial nod to her poetic mentor gives way to a more thorough assimilation of his use of sensorial elements, his drive to purify poetry, and his conception of nature as an ephemeral force with which the human spirit strives to unite. To quote José-Carlos Mainer, Ahora marks "su paso de la vaguedad modernista al mundo de símbolos intuitivos, búsquedas de abstracción y emotividad intelectual propio de Juan Ramón Jiménez" [her passage from "modernista" vagueness to the world of intuitive symbols, quests for abstraction and intellectual emotionalism characteristic of Juan Ramón Jiménez].[26] More important, the very substance of Champourcin's poetry changes. Her horizon broadens, the role of poetry expands for her, and her poetic subject's disposition evolves. The narcissistic self-confinement of the poetic speaker is discarded for a multidirectional focus that encompasses the whole of human existence, or as Ascunce puts it, "el sujeto lírico exige una dicción de acuerdo con el alma-emoción, con la palabra-estética y con el mundo exterior-sensación" [the lyrical subject demands a style in accordance with the soul-emotion, with the word-aesthetic and with the exterior-sensation world].[27] A more confident and animated poetic personality looks within herself, contemplates the world of nature, and examines the power of poetry. Now an active observer cognizant of her power as both poet and woman, the poetic persona embarks on the journey toward transcendence that becomes the hallmark of Champourcin's poetry.

Although "alma-emoción" is only a component of the total being that preoccupies Champourcin, personal feelings still command appreciable attention for her. John C. Wilcox sees her identity with her feelings as evidence of her gynocentrism, of a characteristically feminine vision and a concomitant divergence from masculine discourse as well as from the norms of objectivity affirmed by "influential patriarchs" of European modernism.[28] Although it is true that her poetry provides a notable example of the feminine subjectivity profiled by feminist psychologists, care must be taken not to overlook the nuances and ambivalences within the general outlines of Champourcin's feminine discourse and not to turn difference into a mechanism for the gender-based marginalization that women poets of her generation attempted to collapse. Emilio Miró places her poetry squarely within the "tradicional universo femenino" [traditional feminine universe], not the world of domesticity, but rather that realm relating to the "traducción verbal de las 'galerías del alma'—para decirlo machadianamente—, de los anhelos del espíritu, de las emociones más íntimas y los sueños de la plenitud" [verbal translation of the "galleries of the soul"—to say it in the manner of Machado—of the longings of the spirit, of the most intimate emotions and the dreams of plenitude].[29] Although he evokes the name of a male master of poetry, he divorces Champourcin's verses from mainstream literature. If she textualizes the yearnings hidden within the chambers of the soul, she can be linked as easily to Machado as to the feminine tradition; and her celebration of inner plenitude could be related to Jorge Guillén. What distinguishes her from these male poets is her specific perspective within their schemes. She readily exposes female desire through sublimate poetic transformations or religious overtones; and when she faces the other, she tends to eschew the disengagement and appropriation characteristic of masculine discourse. The plenitude of being in her poems coincides paradoxically with both a transcendence of the concrete and a sensual grounding in the corporal. This dynamic interplay of sensations and spirit sets her off from her male contemporaries, as well as from her female peers.

If *En silencio* . . . portrayed the melancholy and masochism associated with the sentimental "poetisa," *Ahora* presents an atmosphere of brilliant light, technical dexterity, and a sense of affirmation attuned to the confident, animated, and playful spirit of vanguard Spanish poetry of the twenties. In

"Estancamiento" [Stagnation], the first poem of the collection, the budding poetic voice emerges from her dark cocoon intent on revitalizing her world and announces her desire to overcome stagnation and banal beauty:

> Yo remontaré
> el agua estancada
> en el bajel gris
> que fletan mis dudas,
> hasta deshacer
> el tropel de rosas
> . . . .
> que atasca de aromas
> banalmente suaves
> tu alma desnuda.
>
> (87)

> [I will go up
> the stagnant water
> in the gray vessel
> that my doubts load,
> until I break up
> the throng of roses
> . . . .
> that clogs
> your naked soul
> with banally soft aromas]

Instead of pain, sadness, and death, she speaks of the vital energy of life, the joy in nature, and the cosmic scope of passion. The speaking subject finds herself engulfed by pleasurable feelings of wonder and gladness:

> Goce íntimo y quedo en que el alma se admira
> de su propia belleza:
> minuto de egoísmo eterno como el mundo,
> divina complacencia
> de todo lo creado
> al contemplarse mudo
> en la múltiple esfera del corazón humano.
> Delirante alegría
> de palpar la consciencia que hace cierta la vida.
> ¡Silencioso placer de escucharse sin miedo
> y arrancar a la nada nuestros propios secretos,
> mientras huye la tierra, bulliciosa y maldita!
>
> (93)

[Intimate and quiet joy in which
the soul marvels at its own beauty:
a minute of eternal selfishness like the world,
divine self-satisfaction
over all its creations
upon contemplating itself silently
in the multiple sphere of the human heart.
Delirious happiness
of touching the awareness that makes life certain.
Silent pleasure of listening to oneself without fear
and extracting our own secrets from nothingness,
while the noisy and wicked earth flees!]

The specific identity or cause of these feelings is not furnished; what matters in *Ahora* is the state of being as vibrant, generic essence. The joy celebrated comes from a release from the quotidian world, that "tierra, bulliciosa y maldita," and the soul's realization of its own completeness. In contrast to the cheerless, self-absorbed withdrawal in *En silencio . . .* , the retreat from the material world in this book constitutes the arrested perfection of the instant. From the dependency on the present announced in its title, *Ahora* depicts a present that reconfirms human existence and its unity with all creation.

Not only does the present loom before the speaker in these poems, but new horizons and new discoveries as well:

> Esta vida profunda
> que surge de las cosas,
>
> . . . .
> Guarda en remotos pliegues
> la dulce flor secreta
> de un pecho inexplorado . . .
>
> (97)

> [This profound life
> that arises out of things
>
> . . . .
> Keeps in its remote folds
> the sweet and secret flower
> of an unexplored breast . . .]

A sense of wakening echoes throughout the book. The soul of the protagonist of these poems finds itself facing a "víspera de algo" [eve of something] and "la mañana indecisa" [hesitant morning]. To her own question, in one poem, "¿Ir al sol o a la nube?" [To go to the sun or the cloud?] she opts, in another, for the sun. She embarks on the journey toward the light that unfolds in the poet's subsequent collections.[30] Transcendence and rebirth in the imminent future become the overriding desire: "¡Navidades del alma! / Quiero hacer de vosotras la Navidad del mundo" (107) [Christmas time of the soul! / I want to make the Christmas of the world out of you].

The emotion that consistently engenders the existential joy characterizing *Ahora* is love. The poet's drive to unite the human spirit with the eternal life force compels her to sublimate love, to infuse it with cosmic qualities that allow it to transcend the material world. For example, in the title poem of the book, the love that emanates from the unidentifiable "you" sheds all "visible contours," becoming a flame and a flash of light and finally coalescing with the dazzling reflections of universal beauty. Love is not rendered only in spiritual terms; it can clearly be passion, physical contact, and violence of expression. For example, in the poem aptly titled "Pasión," the poetic speaker expresses her intention to restrain and sensitize the other until she can consume ("sorber" [to sip]) "ese amor yerto, / que resquicia su miel en tu pecho cobarde" [that stiff love, / that hoards its honey in your cowardly breast]. Champourcin develops an erotic discourse, as French feminists later recommended, by inscribing the female desire within the text in such a way that the tactile is privileged over the visual and female *jouissance* is affirmed. But, as always, Champourcin quickly transcends the terrestrial realm to revel in the delight of being held in arrested rapture between the sea and the sun:

> Sobre el lecho viviente de una ola esmeralda
> arrebujo mi cuerpo entre líquidas nieves.
> El sol con sus plumones empolva de oro fino
> el rútilo azabache que sombrea mi frente.
> . . . .
> ¡Perfecta embriaguez de la inmovilidad!
>
> (106)

> [On the living bed of an emerald wave
> I wrap my body with liquid snow.
> The sun with its downy feathers dusts with pure gold
> the shining jet that shades my brow.
> . . . .
> Perfect rapture of motionlessness!]

In these poems Champourcin mediates the tangible and the intangible through the conversion of one order of reality into another.

The maturing poet recognizes that the artistic essence of poetry relies not on the literal transcription of sentiments but on a process of replacement, analogy, and transformation. Filtered through these devices of distancing and obliqueness, emotional experiences are deflected, re-emerging only indirectly as objective descriptions and metaphorical allusion. Debicki locates the strengths of Champourcin's early poetry in this ability of hers to materialize the nonmaterial. As he shows, through a whole array of poetic strategies—personification, reification, montage, accumulation, synesthesia, and the "imagen visionaria"—she creates concrete, specific equivalents that embody the sensitivity of her speaker in an impersonal manner. Intangible feelings are objectified through concrete images or by imposing upon them images that create sensorial effects.

Besides serving as a poetic vehicle for objectifying human sentiments, nature itself in *Ahora* becomes an object of contemplation, offering a rich array of sensorial qualities that reinforce the sensual underpinnings in the book. Nature reveals itself in a series of images that take the poems beyond the level of vivid picture to that of intense activation of all five senses and the assumption, through personification, of human existence. Like the poetic speaker herself, nature in *Ahora* is vibrant and erotically charged. Especially in the section aptly termed "Cromos vivos" [Living color prints], the poems are color prints that come alive, as the following poem illustrates:

> El sol ha roto ya las canciones del alba
> y el crujiente abanico de las horas abiertas
> mece su plenitud en la mano del día.
> Han caído las doce del viejo campanario
> y son doce naranjas chorreantes de zumo,
> cargazón deleitosa del tiempo hecho frutal.
> Rasgóse la piel fina contra el áspero suelo.
> Todo es pulpa de oro, luz hecha carne, aroma,
> claro ámbar de paz . . .
> Tejieron los instantes este frágil cestillo
> de tejados, veletas, pinares rumorosos
> y ascéticas llanuras, para que en él cayeran
> henchidas de belleza, lucientes, despaciosas,
> empapando la vida en agridulces mieles,
> las trémulas naranjas que hacen de la tierra
> un fecundo panal.
>
>   (109)

> [The sun has already broken the songs of dawn
> and the rustling fan of the opening hours
> rocks its fullness in the hand of the morning.
> Twelve strokes have sounded from the old bell tower
> and there are twelve oranges dripping with juice,
> the delicious weight of time turned into fruit.
> The fine skin ripped itself on the rough ground.
> Everything is golden pulp, light made flesh, smell
> clear amber of peace . . .

The moments wove this fragile little basket
with roofs, weather vanes, murmuring pine groves
and ascetic plains, so that into it would fall,
all swollen with beauty, shining, slow,
drenching life in bittersweet honey,
the quivering oranges that made the earth
a fertile honeycomb.]

Although regularly favoring morning and sunset, in this poem Champourcin exploits the possibilities for plenitude in noon. The brightest hues—red, orange, and gold—drench her nature scenes, acquiring a palpable, viscous quality. The midday sun is not merely orange in color, it is literally the fruit, releasing a tasty ooze and breaking open its fleshy, fragrant pulp. More startling than the conjunction of the visual, the olfactory, and the gustatory in the second stanza is the synesthetic conversion of the visual effects of the sun into audio attributes in the first stanza. The personified sun replaces ("breaks") the songs of morning with a fuller panoply of sounds. The round, orange-like shape of the sun is transferred to the audio sphere, making possible the metaphorical displacement of the twelve strokes of the noonday bells by "doce naranjas." In the second stanza, the conversion from sun to fruit is complete; the heavenly body descends to the terrestrial "áspero suelo," disappearing behind images that incorporate the five senses. The third stanza begins with an allusion to the traditional metaphor of time as a weaver, but the intangible is quickly turned into an expression of concreteness that further develops the initial metaphor of sun as orange. Time weaves a basket from the lofty yet earthly elements of roofs, weather vane, and pine trees as a container for the oranges that are the sun. These fruits are fertile seeds, the potential for new life, for "un fecundo panal." Reminiscent of ancient sun myths, Champourcin's sun becomes the generative instrument of the earth's fecundity.

Beyond the overlapping sensorial effects in this poem, the image of the orange carries with it suggestive erotic overtones. Fruit symbolizes earthly desires and along with flowers is widely used to link nature with love and particularly with feminine love.[31] The apple, the common fruit of carnal knowledge, is replaced in some cultures by the orange, as in the Islamic religion and in Spanish folk songs, in which the orange often appears in mischievous expressions of love.[32] Instead of using the orange to symbolize feminine seduction or purity, as occurs in traditional masculine discourse, Champourcin uses it to represent pleasure as a multiple sensorial experience and of desire as an act of consumption.

In the poem "Pasión," the sensuous collides with the sensual when the metaphor of the sun as orange becomes entangled in the representation of the erotic impulse as a desire to ingest the other. In what Debicki calls a montage of images, the speaker's eye becomes a set of teeth that bites the sun while the latter lacerates the former's vision.[33] In conjunction with this symbolic infliction of pain, the speaker expresses her erotic desire as a yearning to arouse the emotion of the unidentified "you" through suffering and to suck out his love. As a correlative of this eroticism, nature is configured as a harsh and powerful force that overwhelms with its piercing, stinging, and penetrating properties. The poetic voice refers to the "agujas de plata" [silver needles] of the "mar de vidrio biselado" [sea of bevelled glass]; she calls the weight of time "los puñales del tiempo, / el acero vibrante / de su eterna presión" (104) [the daggers of time, / the vibrating steel / of its eternal pressure]; and in the poem "El sol ha roto . . . " [The sun has broken], she accumulates words connoting harshness or violence: "roto," "crujiente," "Rasgóse," and "áspero." In sum, nature in *Ahora* is imbued with an organic existence through images that allude to the senses and is animated through personification and metaphorical analogy into a dynamic, aggressive force. Nature simultaneously incarnates the phallic aggression of "acero" and "agujas" and the feminine fecundity suggested in "fecundo panal."

Equally forceful is the posture of the poetic voice before the natural vistas she contemplates. The speaking subject in *Ahora* adopts the persona of the hunter who assails the mysteries of nature ("¿Con el mío, cazaré / el corazón de la niebla?" 98 [With mine, will I hunt the heart of the mist?]) and that of the reaper who gathers the fruits of its beauty ("Espigadora alerta, de inseguros trigales, / desgrano sin contar el maíz de los vientos" 102 [An alert gleaner of uncertain wheat fields, / I thresh without counting the winds' corn]). Even when she resorts, in the seventh poem of "Cromos vivos," to the traditional female image of the mother, she does so from a position of maternal strength, as the sustainer of the universe:

> Fui madre de las cosas y madre de la Vida.
> Al seguir mi camino,
> sentí que la ciudad se acurrucaba toda,
> buscándome el regazo.
>
> (110)

> [I was the mother of all things and the mother of Life.
> As I went on my way,
> I felt that the whole city curled itself up,
> looking for my lap.]

In the fourth poem of "Cromos vivos," the actions also clearly illustrate feminine governance imposed upon nature. The poetic voice says, "Con un cepillo de sol / alboroto la melena / de los jardines cautivos" [With a brush of sunlight / I ruffle the long hair / of captive gardens]; "Ciño en

bucles de esmeralda / el mastil uniformista" [I encircle the uniforming
post / with emerald ringlets]; "sutilizo el desorden" [I refine disorder]; and
"Mi ventana es el panal / donde fabrico la miel" [My window is the honeycomb / where I make honey]. Outdoors, she tidies and dresses nature,
while, indoors, she assumes the life-sustaining task of making honey.

This appropriation of the powers and properties of nature on the part
of the female subject promotes an interchange of identities between the
human and natural spheres. In male literature, women have traditionally
been identified with nature in formulae that represent the feminine as the
irrational and passive foil to masculine self-assertion. To elude the self-annihilating powerlessness inherent in this portrayal of woman as the desired
or dreaded other, women writers have to discover alternatives. Champourcin
chose to reverse the negative assumptions about the affinity between nature and woman and view the interconnection as an affirmation of the
self.[34] Nature and speaker reflect one another; in one poem the universe
contemplates its beauty in the human heart and in another, the speaker
"like a new Narcissus" marvels at the mirror nature provides her. Entering
in an enraptured intimacy with nature, she becomes a May queen with a
crown of sun rays:

> Tengo un velo de espumas y una sutil diadema
> que enrosca el sol mimoso a mi cabello lacio.
> Una escala mullida con pétalos de oro
> inquieta dulcemente el ansia de mi paso.
>
> (104–5)

> [I wear a veil of foam and a light diadem
> that coils the affectionate sun around my straight hair.
> A soft ladder with golden petals
> sweetly stirs up the anxiety in my step.]

To describe herself, the speaking subject uses imagery similar to that she
applies to nature. Both are a strong, almost violent force; in the same way
that silence has "púas" [prongs], the mist uses "garras" [claws], and the sea
is made of "agujas de plata" [silver needles], the soul is conceived as
"encrespado acero" [rough steel], with "fervores de espada" [blade fervor].
This conversion of both nature and spirit into metallic matter derives in
part from Champourcin's tendency to equate the two realms and from her
discovery of the "visionary" or irrational potential of metaphoric transformation. In her fervent quest to have nature serve as a "trampoline" to fling
her soul upward, the speaking subject aggressively pursues her goal; she
"hunts" the wind and "bites" the sun.

In paradoxical contrast to these invasive gestures of phallic implication,
she resorts to the traditional image of woman as vessel. Uterine figures, the

goblet and the glass, suggest passive containment and inert materiality, but the crystal vessel also gives liquids a shape that arrests their existence in the world of phenomena and it provides them a protective environment. Especially as goblet, the container represents a durable object that both exhibits and captures beauty. For example, in the fourth poem of "Cromos vivos," the speaker refers to herself, and, probably specifically to her mouth, as a goblet studded with jewels derived from stars and touched by the lips of the other as well as by the fantastical elixir of those same stars. In one stanza of the poem "Fuga" [Flight], the beauty of the soul/goblet enhances, with its brilliant light, the presence of the other's love and, with her purity, dispenses his identity:

> Ha pulido tu amor
> la copa de mi alma
> con el roce fatal
> de su deslumbramiento,
> en el cándido prisma
> de tan leves cristales
> se diluye la gracia
> de tu perfil eterno.
>
> (88)

> [Your love has polished
> the goblet of my soul
> with the fatal rubbing
> of its dazzle,
> in the white prism
> of light glass
> the grace of your eternal
> outline is dissolved.]

In the poem "Firmeza" [Firmness] she also magnifies the spirituality of the poetic subject through a series of images of ascending value that convert the soul first from earthbound "cauce" [riverbed] to the poetic image of the glass and from there to the holy object of the chalice.[35] Champourcin reverses the devalued male portrayal of woman as that which must be contained, making her instead the container that generates life. She gives back to women the power of life that the ancient archetypal image of egg bestowed on the feminine as vessel, and projects a gynocentric vision of selfhood that approximates what Kathryn Allen Rabuzzi terms "motherself" and defines it as the incarnation of space, capable of containing the world within herself.[36]

Just as the orientation and the temperament of the poetic speaker evolve from *En silencio . . .* to *Ahora*, so does the author's concept of poetry. In the

poem beginning "Vieja glosa de los campos . . . " [An old note on the
fields], the poet openly admits her desire to leave behind antiquated aesthetic mannerisms: "Quiero hablar de mi Castilla / sin arcaicos lagrimeos,
/ sin retórico oropel / ni lirismos sensibleros" [I want to talk about my
Castile / without outdated weeping / without rhetorical showiness / or
sentimental lyricism]. No longer an inert receptacle to fill with emotions as
it was in her first book, poetry emerges as a workroom for experimentation
and a vehicle for self-exploration. Champourcin turns from Romanticism
to more contemporary modes, to the irrationalism and "visionary" aspects
of surrealism, and to the ludic quality of *ultraísmo*.[37] Poetry resides outside
the human speaker in a realm without limits and with a supreme harmony:

> Palabras . . .
> Mariposas oscuras del pensamiento ajeno,
> qué inútil vuestra voz
> si ahoga la armonía suprema del instante.
> . . . .
> cuán banales sois ya ante ese libro propio
> escrito por el tiempo
> en el límite falso de una frágil pantalla!
>
> (94)

> [Words . . .
> Dark butterflies of someone else's thought,
> how useless your voice is
> if it drowns out the supreme harmony of the moment.
> . . . .
> how banal you all are in the face of that book of yours
> written by time
> on the false edge of a fragile screen!]

Her attitude toward poetry is part of her recognition of the inadequacy of
the human dimension and her growing aspirations to transcendence. The
poem becomes for her the site of existential transformation and, in Barthes's
terms, more of a text, an experienced activity. No longer contained within
the poem itself, the poetic speaker stands as the manipulator at the center
of the creative process. Champourcin assumes this role without "anxiety of
authorship," describing it instead with a metaphor that Wilcox calls "redo-
lent with phallic aggression":[38]

> La vida fluye abajo, arrastrándose vana.
> Encima de mi frente, los divinos fantasmas
> del sueño verdadero, los éxtasis del alma . . .
> cicatrices de oro, que mi pluma va abriendo
> sobre la hoja blanca.
>
> (111)

[Life flows below, dragging itself in vain.
On top of my brow, the divine phantoms
of the true dream, the ecstasies of the soul . . .
golden scars, that my pen is opening up
on the white page.]

Located at the crossroad between the earthly and the celestial, Champourcin's poetic persona proves to be a fluctuating self, intimately linked to physicality yet aspiring to spiritual plenitude. She is what Kristeva labels a "subject in process," who experiences the moments of instability that constitute creativity and self-actualization.[39]

THE DESIROUS SELF

The expansion of both the power and complexity of the self marks Ernestina de Champourcin's next collection. Well-received, and preceded by a hand-written introduction by Juan Ramón Jiménez,[40] *La voz en el viento* [The voice in the wind] comprises ten sections focusing primarily on love, love for an unidentified "you," who often can be as easily taken to be human as divine. Nature continues to have an impact on the poetic speaker, but she begins to turn away from the world of sensorial phenomena, fixing her sights instead on the transcendent realm of universal beauty and spiritual plenitude. Nevertheless, she continues to ground her expression in the physicality of human experience. She throbs with desire and embraces the quest of fulfillment through love. As both an overwhelming force that subjugates and an avenue that facilitates the transgression of human boundaries, love envelops the feminine self in a dynamic interplay of polar opposites in a paradoxical yet felicitous relation. Self-assured and self-actualizing now, she projects a sense of dominion, at least in the first half of the book.

Poetry emerges as a liberating adventure. The initial and title poem of the collection presents an exultant, cosmic, bareback rider who proclaims her capacity to soar and the power of the word (her wind-steed) to reach "untrod heights" and fill "uninhabited depths":

> ¡Erguida sobre el lomo
> de todo lo inestable,
> derrumbaré certezas
> en nombre del azar!

(115)

> [Sitting straight up on the back
> of everything unstable,

> I will demolish certainties
> in the name of chance!]

Poetic creation has become for Champourcin, as Rafael Espejo-Saavedra indicates, an avenue of existence preferable to love by virtue of its total disengagement from limits of any kind.[41] The poetic speaker confidently describes herself as a creator of her own world, as an artistic creator who inscribes on the page—the soul of the other—her image of ideal love:

> Dibujé una rosa nueva
> en el papel de tu alma.
> ¡Cómo temblaste al sentir
> el roce de mis pinceles
> sobre la hoja arrugada!
> . . . .
> aboceté la estructura
> de mis sueños en la página
>
> (122)

> [I drew a new rose
> on the paper of your soul.
> How you trembled when you felt
> the touch of my brushes
> on the creased page!
> . . . .
> I outlined the structure
> of my dreams on the page]

Champourcin has reversed the common representation of gender, making the male the painted object and the female the painter and thus breaking the long tradition of woman as "blank page."[42] As the initiator of the quest and the designer of her love object, the female speaker in these poems becomes the agent of self-determination.

After the forceful declaration in the opening poem, the poet moves immediately from her preliminary identification with freedom to a series of poems centered on the adventure of liberation. Aptly titled "Viaje" [Journey], the second poem of the collection outlines the nature of her new enterprise. Not physical movement through concrete geographical spaces, this is a symbolic journey beyond the material world, beyond love, and beyond the very self. Reminiscent somewhat of poems of Pedro Salinas, who dismisses the substantive material of "islas, palacios, torres" [islands, palaces, towers] in favor of the intimacy of pronouns, Champourcin alludes to equally generic terms: "puertas," "ribera," and "umbral" [doors, riverbank, threshold]. But unlike her male peer, she seeks to exceed demarcation and the inadequacies of the other. The love she encounters is free, without a preconceived mold; but as she explores her own contours ("ribera"), love threatens her with limitation and disillusion. Consequently, she sets out alone to search for paths beyond the "lintels" of the self.

Poised at the very edge of the self, the poetic speaker is able to look beyond the earthly world. Images of physical ascension convey the emotional elevation she feels. In two poems she is lifted to unreachable heights in a flood of light, or she ascends to the level of abstract beauty through cosmic union with the wind. The titles of both these poems—"Cumbre" [Summit] and "Mirada en libertad" [Freed gaze]—epitomize the rising movement that sweeps across the entire collection.

At the same time the poet insists on images of peaks and stars, of rainbows and celestial light, of heavens and cosmic expanses, a complementary horizontal movement reiterates the sense of quest on a more terrestrial level. The road becomes the symbol of the poet's quest for love, light, and plenitude. The metaphor "life is a journey" stems from the general view of life as purposeful and from the knowledge of its final fatal outcome.[43] Champourcin, however, eliminates this sense of finality and associates the road instead with limitless horizons and fruition. In *La voz en el viento*, the road as a vehicle of poetic meaning has the dual function of a concrete image figuratively analogous to the movement of life, captured in expressions like "smoothed paths," "unknown path," or simply "road," and of material representation of the conduits to plenitude: nature and love. Morning opens before the protagonist of the collection as a road toward new birth in the poem "Génesis" [Genesis]. The road is also comparable to the immensity of love, to human desire, and to the presence of divine love.

The image of the road used in this way holds particular significance for the configuration of a female self because of its implications of progression, self-realization, and transcendence. In *La voz en el viento* the road conveys a sense of motion, but more importantly it materializes, through metaphorical rendering, the poet's aspirations to pass through and beyond sensation and sentiment. Additionally, the road symbol provides an outlet for self-assertion. In "Iniciación" [Beginning], she has the speaker articulate a desire to find a god.

> ¡Abridme paso, pronto!
> . . . .
> ¡Yo acercaré a su sangre la antorcha creadora!
> ¡Yo os lo traeré encendido como un radiante sol!
> ¡Abridme paso todos!
> Cerrad el horizonte, los caminos abiertos.
> Voy tejiendo mi ruta de ausencias enlazadas,
> ¡Con la brisa de un vuelo yo haré que nazca el dios!
>   (130–31)

[Make way for me, soon!
. . . .
I will bring the creative torch close to his blood!
I will bring it to you lit like a radiant sun!
Make way for me everyone!
Close the horizon, the open roads.
I am weaving my route with interlaced absence,
With the breeze of flight I will make god be born!]

The imperative forms, the exclamations, and the future-tense verbs culminate in a declaration of her power to give birth to the god of love. Her confidence in her own potential allows her to strike this priestly, if not god-like, pose.

Even when she alludes to the road in its literal formation of street, Champourcin abstracts the image from its anecdotal frame, focusing on its capacity to project adventure, transgression, or transcendence. The third section of the book, called precisely "Caminos" [Roads], includes five poems centering on the motorcar. In the vein of the *ultraísta* poets, she celebrates the speed and excitement of this modern-day invention ("el susto delicioso / de la escondida curva" [the delightful fright / of the hidden curve]), animates nature ("La calle-balcón desata / una fuga de geranio [The street-balcony unleashes / a flight of geraniums]), and subverts the traditional portrayal of the spent rose with a lighter if not flippant note of irony: "Llora un claxon tu muerte / sin alma en la cuneta" (126) [A car horn mourns your soulless death in the gutter]. Beneath the veneer of ludic playing, the poetic voice declares her own potential for cosmic control over the driver, calling herself the focusing lens that will encircle his hands with the universe, and she asserts her hope for fulfillment through the exhilarating hands of the driver. Thus, even a carefree trip by automobile is converted into a search for cosmic transcendence.

By creating a joyful, assertive, and forceful spirit in these poems, Champourcin in many ways, as Wilcox has discovered, depicts exuberant personae that are both feminine and feminist.[44] Any attribution of feminist to Champourcin must, however, be qualified and adjusted to her simultaneous recourse to traditional conceptions of womanhood. Her "gynocentric focus" is feminist to the extent that it converts inherently feminine images into positive elements of self-definition and highlights love from a woman's perspective. But Champourcin does not protest the restrictive social roles of women; and when she speaks of female self-realization, she does so through a religious posture of submission. Particularly as *La voz en el viento* unfolds in the sections called "La voz transfigurada" [The transfigured voice] and "Poemas ausentes" [Absent poems], the declarations of dominion that command attention in the first half of the book give way to more traditional renditions of the female self. In many of these poems, woman is represented as pure, subordinate, and compliant, as the source of pleasure, and as the vehicle for the transformation of the male. What is noteworthy in Champourcin is her ability to transform traditional feminine qualities into positive motifs of empowerment, presence, and plenitude.

The poetic speaker is continually preoccupied with her purity:

> Desnudaré mi voz para que tú la sientas
> vibrar transidamente en todos los silencios.
> ¡Con qué férvida unción impregnará tu vida
> su inefable pureza de lirio despojado!
>   Limpia, en sí; libre ya de ajenas resonancias,
> logrará eternizar mi único latido
> y ofrecerte en la copa de algún nombre sin eco
> el sorbo que mitigue la fiebre de tus labios.
>
> (141)

> [I will undress my voice so you can feel it
> vibrate fully in all silences.
> With what fervid anointing will its ineffable purity
> of stripped lily impregnate your life!
>   Clean, in itself; free from anyone else's resonances,
> it will manage to make my single heartbeat eternal
> and offer you in the goblet of some name without an echo
> the sip that will mitigate the fever of your lips.]

Without the moral implications of the sexual innocence and abstention generally associated with the female beloved, this is a purity of spiritual and abstract connotations. Detached from "ajenas resonancias," human expression becomes eternal. The female self confidently asserts her capacity to reach higher levels of existence and her role as the agent in elevating both the lover and love to a higher plane.

This attentiveness to the needs of the other can lead to self-surrender. The speaking voice conceives of herself as a prisoner of love who succumbs to the lover's trap. In the first of the sonnets included in *La voz en el viento*, she presents herself as silent, confused, and meek in the face of love:

> Tu presencia me ciñe duramente
> y el grito de mi vida encarcelada
> sucumbe ya, rendido a la celada
> que tus labios abrieron en mi frente.
>   Detén mi paso incierto. Mansamente
> callará en ti mi voz desorientada.
>
> (134)

> [Your presence encircles me tightly
> and the shout of my imprisoned life
> succumbs now, surrendering to the ruse
> that your lips created on my brow.
>   Stop my uncertain step. Meekly
> my disoriented voice will fall silent in you.]

In contrast to conventional portrayals of woman, the female lover here does not resist the advances of love, but welcomes, indeed begs for, the loss of self that love promises. While it is true, as Espejo-Saavedra suggests, that the "prison of love" motif in this poem is more liberating than incarcerating,[45] the traditional paradigm of male conquest and female submission remains constant.

Her willingness to relinquish the essence of her life to the other is total and uncompromised:

> Dejar de ser. Vivir la gloria de tu sueño
> en místico naufragio de sones y palabras.
> Derramar en tu vida la esencia de mi vida,
> sumergir en tus labios el eco de mi voz.
>   Olvidar los caminos y la senda trenzada
> por el sordo latir de mis pulsos febriles.
> Anularme en la sombra de tus manos abiertas
> que apaciguan mi sien con ternura de luz.
>
> (138)

> [To stop existing. To live the glory of your dream
> in a mystical drowning of sounds and words.
> To spill into your life the essence of my life,
> to submerge the echo of my voice in your lips.
>   To forget the roads and the path woven
> by the muffled beating of my feverish pulse.
> To nullify myself in the shadow of your open hands
> that calm my temple with the tenderness of light.]

She depicts the surrender to love with language derived from the representation of the nullification of personal identity associated with the mystical experience. She speaks in terms evoking physical death—drowning, the spilling of fluids, and submergence—and she alludes to existential disappearance— "dejar de ser," "Olvidar los caminos," and "Anular." Without temporal dimension, the infinitives place the protagonist in a suspended state of stasis. When not corresponding to the patterns of the mystical experience, the factor of surrender conforms to the model of maternal self-denial, with the woman speaker declaring herself a perpetual protectoress: "¡Seré tuya aún sin ti! Dejaré de mecerte / en la cuna encendida que tejieron mis besos" (146) [I will be yours even without you. I will stop rocking you / in the inflamed cradle woven by my kisses].

Not only is the female speaker a willing servant of her beloved, she is the vessel of love from which he drinks a beneficial nectar. In the sonnet beginning "Tu presencia me ciñe," the woman's cupped hand offers love in the form of a star. The religious overtones of this gesture of raising the chalice and the word "ungida" [anointed] are repeated throughout the collection. The poetic speaker holds within her physical grasp both intangible human emotions and the beauty of nature. In an intimate dialogue with a rainbow, she asserts, "Múltiple cromo volcado / por ti, sigilosamente, / en el hueco de mis manos" (122) [A multiple color print emptied by you secretly, / in the hollow of my hands]. She sees herself as the guardian of spiritual joy for her lover as well as the medium between the abstract and concrete spheres. This imagery sublimates and even sanctifies the material aspects of human existence. Her metaphors for woman's hands are more traditional than in her previous book, but they reflect the same desire to transcend the purely physical and to ennoble human existence.

The motifs of the vessel of purity, the subordinate beloved, and the prisoner of love do not connote passivity, limitation, or weakness in Champourcin's poetry. Its female self, through love, is freed from the material world and assumes power over both herself and the other, paradoxically, through the very attributes traditionally obstructive of self-fulfillment. Instead of being synonymous with enclosure and serviceability, woman as container in this poetry has possession over the intangibles of life she holds and enjoys the ability to confer material existence upon them—be they rainbows, love, or divine beauty:

> —¡Soy la muchacha término,
> el ancla de cristal
> que detiene las horas.
> Mis cabellos de níquel
> imantan las estrellas—.
> . . . .
> Yo ungí de realidades
> el sueño de tu frente.
> La belleza más próxima
>
> (124)

> [—I am the terminus girl,
> the glass anchor
> that holds back time.
> My nickel hair
> magnetizes the stars—.
> . . . .

> I anoint the dream
> of your brow with realities.
> The nearest beauty]

Self-assured, the speaker boasts of her power to control not only her male companion but the cosmos itself. Although oriented toward the other, the persona that emerges in this poem is both liberated and liberating, self-aware and self-actualizing. This combination of the female as the custodian of the pleasure of the other and the agent of transformation is constant throughout the book.

The poetic speaker conceives of herself as pure yet sensual in the poem "Te esperaré desnuda" [I will wait for you disrobed]:

> Te esperaré desnuda.
> Seis túnicas de luz resbalando ante ti
> deshojarán el ámbar moreno de mis hombros.
> . . . .
> y mis manos que ofrecen su cáliz entreabierto
> a todo lo inasible.
> Te esperaré encendida.
> Mi antorcha despejando la noche de tus labios
> libertará por fin tu esencia creadora.
> ¡Ven a fundirte en mí!
> El agua de mis besos, ungiéndote, dirá
> tu verdadero nombre.
>
> (149)

> [I will wait for you disrobed.
> six tunics of light slipping away before you
> will strip away the dark amber of my shoulders.
> . . . .
> and my hands that offer you the chalice half-opened
> to everything intangible.
> I will wait for you inflamed.
> My torch, clearing the night from your lips,
> will finally free your creative essence.
> Come and fuse with me!
> The water of my kisses, anointing, will say
> your true name.]

She describes herself as a maiden wrapped in six tunics of light, who nonetheless disrobes to reveal her golden nude body. She is both blessed and passionate, identified with a chalice and then a fiery torch. The repetition of "Te esperaré" at the beginning of each of the poem's three stanzas underlines her role as expectant receiver of love; yet her immobility does not denote inactivity. The chalice of her hands captures the intangible ("lo inasible"); she also displays a power to unleash ("libertar") the creative essence of the other; and she anoints him in a final gesture of transformation. The confidence with which she declares her capacity to provoke sexual reactions attests to a bold assumption of agency, but by sanctifying her body, she can successfully incorporate the erotic into her poem within the demands for decorum of her times.

Essential to self-representation in poetry by women is their representation of the masculine other. Traditionally, the male role in the love affair has been that of active player, of the one who desires, seeks gratification, determines the encounter, and regularly abandons the female partner. Just as Ernestina de Champourcin subtly adjusts the conventional depiction of the woman in love as untainted, passive, and compliant, she also modifies slightly the representation of the male as solely an active and aggressive force. He is still the initiator of the sexual act; although she desires physical contact and pleasure, he is the one who must set that operation in motion: "Te espero inmunizada contra todos los hielos. / Sólo tú rasgarás mi cortina de estrellas" (139) [Immunized against all ice / I will wait for you. / Only you will tear my starry curtain]. He can potentially grant her spiritual relief from anguish and sadness: "Quisiera que tus ojos vendaran mi tristeza / con el lino impalpable de su larga mirada" (147) [I would like your eyes to bandage my sadness / with the impalpable linen of your long gaze]. He also is the intangible avenue to her plenitude—the guide, beacon, and final destination of her spiritual search:

> ¡Quiero una luz concreta, surgida de ti mismo,
> que guíe hacia tu puerto los pasos de mi amor!
>
> (141)

> [I want a concrete light, that rises from you yourself,
> that guides the footsteps of my love to your port!]

> guíame lentamente, sin luz, hacia ti mismo,
> pero no apagues nunca la antorcha de tu voz.
>
> (141)

> [guide me slowly, toward yourself,
> don't ever extinguish the torch of your voice.]

The other becomes the conduit to spiritual joy and the eternal. At the same time, however, he is the inert page on which she outlines her dream ("¡Cómo temblaste al sentir / el roce de mis pinceles / sobre la hoja arrugada!" [How you trembled when you felt / the touch of my brushes / on the creased paper!]), the target of the cosmic powers of her gaze ("Yo, lente enfocadora, / ceñiré el universo / al hueco de tus manos" [I, a focusing lens, / will fit the universe / to the hollow of your hands]), and her prisoner ("Eres mi prisionero" [You are my prisoner]).

The masculine other is more an intangible abstraction than a concrete being situated in a specific social environment. He is tied to social references only in the poems of the section "Caminos," where he is the driver of a motor car, the machine that had come to symbolize the carefree, sporting lifestyle of the upper-middle classes of the day. His gloved hands that grasp the steering wheel exude a seductive smell of gasoline and hold the potential for dizzy excitement. Champourcin, like Josefina de la Torre, spotlights the man's hands as the body part of contemplation. This choice derives from her vision of love as a spiritual state rooted in physical contact and becomes particularly significant if we recall that Gustavo Adolfo Bécquer isolated the woman's eyes as the hallmark of her beauty. In male discourse of love, visibility is paramount.[46] The woman is seen more than she sees; she remains visibly alluring yet a physically detached object, and the unsettling threat of her gaze compromises her appeal. The prevalence of the gaze, asserts Luce Irigaray, is foreign to female eroticism. Woman, she says, finds pleasure more in touch than sight.[47] Ostriker, for her part, calls touch "the imperative of intimacy in women's writing and the motif in which we find the elements of a gynocentric erotics, metaphysics, poetics."[48] In Champourcin's poetry, the speaker pleads for tactile attachment: "¡ Dame tus dedos, acres / de olor a gasolina" (125) [Give me your acrid fingers / smelling of gasoline]. His hands soothe, arouse, and sublimate. Union between the self and the other is described as the elimination of boundaries enacted in a set of locked hands: "No hay distancias; la tarde se hace nuestra en el sueño / que reclina las frentes y nos trenza las manos" (147) [There are no distances; the afternoon becomes ours in the drowsiness / that reclines our brows and braids our hands]. Champourcin's poetry confirms what many feminists have seen as women's characteristic privileging of contiguity over remoteness and continuance over division. Rather than the masculine phallic economy of appropriation of the object, according to Jessica Benjamin, women's patterns of desire exhibit "intersubjectivity," a spatial mode grounded on a continuum that includes the space between the I and you, as well as the space within me.[49]

This preference for contact, continuity, and interchange in Champourcin's poetry also accounts, again like de la Torre, for the prominence of the voice, the instrument of verbal communication. She highlights "voice" in the title of the collection and in the section "La voz transfigurada." The voice, along with eyes and hands, are the physical traits of men that women have regularly celebrated, as Evelyne Sullerot points out in her study of eight centuries of feminine writing.[50] In La voz en el viento, through the voice, an intangible connection is formed between the subject and the other on a level midway between a corporal and spiritual union. The voice of the other through metonymic association with lips can acquire palpable features caressed by the speaker. However, more a state than a substance, the voice becomes synonymous with the lover's spirit and with the essence of love itself. The two lovers in perfect concert with nature and between themselves, with hands linked and their voices in unison, are "voces sin voz" [voices without a voice], voices without a material reality. In lines reminiscent of the Biblical "And the word was made flesh," the male voice becomes incarnate before the figure of a kneeling female: "Se hizo carne tu voz y sentí que tu espíritu / inyectaba en mis pulsos el hervor de su fiebre" (143) [Your voice was made flesh and I felt your spirit / inject into my pulse the fire of your fever]. This element of transformation of the male other becomes more evident in the section "La voz transfigurada," where the spiritual transformation of the voice, implied in the title, recasts the speaker's search for a love with mystical dimensions.

The transcendent, deified quality of the male is intensified by numerous associations between him and light. Cano Ballesta oversimplifies when he identifics the male in this poetry with light and the female with darkness.[51] An all-encompassing being, the lover, for Champourcin, has both body and spirit and belongs both to darkness and light. The metaphor of the shadow is used to connote his physical strength, comforting grasp, and lingering worldly presence, while an identification with light bestows a divine essence upon him. Champourcin depicts the physical desire of the lover as a synthesis of light and heat and their orgasmic pleasure as "un naufragio de luz" [a drowning of light], while she at the same time represents him as a beacon she never wants to see extinguished and a distant illumination which she strives to reach. He is a light from beyond this world that carries her past the boundaries of material existence, directs her toward a loftier sphere, and brings a sense of plenitude that combines physical ecstasy with spiritual bliss.

The godlike creature that emerges in this poetry elicits the devotion of an adoring woman who stands ready to confer on him the pleasures available from her body and to engage in a sublimating exchange of desires. This other is far removed from the supreme Other created in masculine discourse that de Beauvoir discusses and also remains at a distance from the other in works of someone like the Spanish contemporary poet Ana Rossetti, who converts male figures into inert objects of desire rooted in banal advertising images. In the poetry of Ernestina de Champourcin, the female speaker is conscious of her erotic desires and the body, but she speaks with the restraint and euphemisms demanded of women in Spain until recent years. Lacking, however, is the ingredient of shame implicit in the concept of *pudor* [modesty] with which Catholicism conditioned women to abnegation. In Champourcin's poetry, self-surrender promises to lead to both the delights of the flesh and the bliss of the spirit. The female self is represented in traditional terms as the expectant lover and the embodiment of purity at the disposal of the other, but this rendition does not preclude agency nor transcendence. The speaking voice confidently asserts her ability to create poetry, the conditions for love, and the beloved himself. Her existence centers not on being but on becoming.

LOVE, DESIRE, AND TRANSCENDENCE

Desire, not love, has been a major preoccupation of postmodern academic research.[52] Dominating this discussion have been the ideas of Jacques Lacan, who defines desire as a psychological drive to unite with that which is needed but always absent. Love, however, is an emotional attachment structured on idealization. The subject constructs an ideal other who promises the attainment of a state of perfection, plenitude, and immortality. Julia Kristeva explains that amatory discourse in Platonic terms is primarily a struggle between sublime Eros and manic Eros, between an effort to idealize the love relationship and the manic force's urging that immediate pleasure be taken from the love object. She observes furthermore that, in Western society at the end of the twentieth century, the idealizing pole of love is under threat while manic Eros predominates.[53] Champourcin intertwines these two versions of Eros. She speaks of sensuality, erotic desire, and sexual union, but her emphasis on the transcendence of corporal limitations and her analogies between physical and divine love show a preference for the sublime and a substantial measure of idealization. She began writing in an era in which the social framework was strongly influenced by religion, a mystic literary tradition was available as a model for amatory discourse, and all vestiges of the romantic formulation of ideal love had not disappeared.

The romantic view that love is an uncontrollable force and that women are the powerless victims of male desire has made contemporary American feminists wary of love.[54] The reaction by feminists like Hélène Cixous to the tradition of love has been to privilege desire. Explorations of desire, however, ultimately reveal that conventional conceptions have consistently prioritized male pleasure and alienated women from their own sexuality and pleasure.[55] The solution in literary criticism to this dilemma has been to delineate ways in which the female can free herself from past alienations through such strategies as self-definition, the assumption of the role of subject, an awareness of the female body, the articulation of desire, and a subversion of the masculine discourse of violence and exploitation.

Champourcin is tentative in her challenge to traditional discourse. She creates a poetic persona who defines herself in terms of conventional femininity, as pure, seductive, and self-surrendering. She views herself in terms of the masculine other: she renounces her essence for his sake, loses herself in nothingness in order to be re-created by the lover, and offers herself as his mirror and muse. The female persona in Champourcin becomes a speaking subject, who describes herself but, for the most part, echoes the traditional masculine conception of women. As Suzette Acevedo-Loubriel has written, she is the one "que se subyuga por sí misma, pero también la que se juzga subyugada" [who subjugates herself, but she is also the one who judges herself to be subjugated].[56] Nonetheless, she significantly diverges from the phallocentrism of masculine depictions in her concentration on female self-definition and in her revelations of exuberance, self-assertion, and even aggressivity. Above all, she displays a sense of consciousness of her own desire and of her power as a woman and a poet.

Champourcin's gynocentric perspective of desire implicitly undermines patriarchal assumptions on domination and autonomy. Rather than dwelling on the gap produced between desire and reality that Lacan highlights, she stresses connection over separation and focuses almost exclusively on communion with the other. In this way, surrender acquires positive meanings for her; and she precludes the self-containment, detachment from the other, and singularity that coincide with autonomy. The drive that Champourcin textualizes is a yearning not for the lost union with the Imaginary but for the experience of a new unity as a means to reaching a higher level of existence. This sublimation of physical desire transforms the erotic in her poetry into a mystical disposition, with the mystical understood not as a rejection of the pleasures of the world, but as the glorification of them. Champourcin's emphasis on the possibility of *jouissance*, on the ecstatic union that completes the self, keeps her poetry linked to physical experience and attaches feminist implications to it. First of all, although not by confrontation, she shows boldness during her times by the mere act of writing about female desire. Then, she displaces the associations made in male literature between desire and capture, possession and domination, by placing her accent on giving, sharing, and transcending. Finally, she reveals the existence, for woman, of pleasure without guilt and love without victimization.

Transcendence is the unifying theme of *La voz en el viento*. The poetic voice yearns to rise beyond the sensorial and the anecdotal in order to reach the realm of the spiritual and absolute. Natural beauty and human love are the avenues leading to that goal. The beauty of nature lifts the lovers toward God, in a poem appropriately titled "Ascensión" [Ascent]:

> Como dos tallos nuevos,
> emprendamos la eterna

conquista de lo azul.
    ¡Subiremos a Dios
por lo bello del mundo!

                                    (121)

[Like two new stems,
let us embark on the eternal
conquest of the blue above.
    We will ascend to God
via the beauty of the world!]

Love and nature share the same destiny and coalesce in metaphorical analogy: "Todos los horizontes despejan sus caminos / ante el surco que trazan
nuestras voces en voces" (123) [All the horizons clear their roads / before
the furrow that our intertwined voices trace]. Ultimately the lovers surpass
natural phenomena to become a part of the universal love and beauty that
are God: "¡Cada paso que demos hacia nosotros mismos / sembrará en lo
invisible un átomo de ti!" (150) [Every step we take toward ourselves / will
sow an atom of yours in all that is invisible!]. A subscription by women to
transcendence can be seen, as Ostriker does in her reading of de Beauvoir,
as a submission to the dominant assumptions of a phallocentric culture
that privileges transcendence over immanence and concomitantly, the masculine over the feminine.[57] However, Champourcin appropriates transcendence to dignify the feminine. She challenges the prevailing equation of
her day that links only men to creativity, intellect, and spirituality while at
the same time inscribing into her articulation of desire a variant of transcendence, which sheds its male value of independent ego and conquest
and acquires a female one of communion.

    The poetic self in Champourcin's poetry embarks on a symbolic jour-
ney in search of ideal love. No poem illustrates better the motif of the
amatory quest in *La voz en el viento* than "Plenitud" [Plenitude], the longest
composition in the book, whose significance as emotional apex is highlighted by its separation from all the other subsections. The poet describes the
birth of desire as a morning march toward luminous heights and the unencumbered, autonomous self feels lonely without an alternative presence:

        ¡Tortura de existir, diferenciada, sola,
        al margen de la esencia que fluye en otras vidas!
        Quise hundirme en el suelo y recibió mis huellas,
        diluirme en el agua y su cristal bruñido
        eternizó mis ojos.

                                            (143)

[Differentiated, solitary torture of living,
on the margin of the essence that flows in other lives!
I wanted to sink into the ground and it received my footprints,
to dissolve myself in the water and its polished crystal
made my eyes eternal.]

She attempts to merge with nature, but only the appearance of the human
lover brings joy; sexual contact transports her beyond the realm of the self;
and her initial impetuosity subsides into post-orgasmic serenity. As consistently occurs in Champourcin, sensuality is enveloped in religious imagery
that sublimates the erotic underpinnings of her poems. Kissing, for example,
becomes the receiving of the holy sacrament in the mass:

> Inclinaste la boca. Yo levanté la mía,
> y un minuto de cielo
> volcó sobre nosotros su cáliz asombrado.
>
> (144)

> [You inclined your mouth. I lifted mine,
> and a minute of sky
> spilled its shaded chalice on us.]

The paradigm of search, encounter, and repose on which "Plenitud" is
grounded accounts for the insistence on the motifs of journey, road, and
ascent. However, the search is but a prelude to plenitude and sexual encounter merely the means to that end. The stress is on the goal of love, but
that love only matters to the extent that it lifts and uplifts, that it drives the
self to exceed itself and experience that "minuto de cielo."

Champourcin underscores her overriding vision of love as basically a
process of spiritual transcendence that combines *jouissance* with mystical
ecstasy by representing the female self as a pure vessel of love and the male
other as a beacon radiating love and by overlaying of religious meanings
on suggestions of eroticism. Her inclusion of motifs of ascension and her
reliance on cosmic images enhance this conception. She intensifies the spiritual quality of love further by identifying it as benevolence. She replaces
the conventional masculine economy of exchange by which love is booty
won through personal achievement or seductive persuasion with an altruis-
tic approach that sees love aimed at the mutual benefit of both the giver
and recipient. The poetic speaker in Champourcin's poetry bestows upon
her lover her purified naked body, the blessed nectar of her lips, and her
chalice-like hands and, further yet, surrenders to him the very essence of
her existence. Her generous acts are gestures made with full consciousness
of the treasures she possesses and their impact. Her love frees the lover, but
it also opens the way for her to rise, through earthly pleasures, to the level

of eternal beauty. By giving, she receives; and the lovers enjoy a happy communion of selves in which the "I" and the "you" are united in reciprocal tenderness: "Navegan nuestros cielos / con rumbo a su recíproca ternura" (134) [Our skies sail toward their reciprocal tenderness]. This system of amorous reciprocity stands in stark contrast to the patterns of desire in men, for whom, as Juliet Mitchell affirms, the language of reciprocity and equality is meaningless.[58] Just as female subjectivity validates reciprocity, a female erotics projects mutuality, continuity, and connection.

Expanding this gender difference, Champourcin casts aside the characteristically masculine attention to the physical appearance and moral qualities of the beloved, preferring an alternative focus on the act of loving and the emotions it provokes. Desire is conceived as springing forth, not from external trappings, but from within the female self as the very essence of her existence or as a treasured body fluid emanating from her. The poetic voice in *La voz en el viento* speaks of her own desire as a juice ("zumo") held in the "goblet," that is, her visage, which the lover will raise to the sun in a gesture suggestive of the priest's elevation of the chalice during mass. At the same time, this miraculous liquid also identifies the lover: "Eres el zumo eterno de esta pausa que vivo" (147) [You are the eternal juice of this pause that I am living]. This interchangeable identification between him and her reinforces the sense of mutuality that sustains Champourcin's vision of love. Not the exclusive dominion of one or the other, desire is an open, liquid force that paradoxically exists both inside and outside the self. It is both an inner essence given away freely and a superior force that must be served.

Another seemingly contradictory aspect of love surfaces in Champourcin's intertwining of physicality and spirituality. Desire is depicted in clearly physical terms ("si el deseo punzante que taladra mis sienes, / es el mismo que seca la pulpa de tus labios?" (145) [if the sharp desire that drills into my temples / is the same one that dries the pulp of your lips?]); and the references to coitus are equally explicit:

> Sólo tú rasgarás mi cortina de estrellas.
> Aún te pertenece ese don infinito
> que a cada nuevo instante me transfigura en ti.
>
> (139)

> [Only you will tear my starry curtain.
> This infinite gift that at every moment
> transfigures me into you still belongs to you.]

> ¿No sientes mis raíces? Tu tallo florecido,
> ebrio de sí, eterniza mi cálida fragancia.

¡Irguiéndolo alzarás la copa de mi frente,
hasta volcar su zumo en los labios del sol!

(148)

[Don't you feel my roots? Your flowering stem,
intoxicated by itself, eternalizes my warm fragrance.
Straightening it, you will raise the goblet of my brow,
until it spills its juice on the sun's lips!]

Yet, as the poetic speaker asserts, she wants to apply a varnish of "mystic presence" to her picture of love. To achieve this goal she describes human love in terms of the mystical experience of surrender of self and with imagery of religious connotations. As Mainer maintains, the poems in the first section of *La voz en el viento* with their schematic titles—"Viaje," "Cumbre," "Cepo," "Pausa," "Huida" [trip, summit, snare, pause, flight]— can suggest "la voluntad de ir más allá de la anécdota, a un mundo de esencias donde Dios comienza a hallar un importante lugar" [the will to go beyond the anecdote, to the world of essence where God begins to find an important place] and the basic structures of the mysticism of San Juan de la Cruz.[59] However, by the midpoint of the collection, the expressions of love become patently sexual and religious images are only a sublimating veneer. For example in "Plenitud," the lover emerges as the incarnation of love in an allusion to the biblical line "And the Word was made flesh." In anticipation of the appearance of her god of love, the poetic speaker kneels to receive him, but the union she awaits is clearly physical.

For many critics *Cántico inútil* [Useless canticle] (1936), the book that followed *La voz en el viento*, represents the culmination of Champourcin's precivil war production. Mainer calls it undoubtedly her best book before her exile; Jiménez Faro writes that it is the book that perhaps best marks her place among Spanish women poets; Landeira affirms that it "stands out in all of her production: it is her longest, most intricate, and most structurally varied volume."[60] *Cántico inútil* concentrates on love and desire with greater insistence than her previous works and broadens the dimensions of its expression. The collection is preceded by five poems by her soon-to-be-husband Juan José Domenchina and begins with poems from the second half of *La voz en el viento*. With the inclusion of these poems from her preceding book, Champourcin assembles a complete presentation of love, desire, and transcendence.

The new poems of *Cántico inútil* continue, with slight variations, the essential stance of the poetic self and the prevailing conception of the other evolved in *La voz en el viento*. Images with mystical implications increase, but at the same time negative imagery and tension surface. The desire for love persists as an irrepressible quest beyond the realm of sensations and sentiments, but the poetic voice focuses more on the different states of human love that hinder or retard ascension and spiritual unity. Her perspective is more contemplative and her tone more somber. The tempo of her poems slows under the weight of their extended lines that often reach the length of the alexandrine. The title *Cántico inútil* predicts the failure of the rapturous hymn that "Plenitud" exemplified in the previous book, and the first, new section of *Cántico inútil*, called "Cumbres sin cielo" [Summits without heaven], suggests that full transcendence is no longer a certainty. However, although doubt and even despair enter the blissful poetic space in which Champourcin's lyrical persona dwells, her basic posture of faith in the realization of love persists.

The idealization of the masculine other seen in *La voz en el viento* intensifies in *Cántico inútil*. The lyrical subject wants comfort from him and a refuge from the sadness and sharp pain ("inquietud punzante" [sharp anxiety]) that begins to bore on her temples. The masculine other does not necessarily respond to her requests. Frequently remaining a silent, distant, and hostile lover, he inflicts pain or knowingly constructs barriers to the fulfillment of her desire for love:

> ¡Si yo viera el camino!
> Pero lo nublas siempre
> con tu palabra hostil
> y tu silencio inerte.
>
> (169)

> [If I were to see the road!
> But you always obscure it
> with your hostile word
> and passive silence.]

Despite his evasion of her, she goes out to the desert to proclaim her belief in him. In the first poem of the section "Noche oscura" [Dark night], she articulates a prayer-like creed of faith that, with its devotional tone together with the biblical motif of crying-in-the-desert, raises the masculine other from benevolent human to divine being. Particularly in the section titled "Dios y tú" [God and you], the correspondences between God and the human lover are firmly established with images referring to the human body juxtaposed or combined with allusions to the deity: "Dios en tu frente, alto, sonriendo en la cima" (*Cántico*, 167) [God on your brow, on high, smiling from the summit] and "Frente de Dios, ¡tu frente! Manos de Dios, ¡tus manos!" (*Cántico*, 168) [God's brow, your brow! God's hands, your hands!]. The identification between the beloved and God cannot be stated more directly than "Eres Dios, y te busco" (167) [You are God, and I am seeking you]. The deification of the indifferent lover converts his remoteness into a reason for steadfast devotion and makes his unresponsiveness proof of his idealized difference.

Looking at herself, the poetic speaker continues to take pride in her sovereign purity and to conform simultaneously to and undermine the norms of femininity. What changes in *Cántico inútil* is the stress placed on the feminine self as the source of love. The poetic protagonist joyfully proclaims: ¡Soy la raíz primera de todos los amores . . . Nada logra su ser sin el zumo que fluye / por mis venas exhaustas" (158) [I am the prime root of all loves . . . Nothing attains its existence without the juice that flows / through my exhausted veins]. With great assertion, she declares herself to be in possession of a "magic essence" that revives, transfigures, and bestows immortality. This equation between the female self and love infuses the poetic persona with an inner power expressed through gestures of maternal nurturance. She physically sustains the other ("Por mucho que te alejes, hasta el bosque más virgen / te llevaré mi agua" 184 [No matter how much you distance yourself, to the most virgin forest / I will bring you my water]); she guides him through life ("mi desvelo / será brújula fiel en tu equipaje" 162 [my vigilance will be the faithful compass in your luggage]); she cures ("Seré para tu cuerpo el lino apaciguante / que sana y que perdona" 159 [I will be for your body the calming linseed / that cures and pardons]); and she ultimately guarantees his salvation ("beberás en mí tu propia eternidad" 158 [in me you will drink your own eternity]). As occurs in *La voz en el viento*, declarations of strength are coupled with affirmations of self-surrender, with the stance of the supplicant becoming more pronounced.

While *La voz en el viento* opened with the poetic personage poised on a hilltop ready for adventure, *Cántico inútil* begins with her in the position of the anxious and lonely supplicant who casts doubt on the arrival of love. Appropriately called "Espera" [Waiting], the initial poem of the collection explains its first word: "amor" [love]. Love is depicted as a conjunction of polarities, of darkness and light, of pain and ecstasy, of distance and desired presence. Love's arrival is not guaranteed, but the incessancy of the wait suggests that aspiration as much as realization gives it a significance. Reinforcing the contrasts established in the first poem, the second poem, aptly called "Fe," [Faith], counterbalances the opening doubt with faith. The poetic voice declares with certainty that she believes love will eventually blossom: "Sé que un día muy claro / brotará del silencio, del agua, del espacio . . . " (154) [I know that one very bright day / it will sprout from silence, from water, from space . . .]. The confidence projected in this statement is accompanied by concessive clauses that indirectly hint at the perseverance of her pursuit and by imperatives and exclamations that exhort the lover to follow her lead. Similarly in the rest of the collection, the glories and sorrows of love will be intertwined as the poetic speaker relentlessly aspires to transcend to celestial heights through human love.

This overriding drive to transcendence compels Champourcin to continue to structure the love quest as a road journey. She unambiguously highlights the metaphorical meaning of the road in the section called "Romances del camino" [Road ballads]. The poetic protagonist is hampered in her search by her unfamiliarity with the roadway and by the roadblocks her lover constructs, but she nonetheless pleads that he be her guide. In the tenth poem of the series, her destination becomes less the state of love than the person loved: "Un camino. Dos pasos . . . / ¡Quiero seguirte siempre / y recoger tu llanto!" [One road. Two steps . . . / I want to follow you always / and gather your tears]. The portrayal of the lover as the road underscores her superimposition of metaphors for God—in this instance that of "Christ as the way"—on human love.[61]

Occasionally in *Cántico inútil* love is envisioned as blissful union, but the celebration of the delights of desire and the joy of love that predominated in *La voz en el viento* is tainted in this new collection with a variety of negative states. Images of ugliness intrude upon the once-peaceful poetic landscape; there are gray snakes, powdered ash, and pale plumage thrown about in a hurricane. "Inhuman ice" threatens the fire of desire, and hatred is personified as painful lashes and fiery shouts. Pain becomes a definite part of love; there is separation, suffering, and failure. The departure of the lover leaves a sense of deep loss within the poetic speaker that manifests itself in the ineffectiveness of her voice: "Ahora, si te llamo, naufragará mi grito" (182) [Now, if I call you, my shout will sink]. Forsaken, she either attempts to flee the pain or suffers the pangs of her anger. Sometimes the absence of the lover is so powerful that it assumes the equivalence of a presence: "El eco de ti mismo se evade lentamente / desgarrando mis venas con su lanza de sol. (*Cántico*, 181) [Your echo slowly slips away / ripping my veins with its lance of sunlight].

The poetic speaker admits to herself that evoked caresses are but tortuous self-deceptions; only loneliness is real. In the poem "Soledades" [Solitudes], an all-encompassing and plural solitude, through dramatic symbols turned into "visiones," takes on the living form of a malevolent devouring animal: "Todas las soledades—grises víboras—muerden / la duda que taladra mis sienes abatidas" (154) [All loneliness—gray vipers—bite / the doubt that bores into my downcast temples].[62] In the poem her loneliness is felt physically, on the forehead, the eyes, and the lips. Three exclamations without verb forms, at the start of successive stanzas, add a note of acute stagnation. The "you" possesses the power to free the lyrical "I" from pain, but the presence of anguish and the remoteness of love make the disappearance of loneliness impossible. Abandoned and alone, the lyrical "I" stands on the brink of nothingness, symbolized in an image of drowning:

¡Silencio tras silencio! Navegarlos sin tregua
y naufragar en todos hasta rozar la nada.
Vivir sólo un instante entre lo que no existe,
rasgar de angustia humana la roca de lo eterno . . .

(186–87)

[Silence after silence! Sailing them relentlessly
and drowning in all of them until rubbing against nothingness.
Living only one instant within everything that does not exist,
slashing the rock of the eternal with human anguish . . .]

The expressions of anguish filtering throughout the book culminate in the penultimate poem of the collection:

Sólo queda un silencio de oscuras mariposas
que afelpan las pisadas crueles del olvido,
un clamor soterrado de júbilos ya muertos,
una dicha que huye de su propio fantasma.

(187)

[There only remains a silence of dark butterflies
that soften the cruel steps of oblivion,
a buried noise of a jubilation now dead,
a happiness that flees its own ghost.]

The disappointments of unrequited love and an unresponsive lover make the poetic speaker dream of a realm spared the hazards of love:

Haremos una tierra inmóvil, desprendida
del ímpetu salvaje que enciende los estíos.
Un pálido universo desnudo de fragancias
que ignore la dulzura de todos los fervores.

(188)

[We will make a motionless land, unleashed
from the wild impulse that ignites summers.
A pale universe stripped of fragrances
that does not know about the sweetness of all passions.]

However, with a rhetorical question, she also declares that the promise of love breeds despair: "Y si todo es inútil . . . ¿Para qué la esperanza endeble y fervorosa / de tantos despertares?" (156) [And if everything is useless . . . why the feeble and passionate hope / of so many beginnings?]. Yet she refuses to eradicate desire completely. Champourcin concludes *Cántico inútil* with a final affirmation of the persistent power of love. With all its contradictions of laughter and tears, gentleness and harshness, elevation and abyss, desire maintains its dominion, compelling the speaker to continue to seek its fire, its "corola de fuego ensombrecido" [corolla of shaded fire].

Fire, a conventional metaphor for physical passion, is used abundantly in *Cántico inútil*. Fire appears in the generic form of "fuego" [fire], and also as "llama" [flame], "antorcha" [torch], and "quemadura" [burn]. Verbs of conflagration—"arder," "encender," "abrasar" [to burn, to ignite, to scorch]—add action to the connotations of potency. Fire is an apt image for Champourcin, for not only does it symbolize vitality, it incorporates the combination of body and spirit that informs her poetry. Fire in the axis fire-earth represents eroticism, solar heat, and physical energy while fire of the axis fire-air is linked with mysticism, purification or sublimation, and spiritual energy.[63] These archetypal values help consolidate the human with the divine. The human lover is infused with the light, the heat, and the fiery essence of that "zenith of suns" to which the female speaking voice wants to ascend, to ascend not of her own accord, but as the impatient recipient of the masculine fire:

> ¿Dime por qué pusiste entre mis manos
> esa antorcha que nunca encenderías
> y me anunciaste el fuego, si querías
> ceñir de escarcha mis fervores vanos?
>
> (164)

> [Tell me why you put between my hands
> that torch you would never light
> and you announced the fire to me, if you wanted
> to encircle my vain fervor with frost?]

In this and other poems of *Cántico inútil* fire is a symbol for the phallic fueling of female sexual combustion:

> ¡Acerca nuevamente
> la antorcha de tus manos
> a la pira fragante
> de mi cuerpo sellado!
>
> (174)

> [Bring the torch of your
> hands close again
> to the fragrant pyre
> of my sealed body!]

Following traditional gender polarizations, Champourcin uses telluric images, particularly water, to represent women. The self is described as "manantial," "linfa," and "dóciles riberas" [spring, lymph, docile banks], and as indelible furrows awaiting seeds. As women poets often do, Champourcin stresses nature's likeness to the lyrical "I." Reacting with neither fear nor reverence, the self is nature. In *Cántico inútil* Champourcin also adapts the metaphor of the flower to a female perspective. She neither associates the woman-as-flower figure with the misogynist Christian tradition that equated woman with the perils of the flesh, nor does she link it any longer to the deflowering of the virgin, as she did in her first collection. The flower is love itself, the love that blooms in the lover's hands and the remembrance of it that the woman holds in hers. From the point of view of the female speaker, an identification with the rose constitutes a positive step toward self-realization: "Déjame ser la rosa del páramo secreto / que destruye y calcina tus más firmes raíces" (184) [Let me be the rose of the secret desert / that destroys and scorches your firmest roots].

Champourcin focuses on physical contact in *Cántico inútil* more than in her previous work. She still refers to caresses and hands, but she dedicates appreciable space to the kiss as an instrument of erotic excitement. Indecorous sexual implications of the kiss are deflected by her customary sublimation of the corporal into the loftier entities of stars and light as illustrated in the poem "El beso" [The kiss]:

> ¡Tus labios en mis ojos!
> Qué dulzura de estrellas alisa lentamente
> mis párpados caídos . . .
> Nada existe del mundo. Sólo siento tu boca
> y el temblor de mi espíritu hecho carne de luz.
> Sé cruel al besarme. Desgarra mis pupilas
> y arranca de su sombra la lumbre de mi sueño.
>
> (157–58)

> [Your lips on my eyes!
> What sweetness of stars slowly smooths down
> my fallen eyelids . . .
> Nothing of the world exists. I only feel your mouth
> and the trembling of my spirit made flesh of light.
> Be cruel when you kiss me. Rip my pupils
> and pull the fire of my dream from its shadow.]

In spite of this metaphorical transformation of the kiss, the forcefulness of desire is unambiguously manifested in the images of the violence of ripping and snatching. The human body in Champourcin's poetry is not, however, the final object of her attention, only a vehicle to her ultimate goal of self-realization. She is not writing the body, as Cixous recommends, for she does not put her own body in the text as much as she revels in the body of the other as the source of pleasure. Nonetheless, Champourcin is unequivocal in anchoring desire in a corporal experience aroused by hands and lips and in sensory phenomena felt as a raging fire, as an unquenchable thirst, and as an act of renewing consumption:

> ¡Bébeme pronto! Agota entre tus labios
> mi linfa humilde y pura.
> Aunque me quede exhausta, brotaré nuevamente
> de la primera roca.
>
> (184)
>
> [Drink me soon. Use up between your lips
> my pure and humble lymph.
> Even though I may be left exhausted, I will pour out
> again from the first rock.]

The union between two bodies, as always, continues to be for Champourcin a mechanism for achieving a communion on a higher, eternal level of existence: "una noche infinita / nos unirá, ya eternos" (173) [an infinite night / will unite our eternal beings]. Love takes place beyond the confines of terrestrial reality among the clouds and the stars and in a future, mythical time frame:

> Cuando todas las piedras del mundo se hagan polvo
> cuando todos los gritos naveguen al silencio
> y en las rutas dormidas camine, solo, Dios . . .
>
> (158)
>
> [When all the stones of the world turn to dust
> when all shouts drift off toward silence
> and God walks, alone, on the slumbering roads . . .]

Ultimately the union with the lover occurs in the spatial and temporal precincts of God. Human love and God are bound together even further by the metaphorical correspondences drawn between the impact of God and of the human lover and by the combination of body images with allusions to transcendence.

For these reasons the structures of Champourcin's love poetry recall the mystical vision evolved by San Juan de la Cruz. Her homage to him is overt. He is the source of the epigraph for one of the poems in "Romances del camino" and various motifs throughout the collection. The title of the section "Noche oscura" echoes the title of one of his books, and the title of Champourcin's work *Cántico inútil* alludes to his *El cántico espiritual* [Spiritual canticle] save the difference suggesting that her "hymn" fails to reach the spiritual heights to which he gives testimony. Like the deity sought in the mystical quest San Juan de la Cruz portrays, the lover in Champourcin is the light, the way, and the refuge in the pursuit of transcendence. Other motifs like the lover as the wounding agent, allusions to the chalice of life, and references to the "dark night" of the soul expand the affinities to mysticism. Especially in the section of *Cántico inútil* "Noche oscura," the female subject speaks of the tortures of the soul she endures in the absence of the lover and of the supreme reward awaiting her for her travails. In her study of the feminist implications of the poetry of San Juan de la Cruz, Rosa Rossi explains that there is a complex but decisive connection between women and mysticism. San Juan's contribution to poetry is particularly significant for feminist thought because not only did he make the voice of mysticism feminine, he gave priority to intuitive, nonrational knowledge over rational, theological discourse.[64] Especially relevant to mysticism is Champourcin's depiction of the union of lovers as the final dissolution of the self into the divine essence of eternal love. Women's presumed psychological propensity to fluidity and permeability of the self, reinforced by the circumstances of their traditional reality, makes mysticism easily a concomitant feature of the feminine personality. Carol Christ argues that because traditional gender roles prescribed that women create a situation akin to the nothingness required in the "dark night," their common experience might encourage a habitual receptivity that readily opens them to a mystical experience of union or integration with a higher power.[65] The difference between Champourcin's articulation of desire, love, and transcendence and that of the mystics is that in her poetry the metaphorical vehicles of expression are religious motifs, while the objective is a love originating in sensuality; but in mystical poetry, the vehicles of expressions are taken from the language of eroticism, while the objective is a state of being that contradicts earthly desires. Despite all the religious overlays, Champourcin writes of human desire as a lived experience of the senses. Love in Champourcin contains nuances of mystical transcendence and neoplatonic idealism, but it is neither totally spiritual nor entirely impossible within the realm of experience. She challenges the dualism in Western thought that privileges man as active being and relegates woman to passive immanence by textualizing transcendence to a spiritual level of "reciprocal tenderness" without eclipsing the exhilaration of human experience.

8

Conclusion

An examination of the life and poetry of the Spanish women poets of the twenties and thirties uncovers an ambivalent, complex relationship between them and the cultural environment of the Generation of 27. Their talents were applauded and nurtured by the major male writers of their day, and their writing benefited from the inspiration they received from a variety of their male contemporaries. They assimilated features of the modes in vogue and they published freely, yet remained marginalized. Despite the social changes effected in Spain during the period and the efforts of these women poets to surpass their spent feminine heritage, their incorporation into mainstream culture was temporary; and the critical recognition they earned proved to be more symbolic than real. Most of them slipped quickly into oblivion. Josefina de la Torre forfeited her career as a poet and Rosa Chacel repudiated hers. Concha Méndez receded into the shadows of her interior world, evading life and poetic development. Only Ernestina de Champourcin and Carmen Conde continued to evolve as poets, enriching their poetic vision with new spiritual dimensions and a social consciousness. But even they remain at the periphery of the canon, the first because of her exile and the second despite her distinction as the first woman elected to the Royal Academy.

However, for a brief moment spanning a little more than a decade, Méndez, de la Torre, Chacel, Conde, and Champourcin enjoyed a connection, albeit a limited one, with their male counterparts as well as among themselves. From the early twenties to the time of the civil war, they shared a common chronology, a certain similarity in education and social circumstances, and several bonds of friendship. A lack of alliance among them specifically in their role as poets prevented the formation, in their time, of a genuine generation of women poets. Nonetheless, common poetic dispositions, themes, tonalities, and language permit the present-day reader to view them in retrospect as a group. The early poetic texts of these five women coincide in their crystallization of a fleeting sense of harmony with the force of life. Although a passing illusion, this state of union with the world around them manifested itself in their poetry in affirmations of self-assurance and plenitude. Their exuberance extended to a confidence in their own creative capacities, their potential for freedom, and their ability to transcend the terrestrial.

Today's readers may be disappointed if their expectations are of aggressive protest, revolutionary forms, or anger toward the establishment. The challenge of these women to the dominant discourse was restrained and oblique. However, placed within the context of their ultra-conservative society, they can be appreciated for their ability to navigate the choppy waters of their cultural environment. Against the backdrop of their times, they emerge as poets who dare to begin to discover themselves as creative subjects and as free beings capable of desire, connection with the other, and transcendence of a variety of limitations. Although they adopted many formal, poetic elements of their male contemporaries, they inevitably projected their own reality as women through these forms.

They defy traditional conceptions of woman by creating self-asserting female personae who are independent, carefree, and active, as in the case of Méndez; who are unabashed and insistent in their declarations of erotic desire and sublimating love, as occurred with Champourcin; or who place themselves at the center of the universe, as Conde's poetic speaker did. They enthusiastically embrace the power of the word, the exciting motifs of modern technology, and the unbound structures of vanguard poetry. They also presume, as in the instance of Chacel, to master the most challenging poetic forms. In their efforts to escape the denigration of feminine writing, in their earliest poetry they ostensibly reject gender-defined difference, clinging instead to a faith in the transcendent power of nature and of poetry to establish their own identity. Nonetheless, traditional feminine postures of modesty, subordination, and abandonment do emerge in their verse. More than the others, de la Torre and Champourcin depict the confrontation between the female speaker and the masculine other in conventional terms and resort to traditional symbols of femininity; yet even the female personae in their earliest poetry are not totally subdued by anguish.

The poetic protagonists conceived by Méndez, de la Torre, Conde, and Champourcin dwell in an edenic world perceived by the senses but unencumbered to a large extent by human sentiment or witnesses. Untouched by the pain provoked by contact with the real world, they live in a timeless realm where female authority, self-possession, and autonomy are possible. Nature, in all its sensuous beauty, provides the medium for pleasure and self-realization. Méndez finds a utopian space of joy, love, and escape in the sea, while de la Torre sees nature more as a refuge for repose. Conde both celebrates and merges with the cosmos; and Champourcin contemplates nature's delights with its frequent erotic overtones at the same time she appropriates its powers. The poetic persona created by Chacel also inhabits a satisfying region. Lodged, not in the realm of nature, but in that of aesthetics, she happily combines the most traditional with the most modern artistic forms. In contrast to the other women, Chacel finds self-affirmation through the people she addresses and commands in her poems. However, like the poetry of her female counterparts, the verse she wrote in the twenties and thirties reveals an assertive female voice.

Love within the schemes of existential harmony drawn by Conde and Champourcin in nature constitutes a correlative avenue of blissful communion. In both of them, love is defined as a tender reciprocity that, far from depriving the female of individuality, engages her, particularly in the case of the latter, in a spiritual union that elevates the human couple to a superior level of eternal existence. The affirmation in Méndez, de la Torre, Conde, and Champourcin of connection and intrinsic identity with the other—be it nature or a human being—confirms the observations made by feminist theorists concerning the psychological tendency in women to blur ego boundaries and to privilege continuity over disjunction.

A preference for bonding does not preclude mobility. Conde relies on the image of cohesion implicit in the self-contained circle, but the thirst in the others for freedom, adventure, or transcendence translates into images of verticality and ascension or into the journey metaphor and other patterns of progression. The speaking subjects in the poetry of Méndez, de la Torre, Chacel, Conde, and Champourcin configure the female self in positive terms of strength and creative potential. They define themselves as active, free, and superior beings who are capable of emulating divine creativity. Self-assured, they speak of themselves, their desires, and their powers. The muteness and invisibility identifying women in masculine literature is replaced in their poetry by a distinctive female presence manifested not only in the examples of female self-definitions but also in the discourse of their poems. Visual imagery, figures in motion, a sense of space, and the use of personification and other kinds of fusion help create a sense of plasticity or concreteness in their poems. Their verbs, syntax, lexicon, and poetic structures further enhance this general drive to infuse life into their poetic world.

The poetry of them all changed with the fall into experience. Already in the thirties they showed signs of an awareness of the somber aspects of life. The civil war introduced Chacel to death, doom, and existential distress. As incipient, abstract desire yielded to tangible encounters, the possibilities for separation, loss, and silence surfaced. In Méndez and Conde the complications of romantic love were juxtaposed with the effects of maternal affection; Champourcin eventually displaced her search for human love with a quest for contact with God. In the poetry of these three as well as in that of de la Torre, a new awareness of the passage of time, the restrictions of mortality, and the inevitability of death compromised their confident declarations of liberation. All five in their own way continued to re-create themselves through their art; de la Torre turned to public performance and Chacel gave herself up to her prose while Méndez, Champourcin, and Conde continued to write in more reflective or meditative tones.

Thus, the poetry written in the twenties and thirties by Concha Méndez, Josefina de la Torre, Rosa Chacel, Carmen Conde, and Ernestina de Champourcin represents the textualization of the birth of their creative impulses and of their initial treatment of absence and presence. Their own youthfulness, coupled with a cultural climate that promoted novelty, freedom, and experimentation, generated joyful expressions of self-realization that minimized the effects of the distressful aspects of existence. Even if only from the periphery, they were able to raise their own voices within their general cultural community. As creators of individual female visions, they undermined the conventional patriarchal portrayal of woman as silent, hidden, and passive, becoming instead agents of representation, the forgers of self-generated images and meaning. Through poetry, they briefly transformed woman into presence and plenitude and symbolically translated absence into a poetic reality.

Notes

CHAPTER 1. INTRODUCTION

1. Montserrat Roig, *¿Tiempo de mujer?* (Barcelona: Plaza y Janés, 1980), 156.

2. *Modern and Contemporary Spanish Women Poets* (New York: Twayne Publishers, 1996), by Janet Pérez, and *Women Poets of Spain, 1860–1990: Toward a Gynocentric Vision* (Champaign: University of Illinois Press, 1997), by John C. Wilcox, are diachronic studies that attempt to show the breadth and development of poetry by women in Spain over a period exceeding a century and a quarter. Wilcox underscores the uniquely female aspects, the "gynocentric vision," of Champourcin, Conde, and Méndez. While I do not deny his premise, I delve into the complexities of the femaleness, the emerging artistic consciousness, and the interaction with masculine constructs of a single generation of Spanish poets in an attempt to elucidate the creative process in women. After I wrote my study, Emilio Miró published an anthology on the five poets I examine: *Antologia de las poetisas del 27* (Madrid: Castalia, 1999). He writes a lengthy introduction summarizing the work of each one and emphasizing their inclusion in former anthologies.

Novels by women have commanded greater attention among Hispanists than the works of women poets. Gender and female subjectivity in the nineteenth century have been treated in two noteworthy books: Lou Charnon-Deutsch, *Gender and Representation: Women in Spanish Realist Fiction* (Lafayette, Ind.: Purdue Monographs in Romance Languages, 1990) and Susan Kirkpatrick, *Las románticas: Women Writers and Subjectivity in Spain 1835–1850* (Berkeley: University of California Press, 1989). Interest in the narrative of Spanish women writers of the post-civil war period has also produced numerous monographs: Joan L. Brown, ed., *Women Writers of Contemporary Spain: Exiles in the Homeland* (Newark, N.J.: University of Delaware Press, 1991); Biruté Ciplijauskaité, *La novela femenina contemporánea (1970–1985): Hacia una tipología de la narración en primera persona* (Barcelona: Anthropos, 1988); Lucía Fox-Lockert, *Women Novelists in Spain and Spanish America* (Metuchen, N.J.: The Scarecrow Press, 1979); Stephen M. Hart, *White Ink: Essays on Twentieth-Century Feminine Fiction in Spain and Latin America* (London: Tamesis Books, 1993); Roberto C. Manteiga, Carolyn Galerstein, and Kathleen McNerney, eds., *Feminine Concerns in Contemporary Spanish Fiction by Women* (Potomac, Md.: Scripta Humanistica, 1988); María Jesús Mayans Natal, *Narrativa feminista española de posguerra* (Madrid: Pliegos, 1991); Beth Miller, ed., *Women in Hispanic Literature: Icons and Fallen Idols* (Berkeley: University of California Press, 1983); Elizabeth Ordóñez, *Voices of Their Own: Contemporary Spanish Narrative by Women* (Lewisburg, Pa.: Bucknell University Press, 1991); Janet Pérez, ed., *Novelistas femeninas de la postguerra española* (Madrid: José Porrúa Turanzas, 1983); and Janet Pérez, *Contemporary Women Writers of Spain* (Boston: Twayne Publishers, 1988); and Noël Valis and Carol Maier, eds., *In the Feminine Mode* (Lewisburg, Pa.: Bucknell University Press, 1990).

3. In her introduction to *The New Feminist Criticism* (New York: Pantheon Books, 1985), 8, Elaine Showalter traces the development of feminist criticism over what she discerns are

three major phases: the earliest phase concentrated on exposing the misogyny of literary practice; a second phase based on the discovery that women had a literature of their own and aimed at a massive recovery and rereading of literature by women; and finally, a phase in which criticism "demanded not just the recognition of women's writing but a radical rethinking of the conceptual grounds of literary study."

4. Elaine Showalter, *A Literature of Their Own* (Princeton: Princeton University Press, 1977).

5. Hélène Cixous, "Sorties," in *New French Feminisms: An Anthology*, ed. Elaine Marks and Isabelle de Courtivron (New York: Schocken Books, 1981), 92.

6. Suzanne Juhasz, *Naked and Fiery Forms: Modern American Poetry by Women* (New York: Harper and Row, 1976) and Sandra M. Gilbert and Susan Gubar, "Introduction: Gender, Creativity, and the Woman Poet," *Shakespeare's Sisters: Feminist Essays on Women Poets* (Bloomington: Indiana University Press, 1979), xv–xxvi. Both studies stress the conflict and dilemmas that the traditional definitions of poetry have caused for the woman poet, with the first one calling the contradiction between gender and vocation a "double-bind situation" and the second one suggesting that the situation can be more accurately labelled a "sort of triple bind."

7. Nancy K. Miller, "Changing the Subject: Authorship, Writing and the Reader," in *Feminist Studies/Critical Studies*, ed. Teresa de Lauretis (Bloomington: Indiana University Press, 1986), 106. Elizabeth Fox-Genovese, "To Write My Self: The Autobiographies of Afro-American Women," in *Feminist Issues in Literary Scholarship*, ed. Shari Benstock (Bloomington: Indiana University Press, 1987), 162–63, voices a similar concern. She recognizes that the death of the subject and the author may accurately reflect the crisis of Western culture and the "bottomless anxieties" of its most privileged subjects, but cautions that there remain plenty of subjects and authors who, never having had much opportunity to write in their own names, are eager to seize the abandoned podium.

8. For the significance of the notion of woman as "blank page" and its impact on female creativity, see Susan Gubar, "'The Blank Page' and the Issues of Female Creativity," in *Writing and Sexual Difference*, ed. Elizabeth Abel (Chicago: University of Chicago Press, 1982), 73–93.

9. See Iris M. Zavala, "Las formas y funciones de una teoría crítica feminista. Feminismo dialógico," in *Breve historia feminista de la literatura española (en lengua castellana)*, vol. 1, *Teoría feminista: Discurso y diferencia*, ed. Myriam Díaz-Diocaretz and Iris M. Zavala (Barcelona: Anthropos, 1993), 71.

10. Ellen G. Friedman, "Where Are the Missing Contents? (Post) Modern, Gender, and the Canon," *PMLA* 108, no. 2 (1993):244.

11. Mary Jacobus, "The Difference of View," in *Women Writing and Writing About Women*, ed. Mary Jacobus (New York: Barnes and Noble Books, 1979), 10–21.

12. These are the functions outlined by M. A. K. Halliday, *Language as Social Semiotics* (London: Edward Arnold, 1978).

13. Toril Moi, *Sexual/Textual Politics* (London and New York: Methuen, 1985), 94.

14. Alicia Suskin Ostriker, *Stealing the Language: The Emergence of Women's Poetry in America* (Boston: Beacon Press, 1986), 1–6.

15. Moi, *Sexual/Textual Politics*, 7.

16. Naomi Schor, "Reading Double: Sand's Difference," in *The Poetics of Gender*, ed. Nancy K. Miller (New York: Columbia University Press, 1986), 249–50.

17. Elaine Showalter, "Women and the Literary Curriculum," *College English* 32, no. 8 (May 1971):859.

18. Nannerl O. Keohane and Barbara Gelpi, eds., *Feminist Theory: A Critique of Ideology* (Chicago: University of Chicago Press, 1982), ix–xi.

19. Juhasz, *Naked and Fiery Forms*, 177.

20. Carlos Morla Lynch, *En España con Federico García Lorca* (Madrid: Aguilar, 1958), 266–67, writes that anyone and everyone connected with literature and the arts attended the wedding of Méndez and Altolaguirre. He says, "Aquí están, fraternalmente reunidos, para asistir a un acto que nadie toma muy en serio, en una atmósfera simpática en que hay mucho espíritu de broma y de chacota pero también amistad, compañerismo y cariño." Seventy years later Champourcin still remembered that festive event: see Catherine G. Bellver, "Conversación con Ernestina de Champourcin," *Ojáncano* 10 (1995), 70.

21. Annette Kolodny, "Some Notes on Defining a 'Feminist Literary Criticism,'" *Critical Inquiry* 2, no. 1 (1975):79.

22. Carmen Conde, "Poesía femenina española, viviente," *Arbor* 297 (1970):222.

CHAPTER 2. SPANISH WOMEN POETS IN CONTEXT: NAVIGATING CHOPPY WATERS

1. José-Carlos Mainer, "Las escritoras del 27 (con María Teresa León al fondo)," in *Homenaje a María Teresa León* (Madrid: Universidad Complutense de Madrid, 1989), 13. Curiously enough, despite his recognition of the absence of women poets from studies of the period, he himself does not include their poetry in his own book *La edad de plata, 1902–1939* (Madrid: Cátedra, 1983).

2. Debicki, Andrew P., "Una dimensión olvidada de la poesía española de los '20 y '30: La lírica visionaria de Ernestina de Champourcin," *Ojáncano* 1, no. 1 (1988):48–60.

3. She is included in Angel Valbuena Prat, *Historia de la literatura española* (Barcelona: Gustavo Gili, 1963), 2:689; but she does not appear in equally notable histories: José María Díaz Borque, *Historia de la literatura española*, vol. 4, *Siglo XX* (Madrid: Taurus, 1980); Angel del Río, *Historia de la literatura española* (New York: Holt, Rinehart and Winston, 1948); and Gerald G. Brown, *Historia de la literatura española*, vol. 6/1, *El siglo XX* (Barcelona: Ariel, 1983). Studies of poetry that omit her include Mainer, *La edad de plata*; Joaquín Marco, *Poesía española siglo XX* (Barcelona: Edhasa, 1986); and Gustav Siebenmann, *Los estilos poéticos en España desde 1900* (Madrid: Gredos, 1973).

4. Her inclusion in Diego's anthology is remembered by Francisco Javier Díez de Revenga, *Panorama crítico de la generación del 27* (Madrid: Editorial Castalia, 1987), 50, 275; and C. Christopher Soufas, *Conflict of Light and Wind* (Middletown, Ct.: Wesleyan University Press, 1989), 19. Víctor García de la Concha, ed., *Historia y crítica de la literatura española*, vol. 8, *Época contemporánea* (Barcelona: Crítica, 1984), 720, alludes to her Teatro Mínimo.

5. Chacel merits a reference in Brown, *Historia de la literatura española*, 234, Mainer, *La edad de plata*, 321, 339, and in Varia, *Historia de la literatura española*, vol. 2, *Desde el siglo XVII hasta nuestros días* (Madrid: Cátedra, 1990). She also earns a place in general English-language guides to literature: Clare Buck, ed., *The Bloomsbury Guide to Women's Literature* (New York: Prentice Hall, 1992), 407, and Martin Seymour-Smith, *The New Guide to Modern World Literature* (New York: Peter Bedrich Books, 1985), 1201–2. Chacel receives more than a single mention in García de la Concha, *Historia y crítica*, and a longer entry than other women writers of the period in Ricardo Gullón, *Diccionario de literatura española e hispanoamericana* (Madrid: Alianza, 1993), 1:340–42.

6. Chacel is not mentioned as a poet in the studies by Díez de Revenga, *Panorama crítico*, or Marco, *Poesía española siglo XX*; and in Del Río's history of literature she is also excluded. In the history by Valbuena Prat, she is listed as an essayist and the publisher of a collection of poems, until its ninth edition, when María del Pilar Palomo adds two sentences of commentary. See *Historia de la literatura española*, vol. 4, *Época contemporánea*, revised by María del Pilar Palomo (Barcelona: Gustavo Gili, 1983), 193. Only four lines are devoted to her in

Federico Carlos Sainz de Robles, *Ensayo de un diccionario de literatura* (Madrid: Aguilar, 1949), 2:414. In contrast, eighty-five lines are given to the poet Pilar de Valderrama, remembered usually as "Guiomar," the secret love of Antonio Machado.

7. Like Champourcin, Méndez is not included in Mainer, *La edad de plata*, or Siebenmann, *Los estilos poéticos*, and is mentioned in Marco, *Poesía española siglo XX*, only as a collaborator with her husband Manuel Altolaguirre in the printing business. Díez de Revenga, *Panorama crítico*, 268, refers to her only as the woman alluded to in Altolaguirre's *Fin de un amor*. Omissions from dictionaries include the 1949 edition of Sainz de Robles, *Ensayo de un diccionario*, Germán Bleiberg and Julián Marías, *Diccionario de literatura española* (Madrid: Revista de Occidente, 1964), and the updated version of Germán Bleiberg, Maureen Ihrie and Janet Pérez, eds., *Dictionary of the Literature of the Iberian Peninsula* (Westport, Conn.: Greenwood Press, 1993). Even more surprising is her exclusion from bio-bibliographical dictionaries devoted to women writers: Carolyn L. Galerstein, ed., *Women Writers of Spain: An Annotated Bio-Bibliographical Guide* (New York: Greenwood Press, 1986) and Linda Gould Levine, Ellen Engelson Marson, and Gloria Feiman Waldman, eds., *Spanish Women Writers: A Bio-Bibliographical Source Book* (Westport, Conn.: Greenwood Press, 1993).

8. After *Vida a vida y Vida o Río*, with an introduction by Emilio Miró (Madrid: Ediciones Caballo Griego para la Poesía, 1979) and *Entre el soñar y el vivir* (Mexico City: Universidad Nacional Autónoma de México, 1981), James Valender published *Poemas, 1926–1986* (Madrid: Hiperión, 1995).

9. *Poemas de la isla*, ed., Lázaro Santana (Las Palmas de Gran Canaria: Gobierno de Canarias, 1989).

10. Ernestina de Champourcin, *Poesía a través del tiempo* (Barcelona: Anthropos, 1991). Shortly after the appearance of this volume, two slim collections of poetry by Champourcin appeared: *Antología poética* (Málaga: Centro Cultural de la Generación del 27, 1991) and *Del vacío y sus dones* (Madrid: Torremozas, 1993).

11. Both versions of the Bleiberg dictionary have entries on Chacel, Champourcin, and de la Torre but not on Méndez. The Gullón book has short notes on Champourcin, Méndez, and de la Torre and a longer entry on Chacel. The *Oxford Companion to Spanish Literature* (Oxford: Claredon Press, 1978) includes Champourcin and Chacel. Predating these is Sainz de Robles, *Ensayo de un diccionario* (1949). Although Méndez did not appear in this edition, she was included in the 1964 revision.

12. Besides the works of Galerstein and Linda Gould Levine et al. already cited, another work of this type has been published: Katharina M. Wilson, ed., *An Encyclopedia of Continental Women Writers* (New York: Garland, 1991). It includes Champourcin, Chacel, Méndez, and de la Torre. Champourcin earned inclusion in Helen Tierney, ed., *Women's Studies Encyclopedia* (New York: Greenwood Press, 1989), 2:330. In Spain, Plutarco Marsá Vancells has published *La mujer en la literatura* (Madrid: Torremozas, 1987); but he includes only Champourcin.

13. It is unclear how much of a role Gerardo Diego played in choosing the women included in his anthology. According to an interview with Champourcin, Ascunce discovered that pressure was put on Diego to exclude Champourcin and other women poets. See Champourcin, *Poesía a través del tiempo*, xii. Yet in another interview, Champourcin states that there was no struggle; Diego simply included her and Josefina de la Torre in the revised edition of 1934 after being criticized for including only men in the first edition of 1932. See Bellver, "Conversación con Champourcin." Paloma Ulacia Altolaguirre maintains that a hurtful act of misogyny kept Concha Méndez out of the anthology: *Concha Méndez: Memorias habladas, memorias armadas* (Madrid: Mondadori, 1990), 16. At the same time as Diego's anthology, another one was published in Belgium in which de la Torre and Carmen Conde represented Spanish female poetry: Mathilde Pomès, *Poètes espagnols d'aujourd'hui* (Brussels: Labor, 1934). Before they disappeared from anthologies after 1950, Champourcin and

Méndez appeared in Juan José Domenchina, *Antología de la poesía española contemporánea, 1900–1936* (Mexico: Unión Tipográfica Editorial Hispano-Americana, 1941). They and nine other women poets (alongside 250 male poets) were included in César González Ruano, *Antología de poetas españoles contemporáneos en lengua castellana* (Barcelona: Gustavo Gili, 1946).

14.   Howard Mancing, "A Consensus Canon of Hispanic Poetry," *Hispania* 69 (1986):53–81.

15.   In 1943, Chacel, Champourcin, and Méndez were still remembered as poets in María Antonio Vidal, *Cien años de poesía femenina: Española e hispanoamericana, 1840–1940* (Barcelona: Olimpo, 1943). Carmen Conde published three anthologies of poetry by women: *Poesía femenina española viviente* (Madrid: Anroflo, 1954); *Poesía femenina española, 1939–1950,* (Barcelona: Bruguera, 1967); and *Poesía femenina española, 1950–1960* (Barcelona: Bruguera, 1971). The first and second ones contain poems by Champourcin and de la Torre while the third has selections only of Concha Méndez. In addition, Méndez is included in Conde's *Antología de la poesía amorosa contemporánea* (Barcelona: Bruguera, 1969). Champourcin, alongside Carmen Conde, is the only female poet of the twenties who gains entry into Luzmaría Jiménez Faro, *Panorama antológico de poetisas españolas: Siglos XV al XX* (Madrid: Torremozas, 1987). The twenties are represented by Rosa Chacel, Concha Méndez, Josefina de la Torre, Ernestina de Champourcin, Nuria Parés, María Enciso, Carmen Conde, and Maruja Mallo in Lorenzo Saval and J. García Gallego, *Litoral femenino: Literatura escrita por mujeres en la España contemporánea* (Málaga: Litoral, 1986). Biographical information on de la Torre can be found in an anthology of prose that deserves mention: Isabel Calvo de Aguilar, *Antología biográfica de escritoras españolas* (Madrid: Biblioteca Nueva, 1954). Finally, in 1996 Luzmaría Jiménez Faro published *Poetisas españolas: Antología general,* vol. 2, *De 1901 a 1939* (Madrid: Torremozas, 1996).

16.   Juan Manuel Rozas, *El 27 como generación* (Santander: Colección "La Isla de los Ratones," 1978), 27–28, inserts women in a concluding list. Both Champourcin and Chacel are dubbed "pure poets" by Emiliano Díez-Echarri and José María Roca Franquesa, *Historia de la literatura española e hispanoamericana* (Madrid: Aguilar, 1966), 1311. This is also the case of Champourcin in José María Castro Calvo, *Historia de la literatura española* (Barcelona: Credsa, 1964), 2:305. In Brown, *Historia,* 234, Chacel is included in a list of exiled novelists; in Castro Calvo, *Historia,* 283-84, she appears in a list as a "cultivadora de la novela del *tempo lento* al modo de Proust y Virginia Wolf" [*sic*], and in Díez Borque, *Historia,* 110–11, she is part of a concluding section on "novelistas de la generación del 27."

17.   In Max Aub, *Manual de la historia de la literatura española* (Madrid: Akal, 1974), she is listed among those who published in *Revista de Occidente* (502), the novelists who tried but failed to create an experimental novel (507), and those who published in *Mono Azul* (508).

18.   Mainer, "Las escritoras del 27," suggests that Angel Valbuena Prat's inclusion of several women in the 1937 edition of his history of literature stems more from gallantry than generosity.

19.   Angel del Río, *Historia de la literatura española,* rev. ed. (New York: Holt, Rinehart and Winston, 1963), 346, limits his comments to "La poesía femenina está representada en esta generación por Ernestina de Champourcin y Concha Méndez."

20.   Guillermo Díaz-Plaja, *Historia de la poesía lírica española* (Barcelona: Editorial Labor, 1948), 420–21. It should be noted that Champourcin is afforded a brief section of her own before the list of the others.

21.   Angel Valbuena Prat, *Historia de la literatura española* (Barcelona: Gustavo Gili, 1937), 2:967; Sainz de Robles, *Ensayo de un diccionario,* 415; *Oxford Companion,* 118.

22.   Champourcin's mother was from Uruguay and her father, born in Barcelona, was of French ancestry. Of Provençal origin, her surname preserves its French spelling and accentuation but is pronounced according to Spanish phonetics without an accent mark. These details are explained in Arturo Villar, "Ernestina de Champourcin," *La Estafeta Literaria,*

556 (1975):11. Ironically, Champourcin's shred of connection to the Basque Country made possible a grant from the Basque government for the publication of her complete works in 1991.

23. Some Hispanists have already offered explanations for this exclusion. Maryellen Bieder, "Women and the Twentieth Century Spanish Literary Canon: The Lady Vanishes," *Anales de la Literatura Española Contemporánea* 17, no. 3 (1992):301–24, points to the aesthetic principles of modernism as the culprit. John C. Wilcox blames the marriage of these women to fellow poets of the Generation of 27, the experience of exile, and the gynocentricity of their verses for their marginalization, in his article, "Ernestina de Champourcin and Concha Méndez: Their Rescision from the Generation of 27," *Siglo XX/20th Century* 12 no. 1–2 (1994):291–92. In the case of Champourcin, Debicki, "Dimensión olvidada," 48, finds sexism and her allegiances to Juan Ramón Jiménez as prime reasons for her exclusion. It is useful to remember that personal alliances, aesthetic philosophy, or political affiliation also marginalized male poets from the canon. The example of Champourcin's husband, Juan José Domenchina, would confirm the hypothesis that those following the route to social, or "impure" poetry, as Pablo Neruda termed it, have been treated more generously by critics than those who traveled the alternative road of "pure" poetry promoted by Juan Ramón. The tension between the two poles is studied by Juan Cano Ballesta, *La poesía española entre pureza y revolución, 1930–1936* (Madrid: Gredos, 1972).

24. Rosa Chacel wrote poetry after 1936 but did not consent to its publication until 1978. Concha Méndez continued to write poetry but at a slower pace, and Ernestina de Champourcin did not resume publication of poetry collections until 1952. Josefina de la Torre published *Marzo incompleto* in the magazine *Fantasia* in 1947. She did not go into exile, but she turned her artistic attention to the performing arts of singing and acting.

25. Ulacia Altolaguirre, *Concha Méndez*, 114; Emma Rodríguez, "Concha Méndez, el rostro ignorado del 27," *El Mundo del Siglo Veintiuno* 2, no. 346 (8 October 1990):35. Acceptance in the Mexican canon was impossible, but Méndez and Champourcin were associated with *Rueca*, a literary magazine published there by women.

26. For example, at the end of the 1950s, *Ora marítima* by Rafael Alberti was allowed to be sold in Spain, probably because it was mistakenly seen as merely a patriotic tribute to the region of his birth. In 1972, his collected works appeared in Spain, with his political verse excluded.

27. Bieder, "Women and the Twentieth Century," 314. Catherine Jagoe argues that even before American literature, Spanish literature changed from a nineteenth-century aesthetic of sentimentality, conventionality, melodrama, religiosity, and pathos to a modernist one resulting in the devaluation of texts formerly produced by women and making "sentimental" and "genius" mutually exclusive: "Noncanonical Novels and the Question of Quality," *Revista de Estudios Hispánicos* 27, no. 3 (1993):431. Shari Benstock contends that Modernism subjected women to exile in the sense of textual expatriation *in patria*, as an exclusion from culture imposed by androcentric definitions and interpretations of Modernism. See "Expatriate Modernism: Writing on the Cultural Rim," in *Women's Writing in Exile*, ed. Mary Lynn Broe and Angela Ingram (Chapel Hill: University of North Carolina Press, 1989).

28. Rosa Chacel, "Esquemas de los problemas prácticos y actuales del amor," *Revista de Occidente* 31 (1931):158–59. Alda Blanco, "But Are They Any Good?" *Revista de Estudios Hispánicos* 27, no. 3 (October 1993):463–70, maintains that the depreciation of a feminine sensibility occurred in the nineteenth century when national identity came to be identified with realism and masculinity.

29. Angela Ena Bordonada makes this point, singling out Manuel Azaña, Rafael Cansinos-Assens, and Angel Guerra in *Novelas breves de escritoras españolas (1900–1936)* (Madrid: Castalia, 1989), 14–15. The most obvious case perhaps was that of José Ortega y Gasset, who in his writings forcefully delineated the defects of women, but, according to Rosa Chacel,

in his personal dealings "no pudo estar más amable ni comportarse mejor de lo que se comportó conmigo." See Kathleen Glenn, "Conversación con Rosa Chacel," *Letras Peninsulares* 3, no. 1 (1990):14.

30. María del Pilar Oñate, *El feminismo en la literatura española* (Madrid: Espasa-Calpe, 1938), 237–38.

31. Edmundo González Blanco, *La mujer según los diferentes aspectos de su espiritualidad* (Madrid: Reus, 1930), 530.

32. Luis Franco de Espés, "Mujeres españolas: María Teresa de León," *El Imparcial*, 8 May 1929, 1.

33. Melchor Fernández Almagro, "Caja de sorpresas," *La Gaceta Literaria* 1, no. 3 (1 February 1927):1. Lest perspective be lost as to the extent of this line of thinking, it must be pointed out that in 1989 Josefina de la Torre's beauty was still given as a reason for her success as a poet. See Lázaro Santana, introduction to *Poemas de la isla*, by Josefina de la Torre, 11–12.

34. "Encuesta sobre la nueva arquitectura," *La Gaceta Literaria* 2, no. 32 (15 April 1928):6.

35. Those who have assumed the authority to determine the canon have included, as Gonzalo Navajas points out, the academics of prestigious universities, a certain segment of society, and patriarchal discourse in general: "Genereración y canon o ley y orden en literatura," *Siglo XX/20th Century* 12, no. 1–2 (1994):157–70. Practical factors such as marketing potential and censorship also figure prominently in the creation of the canon. In the case of women, as Margaret Persin observes, the function of gender is more basic and more universal than other categories such as social context, social identities, and personal affiliations: "Yet Another Loose Can(n)on: The Place and Space of Women's Poetry in Twentieth-Century Spain," *Siglo XX/20th Century* 12, no. 1–2 (1994):196–97.

36. Showalter, *Literature of Their Own*.

37. *Héroe* (Madrid: Turner, 1977) is preceded by a handwritten letter of Vicente Aleixandre, who describes her as a happy helpmate, and is followed by a study by Dietrich Briesemeister, who underlines her role as maternal hostess for the writers who visited her apartment. The printing business run by Méndez and her husband, Manuel Altolaguirre, under the name La Tentativa Poética, published the poetry of such central figures of the Generation of 27 as Pedro Salinas, Rafael Alberti, and Luis Cernuda.

38. See the interviews Sharon Keefe Ugalde held with women poets of today: *Conversaciones y poemas: La nueva poesía femenina española en castellano* (Madrid: Siglo Veintiuno Editores, 1991).

39. Michel Foucault, *Power/Knowledge: Selected Interviews and Other Writings 1972–1977*, ed. Colin Gordon (New York: Pantheon Books, 1980), 131.

40. Joan Kelly, *Women, History, and Theory: The Essays of Joan Kelly* (Chicago: University of Chicago Press, 1984), 20.

41. José Manuel López de Abiada, "El papel de la mujer en la novela española de posguerra," *Insula* 449 (1984):18. Although the socialists and the anarchists ostensibly fostered the rights of women, their theoretical defense of women did not translate into great improvement of their working conditions.

42. Geraldine Scanlon, *La polémica feminista en la España contemporánea, 1868–1974* (Madrid: Akal, 1986), 221–57, traces the efforts of the right to control the development of feminism, through female unions and organizations, under the guise of paternalistic protectionism, and points out that, despite their divergent views, the left did little to change women's place in society. Women from both political poles addressed the issue of women, work, and feminism. María de Echarri, a prominent Catholic social leader, exhorted women workers to maintain their traditionalist values. At the other end of the spectrum, Margarita Nelken, a socialist, published *La mujer ante las Cortes Constituyentes* (Madrid: Editorial Castro, 1931), in which she urged the government to introduce new labor laws, support rights of illegitimate

children, legalize divorce, and abolish prostitution. In her *La condición social de la mujer en España* (Barcelona: Minerva, 1919), she denounced the influence of the Catholic church on women. She believed that women's economic independence and class consciousness would eventually ensure the development of feminism in Spain, but that until that time Spanish women were ill-prepared for suffrage.

43. Rosa María Capel Martínez, *El sufragio femenino en la segunda República* (Granada: Universidad de Granada, 1975), 113. Other helpful sources for the study of women and work during the twenties and thirties are Capel Martínez, *El trabajo y la educación de la mujer en España, 1900–1930* (Madrid: Ministerio de Cultura, 1986); Mary Nash, *Mujer, familia y trabajo en España, 1875–1936* (Barcelona: Anthropos, 1983); and Scanlon, *La polémica feminista.*

44. Capel, *El trabajo y la educación,* 502.

45. Of particular note are the two pedagogical conventions held in Madrid in 1882 and 1892 at which speakers, including Concepción Arenal and Emilia Pardo Bazán, debated the topics of women's rights to education, their aptitude as teachers, and the question of co-education. Pardo Bazán, in a speech titled "La educación del hombre y la mujer: Sus relaciones y diferencias," observed that educational differences were greater between the two sexes than among social classes and that the education of women could not rightly be called such since it consisted essentially of the imposition of obedience, passivity, and sub-mission (Capel, *El trabajo y la educación,* 438–42). Arenal wrote two major works on women's issues, *La mujer del porvenir* (1869) and *La mujer de su casa* (1883), in which she argued that ignorance does not guarantee virtue and that education makes women more rational and therefore better companions for men. A penologist and sociologist, she was an outspoken abolitionist praised throughout the world during her time.

46. Capel, *Sufragio,* 305, singles out the work done on behalf of education by two priests, Andrés Manjón and Pedro Poveda. The first tried to improve the education of workers; the second promoted reforms in teacher training.

47. Pilar Folguera, *Vida cotidiana en Madrid: El primer tercio del siglo a través de las fuentes orales* (Madrid: Comunidad de Madrid, 1987), 118–20, sees three positions with regard to education for women at the turn of the century. The Catholic church, resorting to biological and psychological arguments, enforced inferior education for women although it would later approve a certain amount of training deemed necessary for economic survival. Of the other two, the Marxists had little effect on women's daily lives, while the liberal current provided the central impetus for reform in education, not only for women but also for men. Influenced by the ideas Julián Sanz del Río assimilated in Germany from Carl Christian Krause, the small group of professors called "krausistas" attempted to institute an educational system that was public, free, secular, and co-educational.

48. The Escuela Normal de Maestras had already been formed in 1858, but Castro's school quickly gained a reputation as the best school for girls and for preparing them for the teaching profession. As for the lectures, they were delivered by the leading intellectuals and politicians of the day to audiences of both males and females.

49. See Capel, *El trabajo y la educación,* 363, and *El sufragio,* 88. A slow rate of industrial-ization and of growth in an accompanying middle class, the dominance of the Catholic Church and other conservative forces, and the underdeveloped feminist consciousness in Spain have been blamed for the deficiency, disinterest, and restriction that prevailed in the area of women's education.

50. María Angeles Durán, "Una ausencia de mil años: La mujer en la universidad," in *La mujer en el mundo contemporáneo,* ed. Durán et al. (Madrid: Universidad Autónoma de Madrid, 1981), 53–68. One of the first women to attend a university was Concepción Arenal, but to do so without incident, she dressed as a man. It was not until 1882 that the first woman—Martina Castells—received a doctorate in medicine and 1894 that the first woman—Matilde Padrós—received a doctorate in Arts and Letters. Although technically women were not

forbidden to get a college education, in practice they were denied admission and when they did attend, they were not allowed to practice their professions. Between 1880 and the end of the century only fifteen university degrees had been given to women; and until 1910, by law, a young woman had to secure permission from the government to attend college.

51. According to the charts Capel provides in *El trabajo y la educación*, 381, 473, there was only one woman enrolled at the university level in 1900–1901, but in 1909–10 there were 21; in 1919–20, 345; and in 1927–28, 1,669.

52. Carmen de Zulueta and Alicia Moreno have written a thorough history of the birth, growth, and diasppearance of the Residencia de Señoritas in *Ni convento ni college: La Residencia de Señoritas* (Madrid: Consejo Superior de Investigaciones Científicas, 1993). In *Cien años de educación de la mujer española: Historia del Instituto Internacional* (Madrid: Castalia, 1992), Zulueta traces the history of the Instituto Internacional, founded at the end of the nineteenth century by Americans hoping to teach religious tolerance in Spain. Beyond its original religious intentions, the Instituto introduced some of the most modern teaching methods into Spain. The Instituto Escuela, born from the ideas of the "krausistas," was also a very progressive school; it promoted a close teacher-student relationship, co-education, optional rather than obligatory religious instruction, modern laboratory facilities, and a curriculum that combined academic subjects with sports and manual labor. For the organization of university women, see María Luisa Maillard, *Asociación española de mujeres universitarias, 1920–1990* (Madrid: Instituto de la Mujer, 1990) and Concha Fagoaga, *La voz y el voto de las mujeres: El sufragismo en España, 1877–1931* (Barcelona: Icaria, 1985).

53. Fathers of the professional classes often encouraged their daughters to go to school, not out of feminist enlightenment but to better their opportunities for marriage and as a safeguard in case they did not marry. The aristocracy, meanwhile, was more concerned with a young woman's acquiring social graces than in the development of her intellect. Of foremost importance were the norms of urbanity, courtesy, and propriety (Folguera, *Vida cotidiana en Madrid*, 114–17).

54. The slow and belated development of capitalism, unprogressive labor and educational systems, and an entrenched conservatism among the ruling classes reinforced by the pervasive influence of the Catholic Church hindered the formulation of feminism in Spain. Also as María Lafitte, Condesa de Campo Alange, *La mujer en España: Cien años de su historia, 1860–1960* (Madrid: Aguilar, 1963), 12–15, points out, the Spanish aristocracy, unlike the French, did not enjoy a widespread tradition of literary salons; the lower classes remained oblivious to all discussions of women's rights; and middle-class women sought emancipation for economic reasons, not out of ideological commitment. Women of all classes were conditioned to live by the strictest moral and social traditions and were totally removed from the public struggle for the advancement of their rights. Capel, *Sufragio*, 123, is quick to point out that although María Goyri and Concepción Saiz wrote books on feminism, these were isolated cases of women privileged enough to have benefited from the liberal pedagogical ideas promoted by the Institución Libre de Enseñanza and the Asociación para la Enseñanza de la Mujer.

55. The connection between economic need and the first signs of feminism was recognized early by Nelken in her 1919 publication, *La condición social* (35), and by her contemporary José Francos Rodríguez, who studied the growing need for middle class women to develop a career other than marriage in his *La mujer y la política españolas* (Madrid: Editorial Pueyo, 1920), chapter 12. Summarizing the problem, Mercedes G. Basauri writes, "La urgencia de la mujer de esta clase social por ganarse la vida constituirá uno de los puntos de partida más determinantes. Las estrecheces económicas de la clase media hacen que resulte imposible una dilación de la promoción de la vida profesional, laboral o cultural." "La mujer en el reinado de Alfonso XIII," *Tiempo de Historia*, 46 (September 1978):27.

56. Adolfo González Posada, *Feminismo* (Madrid, 1899), wrote of a radical feminism that

believed in the equality of men and women, a Catholic feminism that focused on improving the education of women, and a "feminismo oportunista y conservadora," a moderate, apolitical brand of feminism that sought certain concrete social, economic, and legal rights for women without demanding total equality. Campo Alange, *La mujer en España*, 199, collapses his three-pronged division into two categories, "un feminismo socialista y revolucionario y otro oportunista y conservador." María Aurèlia Capmany takes issue with the contention that both strains of feminism transformed the condition of women. According to her no transformation at all took place in Spain: *Feminismo ibérico* (Barcelona: Oikos-tau, 1970), 28–29.

57. Pilar Nieva de la Paz, *Autoras dramáticas españolas entre 1918 y 1936* (Madrid: Consejo Superior de Investigaciones Científicas, 1993), 21, makes a persuasive argument for using 1918 as the starting date for modern Spanish feminism. Around that date a social debate on women arose, a number of women's organizations were formed, and the influence of the international feminist movement was felt. Increasing numbers of women were reaping the benefits of the educational efforts initiated by the Krausistas during the last quarter of the previous century, and more women were working outside the home.

58. Alonso Zamora Vicente, *Examen de ingreso: Madrid, años veinte* (Madrid: Espasa Calpe, 1991), nostalgically evokes the Madrid of his childhood as the city that "ansiaba abandonar su cáscara pueblerina para convertirse en gran ciudad." For more detailed accounts of the physical and demographic changes that took place in Madrid in the twenties see Campo Alange, *La mujer en España*,171–89; Capel, *El trabajo y la educación*, chapter 1; and Pilar Folguera, "La historia oral como fuente para el estudio de la vida cotidiana de las mujeres," in *La mujer en la historia de España: Siglos XVI–XX*, ed. María Angeles Durán et al. (Madrid: Universidad Autónoma de Madrid, 1984), 177–211. Leisure characterized the life of the rich woman, while women of all classes were kept economically and psychologically dependent on marriage, uneducated, and divorced from anything beyond the family.

59. Julián Marías, *La mujer en el siglo XX* (Madrid: Alianza, 1980), 187; Luis Aranguren, "La mujer de 1923 a 1963," *Revista de Occidente* 1, no. 8–9 (1963):233.

60. Nieva de la Paz, *Autoras dramáticas*, 38–40, explains that the "mujer de hoy" was introduced in Spain by the press in its physical images of woman identifiable with the Anglo-Saxon woman—tall, thin, and blond with a cigarette or cocktail in her hand. The public reacted with one of two attitudes: either enthusiasm at the possibility of emancipation or horror at the threat to the "true" feminine values of love, marriage, and motherhood.

61. The press of the day carried many articles, often on the front page, concerning the "new woman" and women's sudden entry into the public sphere of sports and "unusual" professions. The abundance of material in this area has already attracted the attention of a number of Spanish scholars who have published studies on women's image as reflected in the press and also on early female journalists. These studies include: María Antonia Galán Quintanilla, *La mujer a través de la información en la II República Española* (Madrid: Universidad Complutense, 1980); Danièle Bussy Genevois, "Problemas de aprehensión de la vida cotidiana de las mujeres españolas a través de la prensa femenina y familiar (1931-1936)," in *La mujer en la historia*, ed. Durán et al., 263-78; Adolfo Perinat and María Isabel Marrades, *Mujer, prensa y sociedad, 1800-1939* (Madrid: Centro de Investigaciones Sociológicas, 1980); Mercedes Roig, *A través de la prensa: La mujer en la historia (Francia, Italia, España)*, (Madrid: Instituto de la Mujer, 1986); Isabel Segura and Marta Selva, *Revistes de dones, 1846-1935* (Barcelona: EDHASA, 1984).

62. Followers in Spain of figures such as Herbert Spencer, Dr. Benedict, R. Kossman, and especially P. J. Moebius adhered to a rationale that "proved" the intellectual inferiority of women. Scanlon, in her chapter 4 of *La polémica feminista*, outlines the prominent "scientific" texts written after 1890 that established the authoritative basis for antifeminist thought among intellectuals and the cultured public. The notions emerging from the new fields of medi-

cine, psychology, and biology were, according to her, more pernicious than those of the Church because they saw in feminism not merely wicked behavior but a threat to the conservation of the species.

63. González Blanco, *La mujer*, 21. He was not alone in his antifeminism. Roberto Nóvoa Santos, *La mujer, nuestro sexto sentido y otros esbozos* (Madrid: Biblioteca Nueva, 1929), believed that intellectual capacity in women was an abnormality and a woman with intelligence was "algo monstruoso, poseedor de caracteres sexuales secundarios de tipo masculino" (15).

64. Ortega y Gasset defined women as biologically inferior to men, as confusing beings lacking in spirituality and passion whose only happiness derives from their submission to the masculine ego. He expressed his ideas on women in works such as "El hombre y la gente," *Estudios sobre el amor*, and "Paisaje con una corza al fondo," collected in *Obras completas* (Madrid: Revista de Occidente, 1964).

65. Padre Graciano Martínez, *El libro de la mujer española: Hacia un femenismo cuasi dogmático* (Madrid: Imprenta del Asilo de Huérfanos, 1921), xiii. The most important Catholic "feminist," Father Martínez supported women's suffrage because he saw in it the potential for a reinforcement of conservative ideas, but he opposed women's active participation in politics.

66. Gregorio Marañón, *Tres ensayos sobre la vida sexual* (Madrid: Biblioteca Nueva, 1926), 137. Another doctor preoccupied with the defeminization of women was the gynecologist Vital Aza y Díaz in *Feminismo y sexo* (Madrid: Javier Morata, 1928). He sees no conflict between maternity and a profession as long as working mothers are protected and their femininity is preserved. He was particularly concerned that changes in fashion had masculinized women. The belief that equality for women produces a loss of femininity continues up to the present day in Julián Marías, *La mujer en el siglo XX*. Through conceptual convolutions, he reasons that equality, by eradicating a natural difference, an "inequality," is at best an ambiguous and undesirable concept that deforms the avenues of sexual fulfillment. Marías revisits the theme of woman in *La mujer y su sombra* (Madrid: Alianza, 1986). He continues to view women as essentially inactive beings rooted in the quotidian and the body, objects of male desire, and "the mysterious continent" available for male exploration.

67. Campo Alange, *La mujer en España*, 198.

68. The word feminist conjured up an image of a disagreeable and aggressive woman, as Campo Alange, *La mujer en España*, 199, explains. Of the documents on egalitarian thought that she anthologizes, María Angeles Durán states that none would qualify as a feminist manifesto: *Mujeres y hombres: La formación del pensamiento igualitario* (Madrid: Castalia, 1993), 23.

69. Francos Rodríguez, *La mujer y la política españolas*.

70. Gregorio Martínez Sierra published this lecture as a book: *Feminismo, feminidad, españolismo* (Madrid: Saturnino Calleja, 1920). He also published *La mujer moderna* (Madrid: Saturnino Calleja, 1920), a book composed of the results of a survey sent to leading intellectuals of the day that focused on their attitudes toward feminism and opinions on women's participation in politics. Martínez Sierra was famous in his day as a "feminist," but as a playwright, he wrote in collaboration with his wife María Lejárraga without giving her due credit.

71. María Luisa Navarro de Luzuriaga, "La mujer, elemento atmosférico," *La Gaceta Literaria* 3, no. 60 (15 June 1929):2 and "Feminidad y feminismo," *La Gaceta Literaria* 3, no. 61 (1 July 1929):2.

72. Chacel, "Esquema," 152.

73. For an examination of the rise of a feminist press in Spain, see Perinat and Marrades, *Mujer, prensa*, chapter 7 and Roig, *A través de la prensa*, 236–73. Not only were increasing numbers of women's magazines being founded, women were writing more often in the general press, and once the Republic was formed, more often on political issues. A number

of prominent women of the day, such as María Goyri, Carmen de Burgos, Margarita Nelken, Celsia Regis, and María Espinosa, were known for their feminist journalism.

74.   Francos Rodríguez, *La mujer y la política*, 301–4, lists the thirty-six points of the organization. Scanlon, *La polémica feminista*, 203–11, traces the development of the ANME and assesses its contribution to the struggle for women's rights. She considers it basically a conservative group because it refused to support suffrage for women and because the political party it formed in the thirties originated in the dated pacifist idea that women's presence in politics promoted peace. Fagoaga, *La voz y el voto*, 127–39, also offers a useful summary of the ANME.

75.   It also sponsored lectures, concerts, exhibitions, and a variety of literary tributes. For instance, Lorca delivered a lecture titled "Imaginación, inspiración y evasión en poesía" to the club; Unamuno read his drama *Raquel encadenada*; and Rafael Alberti created quite a stir when, after arriving for a reading dressed in clown-like attire holding a caged dove in one hand and a turtle in the other, he began to insult the writer-husbands of many of the women present. In an article in *La Gaceta Literaria* 3, no. 71 (1 December 1929):5, Ernestina de Champourcin reported that she found the whole incident amusing, but another woman quoted called it an act of stupidity and cowardice.

76.   Ricardo Baeza, "El blanco y el negro (una lanza por 'Lyceum')," *El Sol*, 21 August 1927, 12, summarizes the contents of the circular. The scorn aimed at the club is also borne out by Campo Alange, *La mujer en España*, 210.

77.   The most complete discussion of the Lyceum Club is Fagoaga, *La voz y el voto*, 178–79, 182–84, 187–88, 190–92. Also informative are Campo Alange, *La mujer en España*, 208–10; Basauri, "La mujer en el reinado," 36–38; Nieva de la Paz, *Autoras dramáticas*, 53, 66–68; Antonina Rodrigo, *Mujeres de España: Las silenciadas* (Barcelona: Círculo de Lectores, 1979), 134–36; Zulueta and Moreno, *Ni convento ni college*, chapter 2.

78.   According to Perinat and Marrades, *Mujer, prensa*, 389–401, women founded 36 new periodicals between 1900 and 1929, but as Bieder points out, this is half as many as in the whole previous century when conditions were less favorable ("Women and the Twentieth Century," 312). As women's issues were incorporated into mainstream periodicals, it might have been less necessary to establish periodicals geared exclusively to women. Also there were some new opportunities for women's writing beyond women's magazines.

79.   "Una encuesta sensacional: ¿Qué es la vanguardia?" *La Gaceta Literaria* 4, no. 84 (1 June 1930):3–4. The surveys in which Méndez appears are found in *La Gaceta Literaria* 2, no. 27 (1 February 1928):1 and 2, no. 43 (1 October 1928):6. Reference has already been made to the survey on architecture that included Chacel.

80.   Bellver, "Conversación," 71.

81.   After her first encounter with Alberti in 1925 at a poetry reading by Lorca, she met with him to hear his advice on writing and to read poetry to each other. She first spoke to Lorca when she called the Residencia de Estudiantes and said, "Habla la novia desconocida de Buñuel." (Buñuel had been her boyfriend for seven years during their summers in San Sebastián.) Through Lorca she met her future husband, Altolaguirre, in 1931. Cernuda became a life-long friend who lived in her home in Mexico until his death in 1963. For details on her relationships with the members of the Generation of 27, see Ulacia Altolaguirre, *Concha Méndez*; and also Max Aub, "Concha Méndez Cuesta," *Conversaciones con Buñuel* (Madrid: Aguilar, 1985), 241–51, and Ulacia Altolaguirre, "Concha Méndez y Luis Buñuel," *Insula* 557 (1993):12–15.

82.   Morla Lynch, *En España*, 335–38.

83.   Wilcox, "Rescision," 292 and Biruté Ciplijauskaité, "Escribir entre dos exilios: las voces femeninas de la generación del 27," *Homenaje al profesor Antonio Vilanova*, ed. Adolfo Sotelo Vázquez and María Cristina Carbonell (Barcelona: Universidad de Barcelona, 1989), 2:119–26. For Méndez's statement see Ulacia Altolaguirre, *Concha Méndez*, 16.

84. Examples of male support included the favorable reviews of two of Champourcin's books that Domenchina wrote. Also, Altolaguirre makes a case for the appreciation of Méndez's theater in "Nuestro teatro," *Hora de España* no. 4 (1937):27–37.

85. Alberto Porlán, *La sinrazón de Rosa Chacel* (Madrid: Anjana Ediciones, 1984), 22. The confinement to the periphery of those few women who intruded into the male preserve of public space is not unique to Spain. Silvia Rogers presents a cogent analysis of how the post-World War II British House of Commons not only limited women's presence to small numbers and reduced spaces but also minimized their representation by reclassifying them as "honorary" men: Rogers in *Women and Space: Ground Rules and Social Maps*, ed. Shirley Ardener (New York: St. Martin's Press, 1981), 50–71.

86. Carmen Bravo-Villasante, "La mujer como autora literaria," *Historia 16* 13, no. 145 (1988):58.

87. Elaine Showalter, "Feminist Criticism in the Wilderness," in *Writing and Sexual Difference*, ed. Elizabeth Abel (Chicago: University of Chicago Press, 1982), 31–32.

88. Susan Kirkpatrick has ably shown in *Las románticas: Women Writers and Subjectivity in Spain, 1835–1850* (Berkeley and Los Angeles: University of California Press, 1989) that despite their initial attempts to create a vision of personal freedom and an individualized female self, by the middle of the nineteenth century, Spanish female poets of the Romantic period tended increasingly to attach themselves to the culture's restrictive feminine ideal by conforming to the norms of the domestic angel (284). Anxiety over this maternal tradition, in the female poets of the twenties, provokes a struggle similar to what Sandra M. Gilbert and Susan Gubar termed the "complicated female affiliation complex": *The War of the Words*, vol. 1 of *No Man's Land* (New Haven: Yale University Press, 1987), 168.

89. Ernestina de Champourcin, "Tres proyecciones," *Síntesis* (Buenos Aires) 30 (November 1929):330–31. In this new "tropel de muchachas ágiles," Champourcin includes Rosa Chacel, Josefina de la Torre, Clemencia Miró, and Carmen Conde. Not all women poets of Champourcin's generation display this implied enthusiasm for the adaptation of these novel tonalities. Conde would later call imitation an obstacle to female authenticity. She writes, "La mujer, al ingresar en el mundo de la creación obedecía a un total mimetismo; impostaba su voz en tono ajeno, y por ajeno falso": "La poesía de la mujer poeta," *Cuadernos de Literatura* 1 (1947):110. The question of imitation, affiliation, and assimilation in early Anglo-American women writers has been studied more extensively than in Hispanic writers. Besides the work of Gilbert and Gubar on the "female affiliation complex," studies helpful to the understanding of the conservative stance of the poets studied here include Mary Jacobus, "The Question of Language: Men of Maxims and *The Mill on the Floss*," in Abel, *Writing and Sexual Difference*, 37–52, and Margaret Homans, "Eliot, Wordsworth, and the Scenes of the Sisters' Instruction," ibid., 53–71. For a partial study of initiation and female creativity among Spanish poets of the twenties see Catherine G. Bellver, "Literary Influence and Female Creativity: The Case of Two Women Poets of the Generation of 27," *Siglo XX/20th Century* 15, no.1–2 (1997):7–32.

90. Guillermo de Torre, "Poesía y novela de amor: Dos libros de Ernestina de Champourcin," *El Sol*, 13 June 1936, 2.

91. Esteban Salazar y Chapela, "Ernestina de Champourcin y su sombra," *La Gaceta Literaria* 6, no. 123 (1 May 1932):16.

92. César M. Arconada, "Ernestina de Champourcin dice . . .," *La Gaceta Literaria* 2, no. 38 (15 July 1928):1. This reticence to apply gender to poetry continues to the present. Ugalde (*Conversaciones*) discovered that the pejorative connotations associated with women's poetry still compel female poets of Spain to reject the notion of a separate and different feminine aesthetic. Narrators do the same. For example, Marina Mayoral acknowledges feminist feelings but still repudiates the label: see Concha Alborg, "Marina Mayoral's Narrative: Old Families and New Faces from Galicia," in Joan L. Brown, 179–97. Likewise, Cristina

Fernández Cubas rejects the notion that she is a feminist even if she mocks certain masculine stereotypes: Kathleen M. Glenn, "Conversación con Cristina Fernández Cubas," *Anales de la Literatura Española Contemporánea* 18, no. 2 (1993):355–63.

CHAPTER 3. CONCHA MÉNDEZ: PLOTTING THE ROUTE FROM OPEN SPACES TO THE REALM OF SHADOWS

1. Elizabeth Janeway, *Man's World, Woman's Place: A Study in Social Mythology* (New York: William Morrow, 1971), 7. Janeway dates the notions underlying the adage "It's a man's world. Woman's place is in the home." to a period no later than the days when ancient Chinese sages conceived the male and female principles of *yang* and *yin*.

2. Daphne Spain, *Gendered Spaces* (Chapel Hill: The University of North Carolina Press, 1992), 3, states that very frequently "women and men are spatially segregated in ways that reduce women's access to knowledge and thereby reinforce women's lower status relative to men's." Shirley Ardener, ed., *Women and Space: Ground Rules and Social Maps* (New York: St. Martin's Press, 1991), offers a collection of studies that show the ways in which space reflects social organization in a variety of cultures throughout the world. Social structures constitute "social maps" realized by placing individuals in prescribed spaces, and once assigned, spaces define the people in them. The female social scientists who contribute to this collection delve into the implications of the experiential situation of women with regard to space, particularly as a vehicle for enclosure and separation. Not unexpectedly, when a male theorist explores the philosophical significance of various kinds of spaces that stimulate the poetic imagination, interior space becomes "felicitous spaces." In his seminal study, *The Poetics of Space* (Boston: Beacon Press, 1969), Gaston Bachelard finds the house, for instance, not a confining space, but a protective, memory-evoking environment with maternal features.

3. According to Mary Ellman, *Thinking About Women* (New York: Harcourt Brace and World, 1968), 92.

4. Examples of young women held prisoners in their own homes seem to have been particularly prevalent in Andalusia. Fascinated by the phenomenon, Rafael Alberti based his poem "La encerrada" and his play *El adefesio* on a beautiful young girl in his neighborhood who was never seen except veiled, in the company of someone, and only at mass. Her authoritarian environment led this intriguing young women to commit suicide, as occurred in Lorca's play. See *La arboleda perdida* (Buenos Aires: Compañía General Fabril Editora, 1959), 189–90. Bridget A. Aldaraca, *El ángel del hogar: Galdós and the Ideology of Domesticity in Spain* (Chapel Hill: University of North Carolina Press, 1991), studies the changing justification for the confinement of women and its manifestation in Spanish literature, particularly in the notion of the angel of the hearth.

5. Sandra M. Gilbert and Susan Gubar, *The Madwoman in the Attic* (New Haven: Yale University Press, 1979), 83–87.

6. Sandra M. Gilbert and Susan Gubar, *The War of the Words*, 168–71.

7. Kirkpatrick, *Las románticas*.

8. Janet Pérez points out that the very titles of novels by women in this era announce a re-creation of a struggle for escape. She singles out titles like *Nada, El cuarto de atrás, Fragmentos del interior*, and *Cinco sombras en torno a un costurero* as evidence of the pervasiveness of enclosure in contemporary Spanish society and fiction: "Contemporary Spanish Women Writers and the Feminized Quest-Romance," *Monographic Review / Revista Monográfica* 8 (1992):39.

9. For Carmen Martín Gaite, "la condición ventanera" differentiates female and male discourse and determines the Spanish woman writer's distinctive literary perspective. She

calls this a perspective that never loses sight of its own boundaries, and she defines woman's gaze as looking without being seen, as looking outward from within an interior "redoubt": *Desde la ventana* (Madrid: Espasa-Calpe, 1987), 36.

10. With the advent of democracy, Spanish women writers gained the freedom to write about formerly taboo subjects, especially about sexuality and homosexuality, but they have only begun to chart the realm of freedom. Elizabeth J. Ordóñez, in *Voices of Their Own: Contemporary Spanish Narrative by Women,* successfully traces the evolution of contemporary Spanish fiction from silence to multivocality, from subversion to transgression, and from somberness to humor. Sharon Keefe Ugalde has studied the multiple efforts of Spanish women poets of the post-Franco era to adapt, revise, or subvert the inherited masculine tradition. In addition to *Conversaciones y poemas,* Ugalde has published numerous articles on the subject.

11. José Ortega y Gasset, *Dehumanización del arte* (Madrid: Revista de Occidente, 1964), 34, 36.

12. Margaret Homans, *Women Writers and Poetic Identity* (Princeton: Princeton University Press, 1990), 215–18.

13. Jorge Guillén, "Concha Méndez: *Poemas. Sombras y sueños,*" *Suma Bibliográfica* 2 (May 1946):25.

14. Mainer, "Las escritoras del 27," 22.

15. Juan Ramón Jiménez, *Españoles de tres mundos* (Buenos Aires: Losada, 1942), 157–58. Juan Ramón Jiménez originally wrote his poetic portrait of Méndez ("Y Concha") in 1931 for the fifth issue of *Héroe,* a short-lived literary magazine published by Méndez and her husband Altolaguirre.

16. Ulacia Altolaguirre, *Concha Méndez,* 41.

17. She tells of her attention-getting exploit in a letter to García Lorca dated 20 July 1925, and on deposit at the library of the Fundación García Lorca. Her airplane incident is retold in "Conversación con Concha Méndez," *La Gaceta Literaria* 3, no. 69 (1 November 1929):3.

18. Antonio Gallego Morell, *Literatura de tema deportivo* (Madrid: Editorial Prensa Española, 1969), 10–12, 33. Guillermo Díaz-Plaja credits the appreciation of nature promoted by the Institución Libre de Enseñanza and the personal influence of Alfonso XIII with generating an interest in sports on all levels of Spanish society. See *Estructura y sentido del Novecentismo español* (Madrid: Alianza, 1975), 186–87. Díaz-Plaja's inclusion of Concha Méndez in his section on sports and Gallego Morrell's inclusion of her in his anthology on the theme attest to its prominence in her poetry and her coincidences with the trend-setters of her day.

19. Emilio Miró, "Algunas poetas españolas entre 1926 y 1960," in *Literatura y vida cotidiana,* ed. María Angeles Durán and José Antonio Rey (Zaragoza: Universidad Autónoma de Madrid and Universidad de Zaragoza, 1987), 310; and José Lorenzo, "Colofón," in *Inquietudes,* by Concha Méndez (Madrid: Juan Pueyo, 1926), 107. Also Luis G. de Valdeavellano, "Los nuevos valores literarios: Concha Méndez Cuesta," *La Epoca,* 4 October 1930, 4, remarks on the atypicalness of her case: "un tipo de mujer no frecuente todavía en el ambiente español: independiente, segura de sí misma, ambiciosa de nuevos panoramas."

20. Wilcox, however, attributes the carefree tone apparent in Méndez's poetry to gender difference and finds in her a deliberately intranscendental vision that oscillates between childlike and "down-to-earth": "Rescision," 293.

21. Francisco Ayala, "Concha Méndez Cuesta. *Surtidor,*" *La Gaceta Literaria* 2, no. 29 (1 March 1928):3.

22. José Díaz Fernández, "Concha Méndez Cuesta," *El Sol,* 29 March 1928, 2.

23. María Dolores Arana, "Concha Méndez: Las dos orillas," *El Día* 9, January 1977, 15. Morla Lynch records the details of her very unconventional wedding in his *En España,* 335.

24. Emilio Miró calls *Inquietudes* "Un verdadero homenaje al primer libro de Alberti"

and of *Surtidor*, he says, "En 1928 . . . Alberti tenía ya sus tres libros de canciones . . . como también las *Canciones*, de García Lorca, y a todos ellos es deudor este segundo título de Concha Méndez, con mimetismos tan ostensibles": "Poetisas españolas contemporáneas," *Revista de la Universidad Complutense* 24, no. 95 (1975):276. José-Carlos Mainer, "Las escritoras del 27," 22, is much more severe, seeing a lack of creativity in her recourse to Alberti as "paratexto."

25. If Méndez was guided in her poetry by Alberti, he in turn was counselled by his "generoso consejero," Dámaso Alonso. This is the phrase that José Luis Tejada uses for the person who guided Alberti in the reading of Spanish poetry: *Rafael Alberti: Entre la tradición y la vanguardia* (Madrid: Gredos, 1977), 39. Alberti himself credits Alonso with a crucial influence over his poetry in *La arboleda perdida*, 155.

26. Ulacia Altolaguirre, *Memorias habladas*, 45.

27. See Solita Salinas de Marichal, *El mundo poético de Rafael Alberti* (Madrid: Gredos, 1968), 12–73.

28. Annis Pratt, *Archetypal Patterns in Women's Fiction* (Bloomington: Indiana University Press, 1981), 16–17.

29. Stanley Richardson, "Spanish Poetry, 1935," *Contemporaries* 2, no. 1 (1935):239.

30. The referentiality of Méndez's poems contrasts with Alberti's intertextuality in *Marinero en tierra*. This dichotomy recalls the observations made by Walter Ong in *Orality and Literacy* (London: Methuen, 1982), 109–13, concerning differences in language employed by male and female English novelists in the nineteenth century. Denied a classical education steeped in Greek and Latin texts, women authors were obliged to use the everyday language they knew and, consequently, developed a fresh, realistic style based on oral language. Unfamiliar with cultural texts, Méndez resorted to the images of her everyday world.

31. Much discussion and research has been conducted on this phenomenon. Feminist psychologists such as Nancy Chodorow and Jane Flax point to the importance of mothering in the shaping of the mechanisms of female psychology. See Chodorow, *The Reproduction of Mothering: Psychoanalysis and the Sociology of Gender* (Berkeley: University of California Press, 1978) and Flax, "The Conflict Between Nurturance and Autonomy in Mother-Daughter Relationships and Within Feminism," *Feminist Studies* 4, no. 2 (June 1978):171–89. The significance of relationships, connections, and unity is also studied by Carol Gilligan, *In a Different Voice* (Boston: Harvard University Press, 1982), who argues that because women's world view is founded on relationships and the preservation of them, connections and unity become necessary for their self-identity. In the field of aesthetics, Judith Kegan Gardiner and others maintain that because female identity is unitary, women writers can be expected to elude canonical genre distinctions, blur the public and the private, and provoke identification by the reader. See Judith Kegan Gardiner, "On Female Identity and Writing by Women," in *Writing and Sexual Difference*, ed. Elizabeth Abel (Chicago: University of Chicago Press, 1982), 177–91.

32. The self-confidence of her poetic personae may be a reflection of the confidence the author herself garnered from her experience as a champion swimmer. When asked if she was not frightened to escape to England on a boat full of undesirables, she replied, "No me da miedo el mar, me da mucho más miedo quedarme en un sitio donde el ambiente me ahoga": See Margery Resnick, "La inteligencia audaz: Vida y poesía de Concha Méndez," *Papeles de Son Armadans* 88, no. 263 (1978):136.

33. Elena Urrutia, "Itinerario espiritual," *Novedades* , 24 October 1976, 5.

34. Carol P. Christ, *Diving Deep and Surfacing: Women Writers on Spiritual Quest* (Boston: Beacon Press, 1980).

35. Resnick, "La inteligencia audaz," 62–66, 138.

36. Quoted in Emilio Miró, introduction to *Vida a vida y Vida o río*, by Concha Méndez, (Madrid: Ediciones Caballo Griego para la Poesía, 1979), 12.

37. Méndez recounts her contempt for the family friend who asked her brothers what they wanted to be when they grew up, but who reponded to her announcement that she wanted to be a captain of a boat with "Las mujeres nunca son nada" (Resnick, "La inteligencia audaz," 132). In her memoirs, she recalls that she escaped from such patronizing treatment, at night, through vivid dreams of adventure (Ulacia Altolaguirre, *Memorias habladas*, 26).

38. Angela Ingram, "On the Contrary, Outside of It," in *Women's Writing in Exile*, ed. Mary Lynn Broe and Angela Ingram (Chapel Hill: University of North Carolina Press, 1989), 4. Paradoxically, women must exile themselves to overcome exile because more than an external circumstance, exile for them is a psychological situation, an internal exclusion. Shari Benstock refers to this exclusion as *matria*, the expatriated other within *patria*, and shows that expatriation for female Modernists had a significance not shared by the men of the time: "Expatriate Modernism,"ibid., 19-40.

39. "Conversación con Concha Méndez," 3.

40. Philip Wheelwright, *Metaphor and Reality* (Bloomington: Indiana University Press, 1968), 112.

41. George Lakoff and Mark Johnson, *Metaphors We Live By* (Chicago: University of Chicago Press, 1980), 3.

42. Ostriker, *Stealing the Language*, 92.

43. Hélène Cixous, "Castration or Decapitation?" *Signs: Journal of Women in Culture and Society* 7, no. 1 (1981):43.

44. Madonna Kolbenschlag, *Kiss Sleeping Beauty Good-Bye: Breaking the Spell of Feminine Myths and Models* (Garden City: Doubleday & Company, 1979), 5. Kolbenschlag works within, or more accurately against, the psychoanalytical interpretation of Sleeping Beauty, of writers such as Bruno Bettelheim in his *Use of Enchantment* (New York: Alfred A. Knopf, 1976), who sees a model for the adolescent dream of everlasting youth and perfection and a paradigm for narcissistic self-involvement without suffering. In their scrutiny of both primary and secondary sources, feminist critics have re-evaluated archetypes, like Sleeping Beauty, perceiving in them signs of restrictions imposed by male desires, fears, and fantasies rather than evidence of a female essence.

45. In recent decades as part of their quest for autonomous self-definition, women poets have refocused the perspective of poetry by speaking of the female body and women's quotidian activities. In defense of the female body and of what she terms the evasion of the Jacob's ladder yardstick, Ostriker censures Simone de Beauvoir for her call for the transcendence of the inferior life of immanence dictated by feminine anatomy (*Stealing the Language*, 95). The vindication of female anatomy evident in the writing of contemporary American women poets as well as in some Spanish ones might suggest a continuing aversion to verticality among women writers and might possibly lead to a criticism of Concha Méndez's early poetry for its lack of focus on distinctively female themes. Her affection for verticality must be seen, however, as a noteworthy expression of freedom in a transitional period when most women wrote about female sentiments in order to conform to literary expectations and not to flout conventions.

46. Carlos Bousoño, *Teoría de la expresión poética* (Madrid: Gredos, 1970), 1:177–78.

47. Dámaso Alonso, *Poetas españoles contemporáneos* (Madrid: Gredos, 1969), 162.

48. Hélène Cixous, "The Laugh of the Medusa," in *The Signs Reader: Women, Gender and Scholarship*, ed. Elizabeth and Emily K. Abel (Chicago: University of Chicago Press, 1983), 291.

49. J. E. Cirlot, *A Dictionary of Symbols*, trans. Jack Sage (New York: Philosophical Library, 1962), 104.

50. In her own personal life, Méndez intruded into masculine space when she introduced herself to the select circle of writers and intellectuals gathering at the Residencia de Estudiantes in the twenties. Through them, she came in contact with the men who were

shaping Spain's avant-garde culture. Later, after her marriage to Manuel Altolaguirre, she shared her workplace and home with these men, when her home became an important publication center for contemporary poetry and a meeting place for many of the writers of the Generation of 27 like García Lorca, Rafael Alberti, and Luis Cernuda. The open, adventurous literary spirit of the new Spanish poetry both shaped and strengthened Méndez's personal inclinations just as her travels of 1928 to 1930 gave her the opportunity to combine physical escape with psychological freedom. Personality, individual experience, social and cultural context, and the power of poetry help account for the patterns of movement in *Canciones*.

51. Emilo Miró, Introduction to *Vida a vida y Vida o río*, 21. Dedicated to Manuel Altolaguirre, this collection was published by Ediciones La Tentativa Poética, a press through which she and Manuel brought out books of fellow poets such as Pedro Salinas, Rafael Alberti, and Luis Cernuda.

52. Wilcox, "Rescision," 302.

53. James Valender, Introduction to *Poemas (1926–1986)*, by Concha Méndez (Madrid: Ediciones Hiperión, 1995), 32.

54. Her son died at birth in March of 1933. In 1937, Concha Méndez fled Spain with her two-year-old daughter. She traveled to Paris, where her husband Manuel Altolaguirre joined them after the war, in 1939. The family left for Cuba, where they lived until 1943, when they finally settled in Mexico. The following year her husband left her to marry a rich woman from Cuba, whom they had met when living there. For additional information on her experience of exile see Ulacia Altolaguirre, *Memorias habladas*, 101–15.

55. Political or geographical exile has been satisfactorily outlined by Paul Tabori in his *The Anatomy of Exile: A Semantic and Historical Approach* (London: Harrap, 1972). He succinctly defines this type of exile as "a person who is compelled to leave his homeland—though the forces that send him on his way may be political, economic, or purely psychological. It does not make an essential difference whether he is expelled by physical force or whether he makes the decision to leave without such an immediate pressure" (38). The phenomenon of exile also encompasses the ontological situation of mankind today that creates what Octavio Paz has referred to as "exilio espiritual," an omnipresent loneliness resulting from the feelings of imprisonment and loss engendered by the very act of living: "La palabra edificante," *Papeles de Son Armadans* 35, no. 103 (1943):41–82. This metaphysical type of exile separates the self from the Universe or Deity and blocks transcendence of the spirit. Socio-political exile includes several variations of exclusion: the "inner exile" that Paul Ilie studies among the writers who stayed in Spain after the civil war, in *Literature and Inner Exile: Authoritarian Spain, 1939–1975* (Baltimore: The Johns Hopkins University Press, 1980); the necessary dissidence that for Julia Kristeva privileges the social stance of the intellectual (See Jane Gallop, *The Daughter's Seduction: Feminism and Psychoanalysis* [Ithaca: Cornell University Press, 1982], 119); and the marginalization of women from full and open participation in society that feminists have analyzed and decried. The term psychological exile can be used to refer either to a subconscious predisposition to feelings of alienation and otherness or to the psychological consequences of a break in intimate human relationships.

56. Biruté Ciplijauskaité, "Escribir entre dos exilios," 123.

57. Miró, introduction, 11.

58. War as a disruption of solidarity within a community and a living memory of bloody battles emerges as a characteristic male preoccupation while women are more likely to concern themselves with the family separation occasioned by war and the intimate details of psychological survival. Méndez's poetry on exile shares some features found in her male counterparts, but she also reveals some themes and develops certain strategies to transcend tragedy attributable to a divergent female perspective on war and exile. For a closer look at her relationship to exile in comparison to her male compatriots, see Catherine G. Bellver,

"Exile and the Female Experience in the Poetry of Concha Méndez," *Anales de la Literatura Española Contemporánea* 18, no. 1–2 (1993):27–42.

59. Biruté Ciplijauskaité, *La soledad y la poesía española contemporánea* (Madrid: Insula, 1962), 199.

60. Ciplijauskaité shows that the question "Is the life of an exile an authentic life?" is the one often posed in the poetry of the Spanish exiles of varying temperaments, from Domenchina to Alberti (*La soledad*, 209–15).

61. George Lakoff and Mark Turner, *More Than Cool Reason: A Field Guide to Poetic Metaphor* (Chicago: University of Chicago Press, 1989), 25.

62. Gilbert and Gubar, *Madwoman*, 50.

63. Ciplijauskaité, "Escribir entre dos exilios," 123; Miró, introduction, 26. Valender, introduction to *Poemas*, 33, concurs basically with Ciplijauskaité except that he sees the evasive attitude as flourishing after *Sombras y sueños*.

64. For a lengthier discussion of Méndez and the female tradition of mothers and daughters, see Catherine G. Bellver, "Mothers, Daughters, and the Female Tradition in the Poetry of Concha Méndez," *Revista Hispánica Moderna* 51 (1998):317–26.

65. Essential writers on this issue are Chodorow, Flax, and Gilligan. Also useful are Adrienne Rich, *Of Woman Born: Motherhood as Experience and Institution* (New York: W. W. Norton, 1976) and Jean Baker Miller, *Toward A New Psychology of Women* (Boston: Beacon Press, 1986).

66. Kathryn Allen Rabuzzi, *Motherself: A Mythic Analysis of Motherhood* (Bloomington: Indiana University Press, 1988), 43, argues that the concept of self experienced by women, following the way of the mother, or "motherself," is relational and multiple, but the implicit Western patriarchal assumption that the self is masculine and the belief that unity is better than multiplicity, that "one" is superior to "many," have served as barriers to women's understanding of what "self" is.

67. Cixous, "The Laugh of the Medusa."

68. Méndez's mother died of cancer while Méndez was in exile in Mexico. As she had done when her son died, Méndez registered her grief over the loss of her mother by writing poetry. See Ulacia Altolaguirre, *Memorias habladas*, 11–12.

69. Contrasting male and female elegies, Celeste M. Schenck, "Feminism and Deconstruction: Re-Constructing the Elegy," *Tulsa Studies in Women's Literature* 5, no. 1 (1986):20–24, discovers that the masculine elegy marks a rite of passage that culminates in a young poet's ascension in stature and his supersession of his elders. Especially in the case of dead mothers, women refuse the absolute separation of death because it is in connectedness, rather than psychic agon of the Freudian tribal context, that they stand to gain stature and self-knowledge.

70. Adrienne Rich, *Of Woman Born: Motherhood as Experience and Institution* (New York: W. W. Norton, 1976), 237.

71. Resnick, "La inteligencia audaz," 132.

72. Valender, introduction, 31–33.

CHAPTER 4. JOSEFINA DE LA TORRE: THE UNRAVELING OF PRESENCE

1. Virginia Woolf, *A Room of Her Own* (New York: Harcourt, Brace and World, 1928), 48–52.

2. Gilbert and Gubar, *Shakespeare's Sisters*, xv.

3. Claudio de la Torre won the Premio Nacional de Literatura in 1924 for his novel *En la vida del señor Alegre*. He also went on to write a number of successful plays.

4. Lázaro Santana, the editor of de la Torre's collected works, explains that her environment was happily conducive to the unhindered development of her talents. He also quotes the comments published in 1917 by Margarita Nelken on the little girl's precocious tendencies for writing poetry: introduction to *Poemas de la isla*, by Josefina de la Torre (Las Palmas de Gran Canaria, 1989), 9–10. There is a discrepancy as to her birthdate, with 1907, 1909, and 1910 being given as possibilities: see Rosetta Radtke, "Josefina de la Torre," in *An Encyclopedia of Continental Women Writers*, ed. Katharine M. Wilson (New York: Garland Publishing), 2:1246. Even if born as early as 1907, de la Torre wrote the poems of her first book in her late teens.

5. De la Torre published poems in magazines such as *España, Alfar, Verso y Prosa*, and *La Gaceta Literaria*. Although *Marzo incompleto* did not appear until 1968, Láraro Santana makes a convincing case for dating its completion before 1936 (introduction, 17). The collection appeared in the magazine *Fantasía* in 1947, and several poems had been published in the magazine *Azor*, in 1933, and in Gerardo Diego's anthology of 1934, facts that point to the likelihood that the majority of the poems were written before 1936. Before this collection, de la Torre had published *Versos y estampas* (Málaga: Litoral, 1927) and *Poemas de la isla* (Las Palmas de Gran Canaria: Colección San Borondón, 1930).

6. Josefina de la Torre began giving singing recitals in Madrid in 1927, and later she became an actress of the stage, the movies, radio, and television. In the late twenties she and her brother formed a theater company, "Teatro Mínimo," in their own home. During the forties she became the lead actress of the Teatro Nacional, at the María Guerrero theater, and she again formed her own theater company with her brother as director. She married actor Ramón Corroto.

7. Santana, introduction, 19.

8. Ibid., 15.

9. Gilbert and Gubar, *Shakespeare's Sisters*, xxii.

10. Juhasz, *Naked and Fiery Forms*.

11. De la Torre's adherence to the stereotypical portrayal of women seems confirmed by the short novel, *Memoria de una estrella*, she published in 1954. Appearing as a novel-of-the-week in a subscription series, the book tells of a beautiful but frivolous woman who searches for stardom but finally finds happiness as an anonymous housewife.

12. Josefina de la Torre, *Poemas de la isla* (Las Palmas de Gran Canaria: Gobierno de Canarias, 1989), 57. All references to her poetry are to this text and correspond to page numbers. This volume of de la Torre's complete works has the same title as her second collection and contains her three published collections of poetry as well as the unpublished *Medida del tiempo*, written after 1940. Lázaro Santana, the editor, excluded poems that appeared in magazines but were never included in a book.

13. Santana names Saulo Torón and Alonso Quesada as greater influences on de la Torre than Salinas, Alberti, Cernuda, or any other of the poets of the Generation of 27 (introduction, 19).

14. Anthony Leo Geist, *La poética de la generación del 27 y las revistas literarias* (Barcelona: Guadarrama, 1980), 188, calls *Gaceta de Arte* (1932–1936) "sin duda la única revista netamente surrealista publicada en España." Totally independent of the Peninsula, it followed the lines of the French movement. *Gaceta de Arte* has been reprinted (Santa Cruz de Tenerife, 1989) by F. Castro, A. Sánchez Robayna, and F. G. Martín. The avant-garde in the Canary Islands includes Pedro García Cabrera, Félix Delgado, Agustín Miranda Junco, and Juan Ismael. See Joaquín Artiles, *Literatura canaria* (Las Palmas de Gran Canaria, 1979).

15. One of her literary descendants, Ana María Fagundo, openly recognized the "canariedad" of her own poetry, the presence in it of the geography of the Canary Islands where she too was born and grew up. But whereas de la Torre evokes the sea and the sun, the contemporary poet identifies her birthplace as a "tierra en punta," because of its volca-

nic mountains, and finds in them a symbol of the "problemática existencia del ser humano": "Mi literatura es mía en mí," in *La Chispa '85: Selected Proceedings*, ed. Gilbert Paolini, (New Orleans: Tulane University Press, 1985), 89. A more self-conscious poet than de la Torre, Fagundo nonetheless shares with her poetic forebear the characteristic Santana singles out as typical of Canarian poets: a distaste for gratuitous complexity and technical ostentation.

16.   The "Romance del buen guiar," at the middle of the collection, is an obvious exception to the reservation of the narrative mode for prose. However, its narrative structure evokes a literary and not a personal past. Reminiscent of the medieval compositions of Gonzalo de Berceo, the poem tells of a lost traveller aided by a mystery woman, probably the Virgin.

17.   Adrienne Rich, *On Lies, Secrets, and Silences: Selected Prose, 1966–1978* (New York: Norton, 1979).

18.   To the discussion of the "anxiety of authorship" experienced by female writers, particularly in the nineteenth century, initiated in 1979 by Gilbert and Gubar in *Madwoman*, Ann Rosalind Jones has added insights into the connection between writing and immorality. She writes that the link between loose language and loose living arises from a basic association of women's bodies with their speech: a woman's accessibility to the social world beyond the household through speech was seen as intimately connected to the scandalous openness of her body: "Surprising Fame: Renaissance Gender Ideologies and Women's Lyric," in *The Poetics of Gender*, ed. Nancy K. Miller (New York: Columbia University Press, 1986), 76.

19.   Mary Jacobus, "The Difference of View," 10–21.

20.   Monique Wittig, "The Mark of Gender," in *The Poetics of Gender*, ed. Nancy K. Miller (New York: Columbia University Press, 1986), 66.

21.   Ostriker, *Stealing the Language*, 63–69.

22.   The question of silence has preoccupied American critics since poet Tillie Olsen spoke at the Radcliffe Institute in 1963 on the unnatural silences, the external circumstances that disrupt the creative process in women. Throughout the 1970s "silence" captured the attention of feminists, but as Elaine Hedges and Shelley Fisher Fishkin explain, by the mid-1980s the focus shifted from external impediments to silences that are intrinsic to a text. This silence, they add, might reveal reticences culturally imposed upon women, the workings of a repressed ideology, or a form of resistance to the dominant discourse: *Listening to Silences: New Essays in Feminist Criticism* (New York: Oxford University Press, 1994), 5. Spanish feminists have also addressed the question of silence. For example Antonina Rodrigo subtitled her 1979 publication, *Mujeres de España*, "Las silenciadas;" and the lead chapter ("Cartografías del silencio") in the more recent *Crítica y ficción literaria: Mujeres españolas contemporáneas*, ed. Aurora López and María Angeles Pastor (Granada: Universidad de Granada, 1989), is a review of the theme by Antónia Cabanilles. American Hispanists, for their part, have not only unearthed ignored or "silenced" female authors, they have also examined the "aesthetic of silence" that Jeanne Kammer calls the unifying characteristic of poetry by women: "The Art of Silence and the Forms of Women's Poetry," in *Shakespeare's Sisters*, ed. Gilbert and Gubar, 163. Margaret Persin, for one, finds silence imbued with power in the poetry of Carmen Martín Gaite ("Carmen Martín Gaite's *A rachas*: Dreams of the Past and Memories of the Future, Text(ure)s Woven of Many Colored Threads," *Monographic Review/Revista Monográfica* 6 [1990]:97); and Ordóñez, *Voices of Their Own*, discusses the varying degrees to which the female voice in contemporary Spanish fiction breaks the silence imposed by pariarchal discourse.

23.   Kirkpatrick, *Las románticas*. Sharon Keefe Ugalde, "Spanish Women Poets on Women's Poetry," *Monographic Review/Revista Monográfica* 6 (1990):135; and *Conversaciones y poemas*.

24.   Joy Buckles Landeira, in *Women Writers of Spain: An Annotated Bio-Bibliographical Guide*, ed. Carolyn L. Galerstein (New York: Greenwood Press, 1986), 314.

25.   The image of the room in literature by Spanish women is probably most readily

associated with Carmen Martín Gaite, whose critically acclaimed novel *El cuarto de atrás* (1978), contains "room" in its very title. Linda Gould Levine maintains that the "back room" of the novel combines the two gender-related realms that Gilbert and Gubar outline in *The Madwoman of the Attic*: the "special imagery of enclosure" of writing by women and the notions of flight and open space common to men's writing: "Carmen Martín Gaite's, *El cuatro de atrás*: A Portrait of the Artist as Woman," in *From Fiction to Metafiction: Essays in Honor of Carmen Martín-Gaite*, ed. Mirella Servodidio and Marcia L. Welles (Lincoln, Nebraska: The Society of Spanish and Spanish-American Studies, 1983), 169. Also helpful to understanding the motifs of enclosure and escape in this novel is Catherine G. Bellver, "War as Rite of Passage in *El cuarto de atrás*," *Letras Femeninas* 12, no. 1–2 (1986):69–77. Gender dichotomy in the treatment of enclosed spaces is also evident in poetry. For example, Biruté Ciplijauskaité finds a more intimate and contained relationship with the house in Concha Zardoya than in her male contemporary Leopoldo Panero: "Dos casas habitadas por la ausencia," *Sin Nombre* 9, no. 3 (1978):32–40.

26. Gilbert and Gubar, *Madwoman*, 87.

27. María Zambrano, *Filosofía y poesía* (Mexico: Fondo de Cultura Económica, 1987), 69.

28. Noël Valis, "The Language of Treasure: Carolina Coronado, Casta Esteban, and Marina Romero," in *In the Feminine Mode*, 268.

29. In addition to silence (not speaking) and ambivalence ("double-voiced discourse"), women poets practiced reticence (restrained speech) well into the middle of the twentieth century. The pregnant pause has served as a defense mechanism both to subvert the dominant discourse and to reveal the marginalization of women. Even in the more open social environment of the United States, Marianne Moore, writing during the same period as Josefina de la Torre, became famous for her reticence and deference (Juhasz, *Naked and Fiery Forms*, chapter 3). Even though some women began to speak more openly about their female experiences, acceptance as a respected poet required "timidities and disguises of a brilliant woman in a world where literary authority is male" (Ostriker, *Stealing the Language*, 52).

30. Angel Valbuena Prat, *La poesía española contemporánea* (Madrid: Compañía Ibero-Americana de Publicaciones, 1930), 129.

31. Gregory Keith Cole, "Women Poets of the Generation of 1927" (Ph.D. diss., University of Kentucky, 1993), 116. A descriptive study with a strong emphasis on the enumeration of literary influences, Cole's work is the only study other than Santana's introduction that treats de la Torre at some length and is one of the few general considerations of her generation of women poets.

32. Santana, introduction, 16.

33. Gilbert and Gubar, *Madwoman*, 642.

34. Nancy K. Miller, "Arachnologies: The Woman, the Text, and the Critic" in her *The Poetics of Gender*, 270–95; Patricia Klindienst Joplin, "The Voice of the Shuttle is Ours," *Stanford Literature Review* 1 (1984):25–53. The power of the Arachne archetype is borne out by the male appropriation of the implications of parody in this female figure. For a discussion of the confrontation by the leading artists of seventeenth-century Spain with their predecessors' interpretations of the erotic mythological tales, see Marcia L. Welles, *Arachne's Tapestry: The Transformation of Myth in Seventeenth-Century Spain* (San Antonio, Tex.: Trinity University Press, 1986).

35. Elaine Showalter, "Piecing and Writing," in *The Poetics of Gender*, ed. Nancy K. Miller (New York: Columbia University Press, 1986), 222–47.

36. Emilia Pardo Bazán, *La mujer española y otros artículos* (Madrid: Editora Nacional, 1976), 28.

37. Capel, *Sufragio*, 84. The predominant public belief was that a woman's learning to read and write opened the door to seduction and that women did not need an education to serve God and fulfill her domestic obligations. See Scanlon, *La polémica feminista*, 49.

38. Martínez Sierra, *Feminismo, feminidad y españolismo*, 165.

39. Capel, *El trabajo y la educación*, 343, 325–27.

40. See Folguera, *Vida cotidiana en Madrid*. The importance of women's learning the art of embroidery continued in Spain beyond the thirties, as the novel *Una primavera para Domenico Guarini* by Carme Riera (Barcelona: Montesinos, 1981) attests. The protagonist recalls the intricate sewing of sheets, tablecloths, and baby clothes by her mother and aunts, but her rejection of her dowry now rotting in some drawer symbolizes her release from women's subjugation to domesticity and to traditional notions of women's "proper" role in society.

41. Sandra M. Gilbert, "Costumes of the Mind: Transvestism as Metaphor in Modern Literature," in *Writing and Sexual Difference*, ed. Elizabeth Abel (Chicago: University of Chicago Press, 1982), 193–219. Dress as a significant marker of gender identity and a means of communication of messages has a long history and a cross-cultural existence. See Ruth Barnes and Joanne B. Eicher, *Dress and Gender: Making and Meaning* (New York: Berg Publishers, 1992.)

42. Amy Katz Kaminsky, "Dress and Redress: Clothing in the *Desengaños amorosos* of María Zayas y Sotomayor," *Romanic Review* 79, no. 2 (March 1988):391.

43. Much of the discussion on the male gaze began with Laura Mulvey's "Visual Pleasure and Narrative Cinema," *Screen* 16, no. 3 (1975):6–18, republished in *Visual and Other Pleasures*, 14–26 (Bloomington: Indiana University Press, 1989), and has focused on film. See, for example, Teresa de Lauretis *Alice Doesn't: Feminism, Semiotics, Cinema* (Bloomington: Indiana University Press, 1984) and Annette Kuhn, *The Power of the Image* (London: Routledge and Kegan Paul, 1985). The question of the gaze is applicable to literature as well as film, and, as Ann E. Kaplan argues, "masculine" looking is not done only by males. See "Is the Gaze Male?" in *Powers of Desire: The Politics of Sexuality*, ed. Ann Snitow, Christine Stansell, and Sharon Thompson (New York: Monthly Review, 1983). De la Torre's contemporary Rosa Chacel provides a good example, according to Abigail Lee Six, of the voyeuristic variety of the gaze enacted by female characters and devoid of the qualities of possession and dominion usually associated with the masculine gaze: "Perceiving the Family: Rosa Chacel's *Desde el amanecer*," in *Feminist Readings on Spanish and Latin-American Literature*, ed. Lisa P. Condé and Stephen M. Hart (Lewiston, N.Y.: The Edwin Mellen Press, 1991), 79–90.

44. Ostriker, *Stealing the Language*, 92. For studies on Rosetti's boldness, consult Sharon Keefe Ugalde, "Erotismo y revisionismo en la poesía de Ana Rossetti," *Siglo XX/20th Century* 7, no. 1–2 (1989–1990):24–29; John C. Wilcox, "Ana Rossetti y sus cuatro musas poéticas," *Revista Canadiense de Estudios Hispánicos* 14, no. 3 (1990):525–40; and Carmela Ferradáns, "La (re)velación del significante: Erótica textual y retórica barroca en 'Calvin Klein, underdrawers' de Ana Rossetti," *Monographic Review/Revista Monográfica* 6 (1990):183–91.

45. Hélène Cixous discusses the impact of decapitation and of the nature of a "female libidinal economy" in "Castration or Decapitation?" 41–55. It is interesting to note that in her consistent ambivalence of imagery and attitude, de la Torre both diverges from and coincides with Cixous's conception of the sea. Like Cixous, she exploits the associations of mother and water in the poem "Hoy, mañana, y siempre más," yet in the poem "Pez frío . . ." she equates her body with an object moving through a negative water environment. The sea is both an archetype for the generative power of the feminine and a metaphorical vehicle for time and alienation.

CHAPTER 5. ROSA CHACEL: MASKING THE AUTHORITATIVE VOICE

1. Dona M. Kercher, "Rosa Chacel," *Dictionary of Literary Biography*, vol. 134, *Twentieth-Century Spanish Poets*, 2d series, ed. Jerry Phillips Winfield (Detroit: Gale Research, 1994), 57–72.

2. Chacel published eight novels, three books of diaries or memoirs, six books of essays, as well as a biography of her husband Timoteo Pérez Rubio and three collections of short stories. In addition to isolated poems published during the twenties and thirties in magazines such as *La Gaceta Literaria, Héroe,* and *Hora de España,* Chacel published a collection of thirty sonnets titled *A la orilla de un pozo* (Madrid: Ediciones Héroe, 1936) that was republished in 1985 (Valencia: Pre-textos). 1978 saw the publication of *Versos prohibidos* (Madrid: Caballo Griego para la Poesía), and in 1992 Chacel published *Poesía, 1931–1991* (Barcelona: Tusquets), which included almost all of her poetry. A two-volume edition of her complete works has appeared: *Obra completa* (Valladolid: Diputación Provincial y Centro de Creación y Estudios Jorge Guillén, 1989).

3. José Angel Ascunce Arrieta, "Ernestina de Champourcin a través de sus palabras," *Insula* 557 (1993):23. Chacel's preference for narrative over poetry is obvious in her reluctance to publish her verse.

4. Although she lost her bid to be elected to the Real Academia de la Lengua, in 1987 she won the Premio Nacional de las Letras, the national award for the best literary production of an entire career. She also won a number of lesser awards, among them a grant from the Fundación March and the Premio de la Crítica (1976). Except for some of her novels, her work did not, however, attract a great deal of critical attention.

5. In the prologue to her 1978 *Versos prohibidos* and in the course of her ten hour interview with Alberto Porlán, she confesses that although she did not practice writing as a young girl, she did compose poems in her head from the age of twelve on her long walks with her father. See Alberto Porlán, *La sinrazón de Rosa Chacel* (Madrid: Anjana Ediciones, 1984), 25. These revelations are repeated in, Chacel, *Poesía, 1931–1991,* 255, 241.

6. Chacel, *Poesía,* 255.

7. Chacel, *Versos prohibidos,* 13.

8. *Poesía, 1931–1991* comprises *A la orilla de un pozo,* first published in 1936, *Versos prohibidos* from 1978, *Homenajes,* published previously in her *Obra completa* (1989), her previously published translation into Spanish of *Hérodiade* by Stéphane Mallarmé, and a few poems never published in book form.

9. Peter S. Temes, "Code of Silence: Laura (Riding) Jackson and the Refusal to Speak," *PMLA* 109 (1994):87.

10. Angel Crespo, "Notas personales sobre los sonetos de Rosa Chacel," *Anthropos* 85 (1988):45.

11. Chacel repeatedly refers to her social ineptness and physical unattractiveness. Once when asked by an interviewer to what she attributed her failure to achieve fame or recognition for so many years, she answered: "Yo siempre atribuí mi fracaso a lo mal vestida y lo gorda que me presento en todas partes. Estoy segura. . . . Si yo hubiera tenido otra presentación habría sido aplaudida desde el principio." (Porlán, *La sinrazón de Rosa Chacel,* 85.)

12. She openly reveals her desire not to detract from her image as a serious novelist when she confesses to Porlán that she has almost always declined to cheapen her work by writing "artículos de verano" even despite her financial difficulties (Porlán, *La sinrazón,* 95–96). Interestingly while she renounces her poetry, Chacel exercises her poetic impulse in her novels for, as Shirley Mangini notes, her first novel has many stylistic coincidences with Spanish vanguard poetry of the twenties. See Mangini, introduction to *Estación. Ida y vuelta,* by Rosa Chacel (Madrid: Cátedra, 1989), 39–42.

13. Chacel confesses to Alberto Porlán, *La sinrazón,* 92–94, that she has a tendency to both eat and drink too much and that there was a period during the civil war in which her drinking was excessive.

14. Ana Rodríguez Fischer, "Entrevista a Rosa Chacel," *Insula* 557 (1993):27.

15. Shirley Mangini, "Entrevista con Rosa Chacel," *Insula* 492 (1987):10. In another

interview she is even more blatant in her derision of feminism, calling it outright stupid. See Mariano Aguirre, "Rosa Chacel: La literatura femenina es una estupidez," *El País* (*Libros*) (Madrid), 30 enero 1983, 5.

16. Sidonie Smith, *A Poetics of Women's Autobiography* (Bloomington: Indiana University Press, 1987), 53. Spanish women writers, as women writers elsewhere, have had to maneuver skillfully through the maze of gendered poetic models. Iris M. Zavala, for example, points to the "malabarismos" that Sor Juana Inés de la Cruz had to make in order to write within the courtly love poetry tradition, which objectified and fetishized women. See Myriam Díaz-Diocaretz and Iris M. Zavala, *Breve historia feminista*, 1:53.

17. Chacel, "Esquema," 131.

18. Rosa Chacel, "La mujer en galeras," *Los títulos* (Barcelona: EDHASA, 1981), 194. She reiterated this opinion in interview after interview and in *Rabañaduras* (Valladolid: Junta de Castilla y León, 1986), 49. Chacel insists that she directs her aversion to feminists, not women: Milagros Sánchez Arnosi, "Conversación con Rosa Chacel en torno a *Alcancía*," *Ínsula* 38, no. 437 (1983):11. Luis Antonio de Villena attempts to encapsulate Chacel's brand of feminisism when he writes that "El femenismo de Rosa Chacel . . . se mueve . . . en dos esferas, sólo aparentemente antagónicas. Seducción, por mujer realizada como mujer, y afán de ser—culturalmente—igual que un hombre": "*Memorias de Leticia Valle*: la seducción inversa," in *Rosa Chacel: Premio de las Letras (1987)*, ed. Ana Rodríguez Fischer (Madrid: Biblioteca Nacional, 1988), 43.

19. Teresa Bordons and Susan Kirkpatrick, "Chacel's *Teresa* and Ortega's Canon," *Anales de la Literatura Española Contemporánea* 17, no. 1–3 (1992):289.

20. Shirley Mangini has called Chacel's first novel "el mejor testimonio del 'arte por el arte,' doctrina propuesta por Ortega y Gasset" (Introduction to *Estación: Ida y vuelta*, 25), and Jesús Pardo has shown that Ortega left his imprint on the content as well as the style of her philosophical essays (introduction to *Obra completa*, 1:9–29). Chacel praised Ortega and numbered herself among his disciples in several articles, such as "Respuesta a Ortega: La novela no escrita," *Sur* (Buenos Aires) 241 (July-August 1956):97–119, and "Ortega a otra distancia," in *La lectura es secreto*, by Rosa Chacel (Madrid: Ediciones Júcar, 1989), 146–55. Although Ortega publicly disparaged the intellectual capacity of women, he recognized Chacel's talents as a novelist and commissioned from her in 1930 a novel based on the life of Teresa Mancha for inclusion in his collection Vidas extraordinarias. Despite the distance implied in any relationship between master and disciple, Chacel discerned a certain psychological kinship between him and her that belies any suggestion of blind subordination on her part: "Ortega," *Revista de Occidente*, 3d series, 24–25 (May 1993):94.

21. Ana Rodríguez, "La tentación poética de Rosa Chacel," *Barcarola*, 30 (June 1989):218, finds evidence in the poems Chacel published in *La Gaceta Literaria* the *ultraísta* fondness for brevity, objects and objectivity, and the novel image. In 1922 Chacel had already contributed to *ultraísmo* by publishing a prose piece titled "Las ciudades" in the journal *Ultra* 2, no. 23 (1 February 1922):3–4. In 1928 she published three poems ("Reconvención," "Censura," and "La triste en la isla") en *Meseta*, no. 4 and three ("Ausencia," "Antinoo," and "Canalillo") in *La Gaceta Literaria*, no. 27. She published her poem "Narciso" in *Héroe*, no. 2, in 1932. Her sonnet to Paz González appeared in the January 1936 issue of *Caballo Verde para la Poesía*, and later that year in *El Mono Azul* (15 October) she published "¡Alarma!," a poem on the bombings in Madrid during the first months of the civil war. Her "Epístola moral a Sérpula" appeared in *Hora de España* 6 (June 1937):45–49.

22. *A la orilla de un pozo* (Valenica: Pre-Textos,1985), 9. Written in the early thirties, this book was first published in 1936 by Héroe, the small press run by Manuel Altolaguirre and Concha Méndez. Poem twenty-three in the collection dedicated to Méndez attests to the friendship between the two; and for their part, Altolaguirre and Méndez featured Chacel in their second issue of *Héroe*.

23. Shirley Mangini, "Rosa Chacel," in *Spanish Women Writers: A Bio-Bibliographical Source Book*, ed. Linda Gould Levine, Ellen Engelson Marson, and Gloria Feiman Waldman (Westport, Conn.: Greenwood Press, 1993), 135. For a fuller discussion of the self, the personal, and the autobiographical in Chacel's novels, see Roberta Johnson, "'Self'-Consciousness in Rosa Chacel and María Zambrano," in *Self-Conscious Art: A Tribute to John W. Kronik*, ed. Susan L. Fischer (Lewisburg, Pa.: Bucknell University Press, 1996), 54–72.

24. Chacel, *Poesía*, 247.

25. Ostriker, *Stealing the Language*, 48–53.

26. Porlán, *Sinrazón*, 31.

27. Mangini, "Entrevista," 11. For a consolidation of Chacel's statements on her assimilation of the precepts of Ortega y Gasset, see Ana Rodríguez Fischer, "Tras la senda de Ortega y Gasset," *Rosa Chacel*, 48–55.

28. Her rhyme scheme is the one that, according to Tomás Navarro, predominates in the sonnets that Alberti incorporated in *Marinero en tierra* as well as those that Guillén included in one section of *Cántico: Métrica española* (New York: Las Américas, 1966), 462–63.

29. Chacel, *Poesía*, 12. Subsequent quotations of Chacel's poetry refer to this collection. The numbers refer to pages.

30. José-Carlos Mainer finds two other features of Golden Age poetry in these sonnets: the use of the concessive construction at the beginning of poems and of apostrophes in the form of anaphora: "Las escritoras del 27," 32.

31. Noël Valis, "The Perfect Copy: Clarín's *Su único hijo* and the Flaubertian Connection," *PMLA* 104 (1989):856–67.

32. Antonio Martínez Herrarte, review of *Poesía, 1931–1991*, by Rosa Chacel, *Hispania* 76 (1993):473.

33. Rosa Chacel, "Poesía de circunstancia," *La lectura es secreto* (Madrid: Ediciones Júcar, 1989), 20–22.

34. Porlán, *Sinrazón*, 54. Chacel equates the erotic with the artistic in all her art because, as Clara Janés explains, they carry the same anxiety and joy and they imply, as Plato wanted, a desire to engender beauty: "Acrópolis," *Cuadernos Hispanoamericanos* 419 (1985):143.

35. For a discussion of doubling in this novel see Mangini, introduction, 28–35.

36. Wheelright, *Metaphor and Reality*, 123.

37. Cirlot, *Dictionary of Symbols*, 101.

38. Lakoff and Mark Turner in their *More than Cool Reason*, 33–32, offer a superbly succinct explanation of the multiple and seemingly contradictory associations within the metaphor of life as fire. What we know about how fires look determines the figurative representation of life as a fire: "For a fire to burn steadily, it must burn very hot in its early stages. . . . As fuel is consumed, it becomes ashes, which are both the residue of the fuel and the result of the burning. . . . At the fire's end, the ashes are on the ground and the embers in the ashes. As the fire dies, the ashes help smother the embers." Thus fire can correspond to the vigor of youth as well as to the diminished vitality of old age, to a confirmation of life and to a verification of death.

39. Mercedes Acillona, "La poesía femenina durante la guerra civil," *Letras de Deusto* 35 (May–August 1986):95.

Chapter 6. Carmen Conde and *Brocal*: Speaking from the Center

1. Dámaso Alonso, "Pasión de Carmen Conde," *Poetas españoles contemporáneos* (Madrid: Gredos, 1969), 344; first published as an article in *Proel* (Santander, 1945). George H.

Engeman, Jr. quotes from what he calls Entrambasaguas's unpublished article in his "Carmen Conde: La pasión del verbo," *Kentucky Foreign Language Quarterly* 13 (1966):18. Already in 1949 Leopoldo de Luis alluded to this declaration by Entrambasaguas in "El sentido religioso en la poesía de Carmen Conde," *Cuadernos de Literatura* 6, no. 16–18 (1949):184. Luis, for his part, in his introduction to the anthology *Carmen Conde* (Madrid: Ministerio de Cultura, 1982), 28, declares that Conde is the greatest "poetisa de lengua castellana."

2. María Isidra de Guzmán, the first woman to receive a doctorate in Spain, had been appointed to the Academy in 1784 by King Carlos III, when she was only seventeen, but this early, remarkable incident was long forgotten, never opening up the "docta casa" to women. Conde occupied chair "K" in January 1979 after delivering an entrance speech titled "Poesía ante el tiempo y la inmortalidad." Her election to the Academy embosses her poetry with a symbolic importance invoked regularly by her commentators, and it is the fact inevitably cited next to her name in her obituaries.

3. Mancing, "Consensus Canon," 53–81.

4. José Albi, quoted in Diana Ramírez de Arellano, *Poesía contemporánea en lengua española* (Madrid: Biblioteca Aristarco de Erudición y Crítica, 1961), 142–43.

5. Susana March, prologue to *Las oscuras raíces*, by Carmen Conde, (Barcelona: Bruguera, 1968), 9.

6. Conde herself calls her generation the Generation of 1930 because that is about when she began publishing. See Zenaida Gutiérrez-Vega and Marie-Lise Gazarian-Gautier, *Carmen Conde de viva voz* (New York: Senda Nueva de Ediciones, 1992), 47, 103.

7. Conde stayed in Spain, but she was not a Franco sympathizer. She lived in Valencia from 1937 to 1939, having followed her husband, who had joined the Republican army. When her husband was jailed in Murcia after the war, she was forced to live with friends, first in Madrid and then El Escorial. The years until his release in 1945 were for her a period of withdrawal, loneliness, and meditation.

8. Emilio Miró, "Algunas poetas españolas," 311. This confirms Julia Kristeva's observation that traditional Western iconography manifests only two attitudes toward the maternal body, a tilting toward the body as fetish or a predominance of a luminous essence beyond corporal representation: *Desire in Language: A Semiotic Approach to Literature and Art*, trans. Thomas Gora, Alice Jardine, and Leon S. Roudiez (New York: Columbia University Press, 1980), 237, 243. The grieving mother in Conde's poetry lacks the silent serenity of the Madonnas in the Renaissance painting Kristeva speaks of, but she possesses the same luminous, detached, and powerful presence.

9. Andrew P. Debicki, *Spanish Poetry of the Twentieth Century* (Lexington: The University Press of Kentucky, 1994), 69.

10. Once released from jail and able to join his wife in Madrid, Oliver studied for his doctorate and became a professor of Latin American literature at the University of Madrid. Carmen and Antonio acquired the papers of Rubén Darío and formed the "Seminario-Archivo Rubén Darío" at the University of Madrid. Conde wrote a biography of Francisca Sánchez, Darío's companion, and gave courses at the Instituto de Estudios Europeos (an affiliate of the University of Chicago) as well as at the University of Valencia in Alicante.

11. "Reporter," "Carmen Conde: Académica, poetisa, sed de eternidad," *República de las Letras* 10 (April 1984):17.

12. The creation of this university was the gift of Conde and Oliver to each other when they married. José María Rubio Paredes, *La obra juvenil de Carmen Conde* (Madrid: Torremozas, 1990), documents Conde's publications in local and regional newspapers on behalf of education and the poor and reproduces the articles Conde wrote in the twenties dealing with the issue of education and aid to the poor. Motivated more by a sense of religious charity than by political commitment, Conde pushed for education for the poor that would not deprive them of their dignity.

13. Her four anthologies of poetry are *Poesía femenina española viviente* (Madrid: Anroflo, 1955; *Once grandes poetisas americohispanas* (Madrid: Instituto de Cultura Hispánica, 1967); *Poesía femenina española, 1939–1950* (Barcelona: Bruguera, 1967); *Poesía femenina española, 1950–1960* (Barcelona: Bruguera, 1971). She published an anthology of female mystics: *Al encuentro de Santa Teresa: Antología de escritoras místicas españolas* (Murcia: Belmar, 1978) and two biographies on women: *Acompañando a Francisca Sánchez* (Managua: Ediciones de la Mesa Redonda Panamericana, 1964) and *Gabriela Mistral* (Madrid: E.P.E.S.A, 1970). Her interest in women writers also led her to write *Cartas a Katherine Mansfield* (Zaragoza: Doncel, 1948) and *La humana realidad de unas criaturas increíbles: Vida, pasión y muerte de las hermanas Brontë* (Madrid: Plenitud, 1949).

14. Rafael Baguena Candela recounts one occasion when Conde attacked the "machismo" of the Academy's dictionary in connection with discussion of the word "cazoleta": "La grandeza de Carmen Conde," in *Tu voz reflejada: Homenaje a Carmen Conde*, ed. Josefina Soria (Murcia: Caja de Ahorros de Murcia, 1990), 27–28. She also fought for the election of a second woman because she did not want her presence to be merely a symbolic exception. In 1983 the novelist Elena Quiroga was admitted to the Royal Academy.

15. Carmen Conde, "Estética poética," *Cuadernos de Agora* 46–48 (August-October 1960):10. Later she qualified her enthusiasm, declaring the works of Spanish women poets did not possess or imitate the immense freedom of expression used by non-Spanish ones: "Evolución de la mujer a través de la literatura en la poesía," *Análisis e investigaciones culturales* (Ministerio de Cultura) 11 (April/June 1982):53.

16. Carmen Conde, "Poesía femenina española, viviente," *Arbor* 297 (1970):221. Elsewhere she does nonetheless express a belief in the existence of a female discourse that differs from the language put into women's mouths by men. See Gutiérrez-Vega and Gazarian-Gautier, *Carmen Conde*, 84–85.

17. Carmen Conde, *Cuadernos de Agora*, 10. Reflecting on statements by Rimbaud, in 1947, Conde began her appeal for an authentic female voice not based on preconceived male ideas of what women should write, in "La poesía de la mujer poeta," *Cuadernos de Literatura* (Madrid) 1 (1947):109–16. As well as embracing gender difference, Conde recognized that equal rights for women are essential to their dignity and self expression. See Gutiérrez-Vega and Gazarian-Gautier, *Carmen Conde*, 171.

18. Carmen Conde, "La poesía de la mujer poeta," 114. This conception of female creativity rooted in the maternal will have its impact on her use, in her poetry, of archetypes of the eternal feminine and of images of the vegetative world for the portrayal of herself as creator. Susana Cabello studies a poem from 1938, "Autobiografía," in which she already defines herself as mediator between the unconscious and the conscious spheres, between chthonic values of instinct and uranic values of logos: "Carmen Conde: On Being a Woman and a Poet," *Letras Femeninas* 10, no. 1 (1984):27–32.

19. Rosario Hiriart, the editor of Carmen Conde's *Brocal y Poemas a María* (Madrid: Biblioteca Nueva, 1984), 22, lists the following authors and critics as having responded to her first collection *Brocal*: Esteban Salazar y Chapela, María Luz Morales, José Ballester, Miguel Valdivieso, Rafael Láinez Alcalá, Margarita Nelken, Rafael Porlán y Merlo, Melchor Fernández Almagro, Concha Espina, Jorge Guillén, Enrique Díez-Canedo, Luis Garay. Her second collection, *Júbilos* elicited equally positive responses, receiving enthusiastic endorsements in a variety of newspapers: *El Sol, Informaciones, Luz, Diablo Mundo, Heraldo de Madrid*, and *Eco*. Conde's rise in the world of publishing was, by her own admission, stellar and effortless. See Carmen Conde, prologue to *Ansias de la gracia* (Madrid: Adonais, 1945), 10.

20. Conde says that, during their courtship, Antonio Oliver Belmás introduced her to the poetry of Juan Ramón Jiménez and to the prose of Gabriel Miró: *Por el camino, viendo sus orillas* (Barcelona: Plaza y Janés, 1986), 1:46. Much to her surprise, Juan Ramón published a few of her first poems in *Ley*, one of his magazines he directed. Conde became ac-

quainted with Miró through his relatives in Conde's hometown, Cartagena.

21. Alonso, *Poetas españoles*, 239.

22. José Luis Castillo Puche, "Mis primeros encuentros con Carmen Conde," in *Tu voz reflejada*, ed. Josefina Soria (Murcia: Caja de Ahorros de Murcia, 1990), 41.

23. *Brocal* was first published in 1929 as part of the Colección de Cuadernos Literarios of La Lectura, a publishing enterprise in Madrid run by Domingo Barnés and Enrique Díez-Canedo. It was published, without its colophon, in Conde's *Obra poética* (Madrid; Biblioteca Nueva, 1967), 27–44. Citations in this study refer to this edition and are indicated by page numbers within parentheses. In 1980 a special limited edition was published (Madrid: Editorial Almodóvar, Colección Estampa III) comprising a preface by the poet and the 49 poems without titles from the first edition and including ten illustrations by the painter Francisco Hernández Cop. Rosario Hiriart prepared *Brocal y Poemas a María* (Madrid: Biblioteca Nueva, 1984).

24. Cabanilles, "Cartografías del silencio," 13.

25. Conde, "Evolución de la mujer," 55.

26. Gaston Bachelard, *The Poetics of Space* (Boston: Beacon Press, 1969), 232–39.

27. Cirlot, *Dictionary of Symbols*, 350.

28. Rosario Hiriart, introduction to *Brocal*, 41.

29. Hiriart (ibid., 42), recounts that when the painter Hernández Cop once asked Conde for the meaning of the bells in this poem, the poet revealed that the tower alluded to in the poem is the one in Murcia at the top of which she and Antonio kissed for the first time one summer morning. The hour—eleven o'clock—remained engraved in the poet's memory.

30. Ibid., 25–26.

31. Emilio Miró, introduction to *Obra poética*, 10.

32. Candelas Newton, "El discurso heroico de Carmen Conde," *Monographic Review/Revista Monográfica*, 6 (1990):62–63.

33. Ostriker, *Stealing the Language*, 109.

34. Emilio Miró, "Carmen Conde y Ernestina de Champourcin," *Insula*, 390 (1979), 6.

35. Marie-Lise Gazarian-Gautier, *Interviews with Spanish Writers* (Elmwood Park, Ill.: Dalkey Archive Press, 1991), 99.

36. Carlos Bousoño, *Teoría de la expresión poética*, 1:177–99.

37. Annis Pratt, *Archetypal Patterns*, 16–21. While in women's narrative the green world is a place evoked in memory, in *Brocal*, it is a lived reality of the present.

38. Moraima Semprún Donahue. "El paisaje ibérico en la poesía de Carmen Conde," *Cuadernos de Aldeeu*, 1 (May–October 1983), 481.

39. Bertrand Russell, *A History of Western Philosophy* (New York: Simon and Schuster, 1967), 649, explains Berkeley's belief that the qualities of things are relative to the percipient.

40. Gutiérrez-Vega and Gazarian-Gautier, *Carmen Conde*, 74.

41. Alonso, *Poetas españoles*, 341.

42. Semprún Donahue, "El paisaje ibérico," 484, lists the multiple meanings of wind in Conde's second book as companion of the flower, faithful friend, and cruel foe. Her identification with the wind was so deep-rooted, Conde says, that once during her childhood, upon seeing her pass by, a neighbor commented that she looked like the wind itself (Gutiérrez-Vega and Gazarian-Gautier, *Carmen Conde*, 172).

43. Newton, "El discurso heroico," 62-63.

44. Susana Cabello, "Carmen Conde on Being a Woman," 28–29.

45. The dangers for the female poet of an identity between women and nature leads Margaret Homans, *Poetic Identity*, chapter 1, to believe that Mother Nature is not a helpful model for aspiring poets.

46. Susan Griffin, *Woman and Nature: The Roaring Inside Her* (New York: Harper & Row, 1980).

47. Miró, introduction to *Obra poética*, 9.

48. Carmen Conde, prologue, *Ansia de la gracia*, 12.

49. González Ruano, *Antología de poetas españoles*, 577. The same interpretation is repeated by Sainz de Robles, *Ensayo de un diccionario*, 2:371.

50. Bonnie M. Brown, "Carmen Conde's *En la tierra de nadie*: A Journey Through Death and Solitude," *Revista/Review Interamericana* 12 (1982):40–45.

51. Gerardo Diego, "Poesía y creacionismo de Vicente Huidobro, *Cuadernos Hispanoamericanos*, 222 (1968), 534.

52. Conde, *Obra poética* 232; Gazarian-Gautier, *Interviews*, 99.

53. José Gerardo Manrique de Lara, "Poesía española de testimonio," *La Estafeta Literaria* (Madrid), 396 (18 May 1968):10.

54. Semprún Donahue, "El paisaje ibérico," 485–87.

55. Gutiérrez-Vega and Gazarian-Gautier, *Carmen Conde*, 101.

56. Luis, introduction, 17–18.

57. Hiriart, introduction, 33.

CHAPTER 7. ERNESTINA DE CHAMPOURCIN: CREATING THE SELF THROUGH TRANSCENDENCE

1. Simone de Beauvoir, *The Second Sex*, trans. and ed. H. M. Parshley (New York: Bantam Books, 1961), 43, xvi.

2. Champourcin is recorded in the *Dictionary of the Literature of the Iberian Peninsula*, ed. Germán Bleiberg, Maureen Ihrie, and Janet Pérez (Westport, Conn.: Greenwood Press, 1993), 402, as "the best-known poet of the Generation of 1927" and for her inclusion in Diego's significant anthology. Emilio Miró, "Cinco poetas en la 'España Peregrina,'" *Cuadernos Hispanoamericanos* 510 (December 1992):138, designates Champourcin "el indiscutible nombre femenino." Luzmaría Jiménez Faro, the editor of the only anthology of Champourcin's poetry, calls her "la única representante femenina" of the poets of 27: Ernestina de Champourcin, *Antología poética* (Madrid: Torremozas, 1988), 11.

3. José Angel Ascunce, prologue to *Poesía a través del tiempo*, by Ernestina de Champourcin (Barcelona: Anthropos, 1991), xii.

4. Debicki, "Una dimensión olvidada," 48.

5. Joy B. Landeira, "Ernestina de Champourcin," in *Spanish Women Writers: A Bio-Bibliographical Source Book*, ed. Linda Gould Levine, Ellen Engelson Marson, and Gloria Feiman Waldman (Westport: Greenwood Press, 1993), 145. Champourcin herself denies that Domenchina had any influence on her poetry. See Bellver, "Conversación," 73.

6. Ernesto Salazar y Chapela, "Ernestina de Champourcin y su sombra," *La Gaceta Literaria* 123 (1 May 1932):16.

7. César M. Arconada, "Ernestina de Champourcin dice . . ." *La Gaceta Literaria* 2, no. 38 (15 July 1928):1. Gerardo Diego, *Poesía española contemporánea* (1934, reprint, Madrid: Taurus, 1962), 460.

8. In an interview in 1990 she said, "La poesía no es una profesión ni una obligación. Es una vocación: se tiene o no se tiene": José María Bermejo, "Ernestina de Champourcin," *El Independiente (Libros)* (Madrid) 1, no. 19 (12 July 1990):4. She repeated this basic stance in a 1993 interview: Ascunce "Champourcin a través de sus palabras," 24.

9. Ostriker, *Stealing the Language*, 6, 31. Homans, *Poetic Identity*, 215, traces the woman poet's art of concealment to Eve, the "first human speaker to learn a nonliteral language." Feminist critics have shown that women's writings reflect their reality of being eternally split between who they are and whom they are instructed to be and divided between the domi-

nant masculine discourse and the muted female one. Key texts on constraint and duplicity in women's writing include Gilbert and Gubar, *Madwoman* and *Shakespeare's Sisters*; Juhasz, *Naked and Fiery Forms* and Showalter, *A Literature of Their Own.*

10. Ascunce, prologue, xxvii, suggests that "Plegarias tristes" refers to Juan Ramón Jiménez's collection *Arias triste* and "Rimas sedientes" to his *Rimas*, but the latter title also certainly evokes the *Rimas* of Bécquer to whom both Champourcin and Jiménez were indebted.

11. By the age of fifteen she had read the Greek classics and, perhaps because of her father's French background, she was also familiar with the French Romantics. Her liberal-minded parents encouraged her to read, but they adhered to the custom according to which young girls were escorted to the university by their mothers. Refusing this condition, she lost her dream of a college education. The best sources for details on Champourcin's biography are Ascunce, prologue and "Champourcin a través de sus palabras," Jorge Cardoso, "Ernestina de Champourcin," *El Mundo del Siglo Veintiuno* 2, no. 119 (23 February 1990):34, Landeira, "Ernestina de Champourcin," and Arturo Villar, "Ernestina de Champourcin," *La Estafeta Literaria* 24 (15 January 1975):10–15.

12. Ascunce, prologue, xxvii–xxix.

13. Arturo Villar, "Ernestina de Champourcin," 11. See also Ascunce, "Champourcin a través de sus palabras," 23. Since women rarely published poetry, when three books by women appeared in the same year, some critics even doubted that the books had been written by women. See Jacques Canales, "El esplendor de la palabra de Ernestina de Champourcin," *La Tarde de Madrid*, 1 October 1987, 26.

14. Fernando Bertrán, "Ernestina de Champourcin y la poesía," *El Consultor Bibliográfico* 2, no. 12 (July 1926):9–13.

15. Anonymous, "Ernestina de Champourcin," *La Vida Literaria*, Supplement of *España y América* 1, no. 4 (April 1927):46; Claudio Gutiérrez Marín, "*En silencio . . . Poesías*," *Revista de Segunda Enseñanza* 24 (June 1926):286; Juan G. Olmedilla, "*En silencio . . .*," *Heraldo de Madrid*, 13 June 1926, 4.

16. Champourcin sent him a copy of her first book and met him personally shortly afterwards, beginning what would become a lifelong friendship with him and his wife, a relationship she would later evoke in her 1981 book of memories of him, *La ardilla y la rosa* (Madrid: Los Libros de Fausto, 1981). Letters from Juan Ramón Jiménez to her and her husband are appended.

17. Cano Ballesta studies the conflict between these two pronounced camps in *La poesía española entre pureza y revolución.*

18. Gilbert and Gubar, *War of the Words.*

19. Rafael Cansinos-Assens, "*En silencio . . . (poesías)* por Ernestina de Champourcin," *La Libertad* (Madrid), 4 June 1926, 6.

20. Champourcin, "Tres proyecciones," 329–35.

21. See Showalter, *A Literature of Their Own*; Gilbert and Gubar, *Madwoman* and *No Man's Land*; Adrienne Rich, *The Dream of a Common Language* (New York: Norton, 1975); and Josephine Donovan, "Everyday Use and Moments of Being: Toward a Nondominative Aesthetic," in *Aesthetics in Feminist Perspective*, ed. Hilde Hein and Carolyn Korsmeyer (Bloomington: Indiana University Press, 1993), 53–67.

22. The arguments made by feminist psychologists to identify women with continuity in the development of their ego and body boundaries could be used to explain Champourcin's lesser need to reject and defeat male predecessors. For the practical reasons, both social and cultural, for the adoption of masculine models, see Bellver, "Literary Influence and Female Creativity," 7–32.

23. Champourcin, *Poesía través del tiempo*, 79–80. Because of its accessibility, this collection is used for the quotations of Champourcin's poetry. Page numbers are indicated in parentheses.

24. Ascunce, prologue, xxx.
25. Kirkpatrick, *Las románticas*, 217.
26. José-Carlos Mainer, "Las escritoras del 27," 23.
27. Ascunce, prologue, xxxi.
28. Wilcox, "Rescision," 299.
29. Emilio Miró, "Algunas poetas españolas entre 1926 y 1960," *Literatura y vida cotidiana*, ed. María Angeles Durán and José Antonio Rey (Zaragoza: Universidad Autónoma de Madrid and Universidad de Zaragoza, 1987), 307.
30. Critics have employed the metaphor of the "avenue to the light" to designate the trajectory of Champourcin's religious poetry, but the light as a guiding beacon surfaces already in *Ahora*. See Luzmaría Jiménez Faro, "Ernestina de Champourcin: Un camino hacia la luz," *Insula* 557 (1993), 21–22 and "Ernestina de Champourcin: Un peregrinaje hacia la luz," prologue to *Antología poética*; also Emilio Miró, "Poetisas españolas contemporáneas," 275.
31. Cirlot, *Dictionary of Symbols*, 109.
32. Pedro Henríquez Ureña, *La versificación española irregular* (Madrid, 1935), 195, affirms that an entire series of traditional Spanish songs is called "Naranjicas." The orange is associated with love in the folklore-inspired poetry of Champourcin's Andalusian contemporaries García Lorca and Alberti. For the orange as a Christian symbol of feminine purity, see Gertrude Jobes, *Dictionary of Mythology, Folklore and Symbols* (New York: Scarecrow, 1962), 1212, and *Funk and Wagnalls Standard Dictionary of Folklore, Mythology and Legend* (New York: Funk and Wagnalls, 1950), 829.
33. Debicki, "Una dimensión olvidada," 50.
34. This feminization of nature already appears in the nineteenth century in Gertrudes Gómez de Avellaneda and Carolina Coronado. Kirkpatrick, *Las románticas*, discovers that, in contrast to the male Romantic poets, both of these women poets stress nature's likeness with the "I."
35. Not all of Champourcin's references to glasses and goblets follow this process of ennoblement. In one poem the morning light is pictured as a fragrant glass of beer with a hint of the ludic spirit of the "greguerías" José Angel Ascunce Arrieta uncovers in some of her poems of this period: "La poesía de Ernestina de Champourcin: Entre lo lúdico y lo sagrado," *Insula* 557 (1993):19–21.
36. Erich Neumann, *Amor and Psyche* (New York and Evanston: Harper & Row, 1962), 86; and Rabuzzi, *Motherself*.
37. Debicki, "Una dimensión olvidada" and Ascunce, "Champourcin a través de sus palabras."
38. Wilcox, "Rescision," 293.
39. Julia Kristeva, "A Question of Subjectivity: An Interview," in *Feminist Literary Theory: A Reader*, 2d ed., ed. Mary Eagleton (Cambridge, Mass.: Blackwell Publishers, 1996), 351.
40. Cipriano Rivas Cherif wrote that never before had such a blend of modesty and public exposure, of abstraction and precision, been published: "Poesía. Poetisa," *El Sol*, 22 March 1932:2. José Díaz Fernández found in these poems the innocent virtue of a muse that was both ethereal and concrete: "Poemas de Ernestina de Champourcin," *Luz*, 26 January 1932:4.
41. Rafael Espejo-Saavedra, "Sentimiento amoroso y creación poética en Ernestina de Champourcin," *Revista Interamericana* 12, no. 1 (1982):136.
42. Gubar, "The Blank Page," 73–93.
43. Lakoff and Turner, *More than Cool Reason*, 1–17.
44. Wilcox, "Rescision," 293–94. In contrast, Ciplijauskaité refuses to assign the term feminist to Champourcin's early poetry, placing it instead within Showalter's first phase ("feminine") of women's writing because it conforms to the notion of female submission to

love and desire for self-sacrifice: "Hacia la afirmación serena: nuevos rumbos en la poesía de mujer," *Revista de Estudios Hispánicos* 29, no. 2 (May 1995):349–64. To reconcile their contradiction, it could be said that she incorporates feminist aspects into her "feminine" writing.

45. Espejo Saavedra, "Sentimiento amoroso," 134.

46. This dependence has been seen as connected to Freud's privileging of the penis and Lacan's emphasis on the mirror stage of psychic development. Much of feminist psychoanalytic theory centers on a confrontation with this aspect of masculine desire. Before feminist explorations of the gaze, John Berger, *Ways of Seeing* (New York: The Viking Press, 1973), discusses men as surveyors and women as "a sight."

47. Luce Irigaray, "This Sex Which Is Not One," in *New French Feminisms*, ed. Elaine Marks and Isabelle de Courtivron (New York: Schoken Books, 1981), 101.

48. Ostriker, *Stealing the Language*, 165–66.

49. Jessica Benjamin, "A Desire of One's Own: Psychoanalytic Feminism and Intersubjective Space," in *Feminist Studies / Critical Studies*, ed. Teresa de Lauretis (Bloomington: Indiana University Press, 1985), 95.

50. In addition, she singles out the "Bluebird" story by Madame d'Aulnoy as the feminine myth of the ideal lover, who never tires of talking to his beloved or listening to her. Evelyne Sullerot, *Women on Love: Eight Centuries of Feminine Writing* (Garden City, N.Y.: Doubleday, 1979), 7, 23.

51. Cano Ballesta, *La poesía española*, 70.

52. A data-base search of "women and desire" in the MLA electronic bibliography for January 1981 to June 1995 produces over 145 entries. Handbooks of feminist criticism include chapters on desire or sexuality, but not love. See, for example, Mary Eagleton, ed., *Feminist Literary Theory: A Reader*, 2d ed. (Cambridge, Mass.: Blackwell Publishers, 1996); Stevi Jackson, ed., *Women's Studies: Essential Readings* (New York: New York University Press, 1993); and Robyn R. Warhol and Diane Price Herndl, eds., *Feminism: An Anthology of Literary Theory and Criticism* (New Brunswick: Rutgers University Press, 1991). Theorists and critics in postmodern times have deconstructed the privileging of male desire in order to understand and challenge traditional gender arrangements. An exploration of female sexuality is seen as more self-affirming for women than love, a phenomenon linked with burdens, suffering, and self-effacement.

53. Julia Kristeva, *Tales of Love*, trans. Leon S. Roudiez (New York: Columbia University Press, 1987), 382–83. For a summary of Kristeva's ideas on love see John Lechte, *Julia Kristeva* (London and New York: Routledge, 1990), 167–84.

54. Pratt, *Archetypal Patterns*, 78, doubts that love and autonomy can be compatible for women. Ostriker, *Stealing the Language*, 165, calls the addiction to love relationships "woman's peculiar curse."

55. Cixous, "Medusa." Also see Elaine Showalter, *Sexual Anarchy* (New York: Viking, 1990), chapter 1.

56. Suzette Acevedo-Loubriel, "Ernestina de Champourcin y la poética de la transcendencia," *Romance Languages Annual* (West Lafayette, Ind.: Purdue Research Foundation, 1995), 390. This critic finds that in her later religious poetry, unlike in her love poetry, Champourcin does not renounce herself as a woman for God's sake. By shedding her human self, she finds herself in Him.

57. Ostriker, *Stealing the Language*, 95.

58. Juliet Mitchell, *Psychology and Feminism* (New York: Vintage Books, 1975), 307.

59. Mainer, "Las escritoras del 27," 28.

60. Mainer, "Las escritoras del 27," 29, Jiménez Faro, *Antología*, 13, and Landeira, "Ernestina de Champourcin," 88.

61. Champourcin's intention to integrate religious significance into these poems is borne out again in the sixth poem, where the epigram from San Juan de la Cruz provides the

image of the fountain, another image of fluid passage with biblical implications.

62. Debicki, "Una dimensión olvidada," 56, maintains that though "víboras" are technically symbols because they are concrete entities that represent emotions, they function as "visiones," as objective correlatives of those same emotions.

63. Cirlot, *Dictionary of Symbols*, 101.

64. Rosa Rossi, "Juan de la Cruz: La 'voz' y la 'experiencia,'" in *Breve historia feminista de literatura española (en lengua castellana)*, vol. 2, *La mujer en la literatura esspañola: Modos de representación desde la edad media hasta el siglo XVIII*, coordinator Iris M. Zavala (Barcelona: Anthropos, 1995), 215–33.

65. Christ, *Diving Deep and Surfacing*, 19.

Selected Bibliography

For the sake of conciseness, this bibliography is not a complete record of all the works and sources I have consulted. I separate the bibliography of my five subjects from my general bibliography as a convenience for those who wish to continue studying any one of them. Of the five poets, I list only the poetry covered in the book and any other writings essential in its preparation. Secondary sources on them are a selected list, particularly in the case of Rosa Chacel, Ernestina de Champourcin, and Carmen Conde, whose bibliographies comprise more than poetry of the twenties and thirties. In the section of general bibliography, I include only works cited in the book or those that served directly in the formation of my analyses.

ROSA CHACEL

PRIMARY SOURCES

"Esquema de los problemas prácticos y actuales del amor." *Revista de Occidente* 31 (1931):129–80.

A la orilla de un pozo. Madrid: Ediciones Héroe, 1936.

"Respuesta a Ortega: La novela no escrita." *Sur* (Buenos Aires) 241 (July–August 1956):97–119.

Versos prohibidos. Madrid: Caballo Griego para la Poesía, 1978.

"Comentario a un libro histórico: *La mujer en el siglo XX*." *Tiempo de Historia* 6, no. 67 (June 1980):64–81.

Los títulos. Barcelona: Edhasa, 1981.

"Ortega." *Revista de Occidente*, 3d ser., 24–25 (May 1983):77–94.

A la orilla de un pozo. Valencia: Pre-textos, 1985.

Rabañaduras. Valladolid: Junta de Castilla y León, 1986.

La lectura es secreto. Madrid: Ediciones Júcar, 1989.

Obra completa. Valladolid: Diputación Provincial de Valladolid, 1989.

Poesía, 1931–1991. Barcelona: Tusquets, 1992.

SECONDARY SOURCES

Acillona, Mercedes. "La poesía femenina durante la guerra civil." *Letras de Deusto* 35 (May–August 1986):94–95.

Aguirre, Francisca. "Rosa Chacel, como en su playa propia." *Cuadernos Hispanoamericanos* 296 (1975):298–315.

Aguirre, Mariano. "Rosa Chacel: 'La literatura femenina es una estupidez.'" *El País* (Madrid), 30 January 1983, 5.

Anthropos 85 (1988).

Berges, Consuelo. "Rosa Chacel y la literatura 'responsable.'" *Insula* 16, no. 183 (1962):5.

Bordons, Teresa and Susan Kirkpatrick. "Chacel's *Teresa* and Ortega's Canon." *Anales de la Literatura Española Contemporánea* 17, no. 1–3 (1992):283–99.

Chamorro, E. "Rosa Chacel: Objetivismo no significa deshumanización." *Triunfo*, no. 472 (19 June 1971):60–61.

Cole, Gregory Keith. "Rosa Chacel." In "Women Poets of the Generation of 1927," 95–108. Ph.D. diss., University of Kentucky, 1994.

Crespo, Angel. "Notas personales sobre los sonetos de Rosa Chacel." *Anthropos* 85 (1988):45–47.

D'Antin, Carolina. "Una escritora española desconocida en España: Rosa Chacel." *Indice* 16, no. 159 (1962):25.

Delgado, Fernando G. "Rosa Chacel y la necesidad del retorno." *Insula* 30, no. 346 (1975):4.

"Una encuesta sensacional: ¿Qué es la vanguardia?" *La Gaceta Literaria* 4, no. 83 (1 June 1930):1–3.

Font, Domènec. "El texto como cuerpo fragmentario." *La Vanguardia* (Barcelona), 5 August 1982, 22.

García Mercadal, Fernando. "Encuesta sobre la nueva arquitectura." *La Gaceta Literaria* 2, no. 32 (15 April 1928):1–3, 6.

García-Osuna, Carlos. "*Versos prohibidos* de Rosa Chacel." *El Imparcial* (Madrid), no. 166 (1978):43.

Glenn, Kathleen. "Conversación con Rosa Chacel." *Letras Peninsulares* 3, no. 1 (1990):11–26.

Infante, José. Prologue to *Memorias de Leticia Valle*, by Rosa Chacel. Madrid: S.A.P.E. (Club Internacional del Libro), 1985.

Janés, Clara. "*Acrópolis*." *Cuadernos Hispanoamericanos*, no. 419 (1985):140–46.

———. "Quien es Rosa Chacel." *La Nueva Estafeta* 45–46 (1982):49–53.

———. "Sobre un tema cualquiera (Autorretrato con paisaje y figuras)." *Cuadernos Hispanoamericanos*, no. 525 (1994):110–27.

Jiménez, Juan Ramón. "Rosa Chacel." In *Españoles de tres mundos*. Madrid: Alianza, 1987, 134–35.

Johnson, Roberta. "'Self'-Consciousness in Rosa Chacel and María Zambrano." In *Self-Conscious Art: A Tribute to John W. Kronik*, edited by Susan Fischer. Lewisburg, Pa.: Bucknell University Press, 1996, 54–72.

Kercher, Dona M. "Rosa Chacel." *Twentieth-Century Spanish Poets*. Vol. 134 of *Dictionary of*

Literary Biography. 2d ser., edited by Jerry Phillips Winfield. Detroit: Gale Research, 1994, 57–72.

Mangini, Shirley. "Entrevista con Rosa Chacel." *Insula* 42, no. 492 (1987):10–11.

———. Introduction to *Estación. Ida y vuelta*, by Rosa Chacel. Madrid: Cátedra, 1989.

———. "Rosa Chacel." In *Spanish Women Writers: A Bio-Bibliographical Source Book*, edited by Linda Gould Levine, Ellen Engelson Marson, and Gloria Feiman Waldman. Westport, Conn.: Greenwood Press, 1993.

Martínez Herrarte, Antonio. Review of *Poesía, 1931–1991*, by Rosa Chacel. *Hispania* 76 (1993):472–73.

Moix, Ana María. "Rosa Chacel." In *24X24: Entrevistas*. Barcelona: Ediciones Península, 1972, 141–46.

Myers, Eunice. "Conversaciones con Rosa *Chacel*." *Hispania* 67 (1984):286–87.

Núñez, Antonio. "Encuentro con Rosa Chacel." *Insula* 26, no. 296–97 (1971):20.

Pardo, Félix. "Los ensayos de Rosa Chacel, una empresa filosófica." Introduction to *Obra completa*, by Rosa Chacel. Vol. 2. Valladolid: Diputación Provincial de Valladolid, 1989.

Porlán, Alberto. *La sinrazón de Rosa Chacel*. Madrid: Anjana Ediciones, 1984.

Rodríguez Fischer, Ana. "Cronología intelectual de Rosa Chacel." *Anthropos* 85 (1988):28–34.

———. "Entrevista a Rosa Chacel." *Insula*, no. 557 (1993):25–27.

———. "Rosa Chacel, un sistema que el amor presidía." *Quimera* 84 (1988):30–35.

———. "Rosa Chacel sobre el piélago del tiempo." *Barcarola* (Albacete) 30 (June 1989):209–16.

———. "Rosa Chacel: El tiempo auroral, 1919–1929." *Insula* 12, no.529 (1991):33–35.

———. "La tentación poética de Rosa Chacel." *Barcarola* (Albacete) 30 (June 1989):217–30.

———. ed. *Rosa Chacel. Premio de las Letras (1987)*. Madrid: Biblioteca Nacional, 1988.

Ruiz Baños, Sagrario. "La poesía clásica de Rosa Chacel." In *Actas del Congreso en homenaje a Rosa Chacel*, edited by María Pilar Martínez Latre, 143–50. Logroño: Universidad de la Rioja, 1994.

Salaün, Serge. *La poesía de la guerra de España*. Madrid: Editorial Castalia, 1985.

Sánchez Arnosi, Milagros. "Conversación con Rosa Chacel en torno a *Alcancía*." *Insula* 38, no. 437 (1983):11.

Scarlett, Elizabeth. "Rosa Chacel." *Under Construction: The Body in Spanish Novels*, 46–98. Charlottesville: University Press of Virginia, 1994.

Sorela, Pedro. "Rosa Chacel, seguidora de Joyce y Gómez de la Serna, premio de las Letras Españolas." *El País* (Madrid), 18 November 1987, 30.

Suñen, Luis. "Rosa Chacel en 'La región luminosa de sus primeros años.'" *La Vanguardia* (Barcelona), 21 November 1978.

Vidal, Gema, and Ruth Zauner. "Rosa Chacel: La pasión de la perfección." *Camp de l'Arpa* 74 (April 1980):69–73.

Ernestina de Champourcin

PRIMARY SOURCES

En silencio. . . . Madrid: Espasa-Calpe, 1926.

Ahora. Madrid: Imprenta Blass, 1928.

"Tres proyecciones." *Síntesis* (Buenos Aires) 30 (November 1929):329–35.

La voz en el viento. Madrid: Compañía Ibero-Americana de Publicaciones, 1931.

La casa de enfrente. Madrid: Signo, 1936.

Cántico inútil. Madrid: Aguilar, 1936.

"Poética." In *Poesía española contemporánea: Antología,* by Gerardo Diego. 1934; Reprint, Madrid: Taurus, 1962, 460–61.

La ardilla y la rosa (Juan Ramón en mi memoria). Madrid: Los Libros de Fausto, 1981.

"Mientras allí se muere (fragmento de novela)." *Hora de España* 19 (1938). Reprint, *Anthropos (Suplementos)* 39 (1993):89–91.

SECONDARY SOURCES

Acevedo-Loubriel, Suzette. "Ernestina de Champourcin y la poética de la transcendencia." *Romance Languages Annual,* 389–93. West Lafayette, Ind.: Purdue Research Foundation, 1995.

Acillona, Mercedes. "Poesía mística y oracional en Ernestina de Champourcin." *Letras de Deusto* 20, no. 48 (1990):103–18.

Arconada, César. "Ernestina de Champourcin dice . . ." *La Gaceta Literaria* 2, no. 38 (15 July 1928):1–2.

Ascunce, José Angel. "Ernestina de Champourcin: La autenticidad hecha poesía." *Diario Vasco* (San Sebastián), 12 February 1991, 67 and 19 February 1991, 59.

———. "Ernestina de Champourcin a través de sus palabras." *Insula,* no. 557 (1993):22–24.

———. "La poesía de Ernestina de Champourcin: Entre lo lúdico y lo sagrado." *Insula,* no. 557 (1993):19–21.

———. "La poesía de exilio de Ernestina de Champourcin: Expresión límite de una depuración creativa." In *Poesía y exilio. Los poetas del exilio español en México,* edited by Rose Corral, Arturo Souto Alabarce, and James Valender. Mexico City: El Colegio de México, 1995, 119–30.

———. Prologue to *Poesía a través del tiempo,* by Ernestina de Champourcin. Barcelona: Anthropos, 1991.

Bellver, Catherine G. "Conversación con Ernestina de Champourcin." *Ojáncano* 10 (1995):68–77.

Bermejo, José María. "Ernestina de Champourcin: La poesía no es una profesión ni una obligación." *El Independiente (Libros)* (Madrid), 12 July 1990, 4.

Bertrán, Fernando. "Ernestina de Champourcin y la poesía." *El Consultor Bibliográfico* (Barcelona) 2, no. 13 (July 1926):9–13.

Canales, Jacques. "El esplendor de la palabra: Ernestina de Champourcin." *La Tarde de Madrid*, 1 October 1987, 26.

Cano Ballesto, Juan. *La poesía española entre pureza y revolución*. Madrid: Gredos, 1972.

Cansinos-Assens, Rafael. Review of *En silencio . . . (poesías)*, by Ernestina de Champourcin. *La Libertad* (Madrid), 4 June 1926, 6.

Cardoso, Jorge. "Ernestina de Champourcin." *El Mundo del Siglo Veintiuno* (Madrid) 2, no. 119 (1990):34.

Ciplijauskaité, Biruté. "Escribir entre dos exilios: Las voces femeninas de la Generación del 27." In *Homenaje al Profesor Antonio Vilanova*, edited by Adolfo Sotelo Vázquez and Marta Cristina Carbonell. Barcelona: Departamento de Filología Española, Universidad de Barcelona, 1989. 2:119–26.

———. "Hacia la afirmación serena: Nuevos rumbos en la poesía de mujer." *Revista de Estudios Hispánicos* 29, no. 2 (1995):349–64.

Cole, Gregory Keith. "Ernestina de Champourcin." In "Women Poets of the Generation of 1927," 177–219. Ph.D. diss., University of Kentucky, 1993.

Debicki, Andrew P. "Una dimensión olvidada de la poesía española de los '20 y '30: La lírica visionaria de Ernestina de Champourcin." *Ojáncano* 1 (1988):48–60.

Díaz Fernández, José. "Poemas de Ernestina de Champourcin." *Luz* (Madrid), 26 January 1932, 4.

Domenchina, Juan José. "Ernestina de Champourcin: *Cántico inútil*." *La Voz* (Madrid), 27 May 1936, 2.

———. "Poetas españoles del 13 al 31." *El Sol* (Madrid), 19 March 1933, 2.

"Una encuesta sensacional: ¿Qué es la vanguardia?" *La Gaceta Literaria* 4, no. 84 (15 June 1930):3–4.

"Ernestina de Champourcin." *La Vida Literaria*. Supplement of *España y América* 1, no. 4 (Abril 1947):46.

Espejo-Saavedra, Rafael. "Sentimiento amoroso y creación poética en Ernestina de Champourcin." *Revista Interamericana* 12, no. 1 (1982):133–39.

Giménez Caballero, Enrique. "Tres veces amor." *El Sol* (Madrid), 22 June 1927, 2.

Gutiérrez Marín, Claudio. Review of *En silencio . . . poesías*, by Ernestina de Champourcin." *Revista de Segunda Enseñanza* (Madrid) 24 (June 1926):285–87.

Janés Olivé, J. Review of *Cántico inútil*, by Ernestina de Champourcin. *La Vanguardia* (Barcelona), 25 December 1936, 2.

Jiménez, Juan Ramón. "Ernestina de Champourcin." In *Españoles de tres mundos*, 107–8. Buenos Aires: Losada, 1942.

Jiménez Faro, Luzmaría. "Ernestina de Champourcin: Un camino hacia la luz." *Insula*, no. 557 (1993):21–22.

———. "Ernestina de Champourcin: Un peregrinaje hacia la luz." Introduction to *Antología poética*, by Ernestina de Champourcin. Madrid: Torremozas, 1988.

Landeira, Joy B. "Ernestina de Champourcin." In *Spanish Women Writers: A Bio-Bibliographical Source Book*, edited by Linda Gould Levine, Ellen Engelson Marson and Gloria Feiman Waldman. Westport, Conn.: Greenwood Press, 1993, 141–47.

Mainer, José-Carlos. "Las escritoras del 27 (con María Teresa León al fondo)." In *Homenaje a María Teresa León*. El Escorial: Universidad Complutense de Madrid, 1989, 13–39.

Miró, Emilio. "Algunas poetas españolas entre 1926 y 1960." In *Literatura y vida cotidiana*, edited by María Angeles Durán and José Antonio Rey, 307–21. Zaragoza: Servicio de Publicaciones de la Universidad Autónoma de Madrid and Secretariado de Publicaciones de Zaragoza, 1987.

———. "Carmen Conde y Ernestina de Champourcin." *Insula* 24, no. 390 (1979):6–7.

———. "Cinco poetas de la 'España Peregrina.'" *Cuadernos Hispanoamericanos*, no. 510 (1992):134–42.

———. "Poetisas españolas contemporáneas." *Revista de la Universidad Complutense* 24, no. 95 (1975):271–310.

Olmedilla, Juan G. Review of *En silencio . . .* , by Ernestina de Champourcin. *Heraldo de Madrid*, 13 July 1926, 4.

Pérez, Janet. "Ernestina de Champourcin." In *Dictionary of the Literature of the Iberian Peninsula*, edited by Germán Bleiberg, Maureen Ihrie, and Janet Pérez. Westport, Conn.: Greenwood Press, 1993, 401–33.

Rivas Cherif, Cipriano. "Poesía. Poetisa." *El Sol* (Madrid), 22 March 1932, 2.

Sabugo Abril, A. "Los Libros de Fausto (Colecciones de poesía, recuerdos y ensayo)." *Nueva Estafeta* 51 (1983):67–72.

Sáez-Agudo, Julia. "Ernestina de Champourcin: Quiero cambiar su imagen tópica." *ABC* (Madrid), 25 February 1981, 38.

Sáez Angulo, Julia. "Ernestina de Champourcin reclama la memoria de Madrid para su marido, el escritor Juan José Domenchina." *Ya* (Madrid), 20 November 1988, 43.

Salazar y Chapela, Ernesto. "Ernestina de Champourcin y su sombra." *La Gaceta Literaria* 7, no. 123 (1 May 1932):16.

Torre, Guillermo de. "Dos libros de Ernestina de Champourcin." *El Sol* (Madrid), 13 June 1936, 2.

Villar, Arturo. "Ernestina de Champourcin." *La Estafeta Literaria* 556 (1975):10–15.

———. "La vida con las palabras de Ernestina de Champourcin." *Alaluz: Revista de Poesía, Narración y Ensayo* 18, no. 2 (1986):5–14.

———. "La voz del tiempo de Ernestina de Champourcin." *Cuadernos Hispanoamericanos*, no. 551 (1996):143–47.

Wilcox, John C. "Ernestina de Champourcin and Concha Méndez: Their Rescision From the Generation of 27." *Siglo XX/20th Century* 12, no. 1–2 (1994):291–317.

———. "Ernestina de Champourcin and Concha Méndez." In *Women Poets of Spain, 1860–1990: Toward a Gynocentric Vision*, 87–133. Urbana: University of Illinois Press, 1997.

Zueras Torréns, Francisco. "Ernestina de Champourcin." In *La gran aportación cultural del exilio español, 1939*, 87–88. Córdoba: Diputación Provincial de Córdoba, 1990.

CARMEN CONDE

PRIMARY SOURCES

Brocal. Madrid: Editorial La Lectura, 1929.

Júbilos. Murcia: Ediciones Sudeste, 1934.

"¿Qué libro fue el primero que se leyó." *Eco* (Madrid) 2, no. 8 (May–June 1934):12–13.

Ansia de la gracia. Madrid: Adonais, 1945.

"La poesía de la mujer poeta." *Cuadernos de Literatura* 1 (1947):109–16.

Poesía femenina viviente. Madrid: Anroflo, 1955.

"Estética poética." *Cuadernos de Agora* 46–48 (August–October 1960):8–12.

Obra poética, 1929–1966. Madrid: Biblioteca Nueva, 1967. 2d ed. 1979.

Once grandes poetisas americohispanas. Madrid: Instituto de Cultura Hispánica, 1967.

Poesía femenina española, 1939–1950. Barcelona: Bruguera, 1967.

"Poesía femenina española, viviente." *Arbor* 297 (1970):73–84.

Poesía femenina española, 1950–1960. Barcelona: Bruguera, 1971.

Brocal. Madrid: Editorial Almodóvar, 1980.

"Evolución de la mujer a través de la literatura: en la poesía." *Análisis e Investigaciones Culturales* 11 (April/June 1982):53–63.

Por el camino, viendo sus orillas. Barcelona: Plaza y Janés, 1986.

SECONDARY SOURCES

Acillona López, Mercedes. "Carmen Conde: Poemas de la guerra civil." *Cuadernos para la Investigación de la Literatura Hispánica* (Madrid) 8 (1987):223–37.

Aleixandre, Vicente. "En pie, Carmen Conde." In *Los encuentros,* 199–204. Madrid: Guadarrama, 1958.

Alemán Sainz, Francisco. "Recado a Carmen Conde." *Monteagudo* (University of Murcia) 62 (1978):9–10.

Allison, Esther M. "Carmen Conde, primera académica española." *Abside* 42 (1978):195–99.

Alonso, Dámaso. "Pasión de Carmen Conde." In *Poetas españoles contemporáneos,* 339–44. Madrid: Gredos, 1969.

Alvar, Manuel. "Tras los símbolos y los mitos en unos poemas de Carmen Conde." In *Símbolos y mitos,* 345–65. Madrid: Consejo Superior de Investigaciones Científicas, 1990.

"Antología breve de algunas notas dedicadas en la prensa nacional a 'Júbilos' de Carmen Conde." *Verdad* (Murcia), 7 June 1934, 4.

Armas, José R. de. "Carmen Conde y el dolor humano." *Yelmo* 48–49 (1981):29–34.

Baguena Candela, Rafael. "La grandeza de Carmen Conde." In *Tu voz reflejada: Homenaje a Carmen Conde,* edited by Josefina Soria, 27–28. Murcia: Caja de Ahorros de Murcia, 1990.

Brown, Bonnie Maurine. "Carmen Conde's *En la tierra de nadie*: A Journey through Death and Solitude." *Revista/Review Interamericana* 12 (1982):40–45.

"Un buen libro de una escritora." *El Sol* (Madrid), 13 Abril 1937, 7.

Cabello, Susana. "Carmen Conde: On Being a Woman and a Poet." *Letras Femeninas* 10, no. 1 (1984):27–32.

"Carmen Conde deja a la Academia sin mujeres." *El País* (Madrid), 9 January 1996, 35.

"Carmen Conde y su libro." *Heraldo de Madrid*, 10 May 1934, 6.

Castillo Puche, José Luis. "Mis primeros encuentros con Carmen Conde." In *Tu voz reflejada*, edited by Josefina Soria, 41. Murcia: Caja de Ahorros de Murcia, 1990.

Champourcin, Ernestina. *La ardilla y la rosa: Juan Ramón en mi memoria*. Madrid: Los Libros de Fausto, 1981.

Cuadernos de Agora 46–48 (1960).

Debicki, Andrew P. *Spanish Poetry of the Twentieth Century*. Lexington: University Press of Kentucky, 1994.

Díez de Revenga, Francisco Javier. "Glosando la juventud de Carmen Conde." *Castilla: Boletín del Departamento de Literatura Española* 15 (1990):69–73.

———. *Revistas murcianas relacionadas con la generación del 27*. Murcia: Academia Alfonso X el Sabio, 1979.

Díez de Revenga, Francisco Javier, and Mariano del Paco. *Historia de la literatura murciana*. Murcia: Universidad de Murcia, 1989.

Dolç, Miguel. "Hacia el orbe poético de Carmen Conde." Introduction to *Días por la tierra: Antología incompleta*, by Carmen Conde. Madrid: Editora Nacional, 1977.

Engeman, George H. Jr. "Carmen Conde: La pasión del verbo." *Kentucky Foreign Language Quarterly* 13 (1966):14–19.

"Fallece a los ochenta y ocho años la poetisa y académica Carmen Conde." *ABC* (Madrid), 9 January 1996, 74.

Gazarian-Gautier, Marie-Lise. "Carmen Conde." In *Interviews with Spanish Authors*, 97–111. Elmwood Park, Ill.: Dalkey Archive Press, 1991.

Gutiérrez-Vega, Zenaida. "La experiencia poética de la guerra en Carmen Conde." *Cuadernos de Investigación de la Literatura Hispánica* 8 (1987):149–55.

Gutiérrez-Vega, Zenaida and Marie-Lise Gazarian-Gautier. *Carmen Conde de viva voz*. New York: Senda Nueva de Ediciones, 1992.

Hiriart, Rosario. "Los cincuenta y cinco años de *Brocal* de Carmen Conde:1929–1984." *Insula*, no. 455 (1984):19.

———. Introduction to *Antología poética*, by Carmen Conde. Madrid: Espasa-Calpe, 1985.

———. Introduction to *Brocal y Poemas a María*, by Carmen Conde. Madrid: Biblioteca Nueva, 1984.

Homenaje a Carmen Conde. Majadahonda: Concejalía de Cultura y Ayuntamiento de Majadahonda, 1996.

Jarnés, Benjamín. "Letras femeninas." *La Luz* (Madrid), 17 April 1934, 10.

López Gorge, Jacinto. "Conversación con Carmen Conde." *La Estafeta Literaria* 631 (1978):10–12.

Luis, Leopoldo, ed. *Carmen Conde*. Madrid: Ministerio de Cultura, 1982.

Manrique de Lara, José Gerardo. "Poesía española de testimonio." *La Estafeta Literaria* 396 (1968):10–11.

Manso, Christian. "Carmen Conde y la guerra civil." *Anales de Historia Contemporánea* (University of Murcia) 7 (1988–1989):143–53.

March, Susana. Prologue to *Las oscuras raíces*, by Carmen Conde. Barcelona: Bruguera, 1968.

Marquerie, Alfredo. "La vida literaria." *Informaciones* (Madrid), 14 April 1934, 7.

Martín, Pilar. "Carmen Conde." In *Dictionary of Literary Biography*. Vol. 108 of *Twentieth Century Spanish Poets*, edited by Michael L. Perna, 88–108. Detroit: Gale Research, 1991.

Miró, Emilio. "Algunas poetas españolas entre 1926 y 1960." *Literatura y vida cotidiana*, edited by María Angeles Durán and José Antonio Rey, 307–21. Zaragoza: Universidad Autónoma de Madrid and Universidad de Zaragoza, 1987.

———. "Antonio Oliver y Carmen Conde." *Insula* 27, no. 302 (1972):7.

———. "Carmen Conde y Ernestina de Champourcin." *Insula* 34, no. 390 (1979):6.

———. Introduction to *Obra poética, 1929–1966*, by Carmen Conde. Madrid: Biblioteca Nueva, 1967.

———. "Poetisas españolas contemporáneas." *Revista de la Universidad Complutense* (Madrid) 24, no. 95 (1975):271–310.

Newton, Candelas. "El discurso heroico de Carmen Conde." *Monographic Review / Revista Monográfica* 6 (1990):61–70.

———. "El texto especular de Carmen Conde." *España Contemporánea* 8, no. 1 (1995):7–20.

Ramírez Arellano, Diana. *Poesía contemporánea en lengua española*, 131–202, 499–505, 539–47. Madrid: Biblioteca Aristarco de Erudición y Crítica, 1961.

"Reporter." "Carmen Conde: Académica, poetisa, sed de eternidad." *República de las Letras* 10 (April 1984):11–19.

Rodrigo, Antonina. "Carmen Conde." In *Mujeres de España: Las silenciadas*, 227–35. Barcelona: Plaza y Janés, 1979.

Rodríguez Cánovas, J. "Júbilo azul." *La Verdad* (Murcia), 6 September 1934, 4.

Rubio Paredes, José María. *La obra juvenil de Carmen Conde*. Madrid: Torremozas, 1990.

Segado del Olmo, Antonio. "Conversación con Carmen Conde." *Monteagudo* (University of Murcia) 62 (1978):15–22.

Semprún Donahue, Moraima. "El paisaje ibérico en la poesía de Carmen Conde." *Cuadernos de Aldeu* 1 (May–October 1983):481–91.

Soria, Josefina, ed. *Tu voz reflejada: Homenaje a Carmen Conde*. Murcia: Caja de Ahorros de Murcia, 1990.

Torre, Guillermo de. "'Júbilos,' o un gran libro femenino." *Luz* (Madrid), 20 April 1934, 9.

Vázquez Zamora, Rafael. "Carmen Conde. *Júbilos*." *Eco* 2, no. 7 (March–April 1934).

Josefina de la Torre

PRIMARY SOURCES

Versos y estampas. Prologue by Pedro Salinas. Málaga: Litoral, 1927.

Poemas de la isla. Barcelona: Imprenta Altés, 1930.

Memorias de una estrella y En el umbral. Madrid: Ediciones Cid (La Novela del Sábado), 1954.

Una mujer entre los brazos. Madrid: Escelicer, 1956.

Marzo incompleto. Las Palmas de Gran Canaria: Imprenta Lezcano (Colección Borondón), 1968.

Poemas de la isla. Edited by Lázaro Santana. Las Palmas de Gran Canaria: Gobierno de Canarias, 1989.

SECONDARY SOURCES

Artiles, Joaquín. "Josefina de la Torre." In *La literatura canaria*. Las Palmas de Gran Canaria: Mancomunidad de Cabildos, 1979, 38.

Bleiberg, Germán and Julián Marías. "Torre, Josefina de la." In *Diccionario de literatura española*. 3d ed., 775. Madrid: Revista de Occidente, 1964.

Calvo de Aguilar, Isabel. "Josefina de la Torre." In *Antología biográfica de escritoras españolas*, 795. Madrid: Biblioteca Nueva, 1954.

Champourcin, Ernestina de. "Tres proyecciones." *Síntesis* (Buenos Aires) 30 (November 1929):329–35.

Conde, Carmen. "Josefina de la Torre." In *Poesía femenina española, 1939–1950*, 345. Barcelona: Bruguera, 1967.

Cole, Gregory Keith. "Josefina de la Torre." In "Women Poets of the Generation of 1927," 109–32. Ph.D. diss., University of Kentucky, 1993.

Díez-Canedo, Enrique. "Panorama del teatro español desde 1914 hasta 1936." *Hora de España* 16 (1938):13–50.

Landeira, Joy Buckles. "Josefina de la Torre." In *Women Writers of Spain: An Annotated Bio-Bibliographical Guide*, edited by Carolyn L. Galerstein, 313–14. New York: Greenwood Press, 1986.

———. "Josefina de la Torre." In *Dictionary of the Literature of the Iberian Peninsula*, edited by Germán Bleiberg, Maureen Ihrie, and Janet Pérez, 1608. Westport, Conn.: Greenwood Press, 1993.

Pedraza Jiménez, Felipe B. and Milagros Rodríguez Cáceres, eds. "Josefina de la Torre." *Manual de literatura española*. Vol. 11, *Novecentismo y vanguardia: Líricos*, 335. Pamplona: Cénlit Ediciones, 1993.

Radtke, Rosetta. "Josefina de la Torre." In *An Encyclopedia of Continental Women Writers*, edited by Katharina M. Wilson. New York: Garland Publishing, 1991. 2:1246–47.

Review of *Versos y estampas*, by Josefina de la Torre. *La Rosa de los Vientos* (Tenerife) 5 (January 1928):15.

Sainz de Robles, Federico Carlos. "Josefina de la Torre." In *Ensayo de un diccionario de la literatura*, 2:1653–54. Madrid: Aguilar, 1949.

Santana, Lázaro. Introduction to *Poemas de la isla*, by Josefina de la Torre. Islas Canarias: Gobierno de Canarias, 1989.

Valbuena Prat, Angel. "Las poetisas: De la Torre. Champourcin. Concha Méndez de Altolaguirre." In *Historia de literatura española*. Barcelona: Gustavo Gili, 1964. 3:689–91.

CONCHA MÉNDEZ

PRIMARY SOURCES

Inquietudes. Poemas. Madrid: Imprenta de Juan Pueyo, 1926.

Surtidor. Poesías. Madrid: Imprenta Argis, 1928.

Canciones de mar y tierra. Prologue by Consuelo Berges. Buenos Aires: Talleres Gráficos Argentinos, 1930.

Vida a vida. Prologue by Juan Ramón Jiménez. Madrid: La Tentativa Poética, 1932.

Niño y sombras. Madrid: Ediciones Héroe, 1936.

Lluvias enlazadas. Havana: La Verónica, 1939.

Poemas. Sombras y sueños. Mexico City: Rueca, 1944.

Antología poética. Selection by María Dolores Arana. Mexico City: Joaquín Mortiz, 1976.

Entre el soñar y el vivir. Mexico City: Universidad Nacional Autónoma de México, 1981.

Poemas (1926–1986). Introduction by James Valender. Madrid: Hiperión, 1995.

Villancicos de Navidad. Mexico City: Rueca, 1944. Málaga: La Librería El Guadalhorca, 1967.

Vida a vida y Vida o río. Introduction by Emilio Miró. Madrid: Caballo Griego para la Poesía, 1979.

SECONDARY SOURCES

Acillona, Mercedes. "La poesía femenina durante la guerra civil." *Letras de Deusto* (Bilbao) 35 (May–August 1986):91–104.

Albornoz, Aurora de. "Poesía de la España peregrina. In *El exilio español de 1939*, edited by José Luis Abellán. Vol. 4 of *Cultura y literatura*, 54. Madrid: Taurus, 1977.

Altolaguirre, Manuel. "Noche de Guerra (De mi diario)." *Hora de España* 4 (1937). Reprint, Barcelona: Laia, 1977, 305–18.

———. "Nuestro teatro." *Hora de España* 9 (1937):27–37. Reprint, Barcelona: Laia, 1977, 317–25.

———. "Vida y poesía: Cuatro poetas íntimos." In *Obras completas*. Madrid: Istmos, 1986. 1:230–48.

Arana, María Dolores. "Concha Méndez: Las dos orillas." *El Día* (Mexico City), 9 January 1977, 15.

Aristeguieta, Jean. "Poesía de Concha Méndez (con motivo de su obra *Lluvias enlazadas)*." *Revista Nacional de Cultura* (Caracas) 51 (1945):92–94.

Aub, Max. "Concha Méndez Cuesta," *Conversaciones con Buñuel*, 241–51. Madrid: Aguilar, 1985.

Ayala, Francisco. "Concha Méndez Cuesta. *Surtidor*." *La Gaceta Literaria* 2, no. 29 (1 March 1928):3.

Bellver, Catherine G. "Mothers, Daughters, and the Female Tradition in the Poetry of Concha Méndez." *Revista Hispánica Moderna* 15 (1998):317–26.

——. "Concha Méndez's *El personaje presentido* and Its Vanguard Counterparts." *Hispanic Journal* 12, no. 2 (1991):292–303.

——. "Exile and the Female Experience in the Poetry of Concha Méndez." *Anales de la Literatura Española Contemporánea* 18, no. 1–2 (1993):27–42.

——. "Los exilios y las sombras en la poesía de Concha Méndez." In *Poesía y exilio: Los poetas del exilio español en México*, edited by Rose Corral, Arturo Souto Alabarce and James Valender, 63–72. Mexico City: El Colegio de México, 1995.

——. "Literary Influence and Female Creativity: The Case of Two Women Poets of the Generation of 27." *Siglo XX/20th Century* 15, no. 1–2 (1997):7–32.

——. "*El personaje presentido*: A Surrealist Play by Concha Méndez." *Estreno* 16, no. 1 (1990):23–27.

——. "Tres poetas desterradas y la morfología del exilio." *Cuadernos Americanos* 4, no. 19 (1990):163–77.

——. "Voyages, Flights and Other Patterns of Passage in *Canciones de mar y tierra* by Concha Méndez." *Pacific Coast Philology* 30, no. 1 (1995):103–16.

Berges, Consuelo. "Los 'raids' náutico-astrales de Concha Méndez Cuesta." Prologue to *Canciones de mar y tierra*, by Concha Méndez, 5–15. Buenos Aires: Talleres Gráficos Argentinos, 1930.

Bo, Efraín Tomás. "*Poemas. Sombras y sueños* de Concha Méndez." *Letras de México* 8, no. 24 (1944):293.

Bradu, Fabienne. "Paloma Ulacia Altolaguirre. *Concha Méndez: Memorias habladas, memorias armadas*." *Vuelta* (Mexico City) 167 (October 1990):39–40.

Briesemeister, Dietrich. Epilogue to reprint of *Héroe*. Madrid: Turner, 1977, 93–118.

Cansinos-Assens, Rafael. "Crítica literaria: *Canciones de mar y tierra* (versos) por Concha Méndez Cuesta." *La Libertad* (Madrid), 17 August 1930, 4.

Castroviejo, Concha. "Una época literaria en los recuerdos de Concha Méndez." *ABC, Mirador literario* (Madrid), 1 October 1970, 11, 13.

Champourcin, Ernestina de. "Tres Proyecciones." *Síntesis* (Buenos Aires) 30 (November 1929):329–35.

Ciplijauskaité, Biruté. "Escribir entre dos exilios: Las voces femeninas de la Generación del 27." In *Homenaje al profesor Antonio Vilanova*, edited by Adolfo Sotelo Vázquez and Marta Cristina Carbonell, 2:119–26. Barcelona: Universidad de Barcelona, 1989.

Cole, Gregory Keith. "Concha Méndez." In "Women Poets of the Generation of 1927," 133–76. Ph.D. diss., University of Kentucky, 1993.

Corbalán, Pablo. "Concha Méndez, impresora." *El Sol* (Madrid), 14 November 1990.

Díaz Fernández, José. "Concha Méndez Cuesta, *Surtidor*." *El Sol* (Madrid), 29 March 1928, 2.

Díez-Canedo, Enrique. "A manera de epitalamio." *El Sol* (Madrid), 5 June 1932, 2.

Echeverría del Prado, Vicente and Ramón Gálvez. "Pausas literarias: Manuel Altolaguirre y Concha Méndez." *Suplemento Dominical de Novedades* (Mexico City), 30 May 1948, 2.

Gil Albert, Juan. "Memorabilia, 1934–1939." In *Memorabilia*, 186–90. Barcelona: Tusquets, 1975.

Guillén, Jorge. "Concha Méndez: *Poemas. Sombras y sueños.*" *Suma Bibliográfica* (Mexico City) 2 (May 1946):25.

"Ha muerto Concha Méndez." *Insula* 42, no. 483 (1987):2.

Jiménez, Juan Ramón. "Y Concha." In *Españoles de tres mundos*, 157–58. Buenos Aires: Losada, 1942, 157–58.

Lorenzo, José. "Colofón." *Inquietudes*, by Concha Méndez, 105–8. Madrid: Imprenta de Juan Pueyo, 1926.

Mainer, José-Carlos. "Las escritoras del 27 (con María Teresa León al fondo)." *Homenaje a María Teresa León*, 13–39. Madrid: Universidad Complutense de Madrid, 1989.

Martínez Ruiz, Florencio. "*Vida a vida y Vida o río* de Concha Méndez." *ABC* (Madrid), 1 June 1979, 39.

Miró, Emilio. "Algunas poetas españolas entre 1926 y 1960." In *Literatura y vida cotidiana*, edited by María Angeles Durán and José Antonio Rey, 309–11. Zaragoza: Universidad Autónoma de Madrid and Universidad de Zaragoza, 1987.

———. "La contribución teatral de Concha Méndez." In *El teatro en España: Entre la tradición y la vanguardia*, edited by Dru Dougherty and María Francisca Vilches de Frutos, 439–51. Madrid: C.S.I.C., Fundación García Lorca, Tabacalera, 1992.

———. "Dos poetas del destierro: Concha Méndez y Juan Rejano." *Insula* 33, no. 378 (1978):6.

———. "Poetisas españolas contemporáneas." *Revista de la Universidad Complutense* 24, no.95 (1975):275–79.

———. Introduction to *Antología de poetisas del 27*. Madrid: Castalia, 1999.

———. Introduction to *Vida a vida y Vida o río*, by Concha Méndez. Madrid: Caballo Griego para la Poesía, 1979.

Morla Lynch, Carlos. *En España con Federico García Lorca: Páginas de un diario íntimo, 1928–1936*. Madrid: Aguilar, 1958.

Nieva de la Paz, Pilar. *Autoras dramáticas españolas entre 1918 y 1936*. Madrid: C.S.I.C., 1993.

———. "Las escritoras españolas y el teatro infantil de preguerra: Magda Donato, Elena Fortún y Concha Méndez." *Revista de Literatura* 55, no. 109 (1993):113–28.

Pedraza Jiménez, Felipe B. and Milagros Rodríguez Cáceres. "Concha Méndez." *Manual de literatura española*. Vol. 11, *Novecentismo y vanguardia: Líricos*, 329–32. Pamplona: Cénlit Ediciones, 1993.

Perea, Héctor. "Memorias de otro mundo." *Libros*, supplement to *Diario 16* (Madrid), 8 November 1990, 1.

Pérez de Ayala, Juan. "Concha Méndez: Una mujer de la vanguardia del 27." *Cómplice* (Madrid) 86 (September 1990):120–23.

Persin, Margaret. "Moving to New Ground with Concha Méndez." *Monographic Review / Revista Monográfica* 13 (1997):190–204.

Poniatowska, Elena. "Concha Méndez: Ser escritor en español es una desgracia." *Novedades* (Mexico City), 19 November 1971, 1, 12.

Quance, Roberta. "Concha Méndez: Una mujer en la vanguardia." *Revista de Occidente* 121 (June 1991):141–45.

"Los raids literarios: Conversación con Concha Méndez." *La Gaceta Literaria* 3, no. 69 (1 November 1929):3.

Resnick, Margery. "La inteligencia audaz: Vida y poesía de Concha Méndez." *Papeles de Son Armadans* 88, no. 263 (1978):131–46.

Richardson, Stanley. "Spanish Poetry, 1935." *Contemporaries* (Cambridge, England) 2, no. 1 (1935):239–41.

Rodríguez, Emma. "Concha Méndez: El rostro ignorado del 27." *El Mundo del Siglo Veintiuno* 2, no. 346 (1990):35.

Smerdou Altolaguirre, Margarita. Introduction to *Las islas invitadas*, by Manuel Altolaguirre, 14–21. Madrid: Castalia, 1973.

Torre, Guillermo de. "*Canciones de mar y tierra* por Concha Méndez Cuesta." *Síntesis* (Buenos Aires) 38 (July 1930):167–69.

Ulacia, Paloma. *Concha Méndez: Memorias habladas, memorias armadas*. Madrid: Mondadori, 1990.

———. "Concha Méndez y Luis Buñuel." *Insula*, no. 557 (1993):12–15.

———. "Entrevista con Marta Sardiñas." In *Los pasos profundos*, by Manuel Altolaguirre. Málaga: Litoral, 1989, 226–31.

Urrutia, Elena. "Después será la soledad." *Novedades* (Mexico City), 22 July 1979, 4, 16.

———. "Itinerario espiritual." *Novedades* (Mexico City), 24 October 1976, 5.

Valbuena Prat, Angel. "Las poetisas: De la Torre, Champourcin, Concha Méndez de Altolaguirre." In *Historia de la literatura española*, 3:689–91. Barcelona: Gustavo Gili, 1964.

Valdeavellano, Luis G. de. "Los nuevos valores literarios: Concha Méndez Cuesta." *La Epoca* (Madrid), 4 October 1930, 4.

Valender, James. "Dos cartas de María Zambrano a Manuel Altolaguirre y Concha Méndez." *Insula*, no. 557 (1993):11–12.

———. Introduction to *Poemas (1926–1986)*, by Concha Méndez. Madrid: Hiperión, 1995.

———. Introduction to *Diez Cartas a Concha Méndez*, by Manuel Altolaguirre. Málaga: Centro Cultural de la Generación del 27, 1989.

Wilcox, John C. "Ernestina de Champourcin and Concha Méndez: Their Rescision From the Generation of 27." *Siglo XX/20th Century* 12, no. 1–2 (1994):291–317.

———. "Ernestina de Champourcin and Concha Méndez." *Women Poets of Spain, 1860–1990*, 87–133. Urbana and Chicago: University of Illinois Press, 1997.

Zambrano, María. Prologue to *El solitario: Misterio en un acto*, by Concha Méndez. Havana: La Verónica, 1941.

GENERAL BIBLIOGRAPHY

Abel, Elizabeth, ed. *Writing and Sexual Difference*. Chicago: University of Chicago Press, 1982.

Acillona, Mercedes. "La poesía femenina durante la guerra civil." *Letras de Deusto* 35 (May–August 1986):91–104.

Alberti, Rafael. *La arboleda perdida*. Buenos Aires: Compañía Fabril Editora, 1959.

———. *Poesía, 1924–1967*. Madrid: Aguilar, 1967.

Alborg, Concha. "Marina Mayoral's Narrative: Old Families and New Faces from Galicia." In *Women Writers of Contemporary Spain*, edited by Joan L. Brown, 179–97. Newark: University of Delaware Press, 1991.

Aldaraca, Bridget A. *El ángel del hogar: Galdós and the Ideology of Domesticity in Spain*. Chapel Hill: University of North Carolina Press, 1991.

Alonso, Dámaso. *Poetas españoles contemporáneos*. Madrid: Gredos, 1969.

Aranguren, Luis. "La mujer de 1923 a 1963." *Revista de Occidente* 1, no. 8–9 (1963):231–43.

Ardener, Shirley, ed. *Women and Space: Ground Rules and Social Maps*. New York: St. Martin's Press, 1981.

Artiles, Joaquín. *Literatura Canaria*. Las Palmas de Gran Canaria, 1979.

Aub, Max. *Manual de la historia de la literatura española*. Madrid: Akal, 1974.

Aza y Díaz, Vital. *Feminismo y sexo*. Madrid: Javier Morata, 1928.

Bachelard, Gaston. *The Poetics of Space*. Boston: Beacon Press, 1969.

Baeza, Ricardo. "El blanco y el negro (una lanza por '*Lyceum*')." *El Sol* (Madrid), 21 August 1927, 12.

Basauri, Mercedes G. "La mujer en el reinado de Alfonso XIII." *Tiempo de Historia* 46 (1978):26–39.

Barnes, Ruth, and Joanne B. Eicher. *Dress and Gender: Making and Meaning*. Oxford: Berg Publishers, 1992.

Barthes, Roland. "From Work to Text." In *Textual Strategies*, edited by Josué V. Harari, 73–81. Ithaca: Cornell University Press, 1979.

Bellver, Catherine G. "Literary Influence and Female Creativity: The Case of Two Women Poets of the Generation of 27." *Siglo XX/20th Century* 15, no. 1–2 (1997):7–32.

———. "War as Rite of Passage in *El cuarto de atrás*." *Letras Femeninas* 12, no. 1–2 (1986):69–77.

Benjamin, Jessica. "A Desire of One's Own: Psychoanalytic Feminism and Intersubjective Space." In *Feminist Studies/Critical Studies*, edited by Teresa de Lauretis, 78–101. Bloomington: Indiana University Press, 1985.

Benstock, Shari. "Expatriate Modernism: Writing on the Cultural Rim." In *Women's Writing in Exile*, edited by Mary Lynn Broe and Angela Ingram, 19–40. Chapel Hill: University of North Carolina Press, 1989.

———, ed. *Feminist Issues in Literary Scholarship*. Bloomington: Indiana University Press, 1987.

Berger, John. *Ways of Seeing*. New York: Viking Press, 1973.

Bettelheim, Bruno. *The Uses of Enchantment*. New York: Alfred A. Knopf, 1976.

Bieder, Maryellen. "Women and the Twentieth Century Spanish Literary Canon: The Lady Vanishes." *Anales de la Literatura Española Contemporánea* 17, no. 3 (1992):301–24.

Blanco, Alda. "But Are They Any Good?" *Revista de Estudios Hispánicos* 27, no. 3 (1993):463–70.

Bleiberg, Germán, and Julián Marías, eds. *Diccionario de literatura española*. Madrid: Revista de Occidente, 1964. Revised edition Germán Bleiberg, Maureen Ihrie, and Janet Pérez, eds. *Dictionary of the Literature of the Iberian Peninsula*. Westport, Conn.: Greenwood Press, 1993.

Bordonada, Angela Ena. *Novelas breves de escritoras españolas, 1900–1936*. Madrid: Castalia, 1989.

Bousoño, Carlos. *Teoría de la expresión poética*. 2 vols. Madrid: Gredos, 1970.

Bravo-Villasante, Carmen. "La mujer como autora literaria." *Historia 16* 13, no. 145 (1988):49–58.

Brown, Gerald G. *Historia de la literatura española*. Vol. 6/1, *El siglo XX*. Barcelona: Ariel, 1983.

Brown, Joan L., ed. *Women Writers of Contemporary Spain: Exiles in the Homeland*. Newark: University of Delaware Press, 1991.

Buck, Clare, ed. *The Bloomsbury Guide to Women's Literature*. New York: Prentice Hall, 1992.

Cabanilles, Antónia. "Cartografías del silencio: La teoría literaria feminista." In *Crítica y ficción literaria: Mujeres españolas contemporáneas*, edited by Aurora López and María Angeles Pastor, 13–23. Granada: Universidad de Granada, 1989.

Calvo de Aguilar, Isabel *Antología biográfica de escritoras españolas*. Madrid: Biblioteca Nueva, 1954.

Campo Alange, María Lafitte, Condesa de. *La mujer en España: Cien años de su historia. 1860–1960*. Madrid: Aguilar, 1963.

Cano Ballesta, Juan. *La poesía española entre pureza y revolución, 1930–1936*. Madrid: Gredos, 1972.

Capel Martínez, Rosa María. *El sufragio femenino en la segunda República*. Granada: Universidad de Granada, 1975.

———. *El trabajo y la educación de la mujer en España, 1900–1930*. Madrid: Ministerio de Cultura, 1986.

Capmany, María Aurèlia. *Feminismo ibérico*. Barcelona: Oikos-tau, 1970.

Castro Calvo, José María. *Historia de la literatura española*. Barcelona: Credsa, 1964.

Charnon-Deutsch, Lou. *Gender and Representation: Women in Spanish Realist Fiction*. Purdue University Monographs in Romance Languages, vol. 32. Erdenheim, Pa.: John Benjamins North America, 1990.

Chodorow, Nancy. *The Reproduction of Mothering: Psychoanalysis and the Sociology of Gender*. Berkeley: University of California Press, 1978.

Christ, Carol P. *Diving Deep and Surfacing: Women Writers on Spiritual Quest*. Boston: Beacon Press, 1980.

Ciplijauskaité, Biruté. "Dos casas habitadas por la ausencia." *Sin Nombre* 9, no. 3 (1978):32–40.

———. "Escribir entre dos exilios: Las voces femeninas de la generación del 27." In *Homenaje al profesor Antonio Vilanova*, edited by Adolfo Sotelo Vázquez and María Cristina Carbonell. Barcelona: Universidad de Barcelona, 1989. 2:119–26.

———. "Hacia la afirmación serena: Nuevos rumbos en la poesía de mujer." *Revista de Estudios Hispánicos* 29, no. 2 (1995):349–64.

————. *La novela femenina contemporánea, 1970–1985: Hacia una tipología de la narración en primera persona.* Barcelona: Anthropos, 1988.

————. *La soledad y la poesía española contemporánea.* Madrid: Insula, 1962.

Cirlot, J. E. *A Dictionary of Symbols.* Translated by Jack Sage. New York: Philosophical Library, 1962.

Cixous, Hélène. "Castration or Decapitation?" *Signs: Journal of Women in Culture and Society* 7, no. 1 (1981):41–55.

————. "The Laugh of the Medusa." In *The Signs Reader: Women, Gender and Scholarship,* edited by Elizabeth Abel and Emily K. Abel, 279–97. Chicago: University of Chicago Press, 1983.

————. "Sorties." In *New French Feminisms: An Anthology,* edited by Elaine Marks and Isabelle de Courtivron, 90–98. New York: Schocken Books, 1981.

Culler, Jonathan. *Structuralist Poetics.* Ithaca: Cornell University Press, 1975.

Davidson, Cathy N., and E. M. Bonner, eds. *The Lost Tradition: Mothers and Daughters in Literature.* New York: Frederick Ungar, 1980.

de Beauvoir, Simone. *The Second Sex.* Translated and edited by H. M. Parshley. New York: Bantam Books, 1961.

Debicki, Andrew P. *Estudios sobre poesía española contemporánea: La generación de 1924–1925.* Madrid: Gredos, 1981.

————. *Spanish Poetry of the Twentieth Century.* Lexington: University Press of Kentucky, 1994.

De Lauretis, Teresa. *Alice Doesn't: Feminism, Semiotics, Cinema.* London: MacMillan, 1984.

Del Río, Angel. *Historia de la literatura española.* New York: Holt, Rinehart and Winston, 1948. Rev. ed., 1963.

Díaz Borque, José María. *Historia de la literatura española.* Vol. 4, *Siglo XX.* Madrid: Taurus, 1980.

Díaz-Diocaretz, Myriam, and Iris M. Zavala, eds. *Breve historia feminista de la literatura española (en lengua castellana).* Vol. 1, *Teoría feminista: discurso y diferencia.* Barcelona: Anthropos, 1993. Vol. 2, *La mujer en la literatura española: Modos de representación desde la Edad Media hasta el siglo XVII.* Barcelona: Anthropos, 1995.

Díaz-Plaja, Guillermo. *Estructura y sentido del Novecentismo español.* Madrid: Alianza, 1975.

————. *Historia de la poesía lírica española.* Barcelona: Editorial Lábor, 1948.

Diego, Gerardo. "Poesía y creacionismo de Vicente Huidobro." *Cuadernos Hispanoamericanos,* no. 222 (1968):528–44.

————. *Poesía española contemporánea (Antología).* 1934; reprint, Madrid: Taurus, 1962.

Díez de Revenga, Francisco Javier. *Panorama crítico de la generación del 27.* Madrid: Editorial Castalia, 1987.

Domenchina, Juan José. *Antología de la poesía española contemporánea, 1900–1936.* Mexico City: Unión Tipográfica Editorial Hispano-Americana, 1941.

Donovan, Josephine. "Everyday Use and Moments of Being: Toward a Nondominative Aesthetic." In *Aesthetics in Feminist Perspective,* edited by Hilde Hein and Carolyn Korsmeyer, 53–67. Bloomington: Indiana University Press, 1993.

Durán, María Angeles. "Una ausencia de mil años: La mujer en la universidad." In *La mujer en el mundo contemporáneo,* edited by María Angeles Durán, et al., 53–68. Madrid: Universidad Autónoma de Madrid, 1981.

————. *Mujeres y hombres: La formación del pensamiento igualitario.* Madrid: Castalia/Instituto de la Mujer, 1993.

Eagleton, Mary, ed. *Feminist Literary Theory. A Reader.* 2d ed. Cambridge, Mass.: Blackwell Publishers, 1996.

Ellman, Mary. *Thinking About Women.* New York: Harcourt Brace and World, 1968.

Fagoaga, Concha. *La voz y el voto de las mujeres: El sufragismo en España 1877–1931.* Barcelona: Icaria, 1985.

Fagundo, Ana María. "Mi literatura es mía en mí." *La Chispa '85: Selected Proceedings,* edited by Gilbert Paolini, 83–92. New Orleans: Tulane University Press, 1985.

Ferradáns, Carmela. "La (re)velación del significante: Erótica textual y retórica barroca en 'Calvin Klein, underdrawers' de Ana Rossetti." *Monographic Review/Revista Monográfica* 6 (1990):183–91.

Fernández Almagro, Melchor. "Caja de sorpresas." *La Gaceta Literaria* 1, no. 3 (1 February 1927):1.

Flax, Jane. "The Conflict Between Nurturance and Autonomy in Mother-Daughter Relationships and Within Feminism." *Feminist Studies* 4, no. 2 (1978):171–89.

Folguera, Pilar. "La historia oral *como* fuente para el estudio de la vida cotidiana de las mujeres." In *La mujer en la historia de España: Siglo XVI–XX,* edited by María Angeles Durán, et al., 177–211. Madrid: Universidad Autónoma de Madrid, 1984.

————. *Vida cotidiana en Madrid: El primer tercio del siglo a través de las fuentes orales.* Madrid: Comunidad de Madrid, 1987.

Foucault, Michel. *Power/Knowledge: Selected Interviews and Other Writings, 1972–1977,* edited by Colin Gordon. New York: Pantheon Books, 1980.

Fox-Lockert, Lucía. *Women Novelists in Spain and Spanish America.* Metuchen, N.J.: The Scarecrow Press, 1979.

Franco de Espés, Luis. "Mujeres españolas: María Teresa de León." *El Imparcial* (Madrid), 8 May 1929, 1.

Francos Rodríguez, José. *La mujer y la política españolas.* Madrid: Editorial Pueyo, 1920.

Friedman, Ellen G. "Where Are the Missing/Contents? (Post) Modern, Gender, and the Canon." *PLMA* 108, no. 2 (1993):240–52.

Funk and Wagnalls Standard Dictionary of Folklore, Mythology and Legend. New York: Funk and Wagnalls, 1950.

Galán Quintanilla, María Antonia. *La mujer a través de la información de la II República Española.* Madrid: Universidad Complutense, 1980.

Galerstein, Carolyn L., ed. *Women Writers of Spain: An Annotated Bio-Bibliographical Guide.* New York: Greenwood Press, 1986.

Gallego Morell, Antonio. *Literatura de tema deportivo.* Madrid: Editorial Prensa Española, 1969.

Gallop, Jane. *The Daughter's Seduction: Feminism and Psychoanalysis.* Ithaca: Cornell University Press, 1982.

García de la Concha, Víctor. *Historia y crítica de la literatura española.* Vol. 8, *Época contemporánea.* Barcelona: Crítica, 1984.

Gardiner, Judith Kegan. "In the Name of the Mother: Feminism, Psychoanalysis, Methodology." *LIT Literature Interpretation Theory* 1, no. 4 (1990):239–52.

————. "On Female Identity and Writing by Women." In *Writing and Sexual Difference,* edited by Elizabeth Abel, 177–91. Chicago: University of Chicago Press, 1982.

Geist, Anthony Leo. *La poética de la generación del 27 y las revistas literarias*. Barcelona: Guadarrama, 1980.

Genevois, Danièle Bussy. "Problemas de aprehensión de la vida cotidiana de las mujeres españolas a través de la prensa femenina y familiar (1931–1936)." In *La mujer en la historia de España: Siglo XVI–XX*, edited by María Angeles Durán et al., 263–78. Madrid: Universidad Autónoma de Madrid, 1984.

———. "Tiempo histórico y tiempo de las mujeres: Notas sobre la prensa femenina entre 1931 y 1936." *Bulletin du département de recherches hispaniques pyrenaica* 29 (June 1984):99–123.

Gilbert, Sandra M. "Costumes of the Mind: Transvestism as Metaphor in Modern Literature." In *Writing and Sexual Difference*, edited by Elizabeth Abel, 193–219. Chicago: University of Chicago Press, 1982.

Gilbert, Sandra M., and Susan Gubar. *The Madwoman in the Attic*. New Haven: Yale University Press, 1979.

———. *No Man's Land: The Place of the Woman Writer in the Twentieth Century*. Vol. 1, *The War of the Words*. New Haven: Yale University Press, 1987. Vol. 2, *Sexchanges*. New Haven: Yale University Press, 1989.

———. *Shakespeare's Sisters: Feminist Essays on Women Poets*. Bloomington: Indiana University Press, 1979.

Gilligan, Carol. *In a Different Voice*. Boston: Harvard University Press, 1982.

Glenn, Kathleen M. "Conversación con Cristina Fernández Cubas." *Anales de la Literatura Española Contemporánea* 18, no. 2 (1993):355–63.

González Blanco, Edmundo. *La mujer según los diferentes aspectos de su espiritualidad*. Madrid: Reus, 1930.

González Posada, Adolfo. *Feminismo*. Madrid, 1899.

González Ruano, César. *Antología de poetas españoles contemporáneos en lengua castellana*. Barcelona: Gustavo Gili, 1946.

Griffin, Susan. *Woman and Nature: The Roaring Inside Her*. New York: Harper and Row, 1980.

Gubar, Susan. "'The Blank Page' and the Issue of Female Creativity." In *Writing and Sexual Difference*, edited by Elizabeth Abel, 73–93. Chicago: University of Chicago Press, 1982.

Gullón, Ricardo. *Diccionario de literatura española e hispanoamericana*. Madrid: Alianza, 1993.

Hall, Nor. *The Moon and the Virigin*. New York: Harper and Row, 1980.

Halliday, M. A. K. *Language as Social Semiotics*. London: Edward Arnold, 1978.

Hart, Stephen M. *White Ink: Essays on Twentieth-Century Feminine Fiction in Spain and Latin America*. London: Tamesis Books, 1993.

Hedges, Elaine, and Shelley Fisher Fishken. *Listening to Silences: New Essays in Feminist Criticism*. New York: Oxford University Press, 1994.

Henríquez Ureña, Pedro. *La versificación española irregular*. Madrid, 1935.

Homans, Margaret. "Eliot, Wordsworth, and the Scenes of the Sisters' Instruction." In *Writing and Sexual Difference*, edited by Elizabeth Abel, 53–71. Chicago: University of Chicago Press, 1982.

———. *Women Writers and Poetic Identity*. Princeton: Princeton University Press, 1980.

Huff, Linda. *A Portrait of the Artist as a Young Woman*. New York: Frederick Ungar, 1983.

Ilie, Paul. *Literature and Inner Exile: Authoritarian Spain, 1939–1975*. Baltimore: The Johns Hopkins University Press, 1980.

Ingram, Angela. "On the Contrary, Outside of It." In *Women's Writing in Exile*, edited by Mary Lynn Broe and Angela Ingram, 1–15. Chapel Hill: University of North Carolina Press, 1989.

Irigaray, Luce. *Speculum of the Other Woman*. Ithaca: Cornell University Press, 1985.

———. "This Sex Which Is Not One." In *New French Feminisms*, edited by Elaine Marks and Isabelle de Courtivron, 99–106. New York: Schocken Books, 1981.

Jackson, Stevi, ed. *Women's Studies. Essential Readings*. New York: New York University Press, 1993.

Jacobus, Mary. "The Difference of View." In *Women Writing and Writing About Women*, edited by Mary Jacobus, 10–21. New York: Barnes and Noble Books, 1979.

———. "The Question of Language: Men of Maxims and *The Mill on the Floss*." In *Writing and Sexual Difference*, edited by Elizabeth Abel, 37–52. Chicago: University of Chicago Press, 1982.

Jagoe, Catherine. "Noncanonical Novels and the Questions of Quality." *Revista de Estudios Hispánicos* 27, no. 3 (1993):427–36.

Janeway, Elizabeth. *Man's World, Woman's Place: A Study in Social Mythology*. New York: William Morrow, 1971.

Jeffreys, Mark. "Ideologies of Lyric: A Problem of Genre in Contemporary Anglophone Poetics." *PMLA* 110, no. 2 (1995):196–205.

Jiménez, Juan Ramón. *Españoles de tres mundos*. Buenos Aires: Losada, 1942.

Jiménez Faro, Luzmaría. *Panorama antológico de poetisas españolas, Siglos XV al XX*. Madrid: Torremozas, 1987.

———. *Poetisas españolas: Antología general*. Vol. 2, *De 1901 a 1939*. Madrid: Torremozas, 1996.

Jiménez Morell, Inmaculada. *La prensa femenina en España desde sus orígenes a 1968*. Madrid: Ediciones de la Torre, 1992.

Jobes, Gertrude. *Dictionary of Mythology, Folklore and Symbols*. New York: The Scarecrow Press, 1962.

Jones, Ann Rosalind. "Surprising Fame: Renaissance Gender Ideologies and Women's Lyric." In *The Poetics of Gender*, edited by Nancy K. Miller, 74–95. New York: Columbia University Press, 1986.

Joplin, Patricia Klindienst. "The Voice of the Shuttle is Ours." *Stanford Literature Review* 1 (1984):25–53.

Juhasz, Suzanne. *Naked and Fiery Forms: Modern American Poetry by Women*. New York: Harper and Row, 1976.

Kaminsky, Amy Katz. "Dress and Redress: Clothing in the *Desengaños amorosos* of María Zayas y Sotomayor." *Romanic Review* 79, no. 2 (1988):377–91.

Kaplan, E. Ann. "Is the Gaze Male?" In *Powers of Desire: The Politics of Sexuality*, edited by Ann Snitow, Christine Stansell, and Sharon Thompson, 309–27. New York: Monthly Review, 1983.

Kelly, Joan. *Women, History, and Theory: The Essays of Joan Kelly*. Chicago: University of Chicago Press, 1984.

Keohane, Nannerl O., and Barbara Gelpi, eds. *Feminist Theory: A Critique of Ideology*. Chicago: University of Chicago Press, 1982.

Kirkpatrick, Susan. *Las románticas: Women Writers and Subjectivity in Spain, 1835–1850*. Berkeley: University of California Press, 1989.

Kolbenschlag, Madonna. *Kiss Sleeping Beauty Good-Bye: Breaking the Spell of Feminine Myths and Models*. Garden City: Doubleday, 1979.

Kolodny, Annette. "Some Notes on Defining a 'Feminist Literary Criticism.'" *Critical Inquiry* 2, no. 1 (Autumn 1975):75–92.

Kristeva, Julia. *Desire in Language: A Semiotic Approach to Literature and Art*. Edited by Leon S. Roudiez. Translated by Thomas Gora, Alice Jardine, and Leon S. Roudiez. New York: Columbia University Press, 1980.

———. "A Question of Subjectitivy: An Interview." In *Feminist Literary Theory: A Reader*, edited by Mary Eagleton, 351–53. 2d ed. Cambridge, Mass.: Blackwell Publishers, 1996.

———. *Tales of Love*. Translated by Leon S. Roudiez. New York: Columbia University Press, 1987.

Kuhn, Annette. *The Power of the Image*. London: Routledge and Kegan Paul, 1985.

Lakoff, George, and Mark Johnson. *Metaphors We Live By*. Chicago: University of Chicago Press, 1980.

Lakoff, George, and Mark Turner. *More Than Cool Reason: A Field Guide to Poetic Metaphor*. Chicago: University of Chicago Press, 1989.

Levine, Linda. "Carmen Martín Gaite's *El cuarto de atrás*: A Portrait of the Artist as Woman." In *From Fiction to Metafiction: Essays in Honor of Carmen Martín Gaite*, edited by Mirella Servodidio and Marcia L. Welles, 161–72. Lincoln, Nebr.: The Society of Spanish and Spanish-American Studies, 1983.

Levine, Linda, Ellen Engelson Marson, and Gloria Feiman Waldman, eds. *Spanish Women Writers: A Bio-Bibliographical Source Book*. Westport, Conn.: Greenwood Press, 1993.

Lévi-Struass, Claude. *Structural Anthropology*. Translated by Claire Jacobson and Brooke Grundfest Schaef. New York: Basic Books, 1963.

López, Aurora, and María Angeles Pastor, eds. *Crítica y ficción literaria: Mujeres españolas contemporáneas*. Granada: Universidad de Granada, 1989.

López de Abiada, José Manuel. "El papel de la mujer en la novela española de posguerra." *Insula*, no. 449 (1984):18.

Mainer, José-Carlos. "Las escritoras del 27 (con María Teresa León al fondo)." *Homenaje a María Teresa León*. Madrid: Universidad Complutense de Madrid, 1989, 13–39.

Maillard, María Luisa. *Asociación española de mujeres universitarias, 1920–1990*. Madrid: Instituto de la Mujer, 1990.

Mancing, Howard. "A Consensus Canon of Hispanic Poetry." *Hispania* 69 (1986):53–81.

Manteiga, Roberto C., Carolyn Galerstein, and Kathleen McNerney, eds. *Feminine Concerns in Contemporary Spanish Fiction of Women*. Potomac, Md.: Scripta Humanistica, 1988.

Marañón, Gregorio. *Tres ensayos sobre la vida sexual*. Madrid: Biblioteca Nueva, 1926.

Marco, Joaquín. *Poesía española siglo XX*. Barcelona: Edhasa, 1986.

Marcus, Jane. "Still Practice, A/Wrested Alphabet: Toward a Feminist Aesthetic." In *Feminist Issues in Literary Scholarship*, edited by Shari Benstock, 79–97. Bloomington: Indiana University Press, 1987.

Marías, Julián. *La mujer en el siglo XX*. Madrid: Alianza, 1980.

———. *La mujer y su sombra*. Madrid: Alianza, 1986.

Marra-López, José. *Narrativa española fuera de España*. Madrid: Guadarrama, 1963.

Marsá Vancells, Plutarco. *La mujer en la literatura*. Madrid: Torremozas, 1987.

Martín Gaite, Carmen. *Desde la ventana*. Madrid: Espasa Calpe, 1987.

———. *El cuarto de atrás*. Barcelona: Destino, 1978.

Martínez, Padre Graciano. *El libro de la mujer española: Hacia un femenismo cuasi dogmático*. Madrid: Imprenta del Asilo de Huérfanos, 1921.

Martínez Sierra, Gregorio. *Feminismo, feminidad, y españolismo*. Madrid: Saturnino Calleja, 1920.

———. *La mujer moderna*. Madrid: Saturnino Calleja, 1920.

Mayans Natal, María. *Narrativa feminista española de posguerra*. Madrid: Pliegos, 1991.

Miller, Beth, ed. *Women in Hispanic Literature: Icons and Fallen Idols*. Berkeley: University of California Press, 1983.

Miller, Jean Baker. *Toward a New Psychology of Women*. Boston: Beacon Press, 1986.

Miller, Nancy K. "Changing the Subject: Authorship, Writing and the Reader." In *Feminist Studies / Critical Studies*, edited by Teresa de Lauretis, 104–16. Bloomington: Indiana University Press, 1986.

———, ed. *The Poetics of Gender*. New York: Columbia University Press, 1986.

Miró, Emilio. "Algunas poetas españolas entre 1926 y 1960." In *Literatura y vida cotidiana*, edited by María Angeles Durán and José Antonio Rey, 306–21. Zaragoza: Universidad Autónoma de Madrid and Universidad de Zaragoza, 1987.

———. "Poetisas españolas contemporáneas." *Revista de la Universidad Complutense* 24, no. 95 (1975):271–310.

Mitchell, Juliet. *Psychology and Feminism*. New York: Vintage Books, 1975.

Moi, Toril. *Sexual / Textual Politics*. London and New York: Methuen, 1985.

Monaghan, Patricia. *The Book of Goddesses and Heroines*. New York: E. P. Dutton, 1981.

Morello-Frosch, Marta. "Autorrepresentaciones de lo femenino en tres escritoras de la literatura latinoamericana." In *La nueva mujer en la escritura de autoras hispánicas*, edited by Juana A. Arancibia and Yolanda Rosas, 143–54. Montevideo, Uruguay: Instituto Literario y Cultural Hispánico, 1995.

Mulvey, Laura. "Visual Pleasure and Narrative Cinema." *Screen* 16, no. 3 (1975):6–18.

Nash, Mary. *Mujer, familia y trabajo en España, 1875–1936*. Barcelona: Anthropos, 1983.

Navajas, Gonzalo. "Generación y canon o ley y orden en literatura." *Siglo XX / 20th Century* 12, no. 1–2 (1994):157–70.

Navarro de Luzuriaga, María Luisa. "Feminidad y feminismo." *La Gaceta Literaria* 3, no. 61 (1 July 1929):2.

———. "La mujer, elemento atmosférico." *La Gaceta Literaria* 3, no. 60 (15 June 1929):2

Navarro, Tomás. *Métrica española*. New York: Las Américas, 1966.

Nelken, Margarita. *La condición social de la mujer en España*. Barcelona: Minerva, 1919.

———. *La mujer ante las Cortes Constituyentes*. Madrid: Editorial Castro, 1931.

Neumann, Erich. *Amor and Psyche*. New York: Harper and Row, 1962.

Nieva de la Paz, Pilar. *Autoras dramáticas españolas entre 1918 y 1936*. Madrid: Consejo Superior de Investigaciones Científicas, 1993.

Nóvoa Santos, Roberto. *La mujer, nuestro sexto sentido y otros esbozos*. Madrid: Biblioteca Nueva, 1929.

Oñate, María del Pilar. *El feminismo en la literatura española*. Madrid: Espasa-Calpe, 1938.

Ong, Walter J. *Orality and Literacy*. London: Methuen, 1982.

Ordóñez, Elizabeth. *Voices of Their Own: Contemporary Spanish Narrative by Women.* Lewisburg, Pa.: Bucknell University Press, 1991.

Ortega y Gasset, José. *Deshumanización del arte.* Madrid: Revista de Occidente, 1964.

———. *Obras completas.* Madrid: Revista de Occidente, 1964.

———. *La rebelión de las masas.* Madrid: Espasa-Calpe, 1958.

Ostriker, Alicia Suskin. *Stealing the Language: The Emergence of Women's Poetry in America.* Boston: Beacon Press, 1986.

Oxford Companion to Spanish Literature. Oxford: Clarendon Press, 1978.

Palacio Valdés, Armando. *El gobierno de las mujeres: Ensayos históricos de política femenina.* Madrid: Librería Victoriano Suárez, 1931.

Pardo Bazán, Emilia. *La mujer española y otros artículos.* Madrid: Editora Nacional, 1976.

Paz, Octavio. "La palabra edificante." *Papeles de Son Armadans* 35, no. 103 (1943):41–82.

Pérez, Janet. "Contemporary Spanish Women Writers and the Feminized Quest-Romance." *Monographic Review/Revista Monográfica* 8 (1992):36–49.

———. *Contemporary Women Writers of Spain.* Boston: Twayne Publishers, 1988.

———. *Modern and Contemporary Spanish Women Poets.* New York: Twayne Publishers, 1996.

———, ed. *Novelistas femeninas de la postguerra española.* Madrid: José Porrúa Turanzas, 1983.

Persin, Margaret. "Carmen Martín Gaite's *A rachas*: Dreams of the Past and Memories of the Future, Text(ure)s Woven of Many Colored Threads." *Monographic Review/Revista Monográfica* 6 (1990):93–112.

———. "Yet Another Loose Can(n)on: The Place and Space of Women's Poetry in Twentieth-Century Spain." *Siglo XX/20th Century* 12, no. 1–2 (1994):195–206.

Perinat, Adolfo, and María Isabel Marrades. *Mujer, prensa y sociedad, 1800–1939.* Madrid: Centro de Investigaciones Sociológicas, 1980.

Pomès, Mathilde. *Poètes espagnols d'aujourd'hui.* Brussels: Labor, 1934.

Pratt, Annis. *Archetypal Patterns in Women's Fiction.* Bloomington: Indiana University Press, 1981.

Rabuzzi, Kathryn Allen. *Motherself: A Mythic Analysis of Motherhood.* Bloomington: Indiana University Press, 1988.

Ramos-Gil, Carlos. *Claves líricas de García Lorca.* Madrid: Aguilar, 1967.

Rich, Adrienne. *The Dream of a Common Language.* New York: Norton, 1975.

———. *Of Woman Born: Motherhood as Experience and Institution.* New York: W. W. Norton, 1976.

———. *On Lies, Secrets, and Silences: Selected Prose, 1966–1978.* New York: Norton, 1979.

Riera, Carme. *Una primavera para Domenico Guarini.* Barcelona: Montesinos, 1981.

Roca Franquesa, José María. *Historia de la literatura española e hispanoamericana.* Madrid: Aguilar, 1966.

Rodrigo, Antonina. *Mujeres de España: Las silenciadas.* Barcelona: Plaza y Janés, 1979.

Roig, Mercedes. *A través de la prensa: La mujer en la historia: Francia, Italia, España, Siglos XVIII–XX.* Madrid: Ministerio de Asuntos Sociales, 1989.

Roig, Montserrat. *¿Tiempo de mujer?* Barcelona: Plaza and Janés, 1980.

Rozas, Juan Manuel. *El 27 como generación.* Santander: Colección La Isla de los Ratones, 1978.

Ruddick, Sara. *Maternal Thinking: Toward a Politics of Peace.* Boston: Beacon Press, 1989.

Russell, Bertrand. *A History of Western Philosophy.* New York: Simon and Schuster, 1967.

Sainz de Robles, Federico Carlos. *Ensayo de un diccionario de literatura.* Madrid: Aguilar, 1949.

Salinas de Marichal, Solita. *El mundo poético de Rafael Alberti.* Madrid: Gredos, 1968.

Saval, Lorenzo, and J. García Gallego. *Litoral femenino: Literatura escrita por mujeres en la España contemporánea.* Málaga: Litoral, 1986.

Scanlon, Geraldine. *La polémica feminista en la España contemporánea, 1868–1974.* Madrid: Akal, 1986.

Schenck, Celeste M. "Feminism and Deconstruction: Re-Constructing the Elegy." *Tulsa Studies in Women's Literature* 5, no. 1 (1986):13–28.

Schyfter, Sara E. "The Fragmented Family in the Novels of Contemporary Spanish Women." *Perspectives in Contemporary Literature* 3, no. 1 (1977):23–29.

Schor, Naomi. "Reading Double: Sand's Difference." In *The Poetics of Gender*, edited by Nancy K. Miller, 248–69. New York: Columbia University Press, 1986.

Segura, Isabel, and Marta Selva. *Revistes de dones, 1845–1935.* Barcelona: Edhasa, 1984.

Seymour-Smith, Martin. *The New Guide to Modern World Literature.* New York: Peter Bedrich Books, 1985.

Silver, Philip. *Luis Cernuda: El poeta en su leyenda.* Barcelona: Alfaguara, 1965.

Showalter, Elaine. "Feminist Criticism in the Wilderness." In *Writing and Sexual Difference*, edited by Elizabeth Abel, 9–35. Chicago: University of Chicago Press, 1982.

———. *A Literature of Their Own.* Princeton: Princeton University Press, 1977.

———. "Piecing and Writing." In *The Poetics of Gender*, edited by Nancy K. Miller, 222–47. New York: Columbia University Press, 1986.

———. *Sexual Anarchy: Gender and Culture at the Fin de Siècle.* New York: Viking, 1990.

———. "Women and the Literary Curriculum." *College English* 32 (1971):855–62.

———, ed. *The New Feminist Criticism: Literature and Theory.* New York: Pantheon Books, 1985.

Siebenmann, Gustav. *Los estilos poéticos en España desde 1900.* Madrid: Gredos, 1973.

Smith, Sidonie. *A Poetics of Women's Autobiography.* Bloomington: Indiana University Press, 1987.

Soufas, C. Christopher. *Conflict of Light and Wind.* Middletown, Conn.: Wesleyan University Press, 1989.

Spain, Daphne. *Gendered Spaces.* Chapel Hill: The University of North Carolina Press, 1992.

Sullerot, Evelyne. *Women on Love: Eight Centuries of Feminine Writing.* Garden City, N.Y.: Doubleday, 1979.

Tabori, Paul. *The Anatomy of Exile: A Semantic and Historical Approach.* London: Harrap, 1972.

Temes, Peter S. "Code of Silence: Laura (Riding) Jackson and the Refusal to Speak." *PMLA* 109, no. 1 (1994):87–99.

Tierney, Helen. *Women's Studies Encyclopedia.* New York: Greenwood Press, 1989.

Tejada, José Luis. *Rafael Alberti: Entre la tradición y la vanguardia.* Madrid: Gredos, 1977.

Ugalde, Sharon Keefe. *Conversaciones y poemas: La nueva poesía femenina española en castellano.* Madrid: Siglo Veintiuno Editores, 1991.

———. "Erotismo y revisionismo en la poesía de Ana Rossetti." *Siglo XX/20th Century* 7, no. 1–2 (1989–1990):24–29.

———. "Spanish Women Poets on Women's Poetry." *Monographic Review / Revista Monográfica* 6 (1990):128–37.

Valbuena Prat, Angel. *Historia de la literatura española.* Barcelona: Gustavo Gili, 1937.

———. *Historia de la literatura española.* Barcelona: Gustavo Gili, 1963. Revised by María del Pilar Palomo. Barcelona: Gustavo Gili, 1983.

———. *La poesía española contemporánea.* Madrid: Compañía Ibero-Americana de Publicaciones, 1930.

Valis, Noël. "The Perfect Copy: Clarín's *Su único hijo* and the Flaubertian Connection." *PMLA* 104, no. 5 (1989):856–67.

Valis, Noël, and Carol Maier, eds. *In the Feminine Mode.* Lewisburg: Bucknell University Press, 1990.

Varia. *Historia de la literatura española.* Vol. 2, *Desde el siglo XVII hasta nuestros días.* Madrid: Cátedra, 1990.

Vidal, María Antonia. *Cien años de poesía femenina: Española e hispanoamericana, 1840–1940.* Barcelona: Olimpo, 1943.

Vidal, Gloria. *El ultraísmo.* Madrid: Gredos, 1971.

Warhol, Robyn R. and Diane Price Herndl, eds. *Feminism: An Anthology of Literary Criticism.* New Brunswick, N.J.: Rutgers University Press, 1991.

Welles, Marcia L. *Arachne's Tapestry: The Transformation of Myth in Seventeenth-Century Spain.* San Antonio, Tex.: Trinity University Press, 1986.

Wheelwright, Philip. *Metaphor and Reality.* Bloomington: Indiana University Press, 1968.

Wilcox, John C. "Ana Rossetti y sus cuatro musas poéticas." *Revista Canadiense de Estudios Hispánicos* 14, no. 3 (1990):525–40.

———. *Women Poets of Spain, 1860–1990: Toward a Gynocentric Vision.* Champaign: University of Illinois Press, 1997.

Wilson, Katharina M. *An Encyclopedia of Continental Women Writers.* New York: Garland Publishing, 1991.

Wittig, Monique. "The Mark of Gender." In *The Poetics of Gender,* edited by Nancy K. Miller, 63–73. New York: Columbia University Press, 1986.

Woolf, Virginia. *A Room of Her Own.* New York: Harcourt, Brace and World, 1928.

Zambrano, María. *Filosofía y poesía.* Mexico City: Fondo de Cultura Económica, 1987.

Zamora Vicente, Alonso. *Examen de ingreso: Madrid, años veinte.* Madrid: Espasa Calpe, 1991.

Zardoya, Concha. *Poesía española del siglo XX: Estudios temáticos y estilísticos.* Madrid: Gredos, 1974.

Zatlin, Phyllis. "Passivity and Immobility: Patterns of Inner Exile in Postwar Spanish Novels Written by Women." *Letras Femeninas* 14, no. 1–2 (1988):3–9.

Zulueta, Carmen. *Cien años de educación de la mujer española: Historia del Instituto Internacional.* Madrid: Castalia, 1992.

Zulueta, Carmen, and Alicia Moreno. *Ni convento ni college: La Residencia de Señoritas.* Madrid: Consejo Superior de Investigaciones Científicas, 1993.

Index

Teresa (Rosa Chacel), 122, 125
theological base for subordination of
women, 94
theory of complementarity, 33–34
time: in Carmen Conde's poetry, 169–70;
in Josefina de la Torre's poetry, 90,
101–3
time frames, when studying Spanish
women poets, 12, 22
"Toledo" (Concha Méndez), 45–46
de la Torre, Claudio, 38, 84, 86
de la Torre, Josefina, 42, 84–119; ambivalence in poetry of, 108; brother
(Claudio), 38, 84; circularity in poetry
of, 109–10; comparison with Carmen
Conde, 143, 146, 147; comparison with
Concha Méndez, 85; comparison with
Ernestina de Champourcin, 200;
comparisons with other poets, 84, 109;
as contemporary of Méndez, Chacel,
Conde, and Champourcin, 16; effect
of exile on, 26; elimination from canon,
13; embroidery in poetry of, 112–13;
emotional consequences and uncertainty in poetry of, 105–6; empty room
imagery, 104–5; enclosure imagery,
105; exclusion from canon, 23;
existence in poetry of, 97; futility of
memory, 103–4; group, women poets
as, 18; hand imagery, 117–18; inaudibility in poetry of, 96; inclusion in
Generation of 27 anthology, 24;
inclusion in Gerardo Diego's anthology
of poetry, 84; incompletion imagery,
103; as individual, 19; Juan Ramón
Jiménez's influence on, 89–90; love and
psychological absence in poetry of,
106–7; love and silence in poetry of,
96–97; manifestation of female
presence, 40; *Marzo incompleto*, 84,
102–3, 105, 115, 118–19; "Mi falda de
tres volantes," 110; nature imagery, 86–
90, 91–94; *Poemas de la isla*, 85, 91–101,
102, 119; poetic career, 84–85; poetic
persona, 19, 85–86, 109–19; power of
the word in poetry of, 94–101;
publication in Gerardo Diego's
anthology, 37; publication in *La Gaceta
Literaria*, 36; publication in *Noreste*, 36;
revival of poetry of, 24; "Romance del
buen guiar," 86; sexual imagery, 115–

17; singing recitals, 38–39; story of
absence, 12; summary, 216–19; support
from family/friends, 85–86; time in
poetry of, 101–3; timelessness in poetry
of, 90; *Versos y estampas*, 85, 86–90, 94,
101–2, 109, 119, 148; water imagery,
86–89; withdrawal from poetry, 14;
woman as weaver or sewer in poetry of,
110–15. **—Works:** Josefina de la
Torre: *Marzo incompleto*, 84, 102–3, 105,
115, 118–19; "Mi falda de tres
volantes," 110; *Poemas de la isla*, 85, 91–
101, 102, 119; "Romance del buen
guiar," 86; *Versos y estampas*, 85, 86–90,
94, 101–2, 109, 119, 148
de Torre, Guillermo, review of Ernestina
de Champourcin's books, 40
touch, sense of: in Carmen Conde's poetry,
166–67; in Ernestina de Champourcin's poetry, 200
transcendence: in Carmen Conde's poetry,
158; in Ernestina de Champourcin's
poetry, 202–15
"Trasatlántico" (Concha Méndez), 61–62
travel imagery, in Concha Méndez's
poetry, 59–62

Ugalde, Sharon Keefe, 100
"Ultima cita" (Concha Méndez), 71
ultraísta mode of poetry writing, 164
ultraísta poets, and Ernestina de Champourcin, 194
Unamuno, 132–33
uncertainty, emotional consequences, in
Josefina de la Torre's poetry, 105–6
Universidad Popular de Cartagena,
founding of, 145
Urrutia, Elena, 58

Valbuena Prat, Angel, 109; on Ernestina
de Champourcin, 25
de Valderrama, Pilar, publication in La
Gaceta Literaria, 36
Valender, James, 73, 83
Valéry, Paul, 175
Valis, Noël, 108, 130
vanguard techniques, of Rosa Chacel, 128
vanguardist mode of poetry, 13
de Vega, Lope, 143
Verso y prosa, 37
Versos prohibidos (Rosa Chacel), 122, 132, 139